FAY CHUNG

Re-living the Second Chimurenga

Memories from the Liberation Struggle in Zimbabwe

With an introduction by Preben Kaarsholm

THE NORDIC AFRICA INSTITUTE, 2006
Published in cooperation with Weaver Press

Indexing terms
Biographies
National liberation movements
Liberation
Civil war
Independence
ZANU
Zimbabwe

RE-LIVING THE SECOND CHIMURENGA
© The Author and Nordiska Afrikainstitutet, 2006
Cover photo: Tord Harlin *The Epsworth rocks, Zimbabwe*
Language checking: Peter Colenbrander
ISBN 91 7106 551 2 (The Nordic Africa Institute)
    1 77922 046 4 (Weaver Press)
Printed in Sweden by Elanders Gotab, Stockholm, 2006

*Dedicated to our children's generation,
who will have to build on the positive gains and
to overcome the negative aspects of the past.*

Contents

Introduction: Memoirs of a Dutiful Revolutionary
Preben Kaarsholm 7

1. Growing up in Colonial Rhodesia 27
2. An Undergraduate in the '60s 39
3. Teaching in the Turmoil of the Townships 46
4. In Exile in Britain 65
5. Learning from the Zambia of the 1970s 71
6. Joining the Liberation Struggle in Zambia 75
7. Josiah Tongogara: Commander of ZANLA 124
8. Post-*Détente* Intensification of the War:
   Nyadzonia and Chimoio 140
9. The Formation of the Zimbabwe People's
   Army (ZIPA), 1976 145
10. The Geneva Conference: Old Enemies and
    New Friends 153
11. Post-*Détente* and the Defeat of the ZANU Left Wing 171
12. I End Up in a Military Camp 189
13. Traditional Religion in the Liberation Struggle 197
14. The Formation of the ZANU Department of
    Education 203
15. The Internal Settlement and Intensified Armed Struggle 229
16. The Lancaster House Agreement 242
17. Prelude to Independence 248
18. The Fruits of Independence 254
19. A Vision of Zimbabwe Tomorrow 327

Appendix 1: The Mgagao Declaration by
Zimbabwe Freedom Fighters (October, 1975) 340
Appendix 2: Curriculum Vitae: Fay Chung 347
Acronyms 351
Index of names 353

Memoirs of a Dutiful Revolutionary

Fay Chung and the Legacies of the Zimbabwean Liberation War

An Introduction by Preben Kaarsholm[1]

Scholars and activists who followed the dramatic events of the nationalist liberation struggle in the 1970s, and the first years of Zimbabwe's independence from 1980 will remember Fay Chung, and associate her name with the high hopes invested in reform and expansion of the country's educational system. They will remember how educational reform was seen to be a central part in a transformation, which went beyond the appropriation of state power, and which – by applying didactic principles developed in refugee camps in Zambia and Mozambique in the 1970s – would help to build a nation of new citizens who were both well-trained and decolonised also mentally. The new education system would be democratic by offering primary education to all, and broadening access to secondary and tertiary training radically. It would also be socialist in its application of principles of 'education with production' and of 'dialogic teaching' inspired by the writings of Paolo Freire. Fay Chung was at the forefront of these aspirations – both in ZANU(PF) and within the Ministry of Education – and kept on fighting for them against increasing bureaucratic obstacles and – eventually – the restrictions imposed by Structural Adjustment, until she resigned from the Ministry in the early 1990s, and left Zimbabwe to work for UNICEF.

---

1. Preben Kaarsholm teaches International Development Studies at Roskilde University, and is a member of the Nordic Africa Institute's editorial board. He has been doing research for many years on culture, politics and urban history in Zimbabwe and South Africa, and is the editor of *Cultural Struggles and Development in Southern Africa* (1991) and *Violence, Political Culture and Development in Africa* (2006). He is grateful to Brian Raftopoulos, David Moore, Terence Ranger and Wilfred Mhanda for commenting on draft versions of the introduction.

Fay Chung's account of her experiences and reflections upon them is an important historical document, and will be of great interest – not only to students and researchers, but also to a more widespread group of readers concerned with the Zimbabwean experiment in social transformation from the 1970s to the present. It will be so also in the light of the tremendous crisis in which this experiment finds itself from the late 1990s, and readers will look forward to Fay Chung's narrative and interpretation of Zimbabwe's trajectory over the last thirty years, from nationalist and socialist uprising, through the promises of the first independent government, to populist dictatorship, state violence, and economic collapse.

The memoirs are significant in several respects. Though written with some formality and restraint, they give insight into the very unusual circumstances of growing up, from the early 1940s, in a Roman Catholic Chinese family – settled in Rhodesia's capital, Salisbury, since 1904. Fay Chung's account of her childhood and youth lets the reader look into the racially segregated life of Rhodesia from the special angle of a Chinese minority, which was so small that it did not really figure within the state's categorisation of population groups. As an adolescent with a Chinese family background, Fay Chung was able to experience the system from a position of both relative privilege and oppression, and therefore perhaps as particularly arbitrary. Her narrative has a special focus on her school experiences, and describes the efforts of liberalisation that took place in the 1950s and early 1960s in the context of Southern Rhodesia's membership of the Central African Federation. Of particular interest is her account of her period of study at the University of Rhodesia and Nyasaland around 1960, then an outpost of liberal reform and debate among intellectuals – an experience that played an important role in deciding Fay Chung's future political orientation.

On completing her first degree, Fay Chung went on to teach African students, first at a secondary school in Gwelo, and then in the tumultuous circumstances of Salisbury's townships, where she experienced the growing radicalisation of nationalist mobilisation, and the tightening of state governance, following the Unilateral Declaration of Independence and the coming to power of Ian Smith's Rhodesian Front party in 1965. From there, she moved on in 1968 to post-graduate studies in English literature at the University of Leeds in England, where she was influenced by the students' rebellion, and was introduced to the political thought of Marx, Lenin, Mao and Machiavelli. She then moved back to Africa, and in the early 1970s worked as a lecturer in the Department of Education at the University of Zambia, being an active member of the growing diaspora of refugees from Rhodesia in Zambia, and – following the escalation of the guerrilla war inside Rhodesia – joined up with ZANU and the liberation struggle in 1973.

The memoirs give the reader unique insights into her experiences as an insider with the nationalist movement in exile – first in Zambia and from 1975 in Mozambique – where Fay Chung had her primary tasks within the ZANU Department of Information and Media and subsequently its Department of Education. Belonging to the 'university group' within ZANU, she was considered a leftist and an intellectual, but avoided direct involvement with the two famous take-over attempts by intellectuals within the movement in the 1970s – the young officers' revolt led by Thomas Nhari in 1974-75 and the more leftist vashandi mobilisation of 1976. She therefore avoided also the unhappy fate which befell the rebels, whose leaders in the Nhari case were executed, and that of the vashandi were incarcerated in Mozambique until Independence in 1980.

Fay Chung was also active as a feminist, and worked to improve the situation of women guerrillas and refugees, who were at times exposed to considerable harassment by male commanders, and expected to provide services as 'warm blankets'. She experienced – or can quote first-hand accounts of – some of the most dramatic moments of the armed liberation struggle, such as the Rhodesian Air Force massacres of refugee schools in Nyadzonia and Chimoio, and – being active at leadership level as well as personally related to some of the main protagonists – was a central witness to some of the most important political divisions and upheavals within ZANU and its ZANLA guerrilla army.

As Head of Information and Media, she helped formulate ZANU's line of political education, and – in her work for the Education Department – together with Dzingayi Mutumbuka outlined the principles for curriculum development and pedagogic strategy, which were tried out in exile, and later served as the basis for initiatives to reform education radically in independent Zimbabwe after 1980.

The narrative dealing with the liberation struggle and the period between 1973 and 1980 is by far the longest and the most important part of Fay Chung's memoirs. Her account of the first years of Independence is less substantial, but it is valuable to have her version of the break-up of the Patriotic Front prior to the first post-Independence elections in 1980, and of the confrontation between PF-ZAPU/ZIPRA and ZANU(PF)/ZANLA around ZANLA's incomplete demobilisation before the elections, and the discovery later of ZIPRA arms caches. These events foreshadowed the civil-war-like antagonism between the two nationalist parties, which cast a shadow over Zimbabwean politics between 1982 and 1987, and underlay the incidents of 'dissident' violence, and the unleashing of the military might of the Zimbabwean state and its Fifth Brigade against villagers in Matabeleland in counter-insurgency operations that were no less brutal than those of the Rhodesian forces in the 1970s.

According to Fay Chung, ex-ZIPRA 'dissidents' – amnestied after the unity agreement between ZANU(PF) and PF-ZAPU in 1987 – were later among the leaders of the War Veterans Association, whose campaigns for compensation from 1997 led to the dramatic shift in Government policy away from Structural Adjustment. This initiated the ongoing political and economic showdown in Zimbabwe, culminating in the 'fast-track' expropriations of land, and the battles by President Mugabe and the ruling party to repress the challenge from the Movement for Democratic Change.

The central focus in the memoirs of the 1980s, however, is on developments in education, and on Fay Chung's work with curriculum reform, and her collaboration with Dzingayi Mutumbuka in his time as Minister of Education and Culture 'to democratise educational opportunity', which – in her mind – constitute one of 'the two major aims of the liberation struggle' alongside 'the redistribution of land'. The efforts to transform the educational system had a rapid and forceful impact with numbers of schools and intake of students in both primary and secondary education being increased dramatically, and the University of Zimbabwe opening its doors to thousands of new black students. At the same time, literacy rates – which in spite of what Fay Chung calls Ian Smith's 'Nazi-type, anti-black policies' had been as high as 70% in the late 1970s – after Independence moved to 80% by the end of the 1980s and 90% at the turn of millennium.

Introduction

As Head of Educational Planning in the Ministry, Fay Chung helped establish new forms of state-community collaboration around primary education, and became the first Acting Head of ZINTEC – the Zimbabwe Integrated National Teacher Education Course – aimed at providing sufficient numbers of teachers to cope with the expansion in enrolment. ZINTEC based itself on ideas of education developed in the camps in Zambia and Mozambique during the war, and such ideas also inspired the work of ZIMFEP – the Zimbabwe Foundation for Education with Production – whose first chairperson was Fay Chung, and whose board and staff were composed of war veterans. ZIMFEP was inspired also by Patrick van Rensburg and the achievements of the Foundation for Education with Production in Botswana, and aimed at erasing boundaries between intellectual and manual labour and at the decolonisation of personalities through the application of 'liberation pedagogy'.

The long-term ambition was to make such transformative ideas dominant also within the mainstream of Zimbabwean public education, but initially they would be pioneered at a number of ZIMFEP schools, catering for refugee children and young ex-guerrillas returning from the camps in Zambia and Mozambique. Substantial NGO and international support was mobilised for this effort – not least from Scandinavia, where Swedish SIDA played a major role, as did the Danish Tvind schools through the programme Development Aid from People to People (DAPP). Fay Chung's memoirs mention in passing some of the problems experienced in this collaboration, but do not offer much detail – nor does she discuss the contemporary role played by DAPP in Zimbabwe, where the organisation has been unflinching in its support for Mugabe. It has its international headquarters at Murgwi north of Harare – designed by the Danish architect, Jan Utzon – which are so monumental that they have been claimed to be visible from the moon (they can admired on www.humana.org). This is an interesting chapter – not only of educational, but also of political history, and one would have liked to hear more about the intricacies of this, and the ways in which within the schools, debates were conducted about how to interpret and develop the legacies of the liberation struggle. Fay Chung describes how the ZIMFEP schools in Matabeleland came under attack from 'dissidents' during the 1980s, but does not mention that they were also targeted by Government forces as strongholds of radicalism, run by war veterans, and suspected of collaboration with the 'dissidents'.

Fay Chung eventually, in 1988, became Minister of Education and Culture – and later of Employment Creation and Cooperatives – but the effort to have the alternative contents and pedagogy spearheaded by ZINTEC and ZIMFEP permeate the whole educational system did not succeed. The memoirs attribute this primarily to the resistance experienced from a state bureaucracy that had been inherited from the Rhodesian state. From 1992 onwards, however, there was also a shift in Government policy, as programmes of Economic Structural Adjustment came to be adopted, and the increase in output of students from the radically extended school system was not matched by employment opportunities. This led to confrontations between the Government on the one side and university students and a new intelligentsia of unemployed school candidates on the other, as well as to reconsiderations of curriculum objectives. Fay Chung describes this as coinciding with a transformation within the ZANU(PF) party itself, in which mafikizolo opportunists were gaining the upper hand, corruption spread, and war veterans were sidelined. At the same time, the collapse of the Soviet Union in 1989 led to what she calls a 'death of ideology' and 'a fatal weakening of the state in Zimbabwe', with the Government's policies becoming increasingly populist and giving in to pressure from neo-liberalism under the banner of Structural Adjustment. In 1993, Fay Chung left the Zimbabwean government, and for ten years worked abroad – first as Director of Education for UNICEF until 1998, and then – until 2003 – as Director of UNESCO's International Capacity Building Institute for Africa.

The last sections of Fay Chung's memoirs reflect on developments in Zimbabwe after 1997, and the onset of the economic and political crisis initiated by the accommodation of war veteran demands for compensation and pensions and the rise of the new democratic opposition. Her account here is considerably more sketchy than in the earlier parts, and will – I am sure – be seen as provocative and controversial by many readers. While highly critical of developments within ZANU(PF) and of Government corruption, Fay Chung is even more scathing about the Movement of Democratic Change and the new opposition, which she sees primarily as agents of the white farmer interest and of international neo-colonial forces, whose human rights and democracy platform she

Introduction

considers little more than a front for the pursuit of more sinister agendas, and whose political methods she describes as 'violent'. By contrast, she represents President Mugabe's efforts and his alliance with war veterans after 1997 – which critics have seen as desperate attempts by the ZANU(PF) elite to hold on to power – as aimed at a return to the revolutionary priorities of the liberation struggle, and views the 'fast-track land reform' implemented as being at the forefront of this return to a progressive and pro-people past.

It would have been ideal if Fay Chung's memoirs could have been presented with a full editorial and critical apparatus of notes and commentary, but this has not been possible. Instead, the Nordic Africa Institute and Weaver Press have decided to give priority to making this important document of recent and contemporary Zimbabwean history available quickly in the hope that it will stimulate and enrich the ongoing discussion on Zimbabwe's development trajectory. No doubt, future historians will want to add to her account, and will provide further critical perspective on Fay Chung's role in the liberation struggle of Zimbabwe and her retrospective version of events. It is important, however, to have her memoirs and points of view made available quickly, as they represent not only a historical document, but also a political one of great significance for the understanding of Zimbabwe's recent history, and – especially – the development of positions of the Left within this history. Why is it that issues of human rights and democracy, on the one hand, and of socialism and economic justice and redistribution have become so separate in Zimbabwean radical politics? Why is it of such importance for Fay Chung as a left-wing socialist to support Mugabe and his turning back of the historical clock to the objectives of a struggle that took place thirty years ago? Why does Fay Chung consider it necessary to distance herself so drastically from the new democratic opposition, which has been emerging in Zimbabwe since 1997 – as represented by trade unions, NGOs, the independent press, the National Constitutional Alliance and the Movement for Democratic Change? Why is it that she does not see such an emergence of democratic agenda with substantial local popular support as a continuation and a step forward in political development from the peace-making Unity agreement of 1987, which ended the civil war in Matabeleland, and as something which could substantially promote social and economic justice rather than work against it? All these are questions, which have been at the centre of interest in recent literature and critical debates about Zimbabwe.[1]

To understand this better, it may help to look a little more closely at some of the most important themes and strands of narrative that run through Fay Chung's memoirs, and examine how they link up with the position on contemporary politics that she adopts in the concluding sections of the book.

A prominent focus in the memoirs is on the internal politics and the divisions within the nationalist liberation movement. A constant background is the split between ZAPU and ZANU from 1963 onwards, the attempts to re-unify the two rival movements in the Patriotic Front during the late 1970s, and the decision by ZANU(PF) to break out of the alliance and go for election victory in 1980 on its own, with momentous consequences for Zimbabwean politics during the first years of independence and until the Unity Agreement in 1987. Fay Chung makes no secret of her lack of trust in Joshua Nkomo as an 'old-style', opportunistic nationalist leader – and does not give much attention to his background in the trade union movement, and a nationalist tradition and socialist perspective different from the one represented by ZANU. On the other hand, she writes with great respect of ZIPRA guerrillas and military

---

1. See e. g. Christine Sylvester, 'Remembering and Forgetting "Zimbabwe": Towards a Third Transition', in Paul Gready (ed.), *Political Transition: Politics and Culture*, London: Pluto Press, 2003; Amanda Hammar, Brian Raftopoulos and Stig Jensen (eds), *Zimbabwe's Unfinished Business: Rethinking Land, State and Nation in the Context of Crisis*, Harare: Weaver Press, 2003; David Harold-Barry (ed.), *Zimbabwe: The Past is the Future*, Harare: Weaver Press, 2004; Brian Raftopoulos and Ian Phimister, 'Zimbabwe Now: The Political Economy of Crisis and Coercion' and David Moore, 'Marxism and Marxist Intellectuals in Schizophrenic Zimbabwe: How Many Rights for Zimbabwe's Left?' – both in *Historical Materialism*, 12(4), 2004; Terence Ranger, 'Rule by Historiography: The Struggle over the Past in Contemporary Zimbabwe' and Preben Kaarsholm, 'Coming to Terms with Violence: Literature and the Development of a Public Sphere in Zimbabwe' – both in Robert Muponde and Ranka Primorac (eds), *Versions of Zimbabwe: New Approaches to Literature and Culture*, Harere: Weaver Press, 2005; Brian Raftopoulos, 'The Zimbabwean Crisis and the Challenges for the Left', public lecture, University of KwaZulu-Natal, June 2005. Cf. also two books by Stephen Chan – *Robert Mugabe: A Life of Power and Violence*, London: I. B. Tauris, 2002, and *Citizen of Africa: Conversations with Morton Tsvangirai*, Cape Town: Fingerprint, 2005.

leaders, and of the attempts by socialist groups on both sides to work for unification across the nationalist divide – as for example in the context of the formation of the unified ZIPA – Zimbabwe People's Army – military force in 1976. But such attempts keep being thwarted in Chung's account, not only by leaders' opportunism, but also by ethnic politics and 'tribalist' antagonism between Shona- and Ndebele-speaking groups – the ZIPA exercise, for example, is fatally undermined when ZIPRA guerrillas are massacred by their ZANLA colleagues at the Mgagao and Morogoro camps in Tanzania. Fay Chung's immediate perspective and personal experience, however, are concerned with ZANU throughout, and it is around the divisions and struggles within ZANU that her memoirs are most rewarding. The reader gets a good impression of internal ZANU politics as something of a nightmare of rivalries, intrigue, faction building, and betrayals, within which the author herself at one point at least comes very close to losing – not only her position, but also her life.

As to the question of leadership of ZANU from 1973 onwards, when the nationalist leaderships were released from detention in Rhodesia, Fay Chung writes off Ndabaningi Sithole completely as an 'old-style', self-seeking 'tribalist', who steals, and of whose irresponsible behaviour towards his constituency among the refugee diaspora in Zambia, she has personal experience. By contrast, Robert Mugabe wins her respect as a humble, listening, and teacher-like human being, and as a politician who represents not only a new type of moral integrity, but also political shrewdness. On another frontline of division – between political leaders and the 'militarists', as represented by the fearsome ZANLA commander Josiah Tongogara in particular – Fay Chung has mixed feelings. She is highly critical of Tongogara in some respects, as when he has the Nhari rebel leaders summarily executed, or in the context of sexual harassment of female guerrillas, but sees him also as necessary for military victory. At the same time, she regards the armed struggle as a guarantee of a radicalism of purpose, which is continuously threatened by the preparedness of politicians to compromise and 'sell out', as in the context of the Geneva conference and Kissinger and Vorster's *détente* efforts in 1976. At yet another level of antagonism, Fay Chung sees herself as belonging to 'the university group' within ZANU in exile, and describes how intellectuals and socialists are regarded with suspicion by both 'old-style' political leaders of populist orientation, and by 'traditional' military leaders. It is in the context of such antagonism that she comes close to being killed in 1978, when she is plotted against by political opponents within ZANU (including Edgar Tekere), transferred to the Pungwe III military camp for 'observation', and only escapes through Tongogara's personal intervention. She refers to this as her toughest experience during the whole of the liberation war.

Of special interest is Fay Chung's account of the socialist vashandi – workers – movement in 1976 within ZANU and ZANLA, and the attempt to give new direction to the liberation struggle at a moment when the political leadership was tied up with negotiations around '*détente*' in Geneva, and Tongogara and the 'traditional' military leadership were still held in prison by the Zambians, suspected of complicity in the murder of Herbert Chitepo in 1975.[1] She has great sympathy for the vashandi project of transforming the nationalist struggle into a socialist one, and describes herself as being seen within ZANU to be close to them and to the leader of their left wing, Wilfred Mhanda (aka Dzinashe Machingura). But the memoirs also give clear expression to her disregard for the vashandi's lack of political and diplomatic skill, which she thinks made it all too easy for their opponents to outmanoeuvre them. By contrast, Robert Mugabe – whom the vashandi had first supported in the ousting of Sithole, but soon came to fear 'would become a fascist dictator', and against whom they naively and mistakenly thought they could turn Tongogara – is described as the clever politician, whose capacity to listen is linked up with a Machiavellian readiness to strike and eliminate when required. On hitting back, therefore, Mugabe and the ZANLA High Command had no difficulty in making short shrift with the vashandi rebels, whose leaders were rounded up to spend the remaining four years before Independence in prison in Mozambique, and only saved from Tongogara's wrath and from being executed – like Thomas Nhari and his fellow rebel leaders in 1974 – by Mugabe's more long-sighted political pragmatism. Fay Chung is not completely uncritical of Mugabe's pragmatism, though, and sees it as also providing openings for the populist trends and neo-liberal openings that come to characterise ZANU(PF) and government policies from the early 1990s. But it is a political skill, which she admires and finds necessary.

---

1. On the Chitepo killing and the significance of narratives about it within nationalist discourse in Rhodesia and Zimbabwe, cf. Luise White, *The Assassination of Herbert Chitepo: Text and Politics in Zimbabwe*, Bloomington: Indiana University Press, 2003.

Introduction

One instance of what Chung considers the vashandi's naivety was their inability to appreciate the importance of traditional religion among the peasantry, from whom the majority of guerrillas were recruited, and to understand the role of spirit mediums within the liberation movement. While in the view of the vashandi's Marxist theory of modernisation this represented nothing but superstition and backwardness, Robert Mugabe understood much better the necessity of not alienating the traditionalists, though his own Roman Catholic background and socialist leanings made him prefer advice from the university group to that of 'soothsayers'. Consequently, on this front also – Chung claims – he was able to get people behind him, when cracking down on the vashandi. In the absence of necessary political alliances, no popular or peasant force rallied to their defence, when they were repressed. Fay Chung's own opinion of the spirit mediums is ambiguous – on the one hand, she sees them as symptomatic of the 'feudalism' that characterises 'the peasant psyche', and of which she has nothing good to say. On the other hand – observing the antagonism between Tongogara and the spirit mediums in the guerrilla and refugee camps, where the mediums take issue with unnecessary blood-letting and the exploitation of women – she sees them as representing an alternative moral authority and counter-power to that of the political and military leadership.[1]

---

1. Wilfred Mhanda, who acted as both ZANLA and ZIPA political commissar, disagrees strongly with Chung's representation of the *vashandi*'s view of spirit mediums and their lack of popular support: 'Nothing could be further from the truth. I had personally worked with very senior spirit mediums from 1975 during the time of our restriction in Zambia after Chitepo's death, and enjoyed their full respect. We had fighters in our camps in Tanzania, who were also spirit mediums, and we cooperated very well with them. After resuming the war in January 1976, I personally arranged for the remains of Mbuya Nehanda to be exhumed and re-buried nearer to Zimbabwe. When the FRELIMO commanders who had provided logistical support for the exercise finally got word of it, they were extremely irate with me, but I stood my ground. It is, however, also true that the Rhodesian forces took advantage of our cooperation with the spirit mediums to infiltrate us.' He thinks that as many as 600 ZIPA fighters were arrested in the repression of the *vashandi* movement, and that the only reason they did not resist more forcefully and mobilise support, was that they were given orders not to by their leaders (personal communication, 19 September 2005).

This is an interpretation, which recalls and is perhaps influenced by the work on spirit mediums by David Lan and Terence Ranger – the latter Fay Chung remembers as a lecturer at the University of Rhodesia and Nyasaland in the early 1960s. Against the picture presented by scholars like Norma Kriger or indeed prominent Zimbabweans war novelists like Stanley Nyamfukudza, Shimmer Chinodya, Charles Samupindi and Alexander Kanengoni, she claims that the behaviour of ZANLA guerrillas towards civilians during the war was consistently 'non-violent', and gives credit to the mediums for this. She also praises them for standing up to Tongogara around the issue of sexual exploitation of female guerrillas, and requiring 'purity' also in this respect from freedom fighters.

But predominantly Fay Chung is highly unromantic in her view of cultural custom and peasant practices, and is as staunchly modernist in her views as she claims the vashandi to have been. She is worried about the traditionalism of the peasantry, on whose support ZANU and the liberation struggle depend, and which she sees as violent and reactionary. If not held in check and educated by a strong revolutionary vanguard party, 'the peasant mind' will re-lapse into cultivation of 'feudal values'. Thus, improving the situation of poor peasants by giving them more land to cultivate may well lead to an increase in polygamous marriages, which to Fay Chung represent not only repression and humiliation of women, but also forms of promiscuity that might have disastrous consequences in today's world because of the HIV/AIDS pandemic.

This critical stance towards the traditionalism of the peasantry is related in the memoirs to a more general scepticism about the relevance of democracy in a developing society like Zimbabwe's. Fay Chung sees the populism that came to dominate ZANU(PF) in the late 1980s – and with a more general weakening of state power – as rooted in the need for politicians to win support in elections. In this process 'ZANU(PF) became captive to the electorate's wishes,' the 'political education programme dominated by socialism and the identification of the people's grievances during the liberation war came to a halt,' and the alliance between the Government and the revolutionary war veterans was undermined. Democratic pluralism is not well suited for a society where 'tribal conflict' is a constant threat – thus the Matabeleland civil war between 1983 and 1987 reinforced the conviction of 'almost everyone'

– according to Fay Chung – that 'a one-party state was the right solution, as such a state would guarantee national unity.' The unity agreement of 1987, which incorporated PF-ZAPU into ZANU(PF), she claims, was 'hailed by almost everyone as a monumental achievement in nation building by strengthening the one-party state.'

Paradoxically – and not mentioned by Fay Chung – the 1987 unity agreement which brought about de facto one-party rule coincided with changes in Zimbabwe's constitution that secured the formal rights of political parties to organise and campaign. But Chung has little patience with or respect for opposition parties as they emerge – from Edgar Tekere's Zimbabwe Unity Movement in the late 1980s to the Movement for Democratic Change at the end of the 1990s – such parties are 'direction-less' and deconstructive of state authority. Likewise institutions with a democratic potential within a pluralist civil society like the trade union movement – whose importance in the development of nationalism in Zimbabwe and the struggle for independence is given little credit in Fay Chung's memoirs – after 1980 come to assume an attitude and role in society, which is 'confrontational' rather than 'problem-solving.' NGOs and independent media are seen to be completely dependent on support and finance from abroad, and on forces that are hostile to the project of building socialism in Zimbabwe. By contrast, in Fay Chung's book, more genuine and relevant 'forms of democracy' were represented by the practices of 'self-criticism' developed during the liberation struggle, and by the ways in which spirit mediums would take issue then with Tongogara for sexual exploitation and elimination of rivals. Such 'forms', unfortunately, after Independence 'were largely displaced by the more dominant settler-colonial practices, as well as by strongly held feudal mores.'

The decay in revolutionary ethos and state autonomy after Independence is attributed by Fay Chung to a number of influences. The 'populism' resulting from the need to cater for the electorate's preferences, rather than political ideals, went hand in hand with forms of corruption and the rise to prominence of mafikizolo opportunist elements within ZANU(PF) and both served to undermine the strength of the party as a vanguard force. This process was accelerated further by changes in international politics, with the collapse of the Soviet Union in 1989 helping to give unchallenged power to neo-liberalism and the neo-colonial ambitions of the West, and with Zimbabwe's giving in to this from the early 1990s by adopting national policies of Economic Structural Adjustment. Fay Chung is not alone in seeing this as representing a 'selling-out' of revolutionary ideals of social transformation – this is a critique which was given voice throughout the 1990s also by groups of war veterans. Some of these did this very articulately in literary works like Alexander Kanengoni's Echoing Silences from 1997, crying out against the betrayed promises of economic justice and land reform, for which people had suffered during the war.[1]

It was also a critique expressed from the late 1980s by Marxist academic intellectuals like Sam Moyo or Ibbo Mandaza, analysing Zimbabwe's development in terms of political economy, and stressing the need for the 'national question' of a more equitable distribution of resources and economic power to be resolved. Like Fay Chung, many of these Zimbabwean critics of Structural Adjustment have tended to see Mugabe's change of policy after 1997 as a 'return' to a radicalism of transformation and anti-imperialist struggle, which had been betrayed – what Mugabe himself has called the 'Third Chimurenga', using a traditionalist term that Fay Chung avoids.[2] In the view of such a left critical position, concerns over human rights, good governance and a

---

1. For Kanengoni's view of the ongoing crisis and his support for Mugabe's policies, see his article 'One-Hundred Days with Robert Mugabe' in the Harare *Daily News* of 4 December 2003. More recently, Kanengoni has been claimed to work for Zimbabwe's Central Intelligence Organisation (CIO) as a 'media specialist' – see Dumisani Muleya, 'CIO Takes Over Private Media' and 'Mediagate: *Mirror*'s Kanengoni Fired', *Zimbabwe Independent*, 12 August and 9 September 2005.
2. Cf. the collection of Mugabe speeches published by the Zimbabwean Ministry of Information as instruction material for youth militias and ZANU(PF) activists – *Inside the Third Chimurenga*, Harare, 2001. For a discussion of the political economists' position, see Raftopoulos, 'The Zimbabwean Crisis and the Challenges for the Left', 2005. Wilfred Mhanda's critique of the notion of a 'Third Chimurenga' is scathing: 'For many of us, the idea of a so-called "Third Chimurenga" was a ploy to legitimise the hero status of those who never participated in the war itself of the likes of Mugabe himself, Chenjerai Hunzwi, Chinotimba among others. None of the genuine heroes of the war and senior commanders like Rex Nhongo, Dumiso Dabengwa and Josiah Tungamirai ever publicly associated themselves with the so-called "Third Chimurenga" characterised by armed bandits murdering unarmed innocent and defenceless civilians' (personal communication, 19 September 2005).

democratic deficit are less important, and should not be allowed to overshadow the need for 'completing' the agenda of 'decolonisation', which was left unfulfilled at the end of the 1980s. What is important, is what Christine Sylvester has called a return to 'the first "will be"' – a turning back of the clock to the political agendas that had first priority at the launching of Independence in 1980.

The paradox and difficulty of such a backward-looking left avant-gardism, however, is enhanced by the fact that in the meantime another leftist agenda has emerged powerfully, for which issues of rights and state despotism have been major concerns, and for which there has been substantial and widespread popular support. This 'other' left position was manifested in the mobilisations by the Zimbabwe Congress of Trade Unions to protest against inflation and the decline in real wages and living standards during the 1990s, by the campaigns for a more democratic dispensation by the National Constitutional Assembly, and – in 1999 – the formation of the Movement for Democratic Change. That the new opposition was not just the result of manipulations by the 'white farmer interest' and international neo-colonial forces was demonstrated beyond any doubt by the results of the constitutional referendum in February 2000 and the parliamentary elections of June 2000. Both occasions indicated that there was widespread backing within the Zimbabwean population for a system of more pluralist representation, and testified to a process of political development in Zimbabwe, which had moved well beyond the concerns for peace and stability, which had been the priority of the period of the Unity agreement in 1987-88. This represented a development – also in the country's political culture – which has since been reversed again by the violence and repression, with which the Zimbabwean government has responded to the challenge of opposition and pluralism.

What will unsettle many readers of Fay Chung's memoirs, I think, is the high-handedness with which – in the concluding sections – she treats this process of political development and the emergence of a new opposition and the Movement of Democratic Change in particular. The rough treatment, which the opposition has been given by the Zimbabwean government and the dominant party, has been well documented in the press and the reports of human rights NGOs – most recently in the context of the brutal murambatsvina campaigns to drive poor MDC supporters and slum dwellers out of the cities. In the light of this, it will be difficult for many readers to reconcile themselves with Fay Chung's view of the opposition as primarily an instrument of support for white farmers and British and American 'neo-colonialism', and of the MDC as responsible for political violence.[1]

What is at stake here, however, is not just a matter of Fay Chung's personal representation, but of something more fundamental, which Brian Raftopoulos has described as the development of 'a severe break ... between the discourse and politics of the liberation struggle ... and that of the civic struggles for democratisation in the post-colonial period,' and between 'redistribution and rights issues'.[2] In response to the economic and political crisis, a deep-seated ambiguity within the Zimbabwean left has manifested itself between one set of agendas which give priority to economic redistribution and land reform and others for whom democratic development and protection of human rights against violations from the state are more urgent issues. According to Raftopoulos, this is partly the fault of a narrow-minded economistic, Marxist left, which – even in the face of the Matabeleland atrocities of the 1980s – ignored the significance of political rights for popular mobilisation and a reform agenda. At the same time, the Movement for Democratic Change must accept part of the blame also. In spite of its original close ties with the trade union movement it has not done

---

1. It should be noted, however, that Fay Chung has distanced herself publicly and in strong terms from the violence of Operation Murambatsvina – see her articles 'ZANU PF Shoots Itself in the Foot' and 'Interviews with the Dispossessed', *Sunday Mirror,* 7 and 14 August 2005. I am grateful to Terence Ranger for providing me with this reference. Fay Chung's intervention is discussed in Ranger's 'Towns and the Land in Patriotic History' – forthcoming in a volume edited by Ennie Chipembere, Gerald Mazarire and Terence Ranger with the title *What History for Which Zimbabwe?* For an overview of Operation Murambatsvina, see the report by the United Nations special envoy, the Executive Director of UN-HABITAT, Anna Tibaijuka, of July 2005 – http://www.unhabitat.org/documents/ZimbabweReport.pdf.
2. Brian Raftopoulos, 'The State in Crisis: Authoritarian Nationalism, Selective Citizenship and Distortions of Democracy in Zimbabwe', in Hammar, Raftopoulos and Jensen (eds), *Zimbabwe's Unfinished Business,* 2003, p. 235 and 218.

enough to develop more of a social democratic agenda that would emphasize the interdependence of social and economic reform and a deepening of democracy. One can of course argue here, that the MDC has been obstructed considerably by Government and ZANU(PF) harassment in doing so.

But the ambiguity is also a matter of battling interpretations over the history and significance of the liberation struggle in Zimbabwe and of Zimbabwean nationalism. In Fay Chung's account, the new opposition and the Movement for Democratic Change are weak and have no popular mandate, because they are not rooted in the liberation struggle and the history of Zimbabwean nationalism, and because they have never sought to 'win the war veterans to their side.' This seems to be a problematic argument, against which it could be stated that the background in civic and trade union mobilisation, on which the new democratic opposition has based itself, constitutes as important a building stone in the history of nationalism and liberation in Zimbabwe as does the armed struggle. It could also be argued that from early on the combined battle for rights, citizenship, equality and democratisation was at the heart of Zimbabwean nationalism and the inspiration it received from the Congress movement of South Africa. And that workers' rights and the bringing together of labour and political demands formed a central part of the agenda of ZAPU, whose figurehead Joshua Nkomo – like Morgan Tsvangirai – came into politics from the trade union movement.

It is also not right to say that the Movement for Democratic Change and the new democratic left in Zimbabwe have not had any support from or interaction with the war veterans. Indeed, very central figures within the MDC – like Paul Themba Nyathi, Augustus Mudzingwa and Moses Mzila Ndlovu – have strong backgrounds as liberation fighters. Others – like Paulos Matjaka Nare, who stood as MDC candidate in Gwanda South in the June 2000 elections and only lost due to massive ZANU(PF) harassment and intimidation of voters – have had rich histories of involvement, not only with the armed struggle for liberation, but also with ZIMFEP and the attempts to carry the radical impetus of this struggle into social transformation in Zimbabwe after Independence, attempts with which Fay Chung identifies herself. Even among the most revolutionary left segments of the war veterans' movement, there has been division, and while some have welcome Mugabe's

'Third Chimurenga' as a return to a socialist agenda, others have been highly critical, and tended to sympathise rather with the MDC and the new democratic opposition. This goes for Wilfred Mhanda, for instance, a leader of the left socialist vashandi movement within ZANU in the mid-1970s, to which – as stated above – Fay Chung was in many ways close, though they disagreed over Mugabe, whom the vashandi expected to one day become 'a fascist dictator.' In the context of today's crisis, Mhanda and his side of the war veterans' movement – as represented in the Zimbabwe Liberators' Platform – have tended to support the MDC and recognise it as 'a legitimate and popular voice', to emphasise the importance of protection for democratic rights and procedure, but also to subscribe to the need articulated by Brian Raftopoulos for the opposition to develop more of a social democratic redistribution agenda.[1]

So the legacy of the Zimbabwean liberation war is far from undisputed, and it is also not easily agreed which forces – within contemporary Zimbabwean politics – have the right to represent this legacy. In her memoirs, Fay Chung seems to support Robert Mugabe's and ZANU(PF)'s attempt – through the 'Third Chimurenga' – to monopolise the history of the liberation struggle, pose themselves as its only rightful heir, and dismiss the challenge of democratic opposition as something alien and hostile to this historical mission. It is important to have Fay Chung's memoirs available in order to be able to gain insights into and to understand this position within contemporary Zimbabwean politics. But it is also important to keep in mind that the memoirs are a partisan statement – putting forward a particular argument from

---

1. W. Mhanda, 'A Freedom Fighter's Story' (interview with R. W. Johnson), *Focus*, December 2000. Cf. 'How Mugabe Came to Power: R. W. Johnson Talks to a War Veteran', *London Review of Books*, 23(4), 22 February 2001, and David Moore's demonstration of the biases and distortions introduced in R. W. Johnson's presentation of Mhanda in *London Review of Books*, 23(7), 5 April 2001. See also Peta Thornycroft, 'The Never-Ending War of Robert Mugabe', *e-africa*, vol. 2, May 2005 – http://www.saiia.org.za/modules.php?op=modload&name=News&file=article&sid=330

a particular point of view and with particular objectives in mind, which must be weighed against other evidence, articulations, and efforts to prevail.

My father's shop, 1953

CHAPTER 1

Growing up in Colonial Rhodesia

It was impossible to grow up in colonial Rhodesia without becoming aware from one's earliest age of the deep hostility between the races. The land issue was the main bone of contention. At the age of four, I would listen to my grandfather talking about the land problem with his old friend, a Somali who owned a butchery near my grandparents' cafe. My grandfather, Yee Wo Lee, had come to Rhodesia in 1904 as a youth of 17, the fifth son in a large Chinese peasant family. As the fifth son, he did not inherit any land in China. Instead, he was given an education. He had gained his initiation into politics as a schoolboy-follower of Sun Yat Sen, and as a result was very sensitive to the colonial situation. He was one of the first people to provide financial support to black nationalists, and his bakery, Five Roses Bakery, situated very centrally in the middle of Charter Road and near the railway station, soon became the meeting place for many nationalist leaders. He was later to pay the rent for ZANU.

With a peasant's attachment to the land, he came to Africa in search of land, but his ambition was thwarted by the racial laws instituted by the colonialists. These laws forbade the sale of the best land to anyone but the whites. The worst land was reserved for blacks. Those who were neither black nor white were not catered for by the land laws. Grandfather was never able to buy the farm he yearned for. From a very early age we learnt that the whites were greedy and would not allow other races to own land.

My grandfather was very deeply interested in politics. Every day he would be reading about the latest developments in world politics, and every day he would be discussing political issues with his best friend, the Somali. I would stand next to my grandfather's chair, at the age of four, listening to the two of them discussing the strengths and weaknesses of world leaders such as Hitler, Churchill, Chiang Kai Shek, Mao Tse Tung, and Roosevelt. My grandfather had been a great supporter of Sun Yat Sen, from whom he had learnt his nationalist politics in China, but was very suspicious of Mao Tse Tung.

Instead of farming, grandfather began his career as a chef on the newly established Rhodesia Railways in 1904 and later at the then Grand Hotel. All his life he loved cooking, and in the Chinese tradition made it into an art. In my grandparents' household it was grandfather who did all the cooking while grandmother ran the business. Grandfather made the most delicious meals, full of carefully thought-out delicacies each day.

Grandfather was also a wonderful storyteller, and each night would regale us with stories of the Monkey King and other legendary Chinese figures. He was determined that we should not grow up to be uncivilised "mountain dogs", the name given to Chinese who had grown up outside China, illiterates who knew nothing about Chinese culture or values. As a result, he took it upon himself to teach us how to use chopsticks, how to write some Chinese, and some parts of Chinese history.

Part of the division of labour between my grandfather and my grandmother was that he would do all the paper work, including the accounts and banking for their businesses. This was probably inevitable, since my grandmother was illiterate. We used to help grandfather to do all the preparations for banking, including counting all the takings from the businesses. He set up a competition in money counting for my sisters and me. Part of the game was that he allowed us to keep any change that fell on the floor. We used this money to buy books, comics, and sweets. Harare, then called Salisbury, was such a small town that we could go with our small change to the centre of town by ourselves, and buy these comics and books from the two bookshops there. Our favourite comic was called *School Friend*, but we also had access to other children's comics from Britain, like *Beano*.

My grandmother had followed my grandfather out to Africa. I did not understand that this was an unusual step for a peasant woman to take until many years later when I made my first visit to China. In 1973, I visited the villages of my grandparents, and found myself surrounded by elderly women whose husbands had left China half a century before and had never returned. My grandmother had refused to be constrained by tradition and had displayed great courage and determination in embarking into the unknown. Unlike the grass widows who had remained in China faithfully waiting for their husbands to return,

Three sisters with Grandmother and late Aunt Yukong Caroline Lee, 1949.

my grandmother took her fate into her own hands and left for Africa, a continent of which she had no knowledge.

My grandmother was illiterate because it was not the custom to allow girls to go to school in her day, even though her father was the village teacher. She had a great respect for learning, however, and was determined that we should have as much schooling as possible. Despite the fact that she never mastered either English or an African language because of her inherited deafness, she nevertheless managed to run a number of very successful enterprises, showing great business acumen. The workers she employed soon mastered Cantonese, so they did not have any problems communicating with her, and because she had their interests at heart they gave her their absolute loyalty. She was also very kind-hearted, forever helping those in need or in trouble.

Besides running the cafe where she made everything that she sold, including soft drinks, sweets, bread, and a form of cake known locally as "*chiponda moyo*" or "heart breakers", because of their sweetness, she also established a bakery. Like many peasant women, she was used to hard work and would be working from about six in the morning till about ten at night every day. She laid the foundations of the family wealth, on which her children could later build.

My two sisters and I had to stay with my grandparents for some years after my mother's death. The three of us shared a bedroom with my aunt, Carol Yukong, behind the tearoom. We used to help my grandmother to run the business whenever she wanted to go out. Somehow, it seemed perfectly logical for a store to be run by three children under the age of five, readily counting money in order to give the correct change, as we exchanged pennies and shillings for sweets, scones, and "heartbreakers". We had to know the basics of business, lessons that were to remain with us throughout a lifetime.

One of my childhood memories was when our neighbours, another Chinese family, the Ahtoys, hit the headlines. A debtor, a white man, who owed them a great deal of money had decided to sell them his house in an all-white suburb, Avondale, as payment for his debts. This caused a furore among the white neighbours, who refused to accept the Chinese family. However, there appeared to be a loophole in the law. The Chinese family refused to move out, and there was no way to evict them from their own house. It was only much later that I came to understand this loophole. The law forbade sale of so-called "white" lands only to indigenous blacks. However, the title deeds of houses in white areas often contained a clause forbidding their sale to non-whites, such as Asians and Coloureds, the term used in Rhodesia for people of mixed race, but this clause could be broken if the white owner was willing to sell. This could be done because the constitution contained a bill of rights that contradicted the racial land laws. Moreover, companies could also purchase property, whatever the race of the company directors.

Many attempts to harass and intimidate non-white owners of houses in so-called white areas took place, the most famous of these being the creation of the "green belt" or no-man's land separating the Indian community in Ridgeview from its white neighbours in the capital city of Salisbury. In order to ensure rigid racial segregation, this green belt of trees and grass separated the white residential areas of Milton Park and Belvedere from the Indian residential area of Ridgeview.

In the 1960s, another attempt was made to oust Asians and Coloureds owning houses in white areas by having 15 white householders sign a petition for their removal. However, although many whites did sign such petitions against their brown neighbours, I am not aware of any succeeding in their intentions. But these attempts did little to lower the racial tensions that marred human relations across colour lines.

My father, Chu Yao Chung, like all other Asians, was also a victim of the land laws. Even though he could afford to buy a house, he was unable to do so until I had completed my university studies in the 1960s. I was then educated enough to uncover the loopholes in the land ownership laws.

Father had come to Rhodesia as a schoolboy and attended Moffat Primary School. He had done some years of schooling in China, but in colonial Rhodesia he was not able to obtain a secondary education in English. After leaving school, he worked as a shoemaker and later as a miner in Bindura, before becoming a businessman in Salisbury after he had married my mother. My mother, Nguk Sim Lee, had been educated in China and trained as a nurse. My grandmother had come out to Rhodesia leaving my mother in China when she was only 12 years old. My mother travelled to Rhodesia to marry my father, but she died giving birth due most probably to the poor level of medical care available in the 1940s.

Another childhood memory was a strike that paralysed Rhodesia in 1948. All Africans refused to work. Everywhere shops closed. Buses and trucks stopped running. The streets were deserted. A few essential services were manned by whites or Coloureds, some of them in army uniform. It seemed to me that the only African who continued to work was our nanny, Elina, who had looked after us from the time my mother died. On our way to school, she would be stopped again and again by strike organisers and supporters.

"Why are you breaking the strike?" she was asked by a black policeman, who was another black person not on strike.

"I must look after these children as they have no mother", she replied. Everyone accepted that explanation.

My mother had died when I was three years old, leaving my father with three young children. My father was busy running his business, and we were left in the charge of our nanny the whole daylong. It was in that situation that we soon picked up a working knowledge of Shona, one of the main African languages in the country. We also came to understand our nanny, her views, her character, and her background quite well as we followed her around through her day. We knew her friends and what they talked about. It was in those early and impressionable days that I came to understand the situation in the country. I did not understand the problem of land from my nanny and from the other servants in the house, but I quickly heard about education. The black people around me felt that they were being deprived of education because whites did not want blacks to be too educated. One of the old workers in my father's business was called Zakia. He was always reading the Bible. He told me that whites would allow black people to know only the Bible, but kept all other knowledge to themselves. This was how white people managed to control the country. Certainly, black people knew a lot about the Bible, and we were taught Bible stories and sang hymns such as "Jesus loves me, this I know". My nanny and subsequent nannies were also excellent at craftwork. I learnt to knit at an early age, and was able to knit myself a jersey before I was ten years old.

Education, or rather the lack of it, was an area that caused bitter resentment. Children were separated by race. White children attended "European" schools, black children attended "African" schools. There was a third category of schools known as "Coloured and Asian" schools, which we attended.

I attended a primary school for Asians. It was called Louis Mountbatten School, named after the British viceroy of India, as most of the pupils were Indians. Our headmaster, Mr. V.S. Naidoo, a South African Indian from Durban, drummed into our heads from the earliest grades that since we were not whites, we would only make our way in the world through education. This message obviously fell on fertile ground, as both the teachers and pupils were exceptionally dedicated to learning. It was only many years later that I learnt that it was not very usual for primary school children to be conversant with Shakespeare and Jane Austen. By the time I went to secondary school, I had already covered quite a lot of the secondary mathematics syllabus. Pupils from Louis Mountbatten School would do exceptionally well later because of the excellent grounding we received there.

One of the most painful memories I have of the school was the daily conversation I had with the headmaster for being late. As we had no one to wake us in time for school, we were generally late. Mr. Naidoo punished all latecomers by hitting our hands with a ruler. For many years I had to receive this punishment. No doubt it was this early training that has made me almost neurotic about keeping good time!

Our primary school was an unusual one in that we were inducted into political awareness without being conscious of it. It was only later that I realised that many of my attitudes and views had been formed at an early age at our school. Every week the school organised well-known leaders to come and address us. These included both whites and blacks. White Christian clerics came to a school where most of the pupils were either Muslim or Hindu. Black nationalist journalists came to speak to us about their work. We were being brought up to look for professional and leadership qualities without being mesmerised by the racism that permeated the society.

Up until the 1950s, there was no secondary school for Coloureds and Asians. I first became aware of this problem when I was about seven years old. My mother's youngest sister, Yu Kong Lee, who had been baptised Caroline Lee, had completed primary school at the age of 11. A brilliant scholar, she was unable to enrol in a secondary school because she was Chinese. My grandfather went to every secondary school in the city to try to get her enrolled, but these schools were for whites only. She was forced to repeat the last grade of primary school for five years until she left school at the age of sixteen. Perhaps the lack of possibilities for professional independence contributed to her premature death at the age of 21. This was the fate of all Asian and Coloured students, except for the few whose parents could afford to send them overseas or to South Africa for secondary and further education. Girls were usually not allowed to go to school away from home. Education, like land, was for whites only.

The situation for blacks was slightly better than for Coloureds and Asians: in the 1950s there was already one secondary school for blacks, Goromonzi High School, which served the whole country. In contrast, there were over 20 secondary schools for whites, although whites then constituted only four per cent of the population. Whites had compulsory and free primary and secondary education, whereas blacks had limited access and also had to pay for what little education they could obtain. A handful of blacks were allowed to obtain secondary education so that they could serve their own communities as teachers and nurses, and also assist the colonial government as lower-echelon civil servants and clerks. Blacks who wanted more education would have to go to South Africa. Those who were able to go were usually men, as few families would allow their daughters to go so far away. For many decades, educated black men had to marry foreign women if they wanted to marry someone of the same level of education as themselves.

I was fortunate that by the time I completed primary school, the first secondary school for Coloureds and Asians, Founders' High School, was opened in Bulawayo. Mr. Naidoo, our primary school head and a dedicated educationist, spent a whole day persuading my father to allow me to attend as a boarder, since the school was 400 miles away. My father, a conservative and traditionalist, did not really believe in educating girls, particularly in a far away boarding school. But Mr. Naidoo was persistent and persuasive, and my father finally relented.

I spent two happy years as a boarder at Founders. Our headmaster, Mr. Baldock, was an Englishman who was dedicated to making our school the best of its kind. For most of us, this was our first experience of having a head and some teachers who were whites, as our teachers had so far been either Indians or Coloureds. Mr. Baldock had a strong sense of justice, and did not use corporal punishment, a system that we had become accustomed to in our primary school. This became clear one day when I broke a rule that I was not aware of. Every Saturday evening we were taken to a film show in the village of Barham Green, a village for Coloureds. These were mainly American films. The school had been built in the middle of this village. One evening we were forced to watch a particularly inane film and I decided to walk back to the school on my own. When the school matron discovered I was missing, she was very upset, not surprisingly as I was only 11 years old. The next day I had to go to Mr. Baldock's office to explain why I had left the cinema early. I told him the film was exceptionally boring, so I had decided to go to bed. He did not punish me. He told me I was born with a silver spoon in my mouth, which apparently meant I was a spoilt brat.

Mrs. Baldock found out that Chinese were allowed to enter the whites-only cinemas, and once asked me to accompany their two small sons to watch a Walt Disney film. Blacks, Indians and Coloureds were not allowed in most of the cinemas. Rhodesian-style racial segregation allowed the Chinese some privileges, and this was one of them.

Founders was a school that emphasized intellectual pursuits. One reason for this was that a large number of older students, some in their twenties, who had been denied access to secondary education before, had enrolled in the school. These were very serious students, and this situation created a culture of dedicated work. Many of us were so keen on reading that we would drape our blankets over our heads, light a candle under the bed, and read. This was against the rules, as we were supposed to go to bed as soon as lights were out. We carried on this dangerous practice usually undetected by the teachers who supervised our dormitories. The only other alternative was to sit in the toilet, which remained lit at night, to read. We did that too. We had a large library run by our English teacher, Mrs. Denise Gubbay, and I soon took to reading a book a day, a habit she encouraged. Our maths teacher, Mr. Yon, had recently graduated from university and gave us a good grounding in mathematics. It was only later that I discovered that we had completed the O level syllabus, which covered the first four years of high school, in only two years.

At the end of my second year at Founders, St. John's School, a well-known Roman Catholic school for Coloureds, established a secondary section. My parents decided to transfer me to St. John's immediately so that I would be nearer home. Moreover, my father had great faith in the nuns, and believed they had special powers to improve a person's character and morality, and as he placed great value on these attributes, I had to leave the government school for a Roman Catholic school. He was not very confident that a government school like Founders would provide the right moral background.

It was at St. John's that I came to understand the colonial set-up more intimately. St. John's was an "orphanage", but the "orphans" were not real orphans. Many of them were the offspring of white men and their black mistresses. The children of such unions were usually rejected by their fathers, and sometimes also by their mothers. These totally abandoned children were raised by the Dominican sisters. They were easily identifiable as they were invariably given the names of Catholic saints such as Francis Xavier or Martin de Porres. They had developed a hard exterior, often persecuting children like myself from more privileged backgrounds. They did this by stealing our panties and our soap. Actually, they were deeply sad children who knew no home other than the school, and no family other than the nuns and priests. I spent two years at that school, and it made me appreciate the privilege I enjoyed of being a spoilt child from a middle class family.

Such was the racist consciousness, some of these children of mixed race would themselves despise and reject their black mothers. One of my most vivid childhood memories was of a black mother coming to visit her ten-year-old daughter at St. John's. As the school had very few visitors, crowds of children would usually gather around to stare at every visitor. So it was that when Hilda's mother arrived to see her, I was one of the crowd of children who had turned out to stare at her. Ten-year-old Hilda was mortified that her black mother had come to the school and she did not want to acknowledge her. This incident made me think. Hilda constantly talked of her father, a white farmer in Sinoia. She was very proud of her father who had rejected her, but she did not want to know her own mother who had come to see her. I was amazed. As a child who had grown up without a mother, I found it appalling that someone would reject her own mother because of race.

On another day, I witnessed a middle-aged white couple drive up to the school. With them was a small black girl, aged about two or three. They entered the "parlour", as the school's reception room was called. A new "orphan" had arrived. Mary, the new orphan, could not understand what had happened to her. She kept calling for her "mummy" and "daddy". She refused to eat. She refused to bath. Eventually she was dragged into the bathroom to be washed. She yelled and screamed and she particularly objected to the foul smelling blue laundry soap that was the only soap available to the "orphans". She had been used to better things. Toilet soap was a potent symbol of privilege at St. John's. I later found that toilet soap and toothpaste were symbols of privilege too among freedom fighters. Mary screamed traumatically for several weeks before she fell into a sullen silence. She finally understood she had been abandoned.

I learnt at St. John's that Coloured children placed a premium on white skin and straight hair. Many Coloured children were indistinguishable from whites, and they were the most envied. Many others were indistinguishable from blacks, and they were either despised or pitied. Teenage girls spent an inordinate amount of time trying to make their skins whiter and their hair straighter. Girls of Chinese origin like myself, in contrast, spent our time trying to make our hair curlier. We all had the image of the perfect beauty in our minds, and she was Caucasian.

The Dominican sisters who ran the school identified closely with the Coloured people. At the time, for some reason, once a nun was placed with a particular race, she tended to remain in that category virtually for life. It was only much later that nuns were able to move among the three racially segregated school types that they worked in. Thus, those nuns who worked in white schools generally remained in white schools, and tended to think like whites. Those who worked in Coloured schools tended to identify with Coloureds. And those who worked in black mission stations tended to identify with their black charges.

I was very impressed by the nuns at St. John's, who showed an exceptional level of dedication. They did all the work more or less by themselves, never shirking even the dirtiest of jobs like toilet cleaning. Every day we would see the humble German nun who cleaned our toilets, which were usually in a disgusting state, doing her job in silent resignation. This was quite a revelation for those of us who had grown up with a house full of black servants, had never made our own beds or washed our own clothes. This was the first time that I had to do household chores. As I was thought to be exceptionally weak and inexperienced at hard work, my task was to clean the classroom, thought to be the easiest of duties. I also had to wash my own clothes for the first time.

The farm that provided the school with pork, vegetables, and fruit, was run by a broad-backed red-faced German nun. She was helped by only one black worker. We would see her trundling with her wheelbarrow across the schoolyard at the end of the day. There was a legend that her predecessor, another German nun, haunted the school, and could be heard trundling her wheelbarrow at night. We were terrified in case we met her ghost. Probably this legend prevented most of us from leaving our dormitories at night. The kitchen, which fed us all, was run by another strong German nun of peasant extraction. She baked the bread for the whole school once a week, so we had fresh bread only once a week, and stale bread the rest of the time. Sister Regis was the nun in charge of the girls, and she managed to be a sympathetic mother to a few hundred of us. Years later we would meet each other while visiting Sister Regis. She was especially fond of the "orphans", for whom she was the only mother they knew.

The priest in charge of St. John's was Father Eric Edmonstone. He was from an old Rhodesian family and was in charge of giving us religious and moral education, a lesson that we had every day. One day, he asked us whether we had heard of "apartheid". I was the only student who had ever heard of it. Living as we did in the midst of Rhodesian-style racial segregation, most of my classmates were totally unaware of its meaning and its ramifications for their lives. They accepted the values and precepts of apartheid without giving it a name. Father Edmonstone discussed moral issues with us, including such issues as race. Morality and the colonial socio-political order were inextricably entwined, and even as school children we could not escape it.

I left St. John's after having passed my O levels. When I began my secondary education at Founders' High School, I had formed the desire to go to university. A number of our teachers there were university graduates, and they imbued in us a desire to emulate them. I had just begun secondary schooling when the University College of Rhodesia and Nyasaland was established. This development had made going to university feasible for many of us. Whereas my aunt's generation could not even attend a secondary school, it was now possible for us to go to university.

It was the days of federation with Northern Rhodesia and Nyasaland, and this brought in a certain degree of racial liberalisation in Southern Rhodesia. A sign of this was that Chinese girls were now allowed into the previously whites-only Roman Catholic high school. This was a school that had rejected my aunt a decade earlier. I was able to enter to do my A levels, but two of my close friends, Irene Steblecki and Dorothy Walker, who were "Coloureds", could not be allowed into the same school because of their race. Even the holy nuns had to obey the laws of educational apartheid. Irene and Dorothy had to take a correspondence course from London for their A levels. Irene and I later went together to the university. It was this discrimination against Irene and Dorothy that first made me critical of the Dominican sisters, whom I had admired as saints before.

My childhood had made me aware of the realities of race, particularly in terms of how race affected land ownership and education. My Roman Catholic upbringing had emphasized the importance of social justice and equality. However, I had no conceptualisation of the possibilities of change. My experience of university was to change this.

CHAPTER 2

An Undergraduate in the '60s

On completion of my A levels, I was accepted at the local university, the University College of Rhodesia and Nyasaland (UCRN). UCRN then offered London University degrees. I entered the university in 1960, when it had been running for four years. There were just over 300 students, of whom about one-third were blacks. There were a handful of us who were neither black nor white.

This was the first opportunity for us to meet with students of all races on an equal footing. Our lecturers were mainly from Britain and had little knowledge or experience of the racist Rhodesian ethics and ethos. For the first time, we were able to confront the nature of our society intellectually.

The university was very far from radical or left wing. Indeed, it was the epitome of middle-class conservatism. Every evening we dressed up for dinner in formal academic gowns and were served at the dinner table by waiters. Our rooms were cleaned everyday by maids. We were being groomed to be the elite, the rulers of the future based on meritocracy rather than on racial superiority. The kind of society we envisaged was basically the same as what we had hitherto experienced, but without the ugly scars of racial prejudice.

It was during this period that I met some of the black students who would later become part of the ruling elite in Zimbabwe, Zambia, and Malawi. We had to learn to juggle personal, social, and political relationships within a racially segregated society. My best friend, Irene Steblecki, who had been at St. John's with me, and I were the only two women students who were neither black nor white. We were given the privilege of having a whole corridor to ourselves in the women's residence, Swinton Hall, complete with a large sitting room to entertain our guests, as the university authorities respected local racial prejudices by separating us by race. There were only four black women students, two from Zambia, one from Malawi, and only one from Rhodesia,

Sarah Chavunduka. They too had a whole corridor and sitting room to themselves!

Being neither black nor white gave us many advantages, as it allowed us to mix freely with all races. The Asians and Coloureds were so few that we were unable or unwilling to form our own racial clique. We numbered less than half a dozen at the time. During my years at the university there were at most two students of Chinese origin on the campus at any one time. There were some whites and some blacks who were willing to mix with other races, although at both extremes there were whites who never spoke to blacks and blacks who never spoke to whites. In the racially segregated halls of residence it was still possible not to share a bathroom with a student of another race. Somehow, bathrooms were a particularly sore point, as many white students would not tolerate sharing a bathroom with a person of another race. One of the courageous steps taken by the Swinton Warden, Dr. Barbara Douglas, in 1961, was to hold a secret ballot for white women students to see which students were prepared to share bathrooms with non-white students. Only a few white women refused to share bathrooms with us, so that by 1961 it was possible to integrate Swinton. The women who had refused to share their bathrooms were able to perpetuate this privilege, as there were some all-white corridors. This move at Swinton enabled the men's residences to follow suit.

The university tried to bridge the racial gulfs that separated the different groups within the society, and in this it was partially successful. In the lecture rooms and tutorials we were not segregated and we were able to study together as equals. The many societies and clubs at the university were also not rigidly segregated, although some attracted only white students and others only black students. I managed to be on the executive of six of these societies. I was especially active in the Catholic Society, having come from a very Catholic background. Many of the white and black students had also been educated in Catholic schools, and although these had been racially segregated, we nevertheless had a great deal in common. The Catholic Society met once a week, and we discussed political, social, as well as religious and moral issues. It was probably due to the Catholic Society that we all developed a very high degree of social consciousness, rejecting racism as unchristian.

There were a few Marxists at the university, mainly among the lecturers, but we accepted them good-naturedly and were not unduly influenced by them. Few of us were interested enough to read Marx or Lenin. The leading intellectual light at the university was the history professor, Terence Ranger. He, together with other anti-racist lecturers and students, organised peaceful protests against the colour bar. This was my first experience of protest. We would go in a racially mixed group and have tea in an all-white restaurant. Innocuous as that sounds today, at the time it was a courageous challenge to the colour bar. We found that we were never chased out when the group consisted of women only. However, things became pretty rough when men were involved. One violent incident that occurred was at the Salisbury swimming pool. For some reason, swimming pools, like bathrooms, were particularly sacred to whites, and an incident took place involving Terence Ranger being pushed into the swimming pool by some irate white racists.

The predominant ideology at the university was that of liberalism, which favoured the development of individual values and individual ideologies. The existentialist philosophy of Jean Paul Sartre, which rejected materialist capitalism while accepting individual responsibility to improve what was wrong around us, was very powerful, particularly among the Catholic thinkers of the day, and influenced our development. The university was well known for rejecting the prevailing racist ideology, epitomised by racial segregation and oppression of blacks on the grounds that they comprised an inferior race, but promoted individual rather than mass action. Nevertheless, the university could not escape being branded as a "communist" institution, although it was in fact very far from being one. It was the practice of the Smith regime to brand any form of criticism or opposition, however mild, as "communist".

It was during my period at university that we heard that a black lecturer named Bernard Chidzero had been prevented from taking up his post merely because his wife, Michelene, was a white French-Canadian. Interracial marriages were forbidden by law, and those who attempted it could face imprisonment.

In my first year at the university I was picked to be a drum majorette, then a "whites only" preserve. Terence Ranger saw this as a breakthrough. However, after a couple of years as a drum majorette I refused to continue, much to the disappointment of those who thought it was important for us to participate in all-white institutions. I begrudged the time I had to spend practising for drum majorettes, a pastime that required two to three hours of rigorous practice every day. It was rather pathetic that we considered these little triumphs to be important breakthroughs.

While some of us were able to form friendships across all races, I do not recall any case of interracial marriage during my period as a student. We were basically a very conservative campus, and respected the separation of our different communities. Our opposition was against state-imposed racism and segregation, but in practice we did not oppose personal choices based on cultural and historical conservatism. As there were only four black women students in my day, most of the black male students were in the habit of dating women from outside the campus, mainly from among the nurses at Harare Hospital.

The 1960s was a period of enormous turmoil in African politics. It was not possible to be unaware of the mass demonstrations taking place, in which tens of thousands of black people gathered against the colonial settler regime. These mass demonstrations were becoming a regular part of the national life. Shops in the city and in the townships would close down during these demonstrations, which saw men and women marching in peaceful protest against the colonial regime. Our black fellow students would go and participate in these rallies. Although the demonstrations were peaceful, they were met with state violence in the form of tear gas and dog attacks. These would cause panic, and some children were crushed on their mothers' backs in the chaos as people tried to escape. Police dogs were generally Alsatians that had been trained to attack black people.

The 1960s was also the period when African nationalism was at its height. Joshua Nkomo was the president of the Zimbabwe African People's Union, ZAPU. It was soon to be challenged by the formation of the Zimbabwe African National Union, ZANU. Both Joshua Nkomo and the new leader of ZANU, Ndabaningi Sithole, came to address us at the university. Perhaps not surprisingly, we were more impressed by Ndabaningi Sithole, whose book, *African Nationalism*[1], had become one of the most popular books on campus. Sithole's argument was that African nationalism had been born in the Second World War when African soldiers fought in the British army against Nazism. This

---

1. Ndabaningi Sithole, *African Nationalism*, 1960.

had brought forth the ideas of freedom from colonialism, which was so closely akin to Nazism, with its foundation of racial superiority and racial domination by the so-called superior race. Joshua Nkomo struck us as a great feudal chief rather than as a modern political leader.

Some of the university lecturers, including Terence and Shelagh Ranger, John Reed, Jaap and Ruth van Velsen, John Conradie, and a host of others, decided to show solidarity with African nationalism by attending these meetings and speaking up against racism. This led to direct conflict between the university and the government, and lecturers and students were jailed and expelled. Many were forced to flee the country. Soon after the Unilateral Declaration of Independence (UDI) in 1965, almost half the lecturers were imprisoned and then expelled. Conflict between university and government was to characterise the next few decades, and has continued even in the post-independence era.

The university provided the first opportunity to come into contact with an academic world that had not been filtered through Rhodesian racism and propaganda. Our school curriculum, particularly at primary school level, had been littered with justifications for colonialism and racism. The syllabuses and examinations were now those of London University, which meant that many topics and views that had been considered taboo could be addressed openly. These topics included the nature of colonialism, the land issue in the country, and the issue of racism. What I had encountered as a child, when my grandparents and my father were not able to purchase land, came into focus historically. Colonialism had meant that the best half of the land had been taken over by whites, with black people being forced to move into "reserves". It was not at all difficult to see the difference between the white commercial farm areas and the "reserves". The white commercial farms comprised beautiful agricultural land with better soil and better rainfall than the "reserves". A few thousand white farmers owned these farms, many of them having received their land as a reward for their participation in the Second World War. Black soldiers who had also fought on the side of the British in the Second World War were rewarded with army overcoats, but no land. White farmers enjoyed generous subsidies through the Agricultural Bank set up to provide them with financial support. An excellent agricultural extension service existed for whites known as CONEX, making it possible even for neophytes to enjoy the highest level of agricultural planning, research, and knowledge. Black peasants were crowded into granite-dominated lands, beautiful to look at, but barren. Many black families remembered the days when they had once inhabited the more fertile farms, which had been forcibly taken from them and given over to white farmers. This bitter memory was engraved in the communal psyche.

Moreover, in these overcrowded black lands there were few facilities. Those fortunate enough to harvest a good crop were not allowed to sell it to the government-controlled marketing board. Instead, they had to find a friendly white farmer who would agree to market it on their behalf. Such white farmers usually charged a heavy commission for their services. Schools and clinics for blacks, where they existed, were provided by missionaries as part of their religious work.

Education for blacks was severely restricted, and in the early days literacy was closely linked with proselytisation. It was not surprising in that situation that blacks firmly believed that they were allowed only religious knowledge, whereas whites were allowed to have access to a wider range of knowledge. This impression was strengthened by the fact that while entry to Grade 1 was generally possible in a mission primary school, restrictions began at Grade 3 and continued every two or three years, with cut-off points at Grade 5, Grade 7, Form 2 (or Grade 9) and Form 4 (or Grade 11). In the 1960s, there were only half a dozen secondary schools for blacks, with only two of them going as far as Form 6 (or Grade 13). Only about two per cent of black children enjoyed the privilege of secondary education at the time.

It was as a university student that I first became interested in education. I began teaching at the university night school, which was run by lecturers and students for the house servants and other workers in the nearby upper class suburb of Mount Pleasant. It had been started by our French lecturer, Dr. Clive Wake, and was run mainly by students. I soon became the head of the primary section of the school, a position I held until I graduated three years later. I encountered once again the thirst for knowledge of my black compatriots. They arrived indefatigably for their evening classes day after day, year after year, despite the fact that most of them worked a 12-hour day. On the other hand, it was a battle to ensure that the university students who had volunteered so enthusiastically to teach at the beginning of the academic year continued to do so consistently. Such was our ignorance and arrogance that none of us had received the benefit of any teacher training. We also knew nothing about administration. We ran the night school to the best of our ability, making elementary mistakes such as doing literacy in English rather than in the mother tongue. As a result of our ignorance, our students took several years to become literate in English. It was many years later that I discovered that we could have developed literacy in the mother tongue within a few months, and that gaining literacy in English would then have been less painful. We learnt to administer without the benefit of any theory or training, and naturally made many gross errors. For example, we learnt through painful experience that we had to test students rather than accept their own assertions about the grade they had completed in school. Some who asserted that they had completed Grade 6 were actually illiterate, whereas others who claimed to have completed the same grade were ready for university. Despite our ignorance and amateurish efforts, there was a lot of goodwill, and our students kept coming. Many of them eventually completed both primary and secondary education. They had few other alternatives.

The university itself ran a pre-university course for older black students, as there were not enough candidates to enrol in the university. This special programme was instrumental in overcoming some of the disabilities created by the racist education system.

Having taught for three years at the night school it was natural for me to think of education as a career, and I decided to enter African education on graduation. Many of my fellow students at the university had also developed a sense of mission. We felt it our duty to somehow improve the situation, to redress the glaring inequities that marred our country. It was impossible, we felt, for us to pursue our totally selfish careers and personal goals. We had to make a difference.

CHAPTER 3

Teaching in the Turmoil of the Townships

When I applied for a post in African education, I found I was received with less than enthusiasm. I was told that I should apply to teach pupils of my own race. As there were only a few hundred Chinese in Rhodesia, this was a laughable suggestion. Although all the Chinese children in the capital city attended the same school, Louis Mountbatten School, a school for Asians, there were so few of us that it was virtually impossible to find two of us in one class. Then I was told that there were too many teachers in African education, and that there was no need for more teachers. However, I had done my research in the area, and I knew that there were in fact very few university graduates within African education. Even if it were true that there were too many teachers, it could not be said that there were enough graduate teachers. At any rate, I refused to be turned down, and after some time my application was accepted.

My family was astonished that I had decided to teach in an African school. My grandmother in particular was anxious to organise my marriage. She had been very keen to see me go to university, but she felt that now I had completed my studies, it was time to marry. My father too felt that it was time for marriage. I was now 21 years old, considered the best time for marriage. My younger sister had already married, having refused to go to university. I was presented with a variety of possible suitors from the Chinese community in the Congo, in Mozambique, and in Rhodesia itself. People of the Chinese diaspora, particularly those from the county of Toisan in southern China, remained closely connected with each other, and marriages were still arranged and could take place across Southern Africa. A marriage could readily be organised for me with a suitably rich Chinese businessman. My grandmother spoke to me about it. Would I insist on marrying a university graduate, as there were not many of them around? There were

My father and stepmother in their shop 1953

a few, and it could be arranged. My stepmother warned me that if I didn't grab the best one now, I would be left with the rotten pumpkins.

Our neighbour, Mr. Ahtoy, was the most vociferous. He openly expressed his opinion that going to university and getting a degree was "going up in the world", whereas going to work in a township school was "going down in the world". Many Chinese had shops in the townships, where they made a precarious living serving these largely impoverished but heavily populated areas. Their main stock in trade was maize meal (the staple diet), sugar, tealeaves, bread, and dried fish – the basic foods of the poor. Mr. Ahtoy could not understand why I would choose to go down in the world. However, I had other ideas and my family was used to my ways and allowed me to have a free hand in making my own decisions. I wanted to teach in African education, and my family did not stop me.

My first post was at Ascot Secondary School in Gwelo, now Gweru. I was the first teacher to arrive at the new school and the builders were still putting the final touches to the buildings. The only other member of staff present was the headmaster, an Englishman who had served in the British army in the Second World War. Many British immigrants had entered the country after that war.

A few weeks later the school opened. Thick crowds of parents and children arrived to enrol. Four classes of 30 pupils each were selected.

The rest were summarily dismissed. An angry scene ensued. Parents and potential pupils protested noisily. An old man in a dark green army overcoat, one of the black soldiers who had served in the Second World War on the side of the British, wept. He had enrolled his son in school at the age of five, but since black children were not allowed to enrol until they were seven years old, he had obtained a birth certificate with the requisite date. Now he was being told his son was too old for enrolment. In the arbitrary selection system where only two per cent of black children could be enrolled in the half-dozen secondary schools for blacks, children were routinely rejected on the grounds of age, residence, or lack of some or other essential bureaucratic documentation. The parents and children refused to leave: they could not understand why a school with 12 classrooms and eight teachers could enrol only four classes.

The flustered headmaster ordered us to lock ourselves, and those fortunate enough to be enrolled, in the classrooms. Immediately afterwards the riot squad arrived. Their task was to clear the school grounds of intruders. Soon tear gas seeped through the doors and windows of the classrooms. The Alsatian dogs attacked the parents and children outside. Screams of terror could be heard. This was the inauspicious inauguration of the school.

The school was run with military discipline, with an inspection of uniforms, socks and shoes each morning. Little attention was paid to the intellectual development of the pupils. The highly inexperienced staff, most of us recent graduates, was left to our own devices. For the children, corporal punishment was the order of the day. Nearly every boy was beaten at least once a week. Girls were more fortunate, as there was a rule that they could be beaten only by a woman teacher. The main transgression was being late for school. School started at 7.30 a.m., although the headmaster himself only arrived at 8.30 each morning. Teachers were required to give in the names of latecomers. As this was the only day secondary school in Gwelo, pupils had to come on foot or by bicycle from all over the city, some travelling over 12 miles each way to school.

It was not long before the teachers refused to report latecomers and the headmaster had to rely on the school clerk for the names of pupils for him to beat. A number of us could not accept the violence with which the boys were beaten. The boys were made to take off their thick khaki shorts so that they could be whipped on their bare bottoms. The headmaster's office was next to the staff room, and each day the violent sound of about 40 boys being beaten and of boys weeping penetrated the walls. It was not surprising that these daily beatings were perceived to be racist and colonialist in origin and intent. It was the norm in the 1960s that the heads of government secondary schools should be whites. The only position a white could hold in an African primary school was also that of the head.

The poverty of our pupils was such that most of them came to school barefooted, carrying their shoes tied together by the shoelaces over their shoulders. These shoes were so precious that they could not afford to be dirtied or worn out. Socks were equally precious. They were always brand new, came packed in the children's school bags, and were hurriedly put on for the morning inspection. Shoes and socks were taken off and neatly packed away immediately after inspection. The fees were R$8 a term and were a major investment by a parent.

As a university student I had been able to afford the luxury of regularly visiting a hairdresser, which cost me about R$8 a visit. Now I was faced with the reality that a visit to the hairdresser cost as much as the school fees for a child for a term. There were two economies in Rhodesia: one where whites routinely spent R$8 for a visit to the hairdresser while blacks who were fortunate enough to be employed earned R$10 a month.

One painful day, a boy in my class called Dube had his shoes stolen. Dube was the youngest in the class, and he was in tears. The theft of his shoes was a serious matter, as it would mean that he would have to leave school, since no child was allowed to attend school without shoes to display during inspection. No shoes meant expulsion. I reacted by refusing to teach the class until his shoes were returned. We managed to spend a whole day in silence staring at each other. So keen were the pupils on their lessons that the next day the stolen shoes were returned. The only punishment necessary at that time was for the teacher to refuse to teach!

The school had adequate textbooks, but no library books. I decided to take the initiative to start a library immediately. I soon managed to obtain about 400 books by begging from embassies and from wellwishers. In my naivety, I trained and left pupils in charge of the library. Within a week all the books had been stolen. These children had never owned books of their own, and the temptation to own a book was too great. Even the encyclopaedias were stolen, as was the usual embassy propaganda. I reacted by closing down the library. No more books would be obtained unless the 400 books were returned. Amazingly, within a few days all the stolen books were back, and we were able to reopen the library. I had to institute strict security measures to prevent books from being stolen by the book-hungry children.

Under the racist system of Rhodesia, the African education system differed radically from the European education system for whites, Coloured, and Asians. Whereas the European system was based on the British system of compulsory education up till the age of 16, with every attempt to encourage learning, African education was a frenzied and irrational race through a jungle of facts that had to be mastered to pass the Rhodesian Junior Certificate. Children who entered our school were the lucky few who had managed to complete primary education, and we had accepted only four per cent of the applicants, but we were expected to shed half of them within two years. The instrument for this task was the Rhodesian Junior Certificate examination. Pupils had little time to develop a love of learning in their desperation to pass the examinations. Education was one of the few ways open to blacks to escape poverty.

"Discipline" was another characteristic of the system, with teachers demanding and obtaining absolute obedience from their pupils, as obedience and passivity were highly prized personality traits. Asking questions and any form of exuberance would have been interpreted as bad behaviour. It was difficult for me to tell how much of this was due to traditional African culture, which required obeisance and subjugation to authority, and how much of it was due to colonial culture, which required passive obedience. Pupils who were unable to impose self-discipline on themselves, faced frequent and even daily beatings at the school, usually from the headmaster himself. Many years later I met an old colleague and remarked that few of the Ascot Secondary pupils we had taught had risen to positions of leadership. In contrast, many of the Harare Secondary pupils whom I later taught became prominent in all walks of life. He told me that many Ascot pupils had become good policemen, a training they had doubtless gained from their schooling.

Gwelo was also the heart of the Rhodesian Front, the extreme right wing party that had won the whites-only elections. Although it had many fascist features, the Rhodesian Front practised a high level of democracy, but only for whites. The Rhodesian Front leader himself, Ian Smith, had a farm not far away. Gwelo was a small town, with little available accommodation. I eventually managed to find a room at a hostel for white women. As there were very few Chinese in Rhodesia, we sometimes found ourselves classified as whites, able to enjoy the same privileges as whites, and I was accepted as a hostel dweller.

Nearly all of the hostel inhabitants were the daughters of neighbouring commercial farmers. These were highly practical young women who cleaned the engines and changed the wheels of their cars themselves. I was soon being given lessons in these practicalities. Having been brought up on farms, they had a kindly paternalistic attitude towards blacks. They advised me never to give a lift to whites, as a white "who didn't own a car couldn't be trusted", but all of them regularly gave lifts to blacks, whom they considered to be trustworthy and harmless. I still remember one kind, barely literate young white girl trying desperately to learn some first aid. She was soon to marry a farmer and was nervous about how she would cope with the sick farm workers. One of the duties of a white farmer's wife was to tend to the illnesses of the workers and their families.

But there was a darker side to white Rhodesia. Not a week passed without a suicide among the small white community in Gwelo. Perhaps it was the schizophrenia so difficult to hide in a small town: the same white men who supported the overtly racist Rhodesian Front also kept black mistresses.

I managed to stay in Gwelo for only one year. I found it difficult to accept the military regime, racism, and sadism that characterised that school. I was fortunate to be transferred to Harare Secondary School, where I remained for the next four years. Harare Secondary, although also a government secondary school for blacks, was very different from Ascot. Situated in one of the most politically volatile townships, where anti-government demonstrations and riots were common occurrences, the school nevertheless managed to survive without any corporal punishment. It was situated amidst many beer halls, as cheap local beer was one of the major means of pacification. Sometimes some of our pupils would come to class drunk. Because the school population was recruited on the basis of race rather than class, the school catered for both rich and poor black children. The few children of the rich exhibited the usual symptoms of their wealth by being more playful and less able to concentrate on their studies than their poorer classmates. On the other hand, the children of the very poor, usually about a third of the class, were obviously not fed properly, particularly in the last ten days of each month. In one family the children had to take turns to go to school. Amazingly, all the boys in that family managed to complete secondary school. Girls were generally less fortunate.

The malnutrition was so severe that a number of women teachers decided to start a soup kitchen. We persuaded a company to sell us some soup at a discount, and began selling it at a cent a cup. Such was the racial acrimony and suspicion of the times that when the soup kitchen was opened, the rumour spread round the school that it was laced with contraceptives to make blacks infertile. This rumour was only scotched when the soup organisers drank the soup. It was quite a picture to see the women teachers queuing up for their cup of soup!

The teachers at Harare Secondary were the usual mixture for an African secondary school of the day, comprising some white missionaries, some white teachers who had been removed from the European education system for misdemeanours as varied as alcoholism and insubordination, and a handful of black graduates, then a rare breed. Despite the difficult situation of almost daily political conflict, combined with the extreme poverty of many pupils, the school managed to obtain excellent results in the Cambridge O levels examinations. Each year, more than 90 per cent of the pupils passed. This was due in large part to the dedication and vision of the headmaster, Mr. Bob Craven, a Yorkshire man who ensured that all teachers and pupils worked well. This was no easy task, given the composition of the teachers and the difficult situation of the pupils. Even the two white alcoholic teachers who nipped off to the Queen's Hotel, a well-known city bar, at the 10.30 a.m. break every morning for a quick drink, performed their teaching duties admirably. Actually, they were among the most brilliant of the teachers! The pupils were allowed to work at the school in the evenings and at weekends, as many of them did not have electricity at home. Many had to share a single room with the whole family.

The school accepted every girl who applied. Many years later the wisdom of this policy became apparent, with many of the top positions in schools and hospitals throughout the country being staffed with women who had obtained their secondary education at our school.

Despite the school's brilliant examination results every year in the O levels, only a handful of our pupils were able to enter the pre-university course known as Advanced or A levels. I remember in 1967 more than 60 students gained first and second class passes at O levels, but only four of them could find places for the A levels that would allow them to enter university. The numbers were kept low so that blacks would never outnumber whites at the local university.

Our pupils, with their brilliant examination results, found jobs in the city as clerks, shop assistants, and messengers. It was not unusual to find a black with eight or nine passes with the top grade of A working as a messenger in an office where a semi-literate white secretary would earn ten times the salary. Better-qualified whites earned 30 times more than the average black. A few of the luckier school leavers found places in teachers' colleges or in hospitals as nurses. The shortage of girls with O levels was to the advantage of the few girls who attended our school, as all of them were able to find training places.

Working in the townships in the 1960s made me more aware of the social and moral problems faced by black people, including many of the children in the school. Because of the paucity of secondary schools, sometimes a rural parent would make enormous sacrifices to send a child to a secondary school such as ours. These children would be sent to live with a relative. All too often this relative would lose the job to which his housing was tied, but the child would be loathe to lose the rare opportunity of attending a secondary school. The boy would remain at school, trying to survive as best he could. Inevitably, some of these children would fall victim to the social pressures in the township. The huge hostels where tens of thousands of men lived as "bachelors" provided a ready sanctuary for such homeless children. The colonial laws made it illegal for black workers to live with their wives in a city. These men lived in hostels, where homosexuality and prostitution were common practice. Destitute children became easy victims. Sadly, many of the young victims of sexual abuse were not able to complete their studies. Young teenage girls were very much sought after. When school ended at 4 p.m., we would see some wealthy men coming in smart cars to pick up our teenage girls. The "sugar daddy" syndrome was already well established. As for the young homeless boys, they were often "befriended" by older men, who would exploit them homosexually in return for supporting them and paying their school fees. Some of the abused children showed signs of severe emotional distress in the classroom, but we teachers were not able to do much to help.

Another problem was political violence, both by the state and by neighbours. The children at the school were also violent, many of them carrying knives in their pockets. One day a boy of 15 threatened to stab a white woman teacher, Mrs. Veronica Ross. He was restrained by his classmates. Mr. Bob Craven, the headmaster, reacted not by expelling the boy or calling the police, but by sending a black teacher to the boy's home. It was thus that we learnt that the boy's father had been arrested for political reasons a few days earlier. As was usual in such cases, his property and his house had been confiscated by the state and his wife and children evicted. The boy was the eldest son. It was a colonial rule that all the property of politically active blacks who joined nationalist parties would be confiscated. Ironically, this rule survived long after independence, when it was used against the political opponents of the ZANU PF government, including white farmers. The boy was allowed to stay in the school, but he failed all his examinations at the end of the year.

During times of violence, the school could not be exempt. On one occasion, it was attacked by the youths whom we had excluded. This was during the period of the school strike of 1964, and only the teachers were in the school. We found ourselves surrounded by angry youths whose intentions appeared to be violent. The Rhodesian police rescued us with the usual teargas and dogs.

On another occasion, some parents came to tell the teachers to evacuate the area as the violence was about to escalate. We were fortunate that the community around us saw us as friends and would come to our rescue in times of danger. Nevertheless, it was not wise to come to the school in the evenings or at weekends, when anyone who was not black could be the object of undiscriminating violence. The "cleaners" who lived on the school premises now had to take on some of the responsibilities of teachers, especially in the evenings and weekends, when children were allowed to study in the classrooms without any other supervision. Actually, the school was cleaned by the pupils, supervised by the teachers. What had been peaceful protests in my days as a university student had now deteriorated into violent rage. Schools, churches, and shops were routinely attacked, and some of them destroyed. I tried to understand the anger and hatred against schools and churches. As schools, particularly secondary schools like our own, catered for only a small elite, they were symbols of privilege from which the majority were excluded. Churches were a symbol of colonialism and oppression to some nationalists. The routine burning of shops was understandable, as these shops contained all the goods that the majority could not buy.

During the nationwide school boycott against school fees in 1964, children who dared to come to school were savagely attacked as scabs. This painful period was not without its moments of humour, such as when an 11-year-old boy, keen to come to school, decided to dress up as a girl to escape being attacked. We burst into laughter when we saw our keen student in disguise! Many brilliant students did not come back at the end of the boycott, and we understood that they had decided to join the armed struggle against colonialism. The politically active students were dropping out, as they saw little hope in change through education.

Sometimes children were caught up in riots, arrested, and sent to prison. A young boy of 15 in my class spent six months in jail. He had been in the middle of a crowd of demonstrators and was alleged to have thrown a stone. We were unable to do anything to get him released, although we tried to see if he could be rescued by the social welfare authorities.

Because of the severe shortage of secondary school places, many community schools began to spring up, following the model created by Josiah Chinamano, a leading ZAPU nationalist leader who had established Highfield Community School. These community schools sought to provide secondary education to the tens of thousands of young blacks deprived of any chance of a secondary education. I was involved in a community school that was started by Father Ted Rogers, a Jesuit priest who had also started the School of Social Work. This school was to become St. Peter's Kubatana School. St. Peter's then depended almost entirely on volunteer teachers like myself, who offered to teach some classes free of charge. Pupils paid a small fee, which was used to employ a few unqualified teachers. We utilised some empty premises that had formerly been a primary school for Coloured children. The main problem with these premises was that the train tracks passed close to the school, so that teachers had to shout above the racket of passing trains. I recall one of my fellow teachers was Wilf Mbanga, who had just left school. He became a prominent journalist and editor. Another was Tim David, a British volunteer who later became an ambassador.

Thousands of children were now able to gain some form of secondary education through community schools. However, conditions were not favourable, mainly because of the use of unqualified and volunteer teachers. While examination results at Harare Secondary School were excellent, those at the community schools were terrible. Our headmaster at Harare Secondary School decided to take any pupils from a community school who managed to pass the Junior Certificate Examination. In this way, some of the top students from the community schools were able to enter into the formal education system, and some of them later were able to make it to university. However, these success stories were few. Only one or two pupils out of a thousand were able to make it from the community school to the formal school system. For the majority of pupils, community schools did not provide a good education.

It was at this time that numerous night schools sprang up, and I was involved in a couple of them. Our task was to provide high school education to adults. I would drive the 14-mile journey from my home in Vainona to Highfield township in the evenings to take my night school class. Some of these night schools were offshoots of the university night school. A few of these adults succeeded in getting into university. I recall one of my students was a Roman Catholic nun. Many young girls joined the convent to escape either from poverty or from the feudal customs that enforced early marriage, polygamy, and deprivation of education. Some of these nuns were able to further their education. This student soon managed to go to university.

Because of the colonial government's determination not to allow many blacks to obtain secondary education, a number of commercial colleges sprang up to provide secondary education to blacks. These generally made a handsome profit, and managed to enrol tens of thousands of students. The demand for education was high, and these commercial schools provided a much-needed service. More students graduated from the voluntary and commercial education system than from the formal government-supported system.

In 1968 the Smith regime decided to halt further expansion of African education. At the time, there were only six secondary schools for blacks, as compared to more than two-dozen for whites. Education was free and compulsory for whites, but expensive and severely restricted for blacks. Because his regime saw education as a dangerous tool that should not be placed in the hands of Africans, Smith decided to stop missionaries, the main providers of education to Africans, from establishing new schools. I was amazed to see the muted opposition by the churches to this draconian move. The main reason was that many churches owned a great deal of property and land, and some felt that open opposition to the state would lead to the confiscation of their properties.

Instead, the Smith regime placed the onus on parents themselves to provide education for their children if they so wished. In 1968, this was a cynical policy as the majority of parents had little education and insufficient money to establish their own schools. Ironically, while the intention was to stop the expansion of education to Africans, it increased the interest of parents in providing education for their children, and many years later, after independence, this made it easier for government to obtain parental support for education.

Although churches were being attacked as symbols of colonialism by protesting township dwellers, churches were also forming the backbone of opposition against racism and injustice. Not far away from our school, the Methodist church was the venue for weekly meetings where people of all races would gather to help those who had been imprisoned for political reasons. There we would meet many of the church supporters who were prepared to face persecution and imprisonment rather than accept the unjust rule of the Rhodesian Front. It was there that we would meet leaders such as Guy and Molly Clutton Brock, Quakers who had dedicated their lives to putting into practice their belief in human equality and social justice. Guy and Molly lived simple lives, eschewing the usual luxuries and conveniences, such as flush toilets and electricity. These meetings focused on social welfare questions, such as how to support the families of and the educational programmes for political prisoners. Politics as such were never openly discussed, probably because the meetings were infiltrated by secret service agents.

Many Quakers were carrying out acts of passive resistance to the Rhodesian regime. One of them was Mr. Knottenbelt, who was the headmaster of Fletcher High School, one of only two schools preparing black students to enter university. In 1965 he refused to raise the new post-Unilateral Declaration of Independence (UDI) Rhodesian flag at his school, deeming UDI to be an illegal rebellion against the British government. For this act of passive defiance he was sacked. He was fortunate enough to find a new post at the University of Rhodesia, which had up till 1965 remained a bastion of liberalism opposed to the racism of the Ian Smith regime.

However, this was soon to change as the Smith regime expelled some dozens of university lecturers on political grounds. Through these expulsions the Smith regime aimed, and to some degree succeeded, in changing the type of university staff able to work at the university.

Two university lecturers, John Reed and John Conradie, were accused of supporting the Zimbabwe African People's Union (ZAPU) by bringing in arms of war on ZAPU's behalf. John Conradie was arrested after being betrayed by a ZAPU colleague and was to spend the next 12 years in prison, where he contracted tuberculosis. His premature death in the 1990s was probably due to his long years of incarceration. John Reed managed to escape to Zambia, where he became professor of literature and languages at the university.

1965, the year of Ian Smith's Unilateral Declaration of Independence, marked an increase in violence everywhere, especially in the cities. Our school in Harare township was soon surrounded by violence. White- and Asian-owned shops around us were burnt down to black hulks. Churches and schools were attacked. Harare township now resembled a city of ruins. The townships had become no-go areas, with violence not only against other races, but also against blacks, as gangs of youths went around demanding party cards. Frequent mass demonstrations through the city centre saw all shops closed as black demonstrators raged through the streets. I remember watching the tens of thousands of demonstrators marching from the townships into the city centre from the vantage point of my father's shop near Charter Road, a mass protest movement that required immense courage from each individual in the face of brutal repression, retaliation, and imprisonment.

One of the ugly characteristics of the townships was the utilisation of the Smith secret service by some township dwellers to get rid of their business and personal rivals. Jealous neighbours would report each other to the colonial authorities. Since these allegations were difficult to prove or disprove, this practice was a way of ensuring that rivals would be incarcerated without trial, with all their property permanently confiscated.

In a system where any political opinion was considered criminal, the mere accusation that a person held a political opinion could end up in the imprisonment of that person without trial. A black teacher who remarked in the staff room that not all Africans supported Ian Smith, had his house raided that night. He had been reported to the police by one of his white colleagues. I also confronted some problems in the staff room when one of my B-stream pupils wrote an eloquent critique of colonialism. Some of my colleagues accused me of dictating the essay to the class. While this was totally untrue, the incident was symptomatic of Rhodesian racism that assumed that blacks could not write English eloquently.

Workers were now afraid to return to the townships to sleep in the vast hostels built by the colonialists. These hostel dormitories, which housed between six and eight male workers in a room, were rented by employers to house their workers from the city council, as blacks were not allowed to own housing in the cities. My father's workers, comprising a mixture of all ethnic groups, now refused to return to their lodgings in the townships and he was forced to put them up in the cramped quarters behind his shop in Rezende Street. The workers were in mortal fear of being killed.

Another palpable fear that haunted younger men was the fear of rape. Young men and boys were sought after by older men, and in a period of chaos and violence, they had no protection. Homosexuality was very common in the townships, where wives were banned, since the colonial regime only allowed "workers" to live in cities. Ninety-nine per cent of these workers were men. A very small number of women worked as domestic servants in the white suburbs, but it was illegal for them to keep their husbands and children in the servants' quarters. Wives and children had to be kept in the "reserves" for blacks. Wives who were caught in a city were liable to be arrested. The police regularly raided township houses to arrest wives who had broken the law by coming into the city. The infamous pass laws were used to arrest any unemployed black found in the cities.

It was in this tense and difficult situation that the liberation movement broke into two parts, ZAPU and ZANU. This division came in 1963. The immediate effect on the townships was to exacerbate the violence that was already endemic. However, whereas the earlier violence was targeted at all symbols of the colonial regime, the new violence was internecine, with ZAPU and ZANU fighting against each other in the townships. Groups of youths roamed the townships demanding party cards from all and sundry. The petrol bombing of each other's houses was becoming a daily occurrence. It was believed that the violence was initially instigated by ZAPU, using the slogan that it was essential to destroy the "snake inside the house", meaning ZANU, before destroying the "snake outside", meaning the colonial-settler regime of Ian Smith. The Smith regime was able to maximise the violence by torching both ZAPU and ZANU houses. White agents, with their faces painted black, entered the townships to burn the houses of political activists. Very cleverly, the Smith regime escaped blame, while the two nationalist parties blamed each other. This violence was particularly painful for the ordinary township inhabitants.

Townships were now divided into the two major political parties. Township dwellers, with their vast experience of survival under the harshest of conditions, reacted by having both party cards, producing whichever was convenient. Worst hit were workers from the neighbouring countries of Malawi, Mozambique, and Zambia, whose poor grasp of either of the two major national languages made them instant victims. A good understanding of both Shona and Ndebele could save one from a severe beating, depending on the linguistic group of the gangs. In a time of extreme poverty and high unemployment it was not difficult to persuade the gangs of unemployed youths who roamed the townships that their poverty was due to some other ethnic group. The poor turned on the poorest of the poor. Their rationale was that the blacks from neighbouring countries had taken scarce jobs from locals.

The breakdown of support for Joshua Nkomo, particularly among the black intelligentsia, was inevitable, as the tactics that had successfully brought independence to neighbouring Zambia and Malawi failed to bring anything substantial in Rhodesia. The usual strategy of peaceful protests and moral appeals to the British government and to the British people did not work in Rhodesia. One reason was that the British government had ceded control of Rhodesia to the colonists as early as 1923. The Rhodesian settlers had built up a haven for whites, particularly the white working class, who were able to enjoy a higher standard of living than their counterparts in Britain of the 1940s,

1950s, and 1960s. That this haven was a haven for whites only, with a small modern economy able to cater for the needs of only a fraction of the total population, was of little concern to the majority of whites, who justified their privileges on the grounds of conquest and racial superiority. They believed that blacks deserved less because they belonged to an inferior race. Whites were born to rule because they belonged to a superior race. Those who challenged this racist ideology were seen as dangerous troublemakers and dubbed "communists", a term that was elastic enough to cover many strange bedfellows.

Two decades of political agitation by black nationalists under Joshua Nkomo had failed to bring any substantive gains for blacks. Younger and better-educated leaders now questioned the wisdom of following the traditional strategies and tactics. This unease was brought to a head when Nkomo allegedly accepted a plan for power-sharing between blacks and whites through which blacks were to be given a small proportion of seats in parliament, with a plan for a gradual transfer of more power to blacks as they "proved" themselves to be more capable of assuming greater responsibility. The Smith regime had reserved for itself the right and power to determine when blacks would be "ready" for a greater share of political and economic power. This decision had been reached after secret negotiations between Nkomo and Smith, during which many of Nkomo's colleagues were either not present or were in disagreement.

Besides this fundamental disagreement over both principle and process, many within the black nationalist elite criticised Nkomo's dependence on white advisors. At the same time he was accused of failing to consult his black colleagues. His advisors included Terence Ranger and John Reed from the university, Leo Baron, a well-known and high respected lawyer in Bulawayo, and Peter MacKay, a British military specialist.

On the other hand, the opponents of ZANU accused it of anti-white racism. ZANU was said to be a minority group of black intellectuals who opposed the entry of whites into black nationalist politics. They were accused of practising a form of reverse racism. Certainly it was true that ZANU's founders included a large number of black intellectuals and professionals, many of its founder members being the first black university graduates in the country. Its first leaders, Ndabaningi Sithole, Leopold Takawira, Robert Mugabe, and Herbert Chitepo, were all university educated. This characteristic of being a party dominated by intellectuals remained with it until the advent of independence. ZAPU, on the other hand, was characterised by a more traditional approach to leadership, with much more support from the business community, more particularly from the wealthy Asian and African businessmen in the urban areas.

The split in the nationalist movement was a godsend for Ian Smith, who could exploit and exacerbate the ensuing violence which wracked the townships. It also gave him a good excuse to imprison the nationalist leaders from both sides, and in so doing deprive the two parties of their elected leadership. Nkomo and most of the ZAPU leaders were held in a game reserve called Gonakudzingwa for the next decade. Their detention programme allowed them visitors from time to time, but they were not allowed to leave the game park. The ZANU leaders were held in a number of prisons all over the country, rather than in detention. There was a difference in degree between being held in "detention" and being held in prison, in that detention was outside prison walls, but escape was virtually impossible. Those held in prison were held under different conditions. They were incarcerated with common criminals. The then president of ZANU, Ndabaningi Sithole, considered very dangerous because of his fiery rhetoric and his charisma, was kept in solitary confinement throughout the period. His only visitor was his interrogator.

Meanwhile, the increasing polarisation by race meant that whites, whose class differences had affected their political affiliation in former times, were now locked into a solid alliance behind Ian Smith's Rhodesian Front. Previously whites covered a wide spectrum of political opinions ranging from the middle-of-the-road liberalism of Garfield Todd to the extreme white racism of Ian Smith, but UDI united all classes behind Ian Smith. The Rhodesians saw themselves as beleaguered, attacked by the international community led by the British government, by all African countries led by the Organisation of African Unity (OAU), and by virtually all blacks within the country. The Rhodesian Front's racist ideology now infected the whole white population, and being seen with a black became tantamount to treason. The paranoia that has remained a powerful part of the political scene was first born in this environment. For example, a good friend of mine, Linda Strange, a white who had retired from public service at the age of 65 in the early 1960s, continued to do voluntary work in the Catholic church and in the Girl Guide movement in mission schools. Soon she was being persecuted for having tea with her black lady associates in her modest flat. Interracial socialisation even by a highly respectable pensioner led to ostracisation and persecution by fellow church members.

The worst divisions were within families. Anyone who was critical of the Rhodesian Front was now an enemy of the state. Young whites who questioned their parents' loyalty to the racist regime were forced to leave home. Many had to go overseas to escape the family tensions. Some Christians who had been schooled in the ideas of social justice found themselves in conflict with the increasingly rabid racism of the government in power. Bishop Lamont, a Roman Catholic prelate, found himself under house arrest. The Catholic Commission for Peace and Justice had now become an enemy of the state. Marriages broke up as loyalty to the edicts of the Rhodesian Front conflicted with church teachings about human rights and human dignity. White racism had now become the sacrosanct ideology of the country, with opponents being classified as "communists" and "kaffir lovers"[1].

Rhodesian Front propaganda, which most whites now accepted, touted Rhodesian Front policies as the frontline against communism and chaos. Blacks represented communism and chaos. UDI Rhodesia had become a totalitarian and fascist state in which the slightest dissent by any black would lead to indefinite terms of imprisonment as well as confiscation of all property. It was clear that the Rhodesian Front's radical racism and its attack on all blacks irrespective of their class or political orientation would lead to war, as armed struggle now became the only viable form of political organisation. So-called "moderate" blacks who desperately wanted to work peacefully with the colonial Rhodesian regime were as liable to arrest as more extreme elements.

The rising violence in the townships mirrored the increasing violence with which the colonial regime attempted to suppress any form of protest. After the Unilateral Declaration of Independence in 1965 and the steps taken in 1968 to halt any expansion of education for blacks, it was clear that only armed warfare would bring an end to

---

1. "Kaffir" is a derogatory and dehumanising term for blacks used by whites who were against any form of political rights for blacks.

colonialism. Zimbabwe would be born of blood, unlike its more fortunate neighbours that had attained independence peacefully. The struggle to liberate Zimbabwe through violence began with the killing of Oberholzer, a white farmer, in 1966, by a group of ZANU activists who called themselves the Crocodile Group. White racism had given birth to its mirror image, black racism.

I realised that my wish to contribute to the development of the country through peaceful means would not work. Although I enjoyed teaching, I recognised that what I was doing would strengthen rather than weaken the Smith regime. It was clear that peaceful evolution was not going to be possible.

CHAPTER 4

In Exile in Britain

I decided to leave Rhodesia to continue my studies in Britain, and enrolled as an M.Phil. student in English literature at Leeds University. I had always enjoyed studying, but my scholastic interests had been overshadowed by a strong urge to contribute to development in practical ways. Now that the Rhodesian government's policies had brought the country to an extreme situation, it was no longer possible for me to delude myself into believing that much could be achieved through peaceful means. This judgment allowed me to indulge my wish for further study.

Initially, I attempted to get a Commonwealth scholarship, but the ministry of education selection committee decided to give the scholarship to a man, apparently because they felt women usually got married, thus making further educational opportunities unnecessary. I then tried to obtain a government bursary, but even this had been politicised and those who obtained such grants had to sign an agreement that they would not criticise the government in any way. Although I was not politically active at the time, I felt I could not sign such an agreement. I was disappointed by the setbacks, but I decided that I could support myself throughout my studies. This was at a time when overseas students paid the same fees as British students, unlike the current system where overseas students have to pay three or four times more. I resigned from my job in Harare township and made my way to England.

I had never been overseas before. The only countries I had visited were the neighbouring countries of Mozambique, where we went with my grandmother on our annual holidays, and Malawi, which I had visited as a university student.

On my way to London, I stopped over in Rome and in Paris. In Rome I was able to attend one of the mass audiences with the Pope arranged by Father Ted Rogers, who was in Rome at the time. This was truly an overwhelming experience, the first time I had been in such a large group of people in one place with one mind. My stopover in Paris coincided with the 1968 students' revolution. I lived in a students' hostel, and could not help listening to the ferment of revolution being discussed.

I arrived in Leeds in the autumn of 1968. The revolution in universities all over Europe had also affected Leeds. The university was situated in the middle of a slum area and prided itself on its left-wing and worker orientation as well as its origins as an industrial university, training engineers and supplying engineering research and development for the industries in the midlands of Britain. It was also building itself up as a Commonwealth university, catering for students from all over the Commonwealth. There were over 100 African students, and the university was a ferment of ideas on African politics. The African Society was strong and I soon found myself its secretary and the editor of its magazine, *Uhuru*. "Uhuru" is the Swahili word for freedom and liberation, and our society was in the throes of participating in this intellectual liberation struggle. Our magazine explored ideas on what liberation would mean for Africa as a whole, placing particular emphasis on the countries that were still under colonial domination, such as Angola, Mozambique, Namibia, South Africa, and Zimbabwe. The African students debated endlessly and excitedly about the future of Africa.

This was the time of Biafra, with fierce debates and student activism on its behalf. Most Nigerian students in Leeds supported Biafra, as there was a predominance of Ibos. Biafra was an attempt by the Ibos to declare their independence from the rest of Nigeria. Their bid for freedom was due to perceived maltreatment by the government of Nigeria. Ultimately, this breakaway movement failed.

It was in Leeds that I first began to read Marx and Lenin. I was immediately attracted to Marx, but seriously put off by Lenin. Marx's idea of class analysis offered a new insight into social evolution. His painstaking scholarship in collecting and analysing data was impressive. His idealism and dedication to creating a better society were both illuminating and exhilarating.

Reading Lenin disturbed me: his emphasis on the use of violence and crime in order to achieve highly laudable goals upset my Catholic value system. I found it difficult to accept the idea that bank robbery and murder in the name of revolution were perfectly acceptable options. Nevertheless, I understood intellectually that Lenin was offering a practical way of making Marx's ideas a reality. Lenin provided the

Machiavellian foundation for Communism to succeed. The issue of how to bring about social, political, and economic change absorbed my thoughts throughout this period: it was the most important question in so many nations during the erupting '60s.

On the one extreme there was the policy of peaceful resistance that had been pioneered by Mahatma Gandhi in India and by the Clutton Brocks in Rhodesia. On the other, there was the possibility of armed warfare, which had been undertaken by Mao Tse Tung in China and Fidel Castro in Cuba. Mao's concept of the just war based on peasant support was the most practical model for Africa, a continent that was yet to be industrialised and where the peasants formed the majority. Fidel Castro and Che Guevara were the heroes of the university students of 1968, and many students sported enormous posters of these two on the walls of their rooms.

On the other hand, this was the beginning of the Cultural Revolution in China, with its persecution of intellectuals and its rejection of all expressions of traditional "feudal" culture. We tried to understand what Mao was attempting to do in unleashing a state of permanent revolution in order to eradicate the remnants of the old worldview and mindset. Was it possible to change the mindset of millions of people through violent revolution? Was the war against intellectuals like ourselves essential for change? Were we, the intellectuals, the enemy, while the peasant was the hero? Was there a definite value to being poor? It appeared that Maoism was a rebirth of asceticism, a return to simpler values and a simpler lifestyle, and a reaction against the materialism of Western capitalism.

Among the Leeds students, in particular the British students, this rejection of Western capitalism was expressed in the dress codes of dirty blue jeans, with hair usually long, dishevelled, and unwashed. Students went out of their way to make new jeans look dirty and old, and bathing was extremely unfashionable. I observed that some of my schoolmates bathed as infrequently as once a month. This was quite a change from my experience of university in Rhodesia, where we were always well-dressed and well-coiffured. Students who dressed in formal suits were soon identified as the "bourgeoisie" by our hippie British colleagues. Most of the foreign postgraduate students like myself fitted into this dress category.

Mao's attack on the intelligentsia made it essential for us to re-examine ourselves. Were we guilty of anti-revolutionary thought? Were we self-seeking careerists? Were we responsible for the suffering of our peoples? For example, could it be said that members of the intelligentsia like myself, were as guilty, if not more guilty, than outright colonialists and racists like Ian Smith? Could we support Mao's rejection of intellectualism as a sterile pursuit that was intrinsically in opposition to the peasant masses? Should we see every peasant as a hero, and every intellectual as "a running dog of capitalism"? Were we intellectuals the class enemies of the peasants and workers? Was Mao justified in trying to cleanse Chinese society of an intelligentsia that had failed and continued to fail to identify with the masses?

Leeds University was a cauldron of political ideas, and we found ourselves discussing African nationalism, the Cuban revolution which had just taken place, the Cultural Revolution in China, Gaddhafi's Green Book as opposed to Mao Tse Tung's Little Red Book, and so on. It was a liberating experience to be able to discuss these issues with African intellectuals from all over the continent. In Rhodesia, it was a crime to read such books or to discuss such issues. You could face imprisonment without trial if you were found with a left-wing book. Rhodesian newspapers were censored daily, and any form of criticism or of thinking that was different from the Rhodesian Front line was excised. The liberal editors of the *Rhodesia Herald* left the pages purged by the government censors blank, to inform their readers how much had been banned. The Rhodesian regime was traditionally anti-intellectual and regarded new ideas with some suspicion.

One of the most important changes in my outlook while at Leeds was that I began to personally accept responsibility for what was happening in Rhodesia. Before I went to Leeds, I saw political responsibility as resting squarely on the shoulders of black nationalist leaders. As a member of a minority racial group, I believed I could act as an individual to do what I could to improve the situation, but I did not feel that I was responsible for major political or social changes. My three years at Leeds changed this. I realised that if skin colour was not to be used as a criterion, then all of us born in the country had an equal responsibility for the liberation of the country. We could not escape merely by saying we were not black, it was not our problem.

While I was in Leeds, I was able to find part-time teaching jobs in nearby colleges, such as at the Kitson College of Engineering, at the polytechnic, and at the Leeds College for Further Education. Teaching in Britain was a new experience. Having been brought up in colonial Rhodesia, I was brainwashed into believing that the British education system and way of life were the best in the world. It was quite a surprise for me to find that the reality did not fit the romanticised fiction that had been created by the colonists. Britain was a class-ridden society, divided within itself. I realised for the first time that many Rhodesians had hailed from working class families and that they had come to Rhodesia in order to escape from the working class environment that had frustrated them by not allowing them to rise to top positions. Colonialism offered them an escape route to new opportunities. Working class children in the Britain of 1968 were quite seriously handicapped. Many were not well educated, despite the compulsory education system. When I was teaching at Harare Secondary, I was extremely demanding of my students, forcing them to reach a high standard of attainment. I was surprised to find that my British students were often satisfied with a very low level of achievement. Even very bright students would not aim to go to university, instead opting for the same jobs as their fathers. There was a strong feeling of class identity that made working class students identify with their parents, rather than to achieve higher positions within their society. Thus, at that time a lorry driver's son would have the ambition to be a lorry driver, even if he had very high intellectual potential.

My teaching experience in Britain over the next three years was critical for my understanding of education. In particular it helped me to grasp the highly varied quality of education within the British system. At the same time, this was an exciting period for education with a great many innovative experiments taking place in British schools, colleges, and universities. The way courses were designed and run was quite different from my experience of the rigid examination-dominated system in Rhodesia. At Leeds University and at the colleges where I taught, lecturers had the opportunity to put into place new curricula and to use new methodologies. The teachers themselves were responsible for the curriculum, whereas in colonial Rhodesia we had to accept highly unsuitable curricula without questioning.

At the end of my period of study, I was determined to go back to Africa. However, I decided to go to an independent African country rather than to go home, and applied for jobs at the University of Dar es Salaam in Tanzania and at the University of Zambia. I was fortunate enough to receive a posting at the University of Zambia, in the school of education, and arrived there in 1971.

CHAPTER 5

Learning from the Zambia of the 1970s

I arrived in Zambia in 1971 to teach at the school of education of the University of Zambia. President Kaunda had made Zambia a refuge for all liberation and democratic movements in Africa. Lusaka was now the headquarters of the Angolan, Mozambican, Namibian, South African, and Zimbabwean liberation movements. Zambia also welcomed professionals from all over Africa, in particular from countries then undergoing traumatic problems, such as Uganda under Idi Amin, and Ghana and Nigeria under their various military regimes. Zambia in its first decade of independence was a place of hope for the whole of Africa. It provided us with an opportunity to meet with African freedom fighters and intellectuals from all over the continent. Zambia promoted a pan-African vision of unity. It also provided us Zimbabweans with the opportunity to learn from both the positive and negative aspects of its post-independence policies and experiences. Here was a wonderful opportunity to study at close hand the challenges of development.

President Kaunda had decided that one of his major contributions to Zimbabwe would be the training of manpower at university level. Zambia had attained independence in 1964 with only 100 graduates in the country, and he was determined to ensure that Zimbabwe would not face the same problems. Thus, he made it possible for some 400 Zimbabwean students to study at the university, a larger number than was allowed in the University of Rhodesia before independence.

In addition to the university students, Zambia was home to a couple of thousand Zimbabwean freedom fighters belonging to the two main liberation movements, ZANU and ZAPU. ZANU controlled two camps for its guerrillas, one known as the Farm just outside Lusaka, and another known as Chifombo close to the Mozambique border. By the mid-1970s the number had risen to over 3,000, as secondary and university students deserted their schools to join the liberation struggle.

A major lesson I learnt from living in Zambia was that it was essential for the intelligentsia to play a very active and, if possible, leading role in government after independence. This was not the case in Zambia, where major decisions were being made by foreign advisors. The UNIP government, while full of good intentions and made up of morally motivated people like Kaunda himself, allowed most of the key decisions to be made by these advisors. Most of these outsiders had no vision of long-term development. And, indeed, they did not have responsibility for long-term development programmes. Most of them were consultants on short-term contracts. As a result, there were many short-lived success stories, but these had little prospect of long-term impact or even survival. While it was true that many principles of development were universal, somehow the application of these principles had to be very local and had to involve the local community in order to succeed. Development could not be imposed from above or from outside.

The school system was a case-in-point of well-intentioned programmes that were, however, unrealistic and problematic. Zambia had decided to nationalise the mission schools after independence, so schools were taken away from the churches and made into state schools. The government intended to provide free primary, secondary, and tertiary education to all. Secondary education would take place in boarding schools, the underlying principle being that this would allow children from different ethnic groups to grow up together. According to this analysis, the main problem facing Zambia was tribalism and ethnic division, a view that had been promulgated by colonial propaganda, and was widely accepted as a proven fact. So the government hoped that an expensive boarding school system would help Zambia to overcome this problem. By the early 1970s, half a decade after independence, the education system was already experiencing serious strains. The end of the Vietnam War had lowered the demand for Zambia's mono-industry, copper. Meanwhile, the escalating conflict in the surrounding countries of Angola, Mozambique, South West Africa (now Namibia), Rhodesia (now Zimbabwe), and South Africa, where liberation movements supported by Zambia were fighting for independence, also affected the economy adversely. Government was unable to keep its promise of free education for all, the result being unhealthy competition for primary school places even in the capital city of Lusaka. The secondary boarding school system proved to be too expensive for government, making expansion impossible. Moreover, the schools were built with World Bank loans. At that time the World Bank required international tenders, which were usually won by overseas companies. As a result, the expansion of the school system had not generated the growth of any local industry. Instead, prefabricated construction materials were imported and installed. When repairs were needed, the materials had to be imported from countries like Sweden or Israel, a difficult challenge for a landlocked country surrounded by countries at war. Moreover, the interest rate was very high, laying the foundations of the debt problem that was to dog Zambia in future decades. The idea of secularising education by removing schools from missionaries proved a constraint rather than an achievement, as government soon found it was not able to provide the resources for the successful maintenance of the schools they had taken over.

Another ill-conceived decision was the nationalisation of industries. For example, the publishing industry was nationalised. As a result, healthy competition was destroyed. The one and only state-owned publishing house was not able to cope with demand in terms of quality and quantity, so many books had to be imported. The nationalisation of the mining industry, Zambia's chief source of income, was equally disastrous. For some reason, mines that had been profitable became liabilities that required constant state subsidies. The Zambianisation programme led to the promotion of many pleasantly mediocre personnel, as the foreign management was, of course, determined not to allow highly capable Zambians to take positions in the mines, fearing that they would easily be replaced.

Planning of development programmes was usually done by international experts, often on flying visits to the country. Local government officials, usually with only two years of high school, eagerly accepted the advice of these experts. As Zambia trained more and more university graduates, these young professionals were unable to find satisfying work within Zambia, as the foreign "experts", allied with the ruling elite, were not interested in having highly qualified Zambians in decision-making positions. These graduates were already leaving the country for greener pastures overseas or in neighbouring countries.

Some of the results of poor planning by so-called "experts" created unnecessary problems: in Western Province, some boarding schools were built in areas that had water for only half the year, as the experts had chosen the location during the wet season, not knowing that for the other half the flood plains become deserts. Another example was a pineapple factory built where there were no pineapples, and a dairy-farming programme devised by a brilliant consultant after a visit of a few days. Not surprisingly, many of these programmes failed.

A major shortcoming of the development system, in particular of the education system, was the failure to use the capacities of the community itself. Development was imposed from above. Plans were made by overseas experts. It was assumed that the local people, mainly peasants and miners, did not have the good sense and expertise to be in charge of their own development. It was clear that one of the fundamental problems was the lack of political participation and power by Zambians.

In many African countries of the 1970s, including Zambia, educated people had an in-built aversion to participation in politics, which was notoriously a "dirty game", allegedly played by ruthless and power hungry politicians, many of whom had risen from the ranks of the trade unions and of the poor. The educated elite were able to do very well without lowering themselves to this level, so there was a natural tendency for them to leave politics to the poor and uneducated. With a largely uneducated population, the educated elite was a privileged minority, often divorced from the realities of the poor. Applying this to the Zimbabwean situation, I thought it was essential for the educated elite like myself to participate at the grassroots level, so that we would avoid many of the problems faced by Zambia.

CHAPTER 6

Joining the Liberation Struggle in Zambia

ZANU IN 1973

It was in this spirit that I decided to join the liberation struggle in early 1973, soon after the ZANU army, the Zimbabwe African National Liberation Army (ZANLA), had scored its first decisive victories within Rhodesia. These victories made me realise that it would be ZANU rather than ZAPU that would one day rule a free Zimbabwe. Having lived in Zambia for a couple of years, I had come to the conclusion that it was essential for the intelligentsia to play a role in the liberation struggle. We, the privileged minority, had to shoulder the same burden as the peasant guerrillas who were spearheading the armed struggle. The liberation struggle would define what would happen in a free Zimbabwe, and we had the opportunity to participate in the most important and formative stages of this struggle. Little did I know at that stage that my participation in the struggle would end in an attempt on my life by the Rhodesian regime, and my subsequent flight from Zambia to Mozambique.

The participants in the struggle included nearly all Zimbabweans who lived in exile in Zambia. The 400 Zimbabweans who were lecturers and students at the University of Zambia formed one important group, to which I naturally belonged. There were also the 90,000 mainly Karanga peasant farmers who had emigrated from the southwestern part of Rhodesia into the fertile farming area of Mumbwa in Zambia. There was a small but wealthy group of Zimbabwean businessmen. And finally, there were the full-time workers in the liberation movements, comprising both guerrillas and political leadership.

I began to work with Zimbabwean lecturers and students at the university to study the challenges and problem areas that Zimbabwe would face in the future. We formed study groups to analyse these different aspects of development in Zimbabwe. These groups worked under the auspices of the Zimbabwe African National Union (ZANU) and comprised hundreds of students. Prominent among the lecturers who worked closely with the students were myself from the school of education; Dzingai Mutumbuka from the chemistry department; Simbi Mubako from the school of law; and Sam Geza from the economics department. The student leaders included Joseph Masangomai, Tungamirai Mudzi, and Ronnie Chiviya.

In addition to the study groups, I ran a joint drama group consisting of university students and the freedom fighters who were stationed in Lusaka. We created and performed plays linked to the liberation struggle. This group travelled all over Zambia, performing for crowds of Zimbabweans who had settled in Zambia. The drama group allowed the university to work closely with the freedom fighters. Those fighters who participated in the drama group included Earnest Kadungure and Joyce Mujuru[1], both of whom were to become ministers in the post-independence government. Sheiba Tavarwisa, who became the deputy head of the ZANU education department from 1976 to 1980 and a member of parliament in the 1980s, was also a member of the team.

This was my first opportunity to meet with the freedom fighters from the war front. Many of them were young students who had left their schools to join the liberation struggle. Most were teenagers, others in their early twenties. Their hunger for education was overwhelming. Many had been starved of educational opportunities under the colonial system, and were very keen to continue their education.

Many of the peasant youths who volunteered came from the Mumbwa community in Zambia. These highly productive farmers had moved northwards in their search for land. As Zambia had a surplus of fertile and unused land, this move was mutually satisfactory, as the Zimbabwean farmers soon made Mumbwa one of the breadbaskets of Zambia. Between 1965 and 1972, ZANLA had suffered a severe shortage of recruits. Initially, only poor peasant youths from Mumbwa were prepared to join the struggle: as a result the oldest and most experienced freedom fighters were not highly educated, many of them having received only a few years of primary education. Some were illiterate. The predominance of the Mumbwa peasant families in the liberation struggle also meant the predominance of members of the Karanga tribe among the early recruits.

---

1. Joyce Mujuru became Vice President of Zimbabwe in January 2005.

The traditional land tenure system in Zambia, based on the granting of land by chiefs, could be highly disadvantageous for the Zimbabweans. Hard-working Zimbabweans would clear virgin land and plant crops, only to find that the chiefs would take back the land with the ripening crops, and instead give the Zimbabweans a new plot of virgin land to clear. Many Zimbabweans came to understand that Zambia was not their country, and that however hard working they were, they would never be allowed to become prosperous. They became convinced that they had to fight for their own country against the white settlers.

Throughout the liberation struggle, the farmers of Mumbwa fed ZANLA, each farmer contributing bags of maize for the soldiers fighting at the front. Many of them lost some or all of their sons in the liberation war. This was the sacrifice they willingly paid for the liberation of Zimbabwe. Ironically, it was only after the independence of Zimbabwe that these Mumbwa settlers were offered Zambian citizenship by President Kenneth Kaunda, who suddenly recognised the possibility of Zambia losing some of its most productive farmers. The Mumbwa peasants had struggled for decades to gain Zambian citizenship. Even more ironically, the Zimbabwe government itself was to deny citizenship to many of these Mumbwa families in 2001–02, in its bid to deny citizenship to its opponents by removing citizenship from those who could claim dual nationality. Zimbabweans born outside Zimbabwe had to renounce their foreign citizenship.

Another disability suffered by Zimbabweans in Zambia was the law that allowed ownership of businesses only by Zambian citizens. While many foreigners, including Zimbabweans, circumvented this law by entering into nominal partnerships, usually with their house servants, the policy remained a sore point and ensured that Zimbabwean businessmen in Zambia were among the most fervent supporters of the liberation struggle.

I soon came to see both the positive and the negative aspects of the liberation struggle. One of the features of that period was that both ZANU and ZAPU used forced conscription: young Zimbabwean men were captured and forced to join the ranks of the liberation soldiers. This included the forced conscription of many students who left colonial Rhodesia in search of scholarships in universities overseas. One such conscript was Josiah Tungamirai, later to rise to the top leadership of ZANLA. After independence, he became head of the Zimbabwean airforce, and after his retirement from the airforce cabinet minister responsible for indigenization of the economy. He died in 2005 from kidney failure. It was more than a decade later, after independence, that he was finally to achieve his ambition of attending university and gaining his bachelor's and master's degrees.

The Zimbabwe African National Liberation Army was born in response to the settler government's total intransigence about any form of majority rule, as expressed in Ian Smith's Unilateral Declaration of Independence in 1965. UDI was intended to entrench white rule for the foreseeable future. A tiny band of volunteers, dedicated to waging armed struggle to achieve majority rule, were willing to take up arms against the Smith regime. Between 1965, the year UDI was declared, and 1972, participation in the armed struggle meant certain death. But desperate situations breed desperate people. Those whose lives were so bad that they had nothing to lose, rose to take up arms.

The 1967 break-up of ZIPRA (Zimbabwe People's Revolutionary Army) brought a larger, better educated, and better-trained group into ZANLA. These ZIPRA guerrillas had developed a deep suspicion of the old-style politicians, whom they believed had so callously sacrificed the lives of hundreds of their soldiers in the Wankie fiasco.[1]

The entry of so many ZIPRA guerrillas into ZANLA, and the marriage of ZIPRA expertise with ZANLA's Chinese training to work with the people before attempting any military enterprises, proved to be the recipe for military success. ZANLA was then a small army headed by Josiah Tongogara, and trained by the Chinese in guerrilla warfare. One of the major tenets of such warfare was to win the support of the people, in this case the Zimbabwean peasantry, so that the guerrilla would merge into the people like "fish in water". The ZANU army had also had the opportunity to gain many years of field experience by fighting side-by-side with FRELIMO, the Mozambican liberation movement. FRELIMO had initially invited ZAPU to join its armed struggle, but the internal problems within ZAPU in 1967 made this impracticable. Although ZANU freedom fighters had had a shorter period of military

---

1. Several hundred ZIPRA and ANC of South Africa freedom fighters entered Rhodesia through uninhabited areas of Wankie. These brave fighters were either killed or captured by a joint Rhodesian-South African force. The escapade was badly planned by non-militarists located in Lusaka.

Josiah Tongogara

training than the Soviet-trained ZAPU army, they had the advantage of actual field experience, as well as the support of the peasantry. Now the two very differently trained armies were to join together into one army, no easy task, under ZANLA. This was one of the many examples of the fluidity of political allegiance in the Zimbabwean liberation struggle, with groups changing sides with some agility.

Two former ZIPRA military leaders, Robson Manyika and Solomon Mujuru[1], became key leaders in the newly amalgamated army, Manyika as chief of staff and Mujuru as commander of the northeast war zone. Thus, the new entrants into ZANLA were immediately given top positions in the leadership, helping to amalgamate the two forces into one. Solomon Mujuru was later to become the first black general to head the Zimbabwean army after independence.

To win the minds and hearts of the people, ZANLA had to be a politicised army that identified with the aspirations of the people. This was the lesson of the relatively unsuccessful years of the 1960s, when local people would betray the guerrillas to the colonial authorities. ZANLA began to build up a cadre of political commissars whose weapons were not the arms of war but concepts, values, and ideology. These commissars were considered to be the most powerful officers in the liberation army, carrying with them the responsibility for winning the support of the populace, without whom the war could not succeed.

---

1. Solomon Mujuru's *chimurenga* name was Rex Nhongo.

The two pillars of political education comprised the code of conduct on the one hand, and the process of analysing the people's grievances on the other. The popular freedom fighter song, *Nzira ye MaSoja,* or the "Soldiers' Guide", sung every day at rallies and based on a mixture of Maoist, Christian, and traditional values, encapsulated the ZANLA *Code of Conduct:*

> "The three main rules of discipline are:
> – Obey orders in all your actions
> – Do not take a single needle or piece of thread from the masses
> – Turn in everything captured
>
> The eight points of attention are:
> – Speak politely
> – Pay fairly for what you buy
> – Return everything you borrow
> – Do not hit or swear at people
> – Do not damage crops
> – Do not take liberties with women
> – Do not ill-treat captives."[1]

The process of analysing grievances followed Paulo Freire's[2] approach, in terms of which the people were invited to voice their grievances and, through dialogue with the freedom fights, come to a consensus on the meaning of the liberation struggle. Key grievances remained the land issue, educational deprivation, poverty, and unemployment. In this way, the people's aspirations could be voiced. Guerrillas had to be good listeners. They had to respect the people's culture and views. They also had to integrate the people's grievances and aspirations into their daily work.

The imperative of laying a sound political foundation, as well as of bringing in and hiding large quantities of weapons, brought about the need to train women as guerrillas for the first time. Women were better suited for doing political work among other women. Women could

---

1. A. Pongweni, *Songs that Won the Liberation Struggle,* College Press, Harare, 1982.
2. Paulo Freire was a well-known Brazilian educator who promulgated a system of teaching based on an analysis of the concerns of the people.

work as nurses and as teachers among the people. Women were also better suited for the long walk from the Mozambican and Zambian borders into Rhodesia carrying loads of weapons on their heads, not only because they were already accustomed to carrying heavy loads of water and firewood, but also because the Rhodesian security forces were less suspicious of women, whereas they suspected every man of being a guerrilla. It was part of the Rhodesian macho mores that war was the responsibility of men, so they were completely unprepared to fight against women. At a time when every able-bodied black man would be routinely arrested and questioned under torture, women were able to move about freely. Thus, 1972 saw not only an intensification of the war effort, but also the entry of women as major players in the liberation struggle.

One such woman was Sheiba Tavarwisa, a primary school teacher who joined the liberation struggle and became one of the first women commanders in ZANLA. Her responsibility in the beginning was to carry arms from Zambia and Mozambique to the frontline in Rhodesia. She was also responsible for working with the peasantry in order to persuade them to support the freedom fighters. When the peasants saw that the fight was being led by women like Sheiba, a highly respected person within her own community, it became much easier to gain moral and logistical support for the war effort. It was said that if women were brave enough to fight the war, then it was incumbent on every person to join too. Sheiba later became the deputy head of the education department of ZANU under Dzingai Mutumbuka. She later died of a kidney disease, a major killer of former guerrillas, and probably the result of hepatitis from polluted water.

On the negative side, it was clear that ZANU was riven with internal conflicts. In 1974, I drew up a plan to utilise the university staff and students to run education programmes for the guerrillas. However, we were not able to implement this plan until many years later. This delay was due to the conflict that had begun to surface within ZANU itself, with leaders such as Henry Hamadziripi and Rugare Gumbo seeking to oust the leader of the external wing of ZANU, Herbert Chitepo. In this situation of division within the leadership, it was not possible to go ahead with new programmes. Chitepo's opponents feared that successful programmes, including successful educational programmes, could be used to boost Chitepo's re-election prospects, and as the next elections were scheduled for 1975, they wanted to delay the implementation of new programmes until after that date. The 1975 elections never took place, as ZANU was soon engulfed by the *détente* exercise that led to the death of Chitepo in March of that year.

I was able to meet many of the young peasants as well as the high school students who had joined the liberation struggle. Before the entry of more than 200 ZIPRA guerrillas into ZANLA in the late 1960s, ZANLA consisted of a dozen dedicated guerrillas. By 1972, ZANLA consisted of only a few hundred dedicated fighters, but after 1973 thousands of young people flooded into Zambia as recruits. By 1974, they numbered over 3,000. The change from forced recruitment to enthusiastic and willing volunteers was due to a number of factors, but most critically to the military success ZANLA scored from 1972 onwards. Whereas the colonial/settler regime looked invincible before that year, its downfall now looked imminent.

The freedom fighters also claimed to have the support of the ancestral spirits, in particular the powerful spirits of Nehanda and Kaguvi in a just war. The liberation struggle saw a revitalisation of traditional religion. Most urbanised and educated young people knew little or nothing about traditional religion. With the liberation struggle, traditional religion, still very powerful among the peasantry, became the main ideology in ZANU's struggle.

ZANLA had also incorporated a system of checks and balances that made it impossible for even as charismatic and as brilliant a leader as Josiah Tongogara to escape censure, either from traditional religious leaders or from internal critics. It was common for ZANLA leaders to hold very frequent self-criticism meetings, a practice copied from the Chinese, who had trained the first group of guerrillas and still participated in the training of ZANLA forces at Mgagao training camp in Tanzania until the attainment of independence in 1980. At such internal criticism meetings, junior commanders, in particular women commanders, would be free to voice their views on leadership failures. One of the most commonly voiced grievances was the mistreatment of women, although the willingness of many women to seek such abuse as a form of social climbing rather weakened the argument of those women leaders who opposed it. More often, such self-criticism centred on military strategies and tactics, as well as logistical shortcomings.

One of the interesting findings from my participation in Zimbabwean politics in the 1970s was the discovery that many students and freedom fighters had entered Zambia through the support of the Rhodesian secret service, the CIO. Their task was to infiltrate ZANU and provide information back to the Rhodesian regime. Some of these people, particularly among the freedom fighters, openly confessed to having been recruited by CIO, and became wholehearted converts to the liberation struggle, while others remained as secret "moles" whose presence would suddenly be discovered during periods of extreme danger. The period of *détente* was to prove such a testing period: many of the opportunist forces that had obtained a much coveted university education through CIO support revealed their confused distrust of the liberation struggle. Smith agents who did not promptly confess and join the liberation forces faced imprisonment, and in some cases, death.

I was beginning to understand the opportunism, born of the experience of deprivation, that characterised township morality. This code of morality dictated that if one was in dire need, it was correct to utilise any opportunity that came one's way to improve oneself. Thus, if the Smith regime offered the opportunity to improve one's position through education, for example, one should welcome this opportunity. Similarly, if the liberation movement offered one a similar opportunity for self-improvement, it was correct to accept this opportunity. The issue of integrity and loyalty to one's principles did not arise.

Despite the heavy infiltration of ZANU and ZANLA by Smith agents, ZANU began to score major victories in the guerrilla war in Rhodesia after 1972, taking the Rhodesian forces completely by surprise. The years 1972-74 were years of victory for ZANU and ZANLA. The main reason for this ability to overcome the problems created by CIO was that most infiltrators concentrated their efforts on ZANU headquarters in Lusaka. Meanwhile, the action had moved to the field. Instead of adopting a mainly military strategy, the freedom fighters decided to live within Rhodesia for prolonged periods, working with local people to win their support.

In 1974, in the midst of this wave of success, the fascist Caetano regime in Portugal fell after a popular uprising. The newly formed socialist government was committed to granting independence to Mozambique and Angola, as well as other Portuguese colonies whose colonial wars had debilitated the Portuguese state for more than a decade. A black government in Mozambique brought the prospect of thousands of miles of border territory opening up to guerrilla infiltration, so that the defeat of the Rhodesian regime on the battlefield was only a matter of time. With both Mozambique and Angola likely to be ruled by Marxist-oriented governments dominated by FRELIMO and MPLA respectively[1], there was a real and frightening prospect of pro-communist regimes dominating the region. Should Rhodesia also fall to a Marxist-oriented government, there was greater likelihood of South Africa and South West Africa (today Namibia) being engulfed in armed conflict under the influence of communists. Western investments in South Africa and South West Africa would almost certainly be threatened in that case. The increasing success of the ZANLA freedom fighters brought the prospect of Southern Africa falling under the control of governments with little or no allegiance to the West. Although ZANU had no connection with the Soviet Union, nevertheless, the majority of their guerrillas had been trained in the Soviet Union when they were under ZIPRA. Moreover, it was well known that ZANU received support from China and Yugoslavia, both communist countries, albeit outside the Soviet spheres of influence. The need for a non-military solution to the conflict was never more clear to the world, and the international community was soon to take action in the form of the *détente* initiative of the US secretary of state, Henry Kissinger in an alliance with Prime Minister John Vorster of South Africa, and later to be joined by the Frontline states bordering on the area of conflict. The aim of *détente* was to bring about a black government in Zimbabwe friendly towards the West and hostile to the Soviet bloc.

---

1. FRELIMO, Frente para o Liberacao do Mocambique, and MPLA, Movemento Popular par o Liberacao do Angola, were both vigorously supported by the Soviet Union. However, of the Zimbabwe liberation movements, the Soviet Union supported ZAPU and not ZANU, leading to ZANU aligning itself with China and Yugoslavia, both communist countries critical of Soviet hegemony. With the identification of the West with the colonial masters, nationalist movements sought and obtained support from any willing source. Besides the Soviet bloc, Zimbabwe liberation movements enjoyed support from many liberal and socialist groups in the West, especially in Scandinavia, Canada, and West Germany.

DÉTENTE

In order to embark on this plan, nationalist leaders from both ZANU and ZAPU were suddenly released from more than a decade of incarceration in Rhodesian jails and detention camps and flown to Lusaka for independence negotiations presided over officially by South Africa and the Frontline states of Zambia, Botswana, and Tanzania (soon to be joined by Mozambique after it had attained independence – Mozambique was under a transitional government led by Joachim Chissano until independence in 1975). In Lusaka, the recently released leaders were to meet their own followers face to face for the first time in over a decade. Negotiations were to begin immediately, with the former prisoners and their externally based colleagues being given little chance to consult extensively.

The arrival of the released leaders came as a complete surprise. They came on a jet owned by LONRHO, whose leader, Tiny Rowland, continued to play the role of godfather to many African regimes. Virtually the whole of the external leadership of ZANU was out of Lusaka when the former prisoners unexpectedly arrived in late November 1974. Secret high-level talks began on 1 December 1974. A number of external ZANU leaders had not yet been able to return to Lusaka. Obviously, surprise and speed were to be important tactics for taking the Zimbabwean side, particularly ZANU, off guard. If the intention of *détente* was to cause disunity and disarray within ZANU, it very soon succeeded in this.

The released ZANU leaders were greeted with jubilation by their followers. A large meeting was organised to enable ZANU members to meet these leaders. For most of us, it was the first opportunity to see and listen to these legendary figures. I managed to get a front row seat. The meeting was held in the yard of a garage owned by a Zimbabwean. This gave the advantage of secrecy, as the venue was surrounded by a high wall. The meeting opened with introductions by Herbert Chitepo. The two main speakers were Ndabaningi Sithole and Robert Mugabe.

Mugabe gave a very detailed and factual speech, outlining exactly what had happened from the time of their release up to that moment. It was clear that he remained, as always, a teacher, anxious to ensure that all his listeners knew and understood the situation in its details and subtleties. He pointed out the possibilities as well as the dangers that the new turn of events offered. Mugabe's didactic approach contrasted with Sithole's emotive flair. Sithole had the magic power that typifies a charismatic leader: in his speech he recounted the triumphal journey after his release, with tumultuous welcomes wherever he went. He had travelled all over the country. It was clear that he believed that independence was imminent: there was nothing that could stop it now. The crowd was so intoxicated by this vision that it suddenly surged forward to lift him up in triumph. Those of us who had chosen to sit in the front row were unceremoniously trampled upon. We were totally unaware of the leadership crisis that was to surface soon afterwards, a crisis that had originated in prison but had been kept a secret to outsiders. This was the palace coup that had replaced Sithole with Mugabe as president of ZANU.

On their release, they announced to the Frontline presidents of Zambia, Tanzania, and Botswana that Mugabe was now the leader of ZANU, but the presidents were suspicious about this prison coup and refused to accept Mugabe. A split in ZANU, at that time the strongest military force in the liberation struggle, would have been good news for Zimbabwe's enemies, but naturally caused alarm among her supporters in the Frontline states. Under pressure from Presidents Kaunda and Nyerere, ZANU papered over its differences and Sithole appeared at the Lusaka talks at the head of the ZANU delegation. But it was *détente* that finally brought an end to Sithole's leadership of ZANU.

Knowing the endemic disagreements between and within the different Zimbabwean parties, President Kaunda, together with Presidents Julius Nyerere of Tanzania and Seretse Khama of Botswana, attempted to negotiate with each party separately. Probably they thought that having all four parties in the same room before they had each agreed to some basic principles would be counterproductive. The bases for agreement were clear:
- there would be an immediate ceasefire by both sides
- the Zimbabwean guerrillas would be absorbed into the Rhodesian army
- the four Zimbabwean parties would unite to form one group
- Smith would concede "majority rule" in a form that had not yet been agreed upon, but which would involve some form of qualitative franchise rather than one person one vote.

However, the problem was first and foremost the ceasefire. ZANLA felt it was just beginning to win the war which had intensified over the previous two years, and that the *détente* exercise was merely an attempt to rob it of victory. In particular, ZANU was not prepared to share the leadership of Zimbabwe with the three other parties, namely FROLIZI (Front for the Liberation of Zimbabwe), ANC and ZAPU. ZANU and ZANLA believed that the proposed independence of Zimbabwe had been won by ZANLA, and that the inclusion of the parties that had not participated in the armed struggle would lead to a weakening of the new state. A popular image used by ZANU and ZANLA was that we had planted the mango tree, but others were going to eat the fruit.

In particular, there was strong opposition to FROLIZI, which many guerrillas believed was nothing more than a tribal union. FROLIZI had been formed by veteran political leaders James Chikerema from ZAPU and Nathan Shamuyarira of ZANU, after the break up of the ZAPU army in 1967 following the Wankie debacle, when many ZAPU guerrillas were either killed or captured by the Smith regime. While it rhetorically claimed to be uniting ZAPU and ZANU, FROLIZI was seen by both ZAPU and ZANU as a tribal formation of Zezurus, whose aim was their tribe's domination of the liberation movement.

Three of the parties, ZANU, ZAPU, and FROLIZI, espoused socialist rhetoric. The Rhodesian regime also called any and every opponent a "communist", such that for the ordinary black citizen of Rhodesia, the word "communist" began to mean any opponent of the settler regime.

A fourth major party was to enter the arena during the *détente* period, the African National Council, ANC, led by Abel Muzorewa. While the three other parties had become externally based as a result of the arrest of ZANU and ZAPU leaders after 1965, ANC was formed as a home-based representative of black opinion during the Pearce commission set up by the British government in 1971 to gauge whether Smith's boast that he enjoyed the support of the majority of black people was true. The commission found that this was not true at all. Muzorewa had arisen as the natural if unelected spokesperson for blacks. During the *détente* period, both ZANU and ZAPU decided to support Muzorewa and the ANC as the voice of black people.

The choice of Muzorewa by both ZANU and ZAPU leaderships, internally and externally, was unanimous because Muzorewa was seen as trustworthy, without either charisma or political experience, and so unlikely to challenge either Ndabaningi Sithole, the then president of ZANU, or Joshua Nkomo, the then president of ZAPU, both imprisoned by the Rhodesian regime since 1965. Both parties urged their followers inside the country to join and support the ANC as the legally permissible representative of black opinion within the country. It was fascinating to find that both ZANU and ZAPU chose the weakest leader, Muzorewa, because they felt they could control him better. This had been a well-established system under the colonial-settler regimes, particularly Smith's, which were in the habit of selecting African leaders known for their pleasant compliance with the real rulers. The ANC was thus to enjoy overwhelming if short-lived support all over the country from both the Smith regime and all the nationalists abroad. Another reason for ZANU's support for Muzorewa was its strong opposition to leadership by Joshua Nkomo. ZANU, having rebelled against Nkomo in 1963, still saw him as a totally unsuitable leader for the liberation struggle. The Zambian government, on the other hand, was strongly in favour of Nkomo as the leader of the newly established coalition.

However, as later events proved, this new unity agreement was soon to founder, because it was not only ZANLA that rejected the ceasefire. Smith himself used the exercise to push forward his attempt at military victory, so nullifying the first basis of the agreement.

Despite the pressure from the Frontline governments, ZANU and ZANLA would not agree to a ceasefire. The Zambian government decided to try some strong-arm tactics to force the issue, by threatening to expel ZANU and ZANLA from Zambia. This caused a rift within ZANU itself. ZANLA, under Tongogara, was determined to continue the war, but a number of political leaders felt that this golden opportunity for majority rule should not be missed.

An even more dangerous split was to surface in ZANU very soon afterwards, and this was a rebellion within the ZANLA army known as the Nhari rebellion. The Nhari group emerged from within ZANLA in opposition to Tongogara and the leadership of the military high command. They were also against the political leadership of ZANU. Their rise and fall marked an important episode in ZANLA's history.

THE NHARI REBELLION

As already noted, ZANLA had increased in size from a mere 200 guerrillas in 1972 to over 3,000 in 1974, and thousands of new recruits were still pouring in. The management problems this entailed were daunting, and were particularly difficult for a leadership that had for years dealt with only a handful of highly experienced and dedicated guerrillas who were fully prepared for and accustomed to the deprivations of war. When ZANLA grew to a few hundred as a result of an influx of better trained and disciplined fighters from ZIPRA, the management problems could still be handled. Now the thousands pouring in included both illiterate peasants and university students, a far more diverse, less disciplined, and more volatile group. These new recruits faced a severe shortage of food, as the old method of feeding the guerrillas based on grain contributions from the Mumbwa farmers was no longer adequate. There was also a short supply of plates – recruits had to receive what little food there was on leaves or in their bare hands. These physical hardships could have been endured, given the high morale and the expectation of victory in the near future, but there was also a serious shortage of guns and ammunition, making it difficult to exploit the many military opportunities that now presented themselves. Thousands of young men were hanging around without food and arms, and they were quickly becoming disillusioned.

The taste of success had also brought about complacency and corruption in the leadership, who were already enjoying the fruits of victory in terms of favours from many admiring women. Junior officers, either more austere or envious, bitterly resented the abuse of women by their superiors. A number of examples of blatant abuse of privilege caused anger. One concerned a teenage girl who was allegedly impregnated by a top ZANLA leader. She subsequently obtained an illegal abortion, which ended up in her being hospitalised. Another case was that of a junior officer, Badza. In a letter found among Tongogara's papers, Badza declared he would create a "Biafra" of Zimbabwe in reaction to his abuse within ZANLA. This was a Zimbabwean version of the David and Barsheeba story being played out, as Badza had lost his wife to his senior commander, who had sent him on a dangerous mission at the front. This personal dispute led Badza to join in a rebellion against the ZANLA leadership.

To make matters worse, junior officers from the Rhodesian army had been meeting clandestinely with their ZANLA counterparts, with both sides venting their resentment against their senior officers. Junior officers on both sides felt that they were left to bear the brunt of the battle at the front, while their seniors enjoyed the comforts of city life, and, in the case of ZANLA, spent too much of their time overseas. For many of the young, the word "overseas" conjured up a life of luxury.

The phenomenal growth of ZANLA meant that the small high command leadership, of only eight members, was now forced to spend a great deal of time negotiating for weapons, ammunition, and food in foreign countries. The high command members were led by Josiah Tongogara. His deputy was William Ndangana, a veteran ZANLA leader who had headed the attack in Chipinge by the "Crocodile Group" that heralded the beginning of the armed struggle in 1965. Third in command was Robson Manyika, formerly head of ZIPRA. He had brought to ZANLA some 200 ex-ZIPRA guerrillas in the aftermath of the ZIPRA crisis in 1967. Other members included Cletus Chigove, head of intelligence, Justin Chauke, in charge of logistics, as well as field commanders Solomon Mujuru, Vitalis Zvinavashe[1], and Joseph Chimurenga. The majority of these were outside Zambia and away from the war front when the Nhari rebellion began. A plot was hatched by the war-weary junior officers in both the Rhodesian army and in ZANLA to take over the leadership of their respective organisations, and to end the war.

A further complication was that the ZIPRA guerrillas who had joined ZANLA a few years earlier soon realised they were better educated and better trained than their veteran ZANLA officers, generally recruited from among the less educated peasantry. Young ex-ZIPRA officers questioned the authority of commanders who had only a few years of education, whereas some of them were college graduates from the best Soviet military academies. Having enjoyed the benefits of this training, they also questioned the wisdom of ZANU's and ZANLA's suspicion of Soviet support, believing that the war would be much more successful if they had more Soviet support and Soviet weapons. ZANU enjoyed Chinese support, not Soviet.

In addition, a group of young Marxists now realised their commanders were not only ignorant of, but also totally indifferent to Marxism. This group believed that the Zimbabwean revolution should be a Marxist one, and that it was therefore imperative to wrest the leadership away from the ideologically bankrupt veterans.

---

1. Vitalis Zvinavashe, whose *chimurenga* name was Sheba Gava, succeeded Solomon Mujuru as army commander in 1990.

The disaffected young officers soon formed what was later known as the Nhari group, after their leader, Thomas Nhari. Nhari was able to unite the disparate elements of discontent and, together with Badza, led the young officers from the front into an attack on the ZANU and ZANLA leadership in Lusaka. It was perhaps happenstance that the attack coincided with the beginning of negotiations for independence in Lusaka, but it was bound to be read as part of the game of *détente* by both that initiative's supporters and opponents. What it in fact meant was that the only group with a real army, ZANU, had a rebellion on its hands, with guerrillas and weapons withdrawn from the front. These guns and bullets were now targeted at its own leaders.

Both the ZANU and ZANLA leaders were taken completely by surprise, and misunderstanding and distrust grew in the disarray. Some ZANU leaders, particularly Chitepo, chairman of ZANU and head of its external wing, and John Mataure, the political commissar, believed they should listen to the young officers. Tongogara, on the other hand, who was the main focus of the young officers' criticism, believed that giving an audience to these officers was tantamount to treason and encouragement of rebellion. It was a period of confusion for members of ZANU and ZANLA faced with the dilemma of which group to believe: the established military leadership under Tongogara, or the young officers complaining of mismanagement, corruption, and neglect.

The majority of Zimbabwean students and lecturers at the University of Zambia actively supported the liberation struggle. It was not surprising that the arrival of the Nhari group in Lusaka included visits to the university, and soon many students were tempted to side with this group, which appeared to be better educated and more revolutionary. Fortunately, some of us lecturers were more suspicious of the rhetoric, and managed to persuade the University of Zambia members of ZANU not to act too hastily by joining Nhari and his group. The group's capture of ZANU and ZANLA leaders through force of arms soon made it clear that the group was in Lusaka not only to air its grievances, but that it was also prepared to kill the leaders if its demands were not met. The experience of some of these young officers of the ZIPRA rebellion against the ZAPU leadership under James Chikerema had convinced them that nothing was to be gained through dialogue and delay. Their rebellion would lose momentum if they did not act quickly and decisively.

The captured leaders, including Josiah Tungamirai and Charles Dauramanzi, were taken to Chifombo, a ZANLA transit camp in eastern Zambia. However, the rebellion was short-lived, as some members of the group began to have second thoughts after the military-style execution of some 70 colleagues who had refused to join the rebellion. With the help of these defectors, Tongogara was able to recapture Chifombo in a clever military manoeuvre involving 300 guerrillas who had been brought from Mgagao training camp in Tanzania. In an irony of history, among the Mgagao group was Wilfred Mhanda, who was to lead the next group of rebels, known as the Vashandi[1] group. Military skill played a great part in putting down the rebellion, aided by the confusion caused by the Nhari group's callous execution of the resistors who had refused to march with them on Lusaka. Thus, while Nhari had gained immediate support, this support vanished as quickly as it had begun.

The aftermath of the rebellion was to divide and confuse ZANU and ZANLA even further, and its repercussions were to echo in ZANU and in Zimbabwe itself decades later. A trial was held at Chifombo, presided over by Herbert Chitepo, in an atmosphere clouded with suspicion. Chitepo had earlier agreed to have an informal meeting with the rebels, and this made some of the veterans, especially Tongogara, suspect that he secretly supported them. Perhaps a more formal meeting, with Tongogara present, and where Tongogara's critics could have laid out their grievances openly, could have saved the situation, although this was unlikely in the tense atmosphere of *détente*. Political leaders like Chitepo were believed to favour a power-sharing agreement for black majority rule, which would certainly have weakened the position of Tongogara and the military. But the need to keep the rebellion a secret made transparency impossible: ZANU's negotiating position at the conference table was based on the fact that it had the biggest and most successful military force, which had brought the Rhodesian regime to the negotiation table. That this military force was involved in internecine and suicidal violence could only strengthen the hand of ZANU's enemies.

---

1. *Vashandi* means "workers" in Shona, referring to the group's espousal of Marxian socialist ideals.

The Chifombo trials took place in the first week of February 1975. Chitepo and all other external leaders, except Mukudzei Mudzi and Noel Mukono, were present. Mudzi had been left in charge of affairs in Lusaka, while Mukono had fled, fearing reprisal for his open support of the rebels. The trial was tape-recorded, and these tapes came into my possession when Tongogara fled from Zambia. Incontrovertible evidence was given that the Nhari group had killed a sizeable number of those who had opposed their plan to leave the front and march on Lusaka. Some 70 opponents of the Nhari group were dead. John Mataure, a prominent and popular political leader who held the position of political commissar, was accused of supporting and aiding the rebels.

Chitepo condemned the rebels and their activities, particularly their killing of their comrades-in-arms. The rebels were given a number of punishments, mainly demotions in military rank. He ordered that they be handed over to the Mozambican authorities for further punishment.

The military leaders under Tongogara, while satisfied with the conduct of the trials, were not satisfied with the punishments meted out. They believed that Chitepo had shown extreme leniency, considering that the rebels had actually disrupted the armed struggle and killed some of their own colleagues. Soon after the trial, the military leaders executed the rebels secretly, without the consent of the political leadership. These extra-judicial executions were to cause further internal conflict within ZANU, with the political leaders dividing against the military leaders.

One of the most controversial issues was the execution of John Mataure, who had not participated with the rebels in the executions at the front, but who had met with them in Lusaka. As a member of the political leadership, not the military, many people believed that his execution by the military high command led by Tongogara was a way of getting rid of a potentially powerful rival, as Mataure would have had credibility both politically and militarily. He could have provided the much-needed bridge between the long divided political and military leaderships.

Another incident occurred when Richard Hove, a prominent political leader and vocal opponent of Tongogara, was captured and taken to Chifombo by the military. His wife Sheila believed that he, like Mataure, would be killed. She appealed to President Kaunda, allegedly refusing to leave his office and stripping off her clothes to bare her breasts, a Zimbabwean symbol of extreme anguish. President Kaunda ordered Hove to be brought to him. And so Sheila saved her husband's life.[1] Soon after this, I had a conversation with Richard. He asked me who I thought would win the power conflict within ZANU, Tongogara or Hamadziripi. I told him that in my view Tongogara was bound to win because he headed the army, and that this stage of the liberation struggle was necessarily a military one. Tongogara held the trump card.

The issue of whether a liberation movement in a foreign country, Zambia, had the right to execute its own members was a live one, with many believing that Chitepo's decision to hand over the rebels to the Mozambican authorities was the only correct choice in the circumstances. The Mozambican rather than Zambian authorities were selected because ZANU believed that the Zambian government supported the *détente* exercise unequivocally for its own internal reasons. Zambia's government was already suffering severe economic crises as a result of its almost total reliance on copper, whose price was fast falling and exacerbating diplomatic relations. The Zambian government blamed the continuing conflict in Rhodesia and the international sanctions against it for the worsening Zambian economic crisis. Many Zimbabweans believed that the Kaunda government would therefore support any group that would weaken ZANU and ZANLA, including the Nhari group, because of ZANU's refusal to hand in its arms as part of the *détente* exercise.

The ZANLA high command, on the other hand, held on to the more Old Testament version of justice of an eye for an eye, a death for a death. They believed the Nhari group had to be killed because it had killed others.

The intense conflict between the political and the military leadership that had remained underground for some time came to a head over the executions. Four members of the political leadership, namely Herbert Chitepo, Noel Mukono, John Mataure, and Henry Hamadziripi, were believed by the military to have supported the rebels. Of the remaining four, Tongogara as army commander, was in a far stronger position than Mukudzei Mudzi, Rugare Gumbo, and Kumbirai Kangai. All the political leaders except Tongogara condemned the

---

1. Richard Hove served as minister in several governments after independence.

executions, but in the circumstances they were unable to discipline either Tongogara or the military. The military leadership had now gained the upper hand, but the battle between the two had not ended. Meanwhile, they appeared as a group at the negotiating table apparently united against *détente*. It was in this uneasy situation that Chitepo was unexpectedly killed. A bomb had been placed in his car, and exploded as he started the engine. He was killed instantly, while his bodyguard, Sadat Kufa Mazuva, was severely injured.

The killing of Chitepo had all the marks of an assassination by the Rhodesian secret service, CIO, whose head, Ken Flower, later confessed to having ordered and implemented it.[1] However, given the timing of the assassination and the well-known internal conflicts within ZANU, it was inevitable that suspicion should fall on ZANU itself, particularly on Tongogara and the military high command, which had only a month earlier executed Mataure and the Nhari group. The Nhari execution and the assassination of Chitepo marked the beginning of the *détente* exercise in earnest. The Zambian government decided to arrest almost every member of ZANU and ZANLA at Chitepo's funeral, thus removing one of the main obstacles to *détente*.

THE AD HOC LUSAKA COMMITTEE

The main strategist behind *détente* was Henry Kissinger, President Nixon's secretary of state. He brought together John Vorster of South Africa and Kenneth Kaunda of Zambia. Vorster gave his "Voice of Reason" speech in October 1974, where he envisaged a zone of peace and prosperity across Africa under the leadership of South Africa. In secret negotiations with Kaunda, Vorster promised not to interfere in either Angola or Mozambique, to withdraw his forces from Rhodesia, and to "force" Ian Smith to concede "majority rule" to Zimbabwe. Zambia's part was to stop the armed struggle being waged by ZANU and ZANLA. As Zambia provided the headquarters and rear base support for both, it was in a good position to withdraw its support whenever it wished. However, President Kaunda's hopes for a peaceful and prosperous Africa were to be dashed, as South Africa was to destabilise and invade both Mozambique and Angola for the next two decades. But in 1974, *détente* appeared to offer a glimmer of hope that had to be explored.

---

1. Ken Flower, *Serving Secretly*, John Murray, London, 1987.

The genius of *détente* was to put forward the idea of a black government that would combine all four Zimbabwean political parties as equal partners. That the history of some of these parties had been one of rivalry, conflict, and mutual distrust, made the prospect all the more attractive to outsiders keen to promote their own interests. If Zimbabweans could also be persuaded that this prospect was in their own interest, then Zimbabwe could emerge as an independent country, free of colonialism, and under a black government, albeit a precariously weak one.

The conflict within ZANU between the political and military leaderships was temporarily shelved when the Zambian government took the drastic step of arresting and imprisoning all ZANU and ZANLA leaders at Chitepo's funeral. According to Zimbabwean custom, the funeral included several days of mourning during which large numbers of people gathered at the home of the deceased. It was there that they were surrounded by Zambian troops and taken into custody. At the same time, over 1,000 trained guerrillas were taken into detention at a place called Mboroma. The Zambian government, having tried to persuade ZANU to cease all fighting and come to the negotiating table, now resorted to the extreme measure of immobilising a whole army on its territory.

On the day of the arrests, the university branch of ZANU was scheduled to have a meeting. To our surprise, only three people turned up, all three of us lecturers. These were Sam Geza, Dzingai Mutumbuka, and myself. We waited for over two hours, grumbling at the failure of our colleagues to understand the seriousness of the situation. At that point, Tungamirai Mudzi, the younger brother of Mukudzei Mudzi, one of the arrested leaders and then the chairman of the university ZANU branch, suddenly arrived. He was accompanied by a young man, a freedom fighter. This young man had left Chitepo's house, which was still full of mourners, to buy cigarettes, and on his return found the Zambian army in the process of arresting everyone. He had instantly fled. University students who had been at the funeral had also been arrested.

We immediately saw this as an attempt by the Zambian government to bring the war in Zimbabwe to an abrupt end. At the time, none of us knew that the military high command had indeed already executed Nhari and his followers, as well as Mataure. Although there were rumours to this effect within ZANU circles, we did not believe them. Even those who felt that the execution of the Nhari group was the right decision did not believe it had already taken place, because the timing was so unpropitious. It was only later that we found out the truth.

After a very brief conference, we decided that we should immediately proceed to the ZANU farm just outside Lusaka to warn those there of the arrests. We only had two cars, my own and Tungamirai Mudzi's. We agreed that both cars should proceed to the farm. I was to go with the guerrilla while everyone else went with Mudzi. The reason for this decision was logical: no one would suspect me of being a Zimbabwean as I was not black. I would proceed first, and the guerrilla would leave the car just before the entrance to the farm. He would make his way into the camp on foot, in case the farm had already been taken by the Zambian army. I would drive straight up to the gate and, if it was guarded by Zambian soldiers, I would pretend to have lost my way. If it had not yet been taken by the Zambian army, I would enter.

Everything went according to plan. Just before reaching the gate, the young guerrilla left my car and disappeared into the thick surrounding bush. I drove up to the gate. To my surprise, the farm had not yet been taken by the Zambians. However, those at the farm had already heard of the arrest of their comrades, as a senior member of the ZANLA general staff, John Mawema, had climbed over the six foot fence surrounding Chitepo's house just as the Zambian army had started to arrest the mourners. He had made his way immediately to the farm.

On my arrival, I found Tongogara and members of the high command just about to leave in two of the ZANLA army trucks. Tongogara welcomed my arrival as a godsend, as he was very worried about the papers that had been left in the house of the ZANLA logistics head, Justin Chauke. These papers included not only the number and types of guns then held by ZANLA, but also the real names and matching pseudonyms of all ZANLA soldiers. Such information would be invaluable to the enemy. ZANLA was now to be a fugitive army, whose leaders and members were under arrest by the Zambian government. Such information would soon be in the hands of the Smith regime, and this would be disastrous for ZANLA. It would have particularly fatal consequences for the ZANLA members and their immediate families, who would now be easy victims of the Smith regime. Anonymity had so far saved these families from persecution.

We decided that Justin Chauke should go with me to his house in one of the shanty compounds outside Lusaka, while the two trucks proceeded towards Mozambique on the Great East Road. Once we had rescued the critical papers, I would drive Chauke to that road and catch up with the two trucks. We managed to reach Chauke's house and take the papers. We then set off on the Great East Road. It was a very dark and misty night, and road was difficult and mountainous, running along the escarpment above the lowlands of Zambia. It was essential to concentrate on my driving.

After some hours, we came across one of the ZANLA trucks waiting for us. As Chauke got out and I prepared to drive back to Lusaka on my own, Wilfred Mhanda got out of the truck. He told me that Tongogara had left his papers in his home, and it was absolutely essential to get these before they fell into the hands of the Zambian authorities.

I drove back to Lusaka, and immediately went to the flat of Sam Geza. It was now four o'clock in the morning. Sam and his wife Ntombana were not yet asleep. I asked him to accompany me to Tongogara's house, located in one of the poorer sections of the city. As we approached the house, we decided that it would be unwise to drive straight up to the gate, in case it was already surrounded by Zambian troops. We parked a few streets away while Geza walked up to the house. He would pretend to be a drunk who had lost his way if the house was surrounded. If it was not, he would rescue the papers.

As it happened, the house was unguarded. Geza made several trips, each time carrying armloads of files and documents. The boot of my car was soon full, and we left the township. We now had to find a good hiding place for Tongogara's personal archives.

We had an opportunity to go through these archives with a fine toothcomb over the next few weeks. Tongogara was a highly intelligent person with a strong sense of history and of the part he was playing in it. His papers showed that he had kept a record not only of every event, but also of his own opinions and views. He had kept letters captured from the Nhari group.

For the next five months until I left Zambia in August 1975, I hid Tongogara's papers in different places. We managed to salvage them intact, and they were handed over to Tongogara himself some years later. This was no mean feat, as my flat was entered and searched one day by unknown persons. They found nothing. In order to hide these materials, I had to use my imagination. It was quite amazing how many "safe" hiding places could be found.

Soon after the arrests at the funeral and the flight of Tongogara and the remaining guerrillas to Mozambique, an emergency meeting was called of ZANU members in Lusaka. The meeting consisted of two main groups: Zimbabwean businessmen in Lusaka and Zimbabwean students and lecturers at the University of Zambia. We were now the only two groups of Zimbabweans in Lusaka not in prison or in detention. Rex Chiwara, then ZANU representative in London, was also at the first meeting. He had just been released from prison, as he had been able to convince the authorities that he had just flown in for the funeral, and had taken no part in the events that preceded Chitepo's death.

Those at the meeting decided that the mass arrests of more than 1,000 ZANLA cadres and leaders was a blatant attempt to stop the liberation struggle. The 300 freedom fighters who were inside Zimbabwe were now totally isolated, unable to get supplies of food, armaments, and other basic necessities such as medicines. Without any rear support, they were likely to be wiped out. The meeting decided there and then that this should not be allowed to happen. A number of committees were formed, with John Mawema, the only full-time freedom fighter in the group, assisted by a rich businessman named Patrick Kombayi, put in charge of ensuring that weapons and supplies continued to flow into Zimbabwe. A second committee formed was the "escape" committee, which was to assist in helping the handful of guerrillas who had eluded the Zambian dragnet to escape either to Mozambique or to Tanzania. Mawema, Peter Mazhandu, and Tungamirai Mudzi were in charge of this committee. I was given the responsibility for the critical area of propaganda and information work, assisted by my colleagues at the University of Zambia, Dzingai Mutumbuka and Sam Geza. The last committee, headed by Kombayi, was in charge of providing food to the wives and children of the imprisoned guerrillas and to the injured combatants, who were generally kept in Lusaka for medical treatment. However, since we were so short of personnel, the leaders of each team could call upon any of us to help when the need arose. Thus, I participated in the work of both the "escape" committee and the food committee.

It was during this period of acute suffering for the 200 stranded wives and children of the imprisoned ZANLA leaders and wounded guerrillas that Rex Chiwara, the ZANU representative in London, approached a number of charities in London for financial assistance. One of the first contributors was Tiny Rowland, the founder of LONRHO, one of the biggest multinational companies operating in Rhodesia. Rowland had always found it useful to cultivate a close friendship with political leaders, whatever their political and ethnic loyalties. He therefore contributed £50,000 to ZANU. Meanwhile, some of the stranded people were able to phone London and were informed by Chiwara that their trials and tribulation in terms of shortage of food were over, as he had just given the money to Sithole to bring back to Lusaka. There was much rejoicing among the hungry, and a huge crowd made their way to Lusaka airport to welcome their leader. They waited patiently for Sithole to explain that they had received a generous contribution, but he said nothing. A long time later, they decided to ask him about the money. He at first denied that he had received any money from Chiwara. It was now Chiwara's word against Sithole's. After some very angry protestations, Sithole admitted to receiving the money, but asserted that the money was for people at the front, not for those in Lusaka. This incident angered everyone in Lusaka. Sithole was fast losing what little support and loyalty he had enjoyed.

Rex Chiwara received another generous donation from Tiny Rowland in 1976, when Sally Mugabe became very ill in Mozambique and had to go to London for treatment. He had elicited these funds to enable her to obtain suitable treatment, but Robert Mugabe felt that this was an attempt to trap him into an illicit relationship with the multi-millionaire capitalist, and Chiwara was subsequently relieved of this responsibility for the London office.

LONRHO continued to play an active part in the liberation struggle for Zimbabwe. By 1974, Tiny Rowland realised that an independent Zimbabwe was likely to be led by ZANU. He therefore sought to strengthen and support elements of ZANU that would be supportive of multinational companies, foreign business interests, and capitalism in general. LONRHO was fortunate that one of its own very senior managers, Cornelius Sanyanga, was a leading member of ZANU. Sanyanga played a key role in trying to weaken the left wing of ZANU, in particular by attacking ZANLA as an ethnic based army controlled by the

Karanga. LONRHO, through its farsighted leader, continued to play a key role in the politics of the post-independence struggle, using its dollars to support those politicians and political leaders who would favour its interests.

It was also at this time that Joseph Masangomai, one of the seemingly most devoted staff members of the ZANU information department, began to organise among us against the leaders in jail. Somehow, he had not been arrested by the Zambian authorities, and he now went around telling us that the arrest of the leaders was a golden opportunity to bring in a better and more educated leadership. Most of the ZANLA leaders did not have O levels, he told us, and a new military leadership could now be formed where the minimum qualification would be O levels.[1] Probably he thought the educational qualification would appeal to us university lecturers.

To me it was clear that the earliest freedom fighters had been recruited irrespective of their education, and that it would be unjust should they be excluded subsequently from any leadership position on the basis of their lack of education. They had been prepared to die for Zimbabwe, despite their low educational qualifications. This injustice was particularly clear to someone like myself who had taught for some years in African education: only about two per cent of blacks were allowed to enter secondary schools at the time, so the educational qualification would disqualify all but this two per cent elite. Masangomai was unable to win support either from the guerrillas or from the university and business groups. He became closely identified with Sithole. He and his wife were killed during the liberation struggle. It is not clear whether he was killed at the command of his leader, Sithole, or by ZANLA guerrillas who soon came to regard him as a turncoat out to confuse the freedom fighters. Some stories were even told of how freedom fighters who had worked with Masangomai inside the country had been captured by the Smith regime, the implication being that he was also a Smith informer. Masangomai had been chairman of the ZANU branch at the University of Zambia for some years, and we had all thought of him as a highly dedicated revolutionary.

---

1. O, or "Ordinary" levels, under the old British education system, was the 11th year of schooling in a 13-year school system.

Not all the ZANLA guerrillas stranded in Lusaka were maimed and injured. Some were fit enough either to return to the front or to join their comrades in Tanzania. At that time, Zambia was seen as all too eager to capture any ZANLA guerrilla in its bid to end the war in Zimbabwe. The escape committee headed by John Mawema utilised the cars of members of the ad hoc committee. These included the cars of Tungamirai Mudzi, Peter Mazhandu, and myself. We now had to ferry guerrillas to the borders with either Mozambique or Tanzania, where they would cross on foot. On one occasion, I was driving so fast that I reached the Luangwa Bridge, guarded by Zambian soldiers, without realising it. The guerrillas in my car had all fallen asleep. They were supposed to cross the Luangwa River, some parts of which were dry at that time of the year, on foot, while I crossed the bridge by car. We had agreed that I would wait for them on the other side of the bridge. However, the Zambian soldiers were unsuspicious of me as I often travelled that road with my students. They allowed me to pass without question, assuming that I had students in my car.

The guerrillas knew that they would have to walk for several days before they reached the safety of either a transit camp in Mozambique or their destination of Mgagao training camp in Tanzania. Generally they refused to eat any food on these journeys, as apparently it was better to fast during operations. They only carried bottles of water, from which they drank from time to time. I had to eat sandwiches and snacks by myself on these long journeys, which often covered over 700 kilometres each way. Fortunately, the Zambian roads were excellent. In this way all the able bodied guerrillas were able to escape.

Two top ZANLA leaders were among those who escaped from Zambia during this period. They were Robson Manyika and Solomon Mujuru. Both escaped to Mgagao, the largest training camp run by ZANLA in Tanzania, where they were able to plan the next stage of the armed struggle.

One very painful and dangerous occasion was when Sam Geza, a fellow lecturer at the University of Zambia, had to escape. It had been agreed that he, together with three guerrillas, would be driven by a man who was always eager to assist, one of the hangers-on in the liberation struggle. For some reason, this man did not turn up on the day. When night began to fall, and we failed to find a suitable driver, it was decided that I would drive the group to the Mozambican border. Just before we left, the original driver turned up with some excuse. He handed Geza a compass to help him on his journey. Geza was genuinely touched, as we all were. We thought this man to be a true revolutionary who had gone to extraordinary efforts to help us. We reached the Mozambican border successfully, but the group was arrested by the Zambian authorities soon afterwards. They managed to trace the group through the compass. Unbeknown to us, the exceptionally eager-to-help man was a Rhodesian spy who had organised Geza's arrest with the Zambian authorities. It was a hard lesson that we had to learn: some of the loudest mouthed "revolutionaries" turned out to be Smith spies.

The absence of all the ZANU workers meant that we now had to do all the work, from political analysis, to information dissemination, ensuring that both ZANU and ZANLA remained united during this painful period, feeding those left stranded in Lusaka, ferrying guerrillas out of Zambia to either Mozambique or Tanzania, and providing logistical support to those at the front. The work of the small ad hoc Lusaka committee had now become critical for the continuation of the struggle. Ian Smith was unable to totally destroy the few hundred guerrillas now virtually isolated within the country, and our logistical support and information work played a major part in the continuation of this courageous military endeavour.

Dzingai Mutumbuka, Sam Geza, and myself were in charge of collecting, analysing, interpreting, and sending all information out. We began doing a newsletter each week. These newsletters had to reach the ZANU representatives, Rex Chiwara in London, Claude Chokwenda in Stockholm, and Tapson Mawere in New York, who would in turn send them to our members and supporters. The Stockholm office was able to persuade many Scandinavian countries that the arrest of the over 1,000 ZANLA combatants in Zambia was part of a political ploy to support *détente* rather than because of criminal activities. It was clear that over 1,000 people could not be jointly accused of the murder of one man, and that man their leader, Herbert Chitepo. The London office was able to reach out to many countries in Europe, including West Germany, France, and the Netherlands, where ZANU had many supporters, particularly among anti-apartheid student groups who supported the liberation of Africa from colonial rule. These groups provided very valuable political as well as financial support throughout the struggle. The New York office ensured that those who had supported the liberation struggle in the United States and Canada continued to do so. It was very important that during this period there was an accurate, reliable, and trustworthy source of information to counteract the disinformation being propagated by the Smith regime and by the supporters of *détente*. In addition, I would send copies to support groups.

We were able to find a number of ways of doing this. My university colleagues, Lionel and Doris Cliffe, were invaluable in helping to find ways to take these newsletters out of the country. I would meet with Doris once a week, each time at a different supermarket. We would "bump" into each other next to the cereals or the jams, and the newsletter would change hands. No one suspected that housewives shopping for groceries were involved in a clandestine propaganda war in support of the liberation of Zimbabwe. We also used the post, which sometimes worked. Throughout the period we were able to ensure that the flow of accurate information to our members continued, thus making it possible for ZANU and ZANLA to remain a united organisation during this difficult time. I also entrusted Lionel and Doris Cliffe with Tongogara's papers when I fled from Zambia, and they were able to return these to Tongogara on his release.

A year later, Lionel Cliffe was arrested by the Zambian government, accused of fomenting demonstrations among the university students. The University of Zambia students demonstrated several times a year, usually to criticise some aspect of government policy. It was part of the Zambian government's strategy to blame discontent on foreigners, particularly on university lecturers from overseas. This was a clever and useful tactic, as no blame fell on any Zambian. Lionel Cliffe was one of those imprisoned and later expelled from Zambia. He shared a cell with one of the ZANLA high command, Joseph Chimurenga, during his incarceration. Another lecturer imprisoned during this period was Robert Molteno, a South African who supported the liberation struggle for Zimbabwe and who later worked with us to free the imprisoned Zimbabwean freedom fighters. Unrest at the university was part of the fallout of *détente*, because the students continued to support the Zimbabwean liberation struggle.

Ian Smith had managed to disarm the majority of guerrillas through the *détente* exercise. With over 1,000 being held at Mboroma in Zambia, several thousand more immobilised in military camps in

Tanzania, and a few hundred more immobilised in Mozambique, Smith now saw the wiping out of the remaining 300 guerrillas within the country as a fairly easy task. He therefore set about a programme of extermination. But this involved attacking the people, particularly the peasants, in the areas near the borders of the country. The Smith forces attacked with increasing ferocity in a desperate attempt to wipe out all support for the guerrillas. Despite the harshness of the conditions, the handful of guerrillas within the country continued to fight on. Their rear support, despite the arrest of their official leaders, continued, with arms, blankets, food, and bullets being organised by the ad hoc support team in Lusaka and entering the country either through friendly Mozambicans, particularly FRELIMO soldiers, or through the huge pantechnicons that plied between Zambia and Rhodesia. Some of these Zimbabwean drivers, working for international transport companies, were prepared to transport arms and other essentials clandestinely, as their trucks were usually empty on the journey back to Rhodesia. This was a traditional means for transporting arms and food for guerrillas, and had been used on many occasions. These drivers did not wish to be known, and have disappeared into the realms of the unsung heroes. They were never paid for their part in the liberation struggle.

On the *détente* front, there was intense activity to portray ZANU and ZANLA as criminals and murderers, guilty of self-destruction through the murder of their own chairman, Herbert Chitepo. The political arena was occupied by the supporters of *détente*, namely Abel Muzorewa, Ndabaningi Sithole, James Chikerema, and Joshua Nkomo, who were desperately trying to come to some agreement with Ian Smith's Rhodesian Front. Despite the powerful support of the United States, Britain, South Africa, and the Frontline African states of Zambia, Botswana, Tanzania, and Mozambique, *détente* was to fail.

One of the most important challenges was to ensure that the various ZANLA groups, now isolated from each other in different countries, should remain as one united force. There was a real danger that they would break up into different factions, with their guns trained on each other. With leaders such as Ndabaningi Sithole and Abel Muzorewa being given access to military camps in Mozambique and Tanzania, it was possible that confusion would soon reign. The worst-case scenario would be the break-up of ZANLA into two or three separate armies controlled by different warlords, and in conflict with each other. The ad hoc committee formed in Lusaka was very much aware of this danger, and it soon fell to me to make journeys into Mozambique and Tanzania to ensure that the guerrillas there remained clearly informed about the issues and developments. I was chosen for the purely pragmatic reason that because I was a woman and I was not black, I could easily enter these countries without suspicion being aroused. Few people would expect me to be a Zimbabwean, so I was naturally perfectly disguised. At that time, Zimbabweans travelled on British passports, which allowed us to travel freely within the region. I was to travel to both Mozambique and Tanzania on several occasions. In Tanzania, the guerrilla commanders came from Mgagao to meet with me. In this way, I was to come to know many of the top commanders in ZANLA. I also travelled to Kenya on one occasion, where I was housed by Ngugi wa Thiongo and his family. They were keen supporters of the Zimbabwean liberation struggle.

It was difficult to inform them that our then president and commander-in-chief of ZANLA, Ndabaningi Sithole, had virtually deserted the armed struggle in order to participate in the *détente* exercise. Despite many efforts to persuade him to support his own organisation and its guerrilla army, he continued to pursue his own agenda, which entailed trying to remove all the external political leaders of ZANU and to change the military leadership. The majority of guerrillas had been fed a diet of unadulterated adulation for Sithole by the ZANU publicity department, and it was a very painful realisation that this overblown portrait was far removed from reality. It was painful for these guerrillas to accept the truth that they were considered as mere gun carriers and cannon fodder, with no say in the direction and process of the liberation struggle. At the same time, no one was prepared to take any step against Ndabaningi Sithole, as the whole movement was already in disarray and attacking Sithole would only worsen the situation. Our task was never to attack him in any way, but to ensure that there was accurate information about what was happening and what decisions were being made.

SITHOLE'S DOWNFALL

During his 11 years of imprisonment, ZANU president Ndabaningi Sithole had been kept in isolation from the rest of his colleagues. During this period, he was allowed to meet only with those people chosen by his captors. This meant in effect he met mainly with his interrogators. From time to time, his captors would allow specially chosen people to see him. Not surprisingly, his grasp of reality was coloured by his isolation and by the information he was fed by his captors and their collaborators.

Two crises marked Sithole's period of imprisonment. One was that his captors placed an *agent provocateur* named John Brumer in his cell. Brumer, who was of East European origin, was able to persuade Sithole that he had been imprisoned for opposing the Smith regime. Sithole fell for this story. On his release from prison, Brumer was assigned by Sithole to bomb some installations. Brumer, actually a Rhodesian secret service agent, duly exploded a small bomb at the Kopje post office in the capital city of Salisbury, with the help, of course, of his employers, the Rhodesian Central Intelligence Organisation, CIO. Brumer recounts placing an incorrectly spelt placard with the word "confrontation" written on it, the wrong spelling apparently to indicate it had been written by an African! Little damage was done to the post office, but this act won him Sithole's full confidence, and he was to use Brumer as an emissary to President Kaunda of Zambia. Brumer was, according to his own account, given the responsibility of persuading Kaunda to allow ZANU guerrillas to train in Zambia.[1]

A second crisis occurred as a result of another plant by the Rhodesian secret service. A South African woman, known as Mrs. X in the subsequent court trials, was allowed to visit Sithole. She soon became a trusted confidante and emissary. He frequently sent letters to his followers outside prison through her. She would hand these over to the Rhodesian secret service first, before taking them to their intended recipients. In one of these letters, Sithole gave instructions for his followers to employ some gangsters to assassinate the Rhodesian leader, Ian Smith. Sithole was tried in a Rhodesian court for this attempted assassination, and during the course of his trial, he publicly renounced the use of any form of armed struggle to gain majority rule. He did this in order to escape conviction.

Sithole's colleagues became increasingly alarmed by his erratic decisions, particularly his association with Brumer, a person they did not

---

1. Recounted by John Brumer in his book, *For the President's Eyes Only*, Hugh Keartland Publishers, Johannesburg, 1971.

know but who was entrusted with the most delicate of tasks. It is also relevant to note the anti-white sentiments of the majority of the old ZANU leaders, and Sithole's misplaced trust in Brumer aroused bitter suspicion. Sithole's association with the infamous Mrs. X, whose repeated acts of betrayal led to his trial and subsequent renunciation of the armed struggle, was even more unsettling, as it was commonly believed that the Ian Smith regime would never hand over power without a military defeat. Renouncing armed struggle was tantamount to giving up the struggle, and would cause confusion among the followers.

Moreover, during this period it was apparently still possible for Sithole to communicate with his imprisoned colleagues through the offices of friendly and helpful jailors, but instead he chose to use Brumer and Mrs. X. His paranoia had already begun, such that he felt threatened by his own colleagues. His fellow ZANU prisoners had therefore decided that he should be removed as president of ZANU and be replaced by Robert Mugabe, who, as secretary general, was the next in the leadership hierarchy following the death of the vice-president, Leopold Takawira, in prison. Takawira had been unable to obtain the insulin that he needed as a diabetic.

After the first *détente* meetings, many of the leaders, including Robert Mugabe, had already returned to Rhodesia, but Ndabaningi Sithole, the president of ZANU and the commander-in-chief of ZANLA, remained in Lusaka.

Following the arrest of the ZANU and ZANLA leadership, many injured guerrillas and the wives and children of many commanders were left stranded in Lusaka. Deprived of the ZANU social services, they had no form of support. Some of the guerrillas had lost their limbs, and were intent on mastering walking again on artificial legs. One brave guerrilla forced himself to do a daily ten-mile hike so that he could get used to his prosthetic leg. The Lusaka University Teaching Hospital had a special unit for manufacturing artificial limbs. This had developed in response to the large number of car accidents in Zambia, but was now routinely used by Zimbabwean guerrillas injured in battle.

Collecting food for 200 people was a difficult task, and took a lot of time. Most of the charitable organisations that would have given support to the destitute said they could not give us money or food, as we were not legal representatives of any organisation. They asked us to approach them through official channels, using the legally recognised leaders of the Zimbabwean liberation movements. It was clearly imperative to get the support of those leaders who had not been arrested, namely those who had been recently released. We decided we had to convince Sithole that it was part of his responsibility to ensure that the wives, children, and the injured be fed. The efforts of the food committee formed by Zimbabwean businessmen and university lecturers had not been rewarded with great success. I was responsible for feeding one house full of guerrillas, and I managed to feed them only once every five days, and this was clearly inadequate. I decided to go and see Sithole on my own, as I thought this would save me from being identified with any one faction within ZANU. ZANU had again splintered, this time into pro- and anti-*détente* factions.

I made my way to the Intercontinental Hotel, then the luxury hotel in Lusaka, and knocked at Sithole's door. The door was opened by his assistant, Sambo. He was surprised to see me as he did not know me at all. I told him that I had come to see the "president". Accidentally, I had said the right word. Sithole was genuinely delighted to see me, and even more delighted to be addressed as "president". I spent the next two hours in conversation with him. Although it was the first time I had ever spoken to him, he immediately became expansive. He was particularly impressed by the fact that people like myself who were not black could support the liberation struggle. He recounted to me a dinner party thrown for him by my uncle, Gavin Lee, soon after his release. What pleased him most was that he was able to sit at the dinner table next to my Aunt Mollie in her home. I realised that Sithole had the old colonial mindset, which considered sitting next to a light-skinned woman in a social context an honour. He would not have felt at all honoured if he had sat next to a black woman! He was also highly impressed that the plane he had boarded to Lusaka had had a black pilot. His was a generation that believed only whites could pilot planes. I later discovered that my uncle, whose interest in politics had led him to entertain many other black political leaders in the same way, had judged Sithole to be mentally unbalanced. I also felt that Sithole was seriously out of touch with reality. In particular, he was unable to understand the plight of his hungry followers, being totally indifferent to the very practical issue of providing food for the wives, children, and injured.

The feeding of the hungry in 1975-76 was a defining moment for the liberation struggle. Sithole constantly refused to accept this responsibility, regarding the wives and children of the imprisoned ZANU and ZANLA guerrillas and the injured ZANLA guerrillas as tainted with guilt for the murders that had been committed by the ZANLA high command. He deliberately distanced himself from them, and definitely refused all responsibility for feeding them.

Patrick Kombayi, the head of the food committee appointed by the ad hoc committee was a brilliant businessman who owned a nightclub in Kafue, a small town near Lusaka. We worked very closely with Kombayi, who showed both exceptional courage and brilliance in devising ways and means to solve the food problem. Later, Kombayi was to try to use his sterling work during the *détente* period to win a position as a top leader within ZANU. He completely failed in this endeavour.

Sam Geza, together with some of the commanders who were stranded in Lusaka, decided to organise a large meeting, including the wives, children, and injured to tell Sithole himself how hungry they were. Sithole reacted angrily at the meeting, particularly on being addressed as "Comrade", a term of honour used within ZANU. "Comrade" had been adopted instead of the more traditional honorifics of "father of" and "mother of". The term was commonly used for anyone who had joined the liberation struggle, whereas those outside the liberation struggle were still addressed in the traditional way.

"I am not your comrade", he shouted angrily.

"What are you then?" replied the perplexed but hungry and angry audience.

"I am your president", he replied.

This was the beginning of a serious misunderstanding between Sithole and his followers. They had idolised him as a god during his 11 years of imprisonment and could not understand that their idol was indifferent to their plight. He did not want to hear about their imprisoned husbands. Nor did he want to hear that they were hungry. The meeting ended in anger when Sithole refused to listen to them, and instead instructed Sambo to take down the names and tribes of everyone present. This instruction was met with indignation by the women in particular, many of them Zambian women who had married Zimbabwean guerrillas during the latter's long exile in Zambia. Mary Dauramanzi, a

Zambian married to a ZANLA commander and mother of seven children, began to shout at him.

"You're nothing but a child. You are happy because they've given you a sweet to keep you quiet, but soon you'll wake up and find they've taken everything away from you."

These words were spoken in the familiar Shona one would use to a child. Because of her ignorance of the subtleties of the Shona language, she had managed to insult him even more than she had intended. Sithole left the meeting in anger, but Mary's words were prophetic.

Sithole's emphasis on tribe at this meeting left his audience both angry and mystified. Fear of tribalism and ethnic politics was endemic during the liberation struggle, with members of ZANU reciting ritualistically that they had no other tribe than Zimbabwe and no other totem than ZANU. Sithole, out of touch and isolated for 11 years, immediately offended this newly founded sense of unity. The *chimurenga* names or *noms de guerre* used by each guerrilla erased all signs of tribe, as these names tended to have no tribal links. Names such as Tichatonga ("we shall overcome"), Hondo ("war"), Kissinger (related to Henry Kissinger's role in the *détente* exercise in Zimbabwe), had no relationship to ethnic grouping. Moreover, the effect of education meant that regional accents were often lost when the most commonly spoken language, Shona, was used. Many Zimbabweans were also fluent in the second major language in Zimbabwe, Ndebele, so that language alone could not identify a person's ethnic grouping. Sithole was never forgiven for demanding information on tribal origins. This meeting was the beginning of a series of misunderstandings between Sithole and the wives of the imprisoned commanders. It led to the boast that Sithole was deposed by the women, who could not accept his failure to listen to their stories of food shortage and the torture of their husbands in Zambian prisons. As the wives were allowed to visit their husbands from time to time, they soon came out with stories of extreme torture endured by their husbands. The women feared that their husbands would be killed. Some of them were becoming hysterical. Lack of food did not improve the situation.

During this period, an incident occurred at Mboroma, the camp where more than 1,000 Zimbabweans were being held in detention. In the tense situation, with Zimbabweans challenging their Zambian jailors, shooting broke out. According to the Zimbabweans, the Zambian guards were aiming to kill the leadership in the camp, in particular Webster Gwauya, who was the ZANLA commander in charge of East Africa, that is, of the military training camps in Tanzania where most of the ZANLA guerrillas received their training. Tsitsi, a young peasant woman who had undergone military training, threw herself in front of Gwauya, and was instantly killed by Zambian fire. Tsitsi's death caused a furore. Sithole was immediately contacted. As the president of ZANU, he was seen as the father of the liberation movement, with guerrillas regarding themselves as members of his family. His refusal to attend Tsitsi's funeral was regarded as a refusal to accept ZANU and ZANLA as part of his family. This was worsened by Sithole's decision to leave for the United States soon afterwards, apparently because his daughter was ill. It was part of the ethics of the liberation struggle that there was no family loyalty greater than the loyalties formed in the struggle, so that Sithole's departure was seen as a statement that his daughter was more important than someone like Tsitsi, who had given up her life to save that of her commander. The deaths at Mboroma marked the end of Sithole as an accepted leader in ZANU and ZANLA, although no official steps were yet taken to disown him. Instead, it was he who officially disowned ZANU, ZANLA, and the armed struggle.

Sithole was so convinced that the *détente* exercise would succeed that he wanted nothing to do with ZANU and the liberation struggle that it had spearheaded in his name. It was a requirement of *détente* that all military activities cease, and the guerrilla army would be disbanded. Not only did he refuse to attend the funeral for the Mboroma dead, but he went all over the world denouncing the ZANU members held in Zambia as a bunch of murderers who deserved to be imprisoned and announcing that ZANU had been disbanded. Sithole sealed his own fate during this period.

It was not lost on the faction led by Abel Muzorewa that they too needed an army, and there was a ready-made army for them in the form of ZANLA. At the time of the Victoria Falls conference, Ndabaningi Sithole was still regarded as president of ZANU and commander-in-chief of ZANLA. That Sithole had spent the preceding months condemning ZANU and ZANLA as criminals and openly stating that ZANU had been disbanded for its criminal activities, did not stop him from claiming that he still enjoyed the allegiance of ZANU's army. In July 1975, Sithole, together with Nkomo, Muzorewa, and Chikerema, were allowed by the Mozambican authorities to enter a camp for Zimbabwean guerrillas. There they met with some hostility, as it was felt that they had not assisted the fighters in any way in terms of food, clothing, medicine, and military training. These were the basic needs of the guerrillas, and anyone who contributed to satisfying these needs was accepted as an ally and supporter. The new leaders had neglected to do so.

Sithole proceeded to form his own military high command, known as the Zimbabwe Liberation Council (ZLC), and appointed as his chief commanders Noel Mukono and Simpson Mutambanengwe. Both had formerly been very prominent ZANU political leaders who had disagreed with the imprisoned head of ZANLA, Josiah Tongogara. Moreover, Mutambanengwe and Mukono had also allegedly supported the Nhari rebellion against Tongogara. Other senior commanders were Felix Santana and Kenneth Gwindingwi, these two being military men rather than politicians. Sithole justified his decision by accusing the old military high command as well as the external ZANU leadership of being criminals and tribalists who were guilty of killing their chairman, Herbert Chitepo.[1] However, the freedom fighters in Zambia and in the Mozambican camp he had visited considered their imprisoned military leaders as the victims of *détente* rather than as criminals.

Sithole's choice of military commanders was bound to be controversial, with all four of them coming from his own ethnic group and all four of them connected in one way or the other with the Nhari group. Moreover, he had immediately sought to impose politicians over military leaders at a time when the military were exceptionally suspicious of politicians. At this time military victory was essential. It was, therefore, not surprising that his attempt to impose this new leadership on the freedom fighters was met with anger verging on violence, such that in November 1975 he could not even enter the Tanzanian military training camps. Sithole had made a monumental misjudgement in discounting the freedom fighters, whom he regarded as mere "gun carriers" whose views counted for little. The ZANLA fighters in Tanzania were now in a position to become the decisive factor in the liberation struggle, and they were not slow to make use of this opportunity.

---

1. N. Sithole's "Statement on the Assassination of H. Chitepo and ZANU," made on 10 May 1975. Published in Goswin Baumhögger, *The Struggle for Independence*, Vol. II, Institute of African Studies, Africa Documentation Centre, Hamburg, 1984, p. 33.

Meanwhile, the freedom fighters held in detention in Zambia or confined to military barracks in Tanzania were becoming increasingly restive. The imprisonment of their leaders had not led to the disintegration of ZANLA. The different parts of the ZANLA forces in Zambia, Tanzania, Mozambique, and Rhodesia itself were able to remain united, despite separation by distance, in different countries, and the fact that their elected leaders were incarcerated in Zambia. It was in this situation that a group of university-educated freedom fighters were able to play a decisive role in keeping ZANU and ZANLA united against the settler-colonialist regime of Ian Smith, rather than in suicidal internal wrangling.

A number of university lecturers had joined the liberation struggle. These included Sam Geza, an Oxford graduate who had lectured in economics at the University of Zambia, and Joseph Taderera, a biochemist who had lectured at the University of Rhodesia and later in the United States. Both were at Mgagao at the time, serving as officers in ZANLA. It was during this period that Simbi Mubako also arrived in Tanzania to confer with the guerrilla commanders. Wilfred Mhanda, also an intellectual, later to be a prominent leader of the Vashandi or Workers' movement within ZANU, held a high position in the military. They were among several hundred university lecturers and students who had decided to leave their campuses to participate in the liberation struggle, and their analytical advantage as well as political sophistication were invaluable during this difficult period. They now formed an influential part of the ZANLA leadership. Their response to the situation was embodied in the *Mgagao Declaration by Zimbabwe Freedom Fighters* published in November 1975.[1] The *Mgagao Declaration* unequivocally rejected Sithole as the leader of ZANU and ZANLA. It gave as reasons his refusal to accept the elected ZANU leadership imprisoned in Zambia; his appropriation for his own use of money contributed for his organisation at a time when his followers were literally starving; his callous behaviour towards his followers killed at Mboroma, since respect for the dead is one of the strongest features of Zimbabwean values; and his appointment of the ZLC leadership in flagrant defiance of the generally held view within ZANLA that the Nhari rebels, whatever the rights and wrongs of their case, played into the hands of the Smith

---

1. See Appendix 1, *The Mgagao Declaration*, 1975.

forces. Sithole had had over a year to assert his leadership over ZANU and ZANLA since his release from prison in later 1974, but had instead made political blunder after political blunder, sacrificing medium- and longer-term gains for immediate ephemeral gains.

The *Mgagao Declaration* solemnly stated that the freedom fighters had the "right to die" for their country. They believed that armed struggle was the only way to win independence in the face of the Smith regime's intransigence, and it ended with an appeal to the OAU and the Tanzanian and Mozambican governments to allow them to return to their own country to fight. Their plea did not go unheard: Kaunda's moderate and conciliatory politics had clearly failed and had to give way to a more aggressive approach. The Front-line presidents, together with the OAU, were soon to come round to full support for armed struggle, after a hiatus of over a year.

By December 1975, it was clear that Ian Smith did not intend to relinquish power and that he had accepted *détente* only as a ruse to disarm the guerrillas when he was losing the war. In the meantime, the Frontline presidents, in particular Nyerere and Samora Machel, had decided that only a resumption of fighting would cause Smith to make any real concessions.

The *Mgagao Declaration* was later confirmed by a meeting of the ZANU central committee held in Mozambique in 1976, just before the Geneva conference. Robert Mugabe now emerged as the new leader of ZANU. The choice of Mugabe was made because of the desire of all to avoid a potentially damaging leadership struggle. Mugabe was the next person in the leadership hierarchy, and he was unanimously accepted as the replacement for Sithole.

ESCAPE

So successful was the work of our small Lusaka committee that we soon attracted the attention of the Rhodesian secret service, CIO, which had already infiltrated ZANU very thoroughly over the years. ZANU was probably the best infiltrated organisation, with Rhodesian moles in very critical areas, according to Ken Flower, CIO head.[1] The two main ways of infiltrating the liberation movement was through recruits and through students. Rhodesian agents, usually young and ambitious

---

1. Ken Flower, *Serving Secretly,* John Murray, London, 1987, p. 109.

black men and women, readily entered through these two routes. From the evidence, it appeared that these agents had participated in the murder of Chitepo, gathered information about internal disagreements and conflicts, and used this information to bring ZANU and ZANLA into further disarray. This period was their heyday.

One of these moles, an agent of Malawian and Zimbabwean descent and trained by the CIA in the United States, had arrived in Lusaka soon after the onset of *détente*. He gained access to Chitepo's home through his student contacts, as Chitepo's daughter, Nomusa, was a student at the University of Zambia. Having participated in the groundwork for Chitepo's murder, he continued to work as an *agent provocateur* for some months after the death of Chitepo in March 1975. He managed to infiltrate some guerrilla groups loyal to Ndabaningi Sithole. It was only when we faced the real possibility of two groups of ZANLA guerrillas having a shootout in the streets of Lusaka in August 1975, that our suspicions were aroused. An incident occurred, which unfortunately involved my car. Some of the guerrillas loyal to Sithole appeared at my house together with the agent and informed me that Sithole had requested the use of my car for that day. As a member of ZANU, it was extremely difficult for me to refuse to allow our own president to use my car, and after grilling the group as closely as possible I agreed to allow them to have the car for several hours. Of course, the car did not reappear that day, and was missing for several days.

In the meantime, members of ZANU, particularly the wives of imprisoned leaders, were in a state of panic. They were convinced that ZANU President Sithole had given orders to the guerrillas who had taken my car to kill them. When I first heard these allegations, I was convinced that they could only be untrue. They appeared to me to be the wild machinations of the Smith propaganda machinery, as it was completely inconceivable to me that a leader would go about killing the wives of his followers. But despite my many attempts to persuade the wives that this story could not be true, they remained absolutely convinced of the reality of these allegations. They had all gone into hiding. Despite their panic, their trust in me was such that I was able to visit them in their hideouts. I was still convinced that these allegations could not be true. It was essential to find some way of calming them and dissipating their panic. Having travelled from hideout to hideout in a car borrowed from one of my neighbours, an American lecturer, I eventually landed at the bottle store owned by the Mazhandus, two brothers who were members of our little committee. When I repeated the wild allegations being made that Sithole was actually giving orders for the elimination of some wives, in particular Mrs. Angeline Tongogara, and of a prominent member of our committee, Patrick Kombayi, they assured me that these allegations were based on the truth. They had given refuge to a number of guerrillas to whom Sithole had given these orders, but who had fled rather than carry them out. They invited me to meet these young men, who could not understand why they should assassinate people whom they saw as on their own side. The guerrilla group that had come to borrow my car was apparently more obedient. This group was now said to be on a mission to punish and even kill those guerrillas who had been undisciplined enough to disobey the orders of the commander-in-chief and had fled rather than carry out orders they believed to be wrong.

When I heard this from the Mazhandus, I became seriously perturbed. I was still convinced that our president, Sithole, could not possibly have given the alleged orders. While participation in *détente* was a rational decision, albeit based on an incorrect reading of the situation, killing one's own supporters was not rational. Nevertheless, I recognised that everyone around me believed the allegations to be true. In particular, there were now two groups of armed guerrillas, hostile to each other, with their weapons trained on each other.

As I left the bottle store to return the borrowed car to my neighbour, I saw my own car on the road. Without a second thought I followed it from Matero township across the city towards the university. It drove into the entrance of a house and I drove in immediately after it. I had not seen my car for four days. As they got out of my car, I confronted them with the words, "Where have you been? Everyone says you have been out to kill people!" I spoke these words out of a mixture of naivety and disbelief: I still did not believe that their mission was possible.

However, the agent's response was such that I was again taken by surprise: "It's Kombayi who has been spreading these stories, and I'm going to kill him now." This was a totally unexpected response, and one I had never heard before. His angry reaction made me believe for the first time that the allegations he was a Rhodesian agent were true. I had never heard a ZANLA guerrilla threatening to or boasting of killing anyone. To do so would have offended the strictures imposed by traditional religion, that wherever possible a living creature was to be respected and not killed, and that even in war, killing was only justified if it was absolutely essential.

The authoritarian in me surfaced and I peremptorily ordered them to remain at the house while I returned the borrowed car. I somehow expected obedience, and I got it. As the house was close to the university, I was able to return the car and get a Zambian colleague to drive me back to the house. Such was my sense of urgency that night that all my neighbours assisted me without question.

On my return to the agent's house, I tried to interrogate those present about what they had been doing over the past four days. The only answer I got was angry and hostile threats against various people's lives from the agent, as he claimed that they had been defaming him for nothing. After several hours of this, I decided that I should go that very night to see Simon Muzenda, then a high ranking officer in the old ZANU leadership who had been recently released from Rhodesian jails. He was later to become the first vice-president of independent Zimbabwe. He had just arrived in Lusaka that week, having been sent by the leadership inside the country to assist in sorting out the chaos in Lusaka. I was now suspicious of the agent, and although I was still determined that Sithole could not possibly have given orders to assassinate his own followers, I was convinced that the two armed guerrilla groups could very easily end up shooting each other in the streets of Lusaka. In such an emergency, it was essential to try to stop the violence before it began. Thus, although it was midnight, I decided to go and see Muzenda. He was at a very low-cost motel, Andrew's Motel, some distance outside Lusaka. As I did not want to drive so far on my own, I ordered two of the guerrillas present, Godfrey and a young woman called Shingirayi, the two most junior guerrillas, to accompany me. I still did not believe that these guerrillas were involved in murderous activities, although I was perceptive enough not to choose either of the two senior guerrillas, who were named Billy and Jimmy.

When I arrived at Andrew's Motel, I found that Muzenda was sharing a small bedroom with John Nkomo of ZAPU. This was a period when the two liberation movements were working closely. Neither had much money, and sharing a very modest motel room was common practice. In order to speak to Muzenda alone, we had to go into the car park. This was about 1 o'clock in the morning. I told him of the danger of the two groups of young guerrillas facing each other in battle in Lusaka, and appealed to him to do something, and then left.

I returned to the agent's house, and insisted on driving all the guerrillas home, although the agent offered again and again to drive all of us home. I was now determined not be to be parted from my car. When I reached the guerrillas' home in the townships, I warned them to be careful not to trust anyone whom they had not worked with before, such as the agent. They were taken by surprise, as they said the agent was the best friend of Tongogara. This is what he had told them. I was able to assure him that this was definitely not the case.

When I finally returned to my flat in the early hours of the morning, I decided to take a torch and examine the boot of my car, as the agent had told me he had had no time to take his luggage out of my boot. What I found there was a radio transmitter. This again took me by surprise. I could not work out the meaning of my find.

The next day the agent came to my flat accompanied by his "sister", a student of mine, and while she kept me entertained, he cleared the boot of my car. However, I was able to keep an eye on him through my large French windows. It was probably because I watched him all the time that he was unable to do as thorough a job as was needed.

It was soon after this that I nearly had an accident in my car. Frightened, I took it to my neighbours, a British couple, Ian and Alison Love, and asked them to assist me in checking out what could be wrong with the vehicle. Ian told me that the electrical wires had been disconnected and had not been reconnected properly. As I had little knowledge of car engines, I decided it was essential to get a properly qualified and experienced mechanic to go over the car. On the other hand, it was impossible to take the car to my garage based on only vague and incoherent suspicions. I was also now afraid that my car would be interfered with during the night, and began to park it at a different house each night. In this way, I ended up involving large numbers of my university colleagues in helping me to hide my car each night over a period of two weeks.

Through my colleague and friend, Sam Geza, we managed to obtain the services of his cousin, an excellent Zimbabwean mechanic, Matthew Geza. My car was hidden on that day in the garden of my friends, David and Mary Kerr. David was British and Mary Malawian. It was on that day that I learnt for the first time that the agent who had posed as a Zimbabwean was actually a well-known member of the Malawian Secret Service, and had achieved notoriety because of his merciless torture of political prisoners. After going through my car, Matthew Geza informed me that the car doors had been unscrewed, and had not been screwed back properly. I learnt for the first time that car doors provide ample storage space. He unscrewed all the doors for me. We found some bullets inside. This was truly a nightmare for me, as it was clear that guns had been stored inside the doors of my car. When he went through the boot of the car, we found a lot of white powder on the floor of the boot. We touched it and tasted it, and could not determine what it was. We also found some tools for radio repair, in line with my initial finding of a radio transmitter in my boot.

Having made these findings, I then decided to go and question the guerrillas Billy and Jimmy as to their activities during the four days they had my car. I arrived at their home in the townships and peremptorily ordered them into a room where I interrogated them one at a time. After several hours of questioning, I came to the conclusion that they had been used by the agent and were not really aware of what was going on. They had been left on several occasions during the four days, which they had spent in the Southern Province of Zambia, near Mazabuka, allegedly while the agent went to look up some girlfriend in the area. Some time later, it was discovered that the Rhodesians had a centre on a farm close to Mazabuka, where arms were stored. I showed Jimmy and Billy what I had found in the car. They identified the white powder as an explosive. I still believed them to be dupes rather than agents themselves. This was probably more because I was extremely disinclined to believe that ZANLA guerrillas could at the same time be Rhodesian agents than because of any real evidence to vindicate them.

Having now identified my car as having contained a radio transmitter, some bullets, and some explosives, I realised I was in serious difficulty. Either they had committed some crime utilising my car, or there would be an attempt to incriminate me in some crime. It was even conceivable that there would be an attempt to kill me. The Rhodesian regime was then offering tens of thousands of dollars for the capture or killing of a freedom fighter, and my death could make someone very much richer. However, it was essential to keep a calm face and to behave as if nothing was amiss. We managed to do this throughout the period. Meanwhile, I had to plan my escape. Unfortunately, the university term was just about to begin and my sudden disappearance would involve letting down my department, but in the circumstances it was essential to act quickly. My colleague, David Kerr, assisted me by driving me in a University of Zambia bus to the airport. We used a bus because as members of the drama section of my department, we often used the university buses to drive students to and from rehearsals. Buses were also used for the frequent travelling theatres that we organised to tour the provinces. Thus, getting into a university bus would give the impression that we were just doing part of our usual work. I arrived at the airport an hour before the plane to Maputo in Mozambique was to take off and bought a ticket on the spot. Within an hour I had left Lusaka, which had been my home for over four years. Thanks to the Rhodesian secret service, I was now thrown into the liberation struggle as a full-time freedom fighter. It was August 1975.

TALKS ABOUT TALKS

Meanwhile, inside Rhodesia, a strong anti-war movement had begun, with many young white Rhodesians refusing to participate in the war against blacks. Instead, they fled the country to settle in Britain, causing an unhappy generational rift in many white families. These young whites were seriously disillusioned with Smith and with the un-winnable and self-destructive war that he had embarked upon. The war had to be fought by older white men. The manpower shortage was so severe that the Rhodesian regime soon began to recruit mercenaries from Europe. The infamous "dogs of war" who had fought in the Congo and in Biafra now arrived. They soon numbered over 1,200. These mercenaries enjoyed killing blacks, and killed for money rather than from conviction, bringing an additional dimension to the liberation struggle. Many of the more respectable older Rhodesians were appalled by the mercenaries, whom they saw as polluting their more virtuous society. Thus, there was also some internal pressure on the Smith regime to come to the negotiating table.

Despite these near perfect conditions for a neo-colonial settlement, month after month passed without progress. The Rhodesian Front blamed the nationalists, whereas the nationalists blamed the Rhodesian

Front. Long hours, days, and weeks were spent discussing the venue of the proposed constitutional conference, with Ian Smith adamantly insisting that such a conference could take place only inside Rhodesia and under his chairmanship.

Smith's intransigence was short-sighted in terms of his own constituency's real interests. If he had followed his mentors, John Vorster and Henry Kissinger, he could have thrown his black opponents into disarray by granting independence to the four negotiators, and by so doing dividing the black nationalist movement even further. However, he stuck instead to his principle that he would not allow a black government in his lifetime. By so doing he destroyed the credibility of his black collaborators, and at the same time made it more difficult for his loyal followers to control their own future political fate.

In the meantime, the Frontline presidents were waiting impatiently for the negotiations to succeed. The presidents were hopeful. President Kaunda in particular had staked his reputation on the success of *détente*. Partly this was because of the precarious state of the Zambian economy. It was commonly believed that this predicament was due to the continued conflict in Rhodesia.

However, Kaunda had another reason for supporting *détente*. As a highly committed Christian he abhorred communism. He was afraid of the possible increase in influence of communism on the two major liberation movements, as only the Soviet Union and Communist China were prepared to arm them. Kaunda was as nervous of the influence of communism in the region as Vorster and Kissinger. He sincerely wanted to stop communism's spread in the region, and saw *détente* as an excellent way to do so. Smith's intransigence was to harm President Kaunda's credibility and influence over his colleagues.

Meanwhile, the South Africans were trying to force the unwilling Smith to the negotiating table. This was what Kissinger expected. This was what the Frontline states also believed possible. The South Africans made it clear that they were not prepared to come to fight on the side of the Rhodesians, at best promising to evacuate the white settlers in the way whites had been evacuated from the Congo in the 1960s. Smith was still myopically convinced that he could gain military victory in the field, despite the glaring evidence that only a few months of resumed guerrilla warfare had brought the country to an economic standstill, with the call-up of all eligible white men for "indefinite periods of continuous service in the security forces".[1] Smith himself was forced to admit the gravity of the situation in a broadcast to the nation in early February 1976.[2]

The decision of the Frontline presidents to withdraw their support for the Kissinger-backed exercise to force both Smith and the liberation movements to the negotiating table was no doubt influenced not only by the predictable intransigence of Smith, but also by the fact that Mozambique had now attained independence. Mozambican President Samora Machel was a long-time partner and supporter of ZANU, as ZANLA had been fighting side by side with FRELIMO in the liberation of Mozambique. The Frontline presidents thus decided to change their strategy and allow a full-scale resumption of the war, convinced that only war would finally bring Ian Smith to the negotiating table.

---

1. From speech by Lieutenant General Peter Walls, as reported in the Daily News of Dar es Salaam on 3 May 1976.
2. Ian Smith's broadcast to the nation, 6 February 1976.

CHAPTER 7

Josiah Tongogara: Commander of ZANLA

Josiah Tongogara led ZANLA to success. A military specialist, he was over six foot tall, with the upright and muscular figure of a soldier accustomed to the rigours of war and the stresses of prolonged periods of living in the bush. Josiah Tongogara commanded both fear and love. Feared on the one hand by his enemies as an ambitious, ruthless, and implacable fighter, he was loved and respected by his supporters and followers as a faithful and caring leader, ever solicitous of his soldiers' welfare; as a leader who deserved to be followed; as a leader to whom people entrusted their children and their lives. Tongogara was able to command respect from both his enemies and his friends. No one could be indifferent to him.

With a distinctive, pockmarked, light brown face, and greeny-brown eyes, his facial expression displayed seriousness and determination. He was not someone you could laugh and joke with. Rather, he was someone who listened with deep concentration and seldom spoke, though when he did speak, he was animated, passionate, and articulate. He had little time for the frivolous, and was often deep in thought. His mind was constantly concentrated on Zimbabwe: on the meaning of the liberation struggle, on the suffering of the people, and on the treachery of politicians and intellectuals. He believed that he would die through the barrel of a gun – he had lived by the gun and expected to die by the gun. This constantly recurring theme in his conversation showed his preoccupation with death: he was prepared to die for Zimbabwe. He expected others around him to be prepared to do the same.

Tongogara displayed a very profound love for his family. Whenever he visited Dar es Salaam, he would phone his wife and children in Lusaka every evening, even though the outdated telephone system in both Tanzania and Zambia in the 1970s made this quite a feat. His family obviously meant a great deal to him, all the more so when he was constantly separated from them by the demands of war. Telephone calls

Josiah Tongogara

from Tanzania to Zambia in those days had to be routed through Britain, and those from Tanzania to Mozambique through Britain and Portugal. This was in the period before satellite transmission. It also meant that telephone calls made by the dispersed Zimbabwean liberation movements could be monitored in both London and Lisbon.

Despite his deep love for his family, he, like many of his senior commanders, demanded the sexual services of some of the young women guerrillas who had joined the liberation struggle in their thousands. Some of these women specially chose to attach themselves to leaders, as "wives" for those fortunate enough to bear children from these temporary unions, or as "girlfriends" for those who did not. Tongogara and his militarists practised their own code of morality based on traditional feudal attitudes: they opposed both contraception and abortion, but felt free to enjoy sexual favours as the reward for their extraordinary role in the liberation war. They recognised all their children from these unions, and were in the habit of taking these children home to be brought up by their legally married wives. Traditional society recognises the special role and responsibility of the first wife in a polygamous marriage, and many of these devoted first wives were prepared to look after their husband's offspring from other liaisons. The guerrilla leaders expected loyalty from these camp "wives", but they themselves were free to have a woman or two in every camp.

Sometimes, women did not enter into these casual unions willingly, but were forced into them. I remember two incidents when I was in Pungwe III, a military camp on the banks of the Pungwe River deep in the heart of Mozambique. I was awakened in the middle of the night by the sound of commotion – many angry voices could be heard shouting from the women's barracks situated a hundred metres from my *posto*[1]. The next morning I was told by a young commander that Tongogara and his retinue had arrived in the middle of the night and had demanded women to entertain them. Such women were euphemistically called "warm blankets". The sycophantic camp commander had immediately gone into the women's barracks and called out the names of several young women for "night duties". These women knew what this meant and refused. The commotion was caused by the fight between the camp commander and the young women, whose fierce opposition to being carried off to grace the beds of the commanders was termed "rebellion". Despite their shouts and screams, they ended up in the beds of the top ZANLA commanders that night.

Another revealing incident occurred when I visited the Pungwe III clinic. Like all clinics and hospitals in the liberation struggle, it was called Parirenyatwa, after the late Dr. Parirenyatwa, one of the earliest leaders to join the liberation struggle. When I arrived at the clinic, I found nobody there. This was strange as there were always nurses and medical officers at the clinic. I decided to call out to see if they were nearby, and to my surprise the nurses emerged from under the high beds made of bamboo. They told me they had gone into hiding when they heard my footsteps, as they thought I was one of the commanders

---

1. *"Posto"* is a word from Portuguese that had entered the Shona vocabulary of the freedom fighters and referred to the little grass huts occupied by individuals, as opposed to the barracks or dormitories occupied by 20 or 30 guerrillas.

who had arrived the night before. They were afraid of being forced into sexual servitude.

These indelicate excesses were accepted by Tongogara's admirers as the fruits of victory, but criticised by the more thoughtful of the freedom fighters. The young men in the military camps, incidentally much more numerous than the young women, accepted these excesses in silence: they believed that they could do nothing against Tongogara as long as the war was on because of his indubitable brilliance and courage as a military leader – Tongogara was necessary for military victory. It was not difficult to see that after the military struggle there would be other struggles, and some of these would be against the victorious militarists.

This feudal attitude towards women was one of the reasons the two rebellions in ZANLA, namely the Nhari rebellion and the Vashandi rebellion, both attracted very large numbers of women. While Tongogara and his top commanders were venerated by their followers, they were regarded with revulsion by many women guerrillas. However, some women commanders who rose to the top exercised the same sexual prerogatives as their male counterparts, taking their pick of the thousands of young men who had joined the struggle.

The only camp commander who to my knowledge refused to comply with this systematic abuse of some of the young women who had joined the struggle, many of them for the most idealistic of reasons, was Sheiba Tavarwisa, a top woman commander and one of the first and most respected of women guerrillas. She was a skilled and wise leader, who managed to maintain her integrity while enjoying the absolute trust of Tongogara, despite the fact that she always refused to comply with his demands for women. Tongogara respected her combination of independence and loyalty.

The only time I saw Sheiba totally distraught was at the death of her husband, Edgar Moyo. Despite his *chimurenga* name, Edgar Moyo was a Shona. Moyo was a ZIPRA commander who had joined ZIPA, the Zimbabwe People's Army, consisting of ZANLA and ZIPRA guerrillas formed directly under the patronage of Presidents Samora Machel and Julius Nyerere in 1975–76. ZIPA was to survive less than a year. Moyo was a brilliant man who had been trained under the KGB in the Soviet Union. He found himself in the unenviable position of being one of the few ZIPRA commanders trapped within ZANLA after the collapse of

ZIPA. He was visibly frightened of Tongogara, and found refuge in Sheiba, one of the most senior women in the liberation struggle. Their happy marriage was shattered when he died, apparently in crossfire between the Rhodesian forces and ZANLA soldiers. However, Sheiba believed that he had been executed on Tongogara's orders. Despite this belief, she remained a loyal supporter of Tongogara. A deeply religious woman, she believed that the ancestral spirits would protect their descendants from harm, and that included the removal of unsuitable leaders. According to traditional beliefs, political leaders could only rule with the support of the ancestral spirits.

Tongogara was surrounded by both admirers and enemies. His admirers called themselves the "veterans", to distinguish themselves as the oldest group of freedom fighters. The veterans were generally hardened soldiers with very little formal education. They were suspicious of, and even hostile towards the younger, more educated guerrillas who had joined the liberation struggle from the schools and universities after the mid-1970s. Their suspicions were further justified by the fact that the two major rebellions in ZANLA, that of the Nhari group and of the Vashandi or Workers' group, had been led by the educated.

Tongogara showed extreme concern for his followers, checking on the details of their housing, bedding, food, and milk for their babies. Whenever he visited a camp, he would make a full inspection, which would include examining the mattresses or more commonly the lack of mattresses for the camp dwellers. He made one of his periodical visits to Pungwe III when my daughter Chipo was just over a year old. He checked out how much powdered milk I had for her. This was one of the very human touches that he commonly cultivated whenever he visited a camp where there were babies. The loyalty of women was a potent political weapon that Tongogara valued and knew how to use. He understood how to win the loyalty of his followers by these little examples of solicitude. His followers trusted him and believed he placed their safety and welfare above his own.

On the other hand, the old-style political leaders regarded Tongogara with some suspicion as he represented the possibility of a "military government" in Zimbabwe after independence, whereas Tongogara himself regarded the old-style nationalists as untrustworthy, corrupt, and liable to betray the military struggle for ephemeral political gains.

The traditional religious leaders also condemned Tongogara and his top commanders for breaking the two inviolable ancestral rules of respect for life and sexual purity. Tongogara himself, while not accepting their moral control of his behaviour, was nevertheless seriously irked by their open condemnation of him. On one visit to Pungwe III military camp, he made the traditional leaders stand up one by one in a rally of thousands of camp dwellers, and threatened to imprison them if they continued to criticise him. Despite these threats, they continued to condemn him, on the pretext that the ancestral spirits spoke through them and they could not control what these spirits wished to say.

Tongogara was also criticised by a third group, the Vashandi, who considered him a failure by their Marxist-Leninist criteria. However, the Vashandi movement included many young militants such as Wilfred Mhanda (whose *chimurenga* name was Dzino Machingura), who admired Tongogara as a new-style leader different from the old-style politicians of the 1960s. This contradictory attitude towards Tongogara later made their defeat inevitable.

In contrast, his many enemies saw him as insatiably ambitious and determined to gain power and become the first president of Zimbabwe. A story is told of his anger against the traditional religious leaders for predicting that the first president of Zimbabwe would be a bald man. Tongogara had a full head of hair. The story was spread by those who believed he harboured the ambition to be the first president of independent Zimbabwe.

How could such differing opinions be held of the same man? Tongogara came to power at a period when the leadership of the Zimbabwean liberation struggle was going through a period of drastic change: the old leadership from the 1950s and 1960s was in danger of losing power to a younger generation of military specialists. There was clear tension between the old leadership, headed by Herbert Chitepo, and the young militarists, headed by Josiah Tongogara. At the same time, a younger generation of intellectuals and students had joined the liberation struggle after 1973, soon after ZANLA's first taste of military victory. It was not clear where and how this younger group would fit into the existing political order: would they accept the old political leadership, who included many university graduates, or would they side with Tongogara and his group of brilliant but not highly educated military specialists? Moreover, it was unclear whether this young university group would become significant in its own right in the liberation struggle or whether it would fall in line under the old divisions.

Tongogara entered the liberation struggle as a lowly soldier. He received his military training in the Nanking military academy in China and forever held the Chinese as his mentors in morality as well as in military skills and strategies. It was from the thoughts and practices of Mao Tse Tung that he learnt that the guerrilla must merge with the people. He taught his soldiers that they were never to mistreat the peasantry, popularly known as the *povo*, Portuguese for the people.

It was probably also from the Chinese that he learnt that it was essential to eliminate his enemies. He saw issues in black and white, and believed that those who opposed or betrayed the liberation struggle for Zimbabwe deserved to be executed, and he did not flinch from playing the role of executioner. He believed he was in a good position to judge those who betrayed the struggle. This Stalinesque aspect of Tongogara's character revealed itself during the Nhari rebellion and its aftermath, which saw the execution of more than a dozen ZANLA soldiers at the hands of the ZANLA high command itself. Their summary executions cast a dark shadow over Tongogara's character as well as on his career as a leader.

Tongogara was not a highly educated man, having received only two years of secondary education. However, he had a brilliant mind, which had benefited from his military training. As a military specialist, he was able to deal with military issues in a highly sophisticated and creative way. He was an avid reader, and eagerly sought to discuss serious political issues with us university teachers. He was thus very much respected by the many Zimbabweans then teaching or studying at the University of Zambia. We were welcomed into his humble township house where we analysed and discussed possible scenarios for the future of the struggle and the future of Zimbabwe. He was particularly close to Dzingai Mutumbuka, then a chemistry lecturer at the university and later the head of the ZANU education department and first minister of education after independence. He was also very close to Simbi Mubako, who was a lecturer in the school of law and later minister of home affairs and a high court judge.

Tongogara's suspicion of the old-style nationalist politicians was shared by the handful of original guerrillas, as well as those who had come from ZIPRA. Tongogara believed that some of the old political leadership were so untrustworthy that they actually worked for the Smith regime while posing as leaders of the liberation struggle. Some of them were even accused of being in the pay of the American Central Intelligence Agency. This suspicion particularly fell on some of the Zimbabwean academics who had spent many years in the United States. One reason for this suspicion was the continuing failure of the armed struggle when it was directed from Lusaka by non-military specialists. Many guerrillas had seen their comrades die in un-winnable battles, and believed that they too could equally easily be sacrificed for personal or political gain.

Although Tongogara himself had read little or nothing of Marx or Lenin, for some time his imbibed Maoism gave him some appeal to the left-wing students who had latterly chosen to join the liberation struggle. Tongogara never made any pretensions to intellectualism: he saw himself as a soldier rather than as a thinker. After the Nhari rebellion, which included many of the most brilliant, better educated, young guerrilla commanders, Tongogara became as wary of the young ideologues as he was of the old-style politicians. The followers who obeyed his every command without question were the uneducated old guerrillas, a devoted group of women guerrillas such as Sheiba Tavarwisa, and the child soldiers. These formed the loyalists with whom Tongogara surrounded himself. They gave him their total and unquestioning loyalty.

Tongogara's indubitable military skills meant that he could adjust his military strategies to suit the various stages of the war, beginning with guerrilla incursions by a dozen dedicated guerrillas, to the stage where he was able to deploy 300 guerrillas at the front, until finally he was able to send in tens of thousands of guerrillas. He moved inexorably and confidently from guerrilla to conventional warfare.

Having had to work with the old-style nationalist politicians, Tongogara himself had become politically adept and understood how to manipulate the elections that were held within ZANU every two years. Through these elections he was able to remove political leaders he did not trust, such as Simpson Mutambanengwe, who was removed in the 1973 elections. Tongogara also did not trust Nathan Shamuyarira, who had left ZANU earlier to form FROLIZI. Nor did he trust the head of the external wing of ZANU, Herbert Chitepo, or veteran politician Henry Hamadziripi. He was particularly suspicious of Hamadziripi, who had tried to manoeuvre Meyor Hurimbo into the top leadership position as head of ZANLA in place of Tongogara. Such was Hurimbo's loyalty to Tongogara that he exposed this plot, causing an irreconcilable rift between Tongogara and Hamadziripi. Incidentally, both Hamadziripi and Tongogara belonged to the Karanga tribe, as did Meyor Hurimbo, making the rather over-simplified explanation of all conflicts within ZANU as "tribal" difficult to maintain. The Karanga formed a substantial part of ZANLA as well as of the Rhodesian army. The fact that "brothers" could be found fighting on both sides of the divide was one of the important factors in the liberation struggle: many Smith soldiers and secret service agents readily crossed over to join the ZANLA forces, and were able to rise to become high ranking officers.

Tongogara's undisguised hostility against Chitepo eventually led to accusations that he had killed Chitepo, despite the fact that there was no evidence to support this claim. Chitepo was killed by a car bomb in March 1975. What was evident was that Tongogara had utilised his position as head of the army to surround Chitepo with "guards" who were personally loyal to Tongogara. These "guards" were not only assigned to protect, but also to spy on Chitepo, and to report on any meetings with and messages to him. It was during this period that the security department of ZANLA, headed by Cletus Chigove, began to play the dual role of providing "protection" while at the same time spying on the person who was being protected. This dual role has continued with the incorporation of the ZANLA security department into the Central Intelligence Organisation after independence. Chitepo was not slow to realise that he was surrounded by hostile forces in the person of the very comrades who were responsible for guarding him.

Tongogara's suspicions against Chitepo stemmed from Chitepo's handling of the trial of the Nhari rebels. As was earlier noted, Tongogara felt that Chitepo had been too lenient on the rebels, given that they had disrupted the liberation struggle and had killed some 70 guerrillas who had refused to join their rebellion. He therefore came to the conclusion that Chitepo was sympathetic towards the rebels, a suspicion fuelled by the fact that Chitepo belonged to the same ethnic group, the Manyika, as did some of the other supporters of the rebels, namely Simpson Mutambanengwe and Noel Mukono.

Tongogara's reaction was to execute by firing squad the rebels who had been left in his custody, a decision that was to have far-reaching effects within ZANLA and ZANU, and to affect the outcome of the liberation struggle for Zimbabwe. In the final analysis, it was the execution of the Nhari rebels that made it impossible for the militarists to again win the upper hand in future power struggles. When Tongogara attempted to quell opposition first by the Vashandi group led by Wilfred Mhanda and Sam Geza and later by a second group of old-style politicians led by Henry Hamadziripi and Rugare Gumbo, he was unable to destroy these two latter groups as effectively as he had done the Nhari group. The power he had given himself as executioner was effectively removed by the new political leaders of ZANU, Robert Mugabe and Simon Muzenda, who were very conscious of the tragic fate of the Nhari group. As a result, as soon as the conflicts with Tongogara came to a head, Mugabe and Muzenda hastily arranged for intervention by the Mozambican authorities, who held these two opposition groups in detention until after independence was agreed upon. Had Tongogara's faction not executed their critics, they could have emerged from the war as a more powerful and coherent group. They used force and executions to impose their views, regarding their political opponents as "sell-outs" and "traitors". Perceived as killers by outsiders as well as by their opponents within ZANU and ZANLA, they became neutralised after independence.

Tongogara's veterans were resurrected finally in the war veterans' revolt of 1997, and they played a pivotal role in the land resettlement programme of 2000-02. Because they were of peasant stock, the issue of land resonated more forcefully with them.

TONGOGARA ON TRIAL FOR MURDER

Soon after the arrests at Chitepo's funeral in March 1975, Josiah Tongogara, together with a large number of military commanders, successfully managed to escape from their base at the ZANU farm outside Lusaka to Mozambique, where they received a warm welcome from their fellow freedom fighter, Samora Machel, soon to become president of Mozambique. ZANLA had worked closely with FRELIMO in the military liberation of Mozambique. Tongogara had formed a close personal relationship with Machel. Informed by the Zambian government that Tongogara and his group were wanted back in Zambia on charges of having murdered Chitepo, Machel insisted on a personal interview with Tongogara. Machel asked Tongogara if he had killed Chitepo.

Tongogara declared that he was entirely innocent of the murder of Chitepo. Machel then made the decision that if Tongogara was innocent, he should be prepared to prove his innocence in a Zambian court. Tongogara was thus escorted back to the Zambian authorities.

While talks about talks between Smith and the nationalists, overseen by the Frontline presidents, continued, Tongogara and members of the external leadership of ZANU languished in jail. An international commission had been formed by the Zambian government to hear of the internecine conflicts within ZANU that had allegedly led to the death of Herbert Chitepo. It was clear that the Zambian government, for unknown reasons, was not prepared to put Tongogara and his team on trial for the murder of the Nhari group, although there were large numbers of witnesses to these killings as well as ample evidence to convict the killers. On the other hand, the Zambian government was determined to find Tongogara guilty of the murder of Chitepo, a crime for which there were no witnesses and no evidence. The international commission did not have the normal checks and balances of a judicial trial, as the accused could not be defended by lawyers, yet it had the power to declare persons and organisations guilty of crimes, including the crime of murder.

As I was now responsible for the ad hoc ZANU information and media department, I decided it was essential for me to know the truth. While I personally believed that Tongogara had not killed either Chitepo or the Nhari group, I realised that this was merely a personal opinion. It was necessary to find out the truth before publishing anything on these allegations. I therefore began to interview many of the guerrillas who had been at Chifombo at the time of the recapture of the camp by Tongogara. I was perturbed to hear from every one of these witnesses that Tongogara and the high command had indeed executed the Nhari group. John Mataure had also been executed. Some of these executions had taken place publicly, witnessed even by children. Edgar Madekurozwa, a medical technician at the Lusaka Teaching Hospital suspected of having harboured the Nhari group in his house, was killed in front of children, for example. From this incontrovertible evidence, it was clear that Tongogara and the high command had indeed killed all those suspected of having been involved in the Nhari rebellion. So convinced were Tongogara and the high command that this was the right step, the executions were carried out and justified publicly.

The killing of the Nhari group was a disastrous decision. The success that the military had experienced on the battlefield had already given them the belief that they had the right to execute those who had "betrayed" Zimbabwe. Yet some of those who had been executed by the high command had clearly not been at the front where the Nhari group had perpetrated its own killings, although they may have been sympathetic to the Nhari group. A number of the executed, like Godfrey Guvara, had worked at the Lusaka office of ZANU. I knew Godfrey quite well, as I sometimes helped with the printing of the Zimbabwean university students' magazine, *Chindunduma*.[1] Godfrey delighted in annoying people in a rather childish and nasty manner. On one occasion when I was trying to wash the black ink from the printing machine from my hands, he came behind me and said, "We will never accept you even if you paint your hands black." On another occasion when I was speaking Shona to one of the women visiting freedom fighters at the office, he made the remark, "Your Shona is so poor, that if I were you I would shut up." These nasty, childish, and racist remarks were typical of Godfrey, a young man who had a chip on his shoulder because he had failed his first year at university. It is quite likely that he was delighted at the uprising led by Nhari, as any defiance of authority pleased him. He could be heard jeering at military leaders like Tongogara who had never completed high school. However, it was quite a shock to me that someone as immature and as inconsequential as Godfrey should have been considered dangerous enough to merit execution.

It was clear to me that the military high command's responsibility for the death of the Nhari group should not be allowed to cloud and confuse the need to continue the struggle for the liberation of Zimbabwe. The ill-advised rebellion by young men and women, some of them fired with the best of ideals, had ended in their tragic deaths. In order to end this sad chapter of ZANU's history it was necessary that the Zambian government be forced to hold a properly constituted trial, based on real evidence, rather than on hearsay, suspicion, and innuendo. Confessions were being extorted by extreme torture, and such evi-

---

1. "Chindunduma" was the name of a revolutionary victory in the first Chimurenga or first liberation struggle in Zimbabwe in the 1890s.

dence was necessarily suspect. Some of us therefore decided to set about the task of forcing a properly constituted judicial trial.

We were determined to ensure that Tongogara's trial would be as fair as possible, and this meant legal representation. While I was still in Lusaka, some ZANU members headed by Simbi Mubako, Ignatius Chigwendere, Dzingai Mutumbuka, and Rex Chiwara were trying to collect funds for a lawyer. Simbi Mubako was then teaching at the University of Southampton, Ignatius Chigwendere was in charge of race relations in the Catholic Institute for International Relations, while Dzingai Mutumbuka was working full time with Rex Chiwara at the ZANU London office, after being forced to flee Zambia. When I arrived in London in February 1976, we decided to form a small committee consisting of both ZANU members and some of those outside ZANU who supported the struggle for the liberation of Zimbabwe. The aim was to carry out a concerted campaign for the free and fair trial of the ZANU accused imprisoned in Zambia. The well-known African history specialist, Basil Davidson, and the Roman Catholic papal representative in Britain, Mgr. Bruce Kent, agreed to support the committee as patrons, thus giving the committee international legitimacy. The committee was named the Zimbabwe Detainees' Defence Committee. The committee included ZANU members such as Simbi Mubako, Dzingai Mutumbuka, Ignatius Chigwendere, and myself. Many well-known people agreed to serve on this committee. The chairman was former Labour councillor, Kees Maxey, an ardent supporter of the Zimbabwe liberation struggle. Judith Todd, a well-known Zimbabwean political activist who was linked to ZAPU rather than ZANU, agreed to work with us for the sake of Zimbabwe. She was an indefatigable treasurer for our fundraising efforts. Two people connected with the anti-apartheid movement in South Africa, the Rev. Michael Scott, an Anglican priest who had worked in Soweto, and Robert Molteno, a well known South African academic who had taught with us at the University of Zambia and was now a publisher in London, also joined us. Lionel Cliffe, a specialist in African politics and economics, who had also taught with us at the University of Zambia, was another very active member. Peter Lowenstein, who later worked for the BBC, and his wife Susan, helped on a day-to-day basis. Later Didymus Mutasa, then studying in Birmingham, joined the committee: we managed to convince him that the arrest and detention of more than 1,000 full-time

ZANU workers and guerrillas in Zambia should not be analysed in terms of tribal conflict between Karanga and Manyika, an explanation that was rampant at the time. It was essential that the liberation struggle should be supported, despite the crimes and mistakes committed by some of its participants. Mutasa's agreement to support the committee was a triumph against tribalism, as he was one of the first Manyika to reject the tribal explanation of the conflict between Tongogara and the Nhari group.

Amnesty International played a very important role in highlighting the torture of the Zimbabwean prisoners and in emphasizing the political nature of their trials. It gave immense publicity to the illegal nature of their detention and trial, and so helped to win international opinion in support of the liberation struggle in Zimbabwe.

Our first task was to raise money and find a lawyer of international stature to undertake the defence of Tongogara against the charge of murdering Chitepo. We had managed to raise £30,000, quite a feat for us, but actually insufficient to pay for a top-class lawyer. Moreover, it was difficult to find a lawyer prepared to take on the responsibility, for it was clear that the trial was a highly political one, with the Zambian government accusing the head of a guerrilla army of having murdered the leader of that same movement. Most lawyers were not prepared to take on such a politically sensitive issue, particularly as it was now well known that Tongogara had led a military-style execution squad that had killed over a dozen of the Nhari rebel group. If Tongogara was able to execute his own followers, it would not be unthinkable for him to have murdered his leader.

Given this situation, we were fortunate enough to find a brilliant lawyer to take on the case, John Platts Mills, a well known socialist. The money we had collected would hardly cover the cost of his travels to and from Zambia, but because he saw that the case involved the liberation of a country, he was prepared to take it on. So it was that John Platts Mills played a critical role in the liberation of Zimbabwe.

It was Platts Mills, a highly experienced politically oriented lawyer, who advised us on the need to lobby for more political support not only in Britain, but from the Commonwealth as a whole. He himself was prepared to use his contacts within the Commonwealth to support us. We were not slow to take his advice, and we began to lobby all political parties in Britain. We managed to present our case to a number of members of the Conservative Party, which was then in opposition. This stood us in good stead, as the Conservatives were to win the elections a few years later and, under Margaret Thatcher, to grant independence to Zimbabwe in 1980. Our painstaking work in explaining the details of the liberation struggle contributed importantly to the support we were to receive from within the Conservative Party. We met with the Labour Party, whose members listened sympathetically, but we received little real support from them. The Labour Party under Harold Wilson had continually failed to support the liberation movements, despite the expectation that as socialists they should have been more sympathetic towards the liberation struggle than the Conservatives. Instead, Harold Wilson had given the green light to Ian Smith to go ahead with his illegal Unilateral Declaration of Independence by assuring Smith that he would never use military force against the Rhodesians. Wilson's rationale, that the British should stand together with their "kith and kin", the white Rhodesian settlers and colonialists, made it impossible for them to take the simple and logical steps that would have ended Smith's illegal regime. We attempted to lobby the Communist Party of Great Britain, but they would have nothing at all to do with us. As they were dedicated to following the policies laid down by the Soviet Union, they spurned ZANU. We approached Archbishop Trevor Huddlestone, so well known for his support of the anti-apartheid struggle, but he refused to assist in any way as he had heard of the killings within ZANLA.

Platts Mills was able to use his Commonwealth links to reach President Nyerere. The Commonwealth Secretariat, headed by Sunny Shridath Ramphal, was to play a key role in the resolution of the Zimbabwean crisis, and it was Platts Mills's political acumen and experience that were instrumental in getting these players on our side. He knew many of these top leaders on a personal basis, and he made it his responsibility to give them the fullest information about what was happening with the liberation struggle and Tongogara's impending judicial trial. The Frontline presidents, led by Nyerere and Machel, also played extremely critical and sensitive roles in bringing about the liberation of Zimbabwe.

The Zimbabwe Detainees' Defence Committee was able to persuade the international community that the Zambian special commission set up to investigate the murder of Chitepo could not be accepted as a judicial trial, as the accused were unable to receive proper legal support. It was essential to have a properly constituted trial following appropriate judicial processes. Evidence elicited through torture could not be accepted. Nor could people who had not given evidence be condemned without appearing in court. Eventually, an open trial was agreed upon. There, Platts Mills's knowledge of police and court procedure enabled him to demonstrate the occasions when the Zimbabwean prisoners were taken out of prison for interrogation under torture. This rendered the evidence elicited from torture untenable in court. Thus he demonstrated that there was not a shred of evidence to convict Tongogara and his followers of the murder of Chitepo. Tongogara and the high command were finally released in September 1976. They had spent 18 months in prison, where, in addition to the poor living conditions and sanitation, they had been subjected to continual beatings and torture. Their release was very much due to the brilliant performance of John Platts Mills, whose defence of Tongogara was to allow the struggle for the liberation of Zimbabwe to resume. Tongogara and the high command were never tried for the deaths of the Nhari group or of Mataure.

DEATH OF TONGOGARA

Tongogara died in a car crash in Mozambique in December 1979, only four months before the achievement of independence by Zimbabwe. The Land Cruiser in which he was travelling overturned while trying to overtake a lorry that was towing a large trailer. As Tongogara's car tried to overtake, the lorry swung to the left, but the attached trailer swung to the right, killing Tongogara instantly. He was sitting on the left-hand front seat beside the driver. The Land Cruiser overturned, but no other passenger was seriously injured. One of the passengers was Oppah Muchinguri, a member of the general staff in charge of funds for the battlefront. A close confidante and follower of Tongogara, she believed his death to be a total but bizarre accident. The followers of traditional religion believed that he was taken away by the ancestral spirits because he had continually transgressed against their rules.

CHAPTER 8

Post-*Détente* Intensification of the War: Nyadzonia and Chimoio

The Smith regime utilised the *détente* exercise to try to eliminate the guerrillas within the country as well as those in the neighbouring countries of Mozambique and Zambia. The end of the formal *détente* negotiations in December 1975 coincided with the decisions of the Frontline presidents to resume their support for the armed struggle. Samora Machel had just taken over in Mozambique, and together with Presidents Nyerere and Kaunda had agreed to support the formation of a new guerrilla army to be known as the Zimbabwe People's Army (ZIPA), consisting of the freedom fighters from ZANLA and ZIPRA.

The Smith regime's determined effort to wipe out all signs of opposition led to an exodus of hundreds of thousands of peasants and their families into refugee camps in Mozambique. It was the freedom fighters and not the Smith regime that were winning the battle for hearts and minds. Broadcasts continued from Dar es Salaam throughout the period. The traditional religious leaders, powerful opinion- and decision-makers in the traditional peasant context, continued to support the liberation struggle, promising certain victory. The extreme cruelty of the settler forces alienated the populace further, driving them to see the freedom fighters as preferable in every way to the regime in power.

Because they could not distinguish the guerrillas from the peasantry, the Rhodesian intelligence began to capture civilians in order to obtain information. Pedzisai, a young girl of 14 who later came to live with me, was an example of what could happen even to young girls who were arrested by the Rhodesian forces. The Rhodesians knew that adolescent girls were usually sent with food for the freedom fighters, so they decided to arrest them. These young women were tied by their ankles and hung in a tree upside down over a barrel of water. They would be dipped from time to time into the water until they were prepared to talk. It was after this ordeal that Pedzisai decided to flee into Mozambique. She managed to reach one of our schools and was able to complete her education.

Prisoners also received electric torture, with electric wires often attached to their sexual organs. Many tortured prisoners suffered permanent physical and mental damage as a result of such extreme suffering. Whenever guerrillas were captured and killed, their dead bodies were displayed as a warning to the people. The Rhodesians claimed to be the bastions of Western civilisation and Christianity fighting against atheistic communism. However, the display of dead bodies as a warning to black people was probably counterproductive, leading to greater support for ZANU. ZANU, on the other hand, claimed to be fighting a just liberation struggle against colonial oppression. It also claimed to be supported by the ancestral spirits. The ideological battleground was to be the people's minds.

One of the signs that the settler regime had lost the battle for hearts and minds was the exodus of thousands of secondary school students to join the liberation struggle. School after school emptied itself of its students. They were prepared to fight and to die if necessary to bring an end to the colonial/settler regime. These young people were to be both the ready recruits into the guerrilla army as well as the nurses and teachers who would look after the people in the contested and liberated zones and in the refugee camps in Mozambique.

Thousands of refugees were housed in Nyadzonia, a refugee camp supported by the United Nations High Commission for Refugees (UNHCR) and located on the banks of the Pungwe River, some 40 kilometres from the border. Both the Mozambicans and the Zimbabwean leaders who ran the camps were unprepared for this deluge of people, and makeshift arrangements had to be made to provide them with the most basic of facilities. Food and medicines were in short supply. Moreover, the war had just resumed after the lull of *détente*.

On 8 August 1976, the Selous Scouts entered Mozambique through Penhalonga, where there was no border post. Arriving at Nyadzonia at 7 o'clock in the morning of 9 August, dressed as FRELIMO troops, with their faces blackened and singing liberation songs, they were welcomed by children who climbed onto the army trucks. The cries of joy changed into screams of horror as the soldiers shot them dead. Nyadzonia had been invaded by enemy troops. Some survivors reported that although their faces were black, their hands were white. Their guide was Nyathi, who had until recently been camp commander at Nyadzonia.

A news reporter from the *Daily News* of Dar es Salaam who visited the scene a few days later described it as follows:

> They came in war vehicles and wore the same uniform as FRELIMO's. As they approached, they were singing revolutionary songs and shouting "Viva FRELIMO!" The people approached them, the children jumping onto the cars. We thought they were FRELIMO because they had the same uniforms.
>
> One of the survivors began by telling us this. A keen-eyed old man, but he seemed not to understand how it was possible.
>
> "Where are your leaders? Go and call them, we want to speak to them", shouted one of the individuals in the group of aggressors, using a loud-hailer.
>
> "Some of us moved to point out the houses where those in charge were. It was at that point that they began to fire on us ... They then said that they were going to kill us", the old man who survived told us, his eyes burning still more.
>
> "Then we heard shots...Those who were nearest fell. They died right there. Then they began to pursue those who were running away towards the river. They got out of their vehicles firing continuously. On the road the vehicles crushed the bodies and everything that was in their way. Many people died at the river, when they were trying to cross it to escape into the bush, above all, children, old people, women and those who didn't know how to swim."
>
> "They burned the houses with people inside", a young survivor who had been living in the camp since March told us.
>
> We heard a child wailing inside a hut. We went in. Beside it were 11 other wounded. They said they did not know the whereabouts of the child's parents. They had probably died as well.[1]

More than 600 refugees were killed. Some 500 sustained injuries, from which some were later to die. The Rhodesian forces blew up the bridge as they escaped back to Rhodesia. Two civilian cars that happened to be

---

1. Report entitled "How Smith's Troops Killed Defenceless Refugees," *Daily News*, Dar es Salaam, 16 August 1976.

at the bridge at the time were also attacked. Three surveyors from the Cabora dam project, two of them foreigners, died in the attack. The Roman Catholic vicar general of Tete, Father Domingo Ferrao, was severely wounded, while a Spanish priest and six Mozambicans were killed. Before crossing back into Rhodesia, they opened fire on the village of Nova Gaia.[1]

Nyathi, former camp commander of Nyadzonia, was a member of the Selous Scouts sent to infiltrate ZANLA. He did so admirably, and soon won promotion to the rank of camp commander for his high-level military skills. However, he was accused and found guilty of extorting money from the peasantry, and for this transgression he was demoted. He was also accused of taking liberties with women freedom fighters, a form of behaviour condoned by the veterans but condemned by the Vashandi. ZANLA was very strict in ensuring that its soldiers did not alienate the people, their lifeline, in any way. Soon after that, Nyathi returned in his true guise as a member of the Selous Scouts, the crack Rhodesian military unit trained in unconventional warfare whose main task was now to fight guerrilla incursions by making pre-emptive strikes into neighbouring countries. In this case, they felt justified in attacking a refugee camp where there were many potential recruits for the guerrilla army, even though none of them had yet received any military training.

Nyathi was captured by ZANLA guerrillas in the streets of Salisbury soon after independence in April 1980. He disappeared, and was believed to have been killed. The head of the Selous Scouts left Zimbabwe soon after that, fearing that the Scouts would be hunted down and killed for their actions at Nyadzonia and elsewhere.[2]

The education department's headquarters were first established in Chimoio, where a school known as Chindunduma, named after one of the battles of the first *chimurenga* or liberation war in 1896, was set up. Tragically, Chimoio was the object of a Rhodesian attack. Chindunduma school and Parirenyatwa hospital were prime targets for the initial bombing and the subsequent assault by the Rhodesian ground forces, intent on killing all potential survivors. Those who did survive the

---

1. Report entitled "UN Office Raps Smith," in *Daily News*, Dar es Salaam, 21 August 1976.
2. R. Reid Daly, Selous Scouts: *Top Secret War*, Galago Publishing, Alberton, South Africa,1982.

bombs suffered from severe napalm burns and shrapnel wounds. Many teachers were permanently injured by shrapnel and napalm. The ZANLA military training camp in the same area was not attacked. It appeared that the Rhodesian forces avoided attacking military camps for fear of heavy losses, but were willing and able to attack schools and hospitals, which were designated as refugee camps in Mozambique. The Mozambican government did not allow military personnel from ZANLA to remain in refugee camps.

It was on 23 November 1977 that planes began to drop napalm and fragmentation bombs over the school near Chimoio. Some teachers and children were instantly killed. Soon after the bombings paratroopers parachuted down. They followed the fleeing children and their teachers towards the hospital where they encountered the nurses and the sick and injured. Those who could not flee in time were killed. After a day of carnage, the paratroopers left. In their wake they left 85 dead, 55 of whom were children. Most of the adults killed were women, as many women worked as teachers and nurses. Among the dead was Peter Tsorai, one of the leading educationists at Chimoio. Those injured by napalm and gunfire numbered over 500, 200 of them very seriously.

Mozambican and ZANLA troops who later came in defence of the refugees were able to inflict some casualties on the attackers. The Rhodesian forces allegedly picked up the dead and wounded white soldiers, but left their dead black soldiers to be buried by the refugees. Even in death Rhodesian apartheid ruled.

The Rhodesian regime's attacks on neighbouring countries served a number of purposes: first and foremost it was a threatening gesture to the governments of these countries that their economic and social infrastructure would be destroyed if they continued to support the Zimbabwe liberation movements; second it was an attempt to intimidate black Zimbabweans to accept white rule as invincible, as even the mildest form of opposition would be punished by death; third it was part of an attempt to internationalise the war within Rhodesia: if Smith could persuade the Western powers that Rhodesia was the bastion of Western values fighting against communism and black chaos, he would have won not only a psychological and political victory, but might even win military and financial support. Smith was to fail on all three counts.

CHAPTER 9

The Formation of the Zimbabwe People's Army (ZIPA), 1976

The Frontline presidents, led by Julius Nyerere and Samora Machel, were seriously concerned about the continued political division of the Zimbabwean liberation movement into two parties, each with its own army. They saw the need for a united liberation movement under one leader, as they feared a civil war in Zimbabwe between the two parties after independence. The Frontline leaders therefore decided to take the initiative to unite ZANLA and ZIPRA with the hope of creating a united army. It appeared to them that it was the political leaders who continually caused the divisions that beset the Zimbabwean liberation movement, whereas the young army commanders were more focused on attaining the objectives of the liberation war. The new army was to be a combination of ZANLA and ZIPRA forces. A joint high command consisting of nine ZANLA and nine ZIPRA commanders was formed under the new name of ZIPA, the Zimbabwe People's Army.

Anxious not to allow a further fracturing of ZANU, the young commanders in ZANLA insisted on having consultations with both their political and military leaders still being held in custody in Zambia. There they received the full blessing of both the external leadership and the high command to join forces with ZIPRA to wage war against the colonial regime. Full-scale resumption of war began in early 1976. Ian Smith had failed to utilise the golden opportunity he had been offered to have a black government of his own choosing in Zimbabwe. His intransigence was to the advantage of ZANU, which had always insisted that the Smith regime was not sincere in its protestations of peace.

Détente had failed, destroying with it the flimsy coalition formed by Joshua Nkomo, Abel Muzorewa, Ndabaningi Sithole, and James Chikerema. This united front split first into two main groups, one led by Abel Muzorewa, the other by Joshua Nkomo. Muzorewa immediately made a virulent attack on the OAU for allowing ZIPA to be formed. He accused the OAU and the Frontline governments of preventing him and his allies from taking control of the freedom fighters. His attack on the OAU and on the Frontline governments meant that Muzorewa was seen as aggressive towards African governments instead of towards the colonial Smith regime. The formation of ZIPA in late 1975 spelt the end of Muzorewa as a credible leader of the liberation forces.

ZAPU, on the other hand, was delighted with the initiative taken by the Frontline states to join together ZANLA and ZIPRA under the aegis of ZIPA. With the external ZANU leadership and the ZANLA military high command still incarcerated in Zambian jails, this was the perfect opportunity not only to provide ZIPRA forces with the much needed field experience that they lacked, but also to fill the vacuum in political leadership. Joshua Nkomo was a highly credible and experienced leader. He was very much in the tradition of African leaders who had led their countries to independence. Moreover, Zambia had long supported ZAPU. Another advantage he enjoyed was that he had been elected president of the "ANC", the name given to every Zimbabwean party during the *détente* period, in a congress held inside Zimbabwe. It was therefore not surprising that the Frontline presidents would intervene to try to unite the different factions under Joshua Nkomo if possible, although in fact they were prepared to accept any leader who could win the support of the majority of Zimbabweans.

ZANU's disarray as a result of the Nhari rebellion and the subsequent execution of the rebels was exacerbated by the problems that it was now experiencing with its leader, Ndabaningi Sithole. The *Mgagao Declaration* (1975) made it clear that Sithole was no longer accepted as a leader by the armed forces of ZANLA. Robert Mugabe was still an unknown factor, kept in isolation in Quelimani by the Mozambican government in order to allow *détente* to be given a chance.

The problem was, how would Zimbabweans be able to choose their own leader? Would the new ZIPA leadership, made up of young military specialists in their twenties provide the new leadership? Would the old leaders Joshua Nkomo, Ndabaningi Sithole, Abel Muzorewa, and James Chikerema lead Zimbabwe to independence? Would ZANU survive this attack on its integrity? Meanwhile, despite these serious leadership problems, the war had to continue.

It was on 1 January 1976 that a combined OAU operation began. Nigerian planes flew into Dar es Salaam to pick up Zimbabwean guerrillas to transport them to the Zimbabwean border via Mozambique. I was in Dar es Salaam at the time. There were torrential rainstorms. Young guerrillas came on open trucks from Mgagao to board the Nigerian planes. Saul Sadza, then the commander in charge of operations in Dar es Salaam, went to fetch these newly trained soldiers. Instead of sitting in the front next to the driver, he stood with the young soldiers crowded in the back of the truck. Like them, he travelled several hundred miles from Iringa to Dar es Salaam totally drenched. He told me that he did this out of comradeship, to make the young guerrillas feel that he shared their hardships. "More than half of them will die in this war", he told me. "It was the least I could do." Sadza himself died a year later, operating in the war zone inside Zimbabwe. He was killed by a bomb placed in a radio presented to him as a gift by a traitor. It was a time when everyone in Zimbabwe appeared to support the liberation struggle, but it was also a time of treachery. Many who joined the struggle as supporters were actually enemy agents, paid to kill.

The unification of the two separate armies into ZIPA provided the opportunity to try to amalgamate the two liberation movements. The freedom fighters of both ZANLA and ZIPRA were brought together in two camps in Tanzania, in Morogoro and Mgagao. This well-meaning gesture by the Tanzanian authorities ended in the tragic massacre of ZIPRA guerrillas by ZANLA guerrillas at both locations. The former resented the use of slogans, many of them hostile to ZAPU leader Joshua Nkomo, who was seen by ZANLA as collaborating with the Smith regime through his tireless efforts to come to a negotiated settlement. ZANLA guerrillas believed that ZIPRA forces intended to take over the political leadership of the newly combined forces. Tensions were high, and ended in violence. A number of ZIPRA guerrillas, estimated at about 50, were killed.

The massacres at Morogoro and Mgagao in August 1976, with the subsequent flight of ZIPRA survivors, meant the end of the united army under ZIPA. The end of the Tongogara's leadership was heralded by his killing of the Nhari rebels, that of the ZIPA commanders by their failure to prevent the massacre of the ZIPRA guerrillas. ZAPU decided to withdraw its forces from the joint army. From then on, each army would operate independently. A small number of ZIPRA cadres decided to remain within ZANLA, including the first medical doctor to join the war effort, Mudzingwa, originally a ZIPRA officer. However, ZIPA was to continue in name until the end of 1976, but now consisted of only ZANLA, but a ZANLA under the leadership of the Vashandi commanders.

The arrest of the external leadership of ZANU as well as of the ZANLA military leadership by the Zambian authorities in March 1975, followed soon after that by the immobilisation of ZANLA forces in both Mozambique and Tanzania as part of the *détente* exercise, made it possible for a new leadership to emerge in the military and refugee camps. Solomon Mujuru was the only member of the old leadership in ZIPA. He found himself surrounded by a new breed of leaders, young men and women in their teens and twenties who had joined the liberation struggle straight from secondary schools and universities. This younger group of military leaders had been influenced by the ideas of Marx and Lenin, and sincerely believed themselves to be participating in a revolution that would overthrow not only colonialism, but also the bourgeois capitalist form of government. This was quite a different objective from that of the old nationalists of the 1950s and 1960s who had wanted African representation, but without major changes in the form of government. The young leaders were also a different breed from the militarists, the "veterans", who believed in the supremacy of military might, but had little idea about the type of government they wanted after independence.

The change in the leadership from the veterans to the Vashandi brought a marked change in all the camps. The abuse of women ceased abruptly. The formation of the Chitepo Academy as the ideological think tank of the struggle brought about a decidedly left wing flavour to the liberation struggle. The study of Marx and Lenin became a major preoccupation. Many of the young commanders took the rhetoric that had been used by some ZANU leaders very seriously, and for the first time tried to transform their Marxist-Leninist ideals into practical reality.

It was under these young commanders that the *Mgagao Declaration* was compiled. This made it clear that the top ZANLA officers were willing to accept Robert Mugabe as the president of ZANU. However, this acceptance was conditional, based on the demand that he provide them with the Marxist-Leninist leadership that they espoused. They had been willing to accept the guidance of two well respected university professors who had travelled to Mgagao in late 1975 to confer with the guerrillas, Simbi Mubako and Joseph Taderera, who had advised that while it was now essential for ZANU and ZANLA to disavow Ndabaningi Sithole, who was causing confusion in his wake, it was best to allow the next in line to become the interim leader. This would provide the smoothest transition. It was thus that the leadership of the liberation struggle that had so troubled everyone was settled.

During the period that Tongogara remained incarcerated in Zambia, many of the young commanders believed that he was the right man to lead them. They believed that he was ideologically as well as personally a better leader than any of the old-style politicians. Their painful experiences with Ndabaningi Sithole had led them to be sceptical of the ability of the old leadership to cope with new problems, as well as with the new ideology of Marxism-Leninism. In particular, their romanticisation of the armed struggle made them believe that those who had received military training and had participated in warfare were somehow superior to those who had waged the liberation struggle in other ways.

This idolisation of Tongogara did not last long. Immediately after the ZANU leaders were released from Zambian prisons, they agreed to attend the constitutional conference to be held in Geneva. Vashandi commander Wilfred Mhanda, like many other left-wing analysts, believed that the constitutional talks had been organised to sabotage the armed struggle just at a time when the Rhodesian forces were about to be defeated. The speed with which the conference was pulled together confirmed their suspicions that the aim was to provide a neo-colonialist solution to Zimbabwe, through the installation of leaders who could easily compromise the welfare of the majority of Zimbabweans in a bid to promote their own political careers. They therefore refused to attend the Geneva conference. The absence of key military commanders meant that the ZANLA army would probably not accept any agreement that was reached at Geneva. It was essential that Wilfred Mhanda and his group attend the conference, and they were forced to do so by President Samora Machel.

Wilfred Mhanda arrived in Geneva dressed in Che Guevara style with a black beret and blue jeans. He habitually shaved his head completely. Short and stocky, bristling with intelligence and with ideological righteousness, he exhibited a high level of puritanical restraint as compared to other leaders who had just emerged from jails or from the battlefront.

It was clear that both the old external leadership of ZANU, known as the *Dare*, comprising Henry Hamadziripi, Mukudzei Mudzi, Rugare Gumbo, and Kumbirai Kangai, as well as the old military high command led by Josiah Tongogara regarded the Vashandi as dissidents. Before their arrests in March 1975, the political and military leaderships of ZANU had been at loggerheads, but now they were temporarily united against their young critics. The Vashandi were openly called bandits because they refused to accept the political leadership of their elders. It was clear that post-Geneva events would include a brutal suppression of the Vashandi group, who could suffer the same fate as the Nhari group.

ZIPA was defeated not on the battlefield but in the conference room. Their romanticisation of the armed struggle also seriously obfuscated their analysis of the political situation within the liberation movement, so that they were easily defeated by Tongogara's more pragmatic and ruthless strategies. The young freedom fighters of ZIPA saw any dealings with Smith and the British as tantamount to betrayal of the liberation struggle for which they were prepared to give their lives. Speaking in an interview with the Mozambican information agency in September 1976, Wilfred Mhanda made it clear that ZIPA saw itself not only as an army, but also as political movement, along the lines of China, Cuba, North Korea, and Vietnam. ZIPA was able to accommodate and shoulder "both the military and the political tasks of the revolution". In a radio announcement, ZIPA made its position clear:

> ... we completely and unreservedly oppose the Kissinger proposals. We totally reject Kissinger's vicious scheme in its entirety which is aiming at sabotaging the Zimbabwean struggle and simultaneously preserving Western interests in Zimbabwe ... The United Kingdom is an avowed enemy of the Zimbabwe people, as evidenced by the role of the British government in the history of Zimbabwe.[1]

Machingura (i.e., Mhanda) also made it clear that ZIPA owed no allegiance to any of the traditional nationalist parties or leaders.

---

1. Based on Interview with D. Machingura by the Mozambican Information Agency on 30 September 1976, and ZIPA Memorandum on the Kissinger Proposals, issued on 30 September 1976. These are published in Goswin Baumhögger, *The Struggle for Independence*, Vol. II, Institute of African Studies, Africa Documentation Centre, Hamburg, 1984, pp. 165, 167

Machingura's intransigence was a major blow to the unity within ZANU and ZANLA, which had managed to survive *détente* and its many problems so robustly. The Vashandi who, in fact, now controlled every training and refugee camp in Mozambique and Tanzania, adamantly refused to participate in the negotiations, branding all would-be participants as traitors. It was this ideological intransigence and tactical rigidity that was to bring about their downfall.

On their return to Mozambique, they were unceremoniously arrested and imprisoned by Tongogara during an attempt to hold a political dialogue with him and his high command. They had arranged to meet at a venue in Mozambique's second city, Beira, but Tongogara had the venue surrounded with troops personally loyal to him beforehand, and when the Vashandi arrived, they were promptly arrested. They were to spend the next five years in prison and in detention. Tongogara was not prepared to dialogue with the self-proclaimed Marxist-Leninists, since he regarded any allegiance to Marxism-Leninism as a form of rebellion against himself and against ZANU and ZANLA, and was prepared to crush it as ruthlessly as possible. Vashandi camp commanders and leaders in Mozambique and at the front were arrested in an unbridled show of force, some of them trussed up in sacks. It is to the credit of the leadership of Robert Mugabe and Simon Muzenda that the Vashandi were not executed like their predecessors, the Nhari group. Instead, they were immediately handed over to the custody of the Mozambican government and lived to see the independence of Zimbabwe that they had fought for.

The failure of the "broad masses" to support the Vashandi, when the Vashandi so confidently believed that they were upholding the interests of these "broad masses" was noteworthy. One of the reasons for this was Vashandi's highly critical attitude towards the traditional religious leaders, the vana sekuru, who were so influential with the peasantry and the rank and file during the liberation struggle. The traditional religious leaders represented the spiritual support of the ancestors for the fighters and the people. Vashandi saw any form of religion as the "opium of the people", and freely criticised the people's adherence to their beliefs as a form of backwardness. While the traditional religious leaders refused to respond to this criticism, other than to say that they were protected by their spirits, their failure to take sides with either the Vashandi or the veterans meant that they were entirely neutral in the internal conflicts within ZANU and ZANLA.

While traditional religious leaders did not respond to the Vashandi's criticism, they themselves were also very critical of Tongogara and his veterans. That the Vashandi were never able to ally with any of the traditional forces in a society that was still closely tied to traditional socio-economic structures and values contributed to the fragility of their power base. So confident were they of their ideological correctness and of their grassroots support that they had done little or nothing to gain the support of those around them.

The Vashandi were equally dismissive of the old-style politicians, now led by Robert Mugabe. While they were prepared to dialogue with Tongogara, whom they regarded as more "progressive" because of his remarkable performance as a military specialist, they were not ready to dialogue with the leaders whom they called "nationalists", using this as a derogatory term. It was perhaps not surprising that the old-style politicians were also not prepared to side with the young Vashandi, abandoning them to their fate. This was a colossal error on the part of the Vashandi, ensuring the failure of the very values that they espoused. Their negotiating skills were limited, and their uncompromising rigidity ultimately gave them no room for manoeuvre.

CHAPTER 10

The Geneva Conference: Old Enemies and New Friends

The Geneva conference heralded yet another attempt to bring about a speedy resolution of the political and military crises. Undoubtedly, the urgency for a quick settlement came from the resumption of guerrilla warfare by the combined ZANLA and ZIPRA forces, known as ZIPA, in January 1976. Within a few months, the country was embroiled in a far worse security situation than ever before. The Rhodesians could not cope and had to call in the South African military to assist. The latter were happy to get the combat experience that they needed. However, despite the military and aerial might of the South Africans, it was clear to all that this would be an un-winnable war for the Rhodesians. Even the Rhodesian Front government, which had resisted negotiations for so long, recognised that it was facing a critical situation.

Mozambican independence in July 1975 meant that Rhodesia was now wide open to incursions along thousands of kilometres of borders that could not be effectively guarded. The Rhodesian regime was clearly losing the battle for hearts and minds, with the guerrilla army swelling from just over 3,000 before *détente* began in 1974 to potentially tens of thousands at the end of *détente* in mid-1976, as hundreds of thousands of refugees flooded into neighbouring countries. With them flowed the young men and women who were now willing to sacrifice their lives to free Zimbabwe from colonial and settler domination.

The British government, assisted by the United States, the South African, and the Frontline governments, was ready to make another attempt at peace making. The Swiss government agreed to host the conference, and many other Western governments contributed both financially and diplomatically to the joint effort, their objective being to stop Southern Africa coming under the control of the communists.

The American secretary of state, Henry Kissinger, once again played a key role in bringing all parties to the negotiating table, persuading the unwilling British government to chair the conference. In an historic meeting with Ian Smith, Kissinger was able to persuade Smith to accept the concept of "majority rule", something that Smith had adamantly refused to countenance before. The capitulation of the Rhodesian Front was not only due to the attractive conditions offered by Kissinger, but also to the deteriorating situation within the country, with the economy at a standstill and guerrilla incursions becoming increasingly successful. Smith was well aware that the situation inside the country was rapidly moving beyond his control. A constitutional solution, even a temporary one, would give his government the necessary respite to recoup, particularly if the United States and Western governments were to pour aid into the country in the interim. The Smith regime understood well the West's reluctance to see a further growth of communist influence in the region, and that Rhodesia's geographic position meant that the country's future would have a profound impact on the whole region. Allowing the nation to fall into the hands of forces hostile to the West would have a dramatic and disastrous effect on the balance of political power worldwide, as well as threatening Western economic interests in the region. Kissinger had been trying all along to protect the capitalist interests of the West, and had been thwarted by the Smith regime's absolute refusal to allow any form of black majority rule, even of the most moderate pro-Western type as represented by the ANC, led by Bishop Muzorewa, and ZAPU, led by Joshua Nkomo. The likelihood of military victory by ZIPA was real, and this would usher in a pro-communist regime of the very type that both Kissinger and Smith most feared. The Rhodesian Front deputy minister in the office of the Rhodesian prime minister, Ted Sutton-Price, made this position clear:

> The Rhodesian Front accepted the [Kissinger] package only because of pressure – there are $60m. in exports in the pipeline. Without exports moving, the government could not support an agricultural crop next year. The railway system was moving few goods … The fuel supply is down to 19.6 days.
>
> The Kissinger deal – an interim government, two years to sort out the constitution and then majority rule – is not seen as one-man one-vote … If the agreed constitution was not liked after two years, parliament could reject it. At worst Rhodesia would be in a better position to fight the war than at present. It would have two years'

trading on the open market with sanctions lifted. The economy would be revived with the $2,000 million development fund. There would be two years to build up arms and war materials for the armed forced... The market for recruiting the armed forces would be widened.[1]

The last reference was to the practice of recruiting mercenaries. The regime's economic crisis had now made recruitment from this source more difficult.

Meanwhile, as we have seen, the ZIPA commanders totally rejected any participation in the Geneva talks, which they regarded as a form of capitulation to colonialism. They were unable to grasp the need for other forms of liberation struggle, such as the legal and diplomatic struggle. Because they saw very clearly that military victory was inevitable, and that they had the unequivocal support of ordinary Zimbabweans, they were unable to see the reality that outside forces such as the Frontline states, South Africa, Britain, and the United States were also interested parties, and that these forces could play a decisive role in the liberation of Zimbabwe. It was in this difficult situation that the Geneva conference opened at the end of October 1976.

The ZANU delegation arrived from all corners of the world. From within Rhodesia came a large contingent, initially calling itself the ANC, but within a short time these people crossed over to join their colleagues in ZANU. From Mozambique came a mixed group including veteran politicians from the 1950s and 1960s such as Robert Mugabe, Simon Muzenda, and Edgar Tekere, now the top three leaders in the new ZANU. The old military high command, led by Josiah Tongogara, fresh from a year's imprisonment and torture in Zambian jails arrived, and included Robson Manyika, Solomon Mujuru, and Meyor Urimbo. The ZIPA commanders, comprising Wilfred Mhanda, Webster Gwauya, and Pfepferere, formed an unwilling part of the delegation, since they saw the Geneva conference as robbing them of outright victory by forcing them into an untimely compromise. Also from Mozambique came Joseph Taderera, a man set apart from the old leadership,

---

1. Report in the *Sunday Times*, London, on 31 October 1976, entitled "Revealed: How Smith Plans to Keep Power", published in Goswin Baumhögger, *The Struggle for Independence*, Vol. II, Institute of African Studies, Africa Documentation Centre, Hamburg 1984, p. 202.

not a member of the old military high command, but also not a member of the Wilfred Mhanda-led Vashandi Group. Nathan Shamuyarira, who had retreated to the University of Dar es Salaam after the failure of FROLIZI, now returned as part of the ZANU delegation, as did the old *Dare*, the external leadership of ZANU, comprising Henry Hamadziripi, Rugare Gumbo, Mukudzei Mudzi, and Kumbirai Kangai. From the capitals and the universities of the West came exiled Zimbabweans connected to ZANU in one way or the other. From Zambia came the businessmen like Patrick Kombayi, who had done so much over the past year to ensure that the military struggle continued. This was a highly diverse collection of people with very different political views, ranging from the extreme left wing, such as the young ZIPA commanders, to the extreme right wing, members of which did not differ very much from Ian Smith's racist right-wing regime, except that they replaced Smith's white racism with their own brand of black racism. The extreme right wing came mainly from the old nationalists of the 1960s. The class composition of the ZANU delegation also varied greatly, including the representatives of the war veterans on the front, many of whom were peasants; labour leaders representing the black urban workers; rich businessmen and middle class professionals.

Over the 13 years of the existence of ZANU, its members had been separated in different countries. Many of these groups had never met before. Clearly, the Geneva conference was going to be one of the watersheds of Zimbabwean politics. Out of this highly disparate group there was now the challenge of building one political party, with one leader. This task was to fall to Robert Mugabe. *Détente* had finally destroyed Ndabaningi Sithole. Robert Mugabe had taken over the mantle of leadership in early 1976. Geneva was to be his first opportunity to exercise his leadership skills over a more diversified ZANU than was represented in the military and refugee camps of Mozambique. The ZANU members at Geneva came from within Rhodesia and from all over the world, as Rhodesian repression had led to a huge diaspora of Zimbabweans.

Like Sithole, Mugabe had spent 11 years in Smith's prisons. A staunch Roman Catholic of ascetic tastes, he was more fortunate than Sithole in that during his period in prison he was able to earn more than half a dozen degrees through distance education and to run a school for other inmates. One of his young students was Emmerson

The Geneva Conference

Mnangagwa, who gained his secondary education in prison under the tutelage of Mugabe. Mugabe's professional training and experience as a teacher marked his leadership. He valued intellectual ability. He also believed it was essential to be a morally upright leader, something he had learnt from his Roman Catholic tutors, as well as from the tenets of traditional religion, which held that political leaders only held power if they were morally justified to do so in the eyes of the ancestral spirits.

During this period, Mugabe also displayed a great deal of humility, aware that much had happened during the 11 years he had spent incarcerated by the Smith regime. He was prepared to listen patiently to the views of all the different groups and personalities that formed ZANU. One characteristic of his personality was that, having listened carefully to everyone, he was able to keep his own opinions to himself. It was not easy to tell what his real opinions were, an important characteristic for a politician in a party like ZANU that contained all sorts and shades of opinions on almost every subject. It was also important for him to be a wise judge of character, as ZANU also contained all sorts of disparate people, the common factor being their opposition to Ian Smith and his Nazi-type anti-African policies. ZANU contained the most idealistic of people, such as the young ideologues who had formed ZIPA. It also accommodated criminal elements that had fled from the arms of the law within Rhodesia. It contained cunning politicians who had had decades of experience in the skills of politicking. One constant issue was which group would dominate ZANU. Mugabe, as the new leader, had to work his way through this intricate maze. If he offended a very powerful group, for instance the militarists who were spearheading the struggle, he would soon be overthrown. This was a period in Zimbabwe's history when military victory was essential as well as imminent. This was the tightrope that Mugabe had to walk.

Having spent more than a decade in prison, Mugabe did not know the new members of his own party, ZANU. They were indeed perfect strangers. Moreover, many of these colleagues had just been released from Zambian prisons, having been ostensibly imprisoned on suspicion of having killed Mugabe's friend and colleague, the leader of the external wing of ZANU, Herbert Chitepo. Clearly the Zambian government had had its own political agenda in accusing the external ZANU leadership of killing Chitepo: it wanted to stop the war in Zimbabwe in order to bring in a government sympathetic to Zambia's own capitalist and Christian ideology. Zambia did not want a left-wing socialist government next door, and it did not want to help bring about a government that would definitely impact on the tenure of Kaunda and his ruling party, UNIP. Mugabe knew that the ZANU detainees had been severely tortured and had made all sorts of confessions, including that they had killed Chitepo. As noted earlier, the brilliant socialist lawyer, John Platts Mills, had managed to prove that the confessions made under torture could not be accepted in a court of law. There was no evidence other than these confessions. As a result, the prisoners had been released.

Nevertheless, Mugabe knew very well that there had been serious tensions within ZANU between the political leadership led by Chitepo and the military leadership led by Tongogara. The ZANU army, ZANLA, had been formed during Mugabe's prison term, and he did not have any first-hand knowledge or control over its formation and over what it had been doing. He did, however, recognise that the stage of the struggle was necessarily a military one and that Zimbabwe would never gain its independence without military victory. He knew that there was severe suspicion of and antipathy towards politicians as a whole, but particularly against the old-style politicians of the 1950s and 1960s. Mugabe had to build a solid bridge uniting the politicians and the militarists if ZANU was to succeed, even to survive. This would be a gruelling test of his leadership skills.

Already Mugabe had had a personal taste of the hostility of the commanders on the ground to the old political leadership. While he had been placed in exile in Quelimani by the Mozambican government, he had sent one of his most trusted deputies to link up with the ZANLA guerrillas. The results were catastrophic, with the commanders actually making public statements that they would never have anything to do with his emissary, and that they were not sure they would accept the leadership of Mugabe if he were of the same mould.

Mugabe's immediate deputy was Simon Muzenda, a humble carpenter with the amazing ability to join together all sorts of groups into one coherent body. Muzenda was of critical importance in strengthening Mugabe's political base among all the disparate groups that now formed ZANU, the only credible opposition to the Ian Smith regime and the only political movement with a powerful army behind it. Muzenda's humility meant that he never made claims to being superior

The Geneva Conference

to anyone. He never gave orders to anyone. He was always able to listen to every point of view and accurately judge the strengths and weaknesses of the protagonists' characters. Every group saw him as trustworthy. Every group saw him as neither a rival nor a contender. His record in diffusing the tensions and conflicts engendered by Ndabaningi Sithole towards the end of Sithole's tenure, when rival groups of guerrillas faced each other in the streets of Lusaka, had shown his remarkable abilities. Knowing that the young guerrillas had formed into two hostile groups, he calmly managed to diffuse the tension by merely giving them orders to leave Lusaka. Outside Lusaka, they were no longer able to receive the confusing commands then being given by Ndabaningi Sithole, who was intent on getting rid of perceived opposition against his leadership within the party. Muzenda had never tried to weaken or attack Sithole, but when Sithole's leadership was over, he did emerge as the leading supporter of Sithole's successor, Mugabe. Later he was to save the lives of the Vashandi and the Hamadziripi groups who had been captured and imprisoned by Tongogara, consolidating his reputation as a peacemaker of remarkable political astuteness and decisiveness.

The number three in ZANU, Edgar Tekere, was a totally different proposition. Intensely ambitious and a brilliant and ruthless political manoeuvrer and close confidant of Mugabe, he enjoyed absolute loyalty from his followers, but quickly formed enemies among all other groups. In particular, the ZIPA group soon became Tekere's implacable enemies. Tekere, for his part, was intensely anti-ZIPA, whose ultra-democratic style of behaviour offended his traditional sense of order and hierarchy. He was also hostile to the large group of university lecturers in ZANU, and used every opportunity to discredit and destroy them. He was clearly afraid that the university group would exert too much influence over Mugabe.

The external leadership of ZANU had worked independently of the leaders who had been in prison, and now formed a distinctive group. One of the most experienced politicians in the external leadership was Henry Hamadziripi, a trade unionist. Highly experienced at traditional politics, Hamadziripi had made a name for himself within ZANU as a tireless opponent and critic of Herbert Chitepo as well as of Josiah Tongogara. At Geneva, it became clear that he might also disapprove of the choice of Robert Mugabe as the top leader of ZANU. Thus, although the former external leadership was seriously divided into two groups, one led by Tongogara and the other by Hamadziripi, both groups could potentially challenge Mugabe's leadership. The leadership task that Mugabe faced at Geneva was to unite the external leadership with the internal leadership that had recently emerged from Rhodesian jails.

One of the first steps Mugabe took at Geneva was to bring back to ZANU some of those political elements that had left in the early 1970s, such as his old friend Nathan Shamuyarira. Shamuyarira had left ZANU in 1973 to form FROLIZI. By 1976 it was clear that FROLIZI would not be able to challenge ZANU for power, and many former FROLIZI leaders had either retired from politics, or, like Shamuyarira, were able to survive and return to ZANU. Mugabe's decision to bring back Shamuyarira into the leadership was to weaken his hold on the military. The military were hostile to Shamuyarira and to FROLIZI, seeing them as a tribal Zezuru formation.[1] Mugabe himself was also a Zezuru. Tribalism was universally seen as anathema within ZANU. However, every ethnic group suspected every other ethnic group of being tribal.

Another of the leaders from the 1960s at Geneva was Eddison Zvobgo. A brilliant academic and lawyer, he had spent a few years in the United States at Princeton and Harvard universities. He had cleverly realised that Ndabaningi Sithole was bungling his own chances of becoming the first president of an independent Zimbabwe, and had moved on to support Mugabe's bid for leadership. Zvobgo played a major role in forging the political strategy for ZANU PF to come to power at independence in 1980. Nevertheless, he too was regarded with some distrust by the military leaders like Tongogara, who were suspicious both of the old nationalists and of intellectuals in general. The military routinely suspected all those who had spent some years in the United States of having pro-American sympathies and of having ties with the CIA, and Zvogbo was not exempt from this suspicion. Zvogbo had belonged to Muzorewa's ANC, and although he had chosen to return to ZANU, he could not overcome the shadow of suspicion that still hung over him at Geneva.

---

1. The Zezuru are a sub-group of the Shona people, which constitutes about 80% of Zimbabwe's population.

The Geneva Conference

Mugabe was fortunate that some of the main Zezuru groups had become hostile towards him during the *détente* period. According to their tribal interpretation of the *détente* period of history, the ZANU army, ZANLA, had become dominated by the Karanga,[1] and the correct step was to deny ZANLA any further support or legitimacy. Mugabe was politically astute enough to know that this would have been a suicidal step for him to take. Instead, throughout the *détente* period he had provided strong support for the imprisoned ZANU leaders in Zambian jails, despite the fact that some of them were Karanga. It was this alliance with the militarists that now stood him in good stead. Even though the militarists questioned his inclusion of Shamuyarira in the leadership, they were prepared to accept this for the moment. They owed their survival in part to Mugabe's steadfast support for them during their 18 months of imprisonment and torture.

There were also the young Marxists, the Vashandi or Workers' Movement, who had taken over the ZANLA and also the ZIPA leadership during the period that the old ZANLA high command was imprisoned in Zambia. Few of them were really workers: they comprised mainly young students who had cut their teeth on the liberation struggle. Their leader, Wilfred Mhanda, a brilliant analyst and highly articulate speaker, was implacably opposed to any form of corruption or compromise with the colonial masters.

Many others flocked to Geneva. As already noted, one such person was Patrick Kombayi, a brilliant businessman who had helped fill the leadership vacuum caused by the arrest of all full-time ZANU and ZANLA members in Zambia between 1975 and 1976. A brilliant strategist as well as an amazingly courageous man, he harboured ambitions to become the president of ZANU. For his indubitable achievements, he demanded to be recognised as a top leader within ZANU, but Robert Mugabe would not allow this. Consequently, Kombayi demanded to be repaid for all his financial inputs into the liberation struggle. Mugabe had once been Kombayi's teacher in primary school in Gwelo, and probably this relationship had influenced his judgement against Kombayi. Although Mugabe was in some ways a populist, adopting the policies that would carry the most favour at a particular time and place, he was very adamant with regard to who should be in the leadership of

---

1. The Karanga are another sub-group of the Shona people.

ZANU. While he brought Shamuyarira back into the leadership, he was totally against allowing Kombayi in.

It was in Geneva that I found myself being threatened with a beating by Kombayi. Kombayi was a big and powerfully built man. He had formed the idea that the young military commanders in Dar es Salaam and Mgagao in Tanzania had wanted to elect him as the next ZANU president, but they had decided not to do this because I had told them he was a businessman. I did not recall anything of the sort, but as I was the courier moving from Lusaka to Dar es Salaam during 1975 and 1976, trying to ensure that the ZANLA forces remained united, I had had the opportunity of talking with many of the commanders who would come from Mgagao to Dar es Salaam to meet me to find out what was really happening. It was this frequent contact that made Kombayi believe that I was instrumental in depriving him of the presidency of ZANU. Kombayi believed that due to the Marxist ideology of some of the ZANLA commanders, they had refused to elect him because of his capitalist leanings as a highly successful businessman. I did not believe I had played any role at all in the choice of who would become the next president of ZANU after the downfall of Ndabaningi Sithole. I managed to stave off a beating by publicly confronting him, but the disagreement marked the end of the close working relationship we had established during the *détente* period.

Joe Taderera was another would-be challenger to Mugabe. Having left a well-established position as a university professor in the United States to join the liberation struggle, he had an advantage over Mugabe in that he was able to spend some time during 1975 and 1976 doing military training at Mgagao. Undergoing military training made a leader more acceptable to the military commanders. However, it was Joe, together with Simbi Mubako, who had advised the Mgagao commanders to avoid a leadership struggle at such a crucial period of the liberation struggle by accepting Robert Mugabe, who was next in the hierarchy of ZANU leaders elected at the first ZANU congress in Gwelo in 1963. They had listened to this advice, and had unanimously voted for Mugabe at the 1976 congress before the Geneva conference.

A brilliant academic and a clever politician, Joe was, however, not wholly trusted by those around him. Unlike Muzenda who was trusted by all, Joe somehow was tainted with ambition: everyone saw him as a would-be top leader rather than as a would-be follower. Rumours circulated that he was in touch with the CIA, although such rumours were common about anyone who had spent any length of time in the United States. His political ambitions came to nought when he participated, together with Cletus Chigove, in an abortive coup attempt by capturing Edgar Tekere and Herbert Ushewokunze in Chimoio in early 1978. Instead, he and Chigove were themselves captured by a military contingent loyal to Tongogara and led by Solomon Mujuru. He was imprisoned by ZANLA and subsequently handed over to the Mozambican authorities, and was to spend three years in detention in Nampula before returning to Zimbabwe at independence. On his return he initially refused to work with ZANU, but later he rejoined shortly before his death in a car accident.

Finally there was Tongogara's inner circle of veterans who had fought through the worst rigours of war. Brilliant militarists, they were generally not well educated. They distrusted both the old politicians and the self-acclaimed Marxists. They were suspicious of intellectuals, particularly after the Nhari rebellion when some of the most educated guerrillas had tried to overthrow Tongogara's leadership. Tongogara was clear that anyone who mentioned the names of Marx, Engels, and Lenin, were his enemies. In 1976, it was not yet clear whether Tongogara and his war veterans would accept an intellectual and a civilian such as Mugabe as their leader.

The traditional religious leaders were not represented at Geneva. However, they comprised a powerful group of opinion-makers within ZANU. While Mugabe himself consciously distanced himself from the traditional religious leaders as symbols of superstition and backwardness, he was careful not to offend them. Other ZANU leaders would openly court these religious leaders, but Mugabe did not.

One of the results of the cross-party negotiations was the walk-out of a large number of the ANC delegation to join ZANU PF. Led by the Reverend Canaan Banana, and including veteran politicians James Bassoppo Moyo and Herbert Ushewokunze, all of whom were highly respected political leaders within Zimbabwe, their defection left Muzorewa's ANC mortally wounded. Canaan Banana was to become the first president of Zimbabwe, and Herbert Ushewokunze served in a number of ministerial posts after independence. James Bassoppo Moyo served as a parliamentarian.

Canaan Banana was a gentle, unassuming, and intelligent man, well liked by everyone. Little did we know that he would become the first president of Zimbabwe. At the time, he had just come out of one of Smith's notorious prisons and was very keen to go shopping for presents for his wife Janet. I was able to accompany him on a shopping spree as his advisor on presents for his wife. His alleged homosexual tendencies were not then in evidence, and he gave the impression of being a devoted husband as well as a highly religious leader. As a top leader of the ANC delegation, his decision to desert the ANC to join ZANU was of critical importance in strengthening ZANU as the key player after independence.

Herbert Ushewokunze, a medical doctor, was also a founder member of ZANU. A brilliant and charismatic leader, he was also irascible and impatient of the slow-witted or the inefficient. He later became the head of the health department in ZANU and served in several ministerial portfolios after independence. At Geneva, he was an ardent supporter of Mugabe, but after independence this relationship deteriorated considerably, particularly during his time as minister of home affairs, when he was suspected of training a personal militia totally loyal to himself.

James Bassoppo Moyo was a social welfare worker and remained a genial supporter of the liberation struggle throughout his life. He had formed a friendship with my father, and I was able to give him a few beautiful Swiss watches as presents for my family when he returned to Rhodesia after the conference. He struck me as a beautifully innocent person who could easily be tricked by the more devious of his enemies. I had always kept in contact with my family, usually by phone, but the situation was now becoming difficult, as telephone calls were monitored. My parents were now suffering from constant interrogations by the CIO.

It would take a great deal of skill to meld this disparate group into one coherent body, and this was the task that faced Mugabe.

The move of the majority of ANC leaders to join ZANU was a major coup for ZANU. ZANU had been thoroughly demonised by the Smith regime, depicted as communists and murderers. The ANC, on the other hand, had been depicted as the "good blacks" who were ready to work hand in hand with the whites. Bishop Muzorewa was the epitome of the good black. The fact that most of the ANC leaders defected in

The Geneva Conference

Geneva to join ZANU undermined Muzorewa's claim to legitimacy. It also strengthened ZANU's claim to the leadership of the Zimbabwe liberation struggle. Leaders like Banana, Bassoppo Moyo, and Ushewokunze were not militarists. They were respected leaders who could not be called "communists". Their entry into ZANU heralded the widening of support for ZANU from a minority-supported group to a majority-supported group.

The ANC was further weakened when Muzorewa, an inexperienced politician whose naivety often entrapped him in compromising positions, admitted in reply to a question in a press conference that he had been meeting with the head of the Rhodesian secret service, Ken Flower. As this service was well known for its attempts to kill freedom fighters, using letter bombs, bombs placed in radios, and clothes impregnated with poison, this admission caused further damage to his credibility as an independent leader. He was being more and more tainted by his closeness with the Ian Smith delegation. It was not long before he emerged as a puppet and servant of the Smith regime.

The ZAPU delegation, led by veteran politician Joshua Nkomo, was housed in the Hotel Intercontinental, a five star hotel. It was to be the only delegation wholly housed in a five star hotel. The different styles of the various movements showed themselves immediately in the type of hotel the movements occupied. Bishop Abel Muzorewa's ANC delegation was housed, like the ZANU delegation, in a modest hotel. Ndabaningi Sithole's delegation, also confusingly called ZANU, later to be called ZANU Sithole, and still later ZANU Mwenje and ZANU Ndonga, was the only delegation that was not housed in a single hotel. Instead, Sithole himself stayed in a five star hotel, whereas the members of his delegation were in various cheap boarding houses and hostels, jokingly called "flea beds". The hierarchy was clear. The Rhodesian Front delegation, headed by Ian Smith, and including the Rhodesian secret service chief, Ken Flower, was in yet another modest hotel. ZANU chose the Royal Hotel, a two star hotel that accommodated the whole ZANU delegation. There was to be much movement between these delegations over the next few months. Some people were able to move between all delegations, apparently on friendly personal visits. They returned with the usual "gossip" or informal information about how things were going in the other camps. They were also the potential conduits for new political alliances across all the political boundaries.

Many other Rhodesian interest groups were also present, including representatives of white farmers and white industrialists, eager to get to know the personalities who led the liberation movements. They frequented the pub at the Royal Hotel, the ZANU hotel, in order to meet the mysterious guerrillas who were rapidly gaining ground in the battlefield. They were able to speak to these fellow countrymen over the usual beer every evening. Getting to know the enemy was a critical activity at Geneva, and was to form the basis of new alliances many years later. Many white farmers spoke fluent Shona, and they went out of their way to make friends with the possible new leaders of a free Zimbabwe.

Also present were several groups of young women, obviously brought there to entertain and perhaps entrap the guerrillas from the war zones. For some reason, most of these young ladies were either whites or Coloureds. There were no blacks. A group had been specially flown in from Bulawayo. Others had made their own way to Geneva.

In the ZANU camp, the Royal Hotel, we found ourselves seriously understaffed. This was our first experience of a quasi-constitutional conference and we were not yet aware of the staffing requirements. The secretariat, headed by Edgar Tekere, consisted of Mabel Mundondo, who had taken leave from her job in the BBC, Sepiwe, a student in London, Joseph Taderera, Meyor Urimbo, Dzingai Mutumbuka, Ruvimbo Tekere (then the wife of Edgar Tekere), Wilfred Mhanda, and myself. So heavy was the workload, that we found ourselves having to work from about six in the morning until midnight. Moreover, the delegation soon decided that it did not want to eat foreign food, so we had to organise a cooking roster to provide the traditional dish of *sadza*, *nyama*, and *muriwo* for the delegation.

Sessions at the conference itself were punctuated by meetings of the new and enlarged ZANU central committee, and secret or not so secret meetings with other delegations. For example, the ZANU and ZAPU legal committees worked very closely together, with Walter Kamba, Simbi Mubako, Honor Mkushi, and Simplisio Chihambakwe on the ZANU side working side by side with Reg Austin and Sibanda from the ZAPU side. ZANU and ZAPU were now working closely together, and many of the details that were to form the final independence constitution in 1980 were hammered out in Geneva.

The Geneva Conference

The historical links between the two ZANUs, now known as ZANU PF and ZANU Sithole, meant that there was much to-ing and fro-ing between the two, with old friendships being renewed across the political boundaries.

There was also a great deal of interchange between the ANC and the ZANU delegations. There was no problem about friends and relatives meeting each other, whatever their political affiliations. Evelyn Kawonza, then head of the ANC secretariat and in charge of the women's department in the ANC, would come and see her cousin, Akim Mudende, a young ZIPA commander. Since relatives could be found in all the different delegations, it was quite natural that they should constantly visit each other.

At the conference sessions, all the delegations sat around the same table. From the beginning it was clear that there was little intention of coming to an agreement at this conference. Instead, Geneva provided the first opportunity for the British and for the various negotiating parties to get to know the characters and personalities of the various leaders and potential contenders for power, and to size them up as potential allies or opponents. It was more like a sparring match to gauge the strength of the various leaders and groups. The exercise was an exhausting test of potential and wills. If these were the leading players in the future of Zimbabwe, it was important for them to know each other well.

The first three weeks of the conference were spent discussing the date for independence, a futile debate that always ended inconclusively. It was part of the political game to discuss inconsequential details in the formal meetings, while the really substantive negotiations took place outside. Two weeks after the conference had begun, Ian Smith decided to return to Rhodesia. Soon after that the Rhodesian forces began renewed attacks into neighbouring states, in particular Mozambique. Attacks were also made on Botswana. These were intended as a warning to these two countries that further support for the freedom fighters would result in merciless attacks on their civilians.

The Geneva conference was marked by a huge fire that engulfed the Royal Hotel, where the ZANU delegation was staying. The fire started in the room of Solomon Mujuru on the fourth floor and soon spread throughout the floor. I was on the third floor. I woke up in the middle of the night with smoke seeping into the room, and when I looked out the window, I saw the hotel was in flames. My first reaction was that enemy agents had attempted to kill us by torching our hotel. Alternatively, I thought that perhaps the ZIPA hotheads had started the fire. I decided to telephone for the Geneva fire department. I managed to get through immediately, and they informed me that they already knew of the fire and the fire engines were *en route*. Meanwhile, Meyor Hurimbo was going from door to door checking to see if anyone was still asleep in the middle of the fire. Just as I put down the phone, Hurimbo was at the door warning me to evacuate. Simon Muzenda was also moving from floor to floor by elevator, checking on everyone's safety. He was not aware that elevators should not be used during a fire. In the crisis of the fire, Hurimbo and Muzenda's strong sense of responsibility revealed itself spontaneously.

When I looked out of my window, I saw Joe Taderera and Wilfred Mhanda outside, holding a blanket and shouting to me to jump. I had sufficient time to debate with myself whether it was necessary to jump or not. As the fire brigade was already on its way, I estimated that they would arrive within 10 minutes, as Geneva is not a very large city. There was no need for me to jump to save my life. However, I realised that I could perhaps play a more useful role outside. I decided to jump, and landed neatly in the middle of the blanket held by Taderera and Mhanda. They were standing on the roof of the ground floor building, so it was not a very long jump. I discovered that I was the only one with my shoes and coat on. It was the middle of the Swiss winter, and dozens of Zimbabweans were running about outside without shoes and in their pyjamas.

I did indeed play an unexpectedly useful role. Taderera and Machingura were now shouting at Robert Mugabe to jump from the fourth floor. I realised that from that height he was likely to be seriously injured if he did jump. Moreover, there was no need for him to jump as his room was far from the fire, and I knew that the fire engines would arrive any minute. I therefore shouted at him not to jump. In the confusion he did not jump, but instead threw down his files. Fortunately, the fire engines arrived soon afterwards, bringing some order to the chaos. One of the older members of our delegation, Robert Marere, actually did jump from the fourth floor. One of the bones on his spine suffered a fracture, but he was lucky that his spine was not severed. He spent some time in a Geneva hospital.

Meanwhile, other members of the delegation had found different solutions. Tongogara and Akim Mudende had locked themselves in the bathroom, closing the cracks with wet towels to prevent smoke entering the room. All of us felt that we had had a narrow escape from death.

The question of who had set the hotel on fire occupied us for some time. Within ZANU it was believed to have been caused by a Smith agent, a young over friendly lady with revolutionary pretensions who had somehow found her way to one of the commander's rooms. However, the Swiss authorities firmly asserted that it was an accident caused by someone leaving a cigarette alight. I believe the hotel would not have had insurance coverage if it had been sabotage. The fire had caused extensive damage to two floors of the large multi-storeyed building.

The Frontline states sent their top advisors to Geneva. From Mozambique came Aquino da Braganca. Aquino was killed in the air crash that also took the life of Samora Machel. From Zambia came Mark Chona, and from Tanzania Foreign Minister Salim Salim.

Geneva was also an opportunity for supporters of the liberation movement from all over the world to come and meet the leaders of the movement they had supported for so many years. Members of the Anti-Apartheid Movement came to meet us, as did numerous support groups from all over Europe. Some of these groups of young people from Germany, France, Holland, Switzerland, and the Scandinavian countries, had done much to support the liberation struggle in practical ways, such as by collecting old clothes for us, or buying shoes and medicines. The prime minister of Sweden, Olof Palme, came to show his support, as did Jane Fonda and her then husband, Senator Tom Hayden. Sweden provided substantial political and financial support to ZANU both before and after independence. Members of the Zimbabwe Detainees Committee such as its chairman, Kees Maxey, and Lionel Cliffe, who had done so much to support us during the crisis in Zambia, also came to meet the new leaders of ZANU.

Over the eight weeks of the conference, no agreement could be reached on the crucial question of who would control the army and the police during the interim government. Smith was adamant that he should control these two portfolios, and all four nationalist delegations were equally adamant that they would not accept this.

The conference adjourned for Christmas 1976, and was never to reconvene.

CHAPTER 11

Post-*Détente* and the Defeat of the ZANU Left Wing

Although the *détente* initiative failed, its key objective of weakening the left wing of ZANU was highly successful. The resumption of the armed struggle in January 1976 under the aegis of ZIPA and under the patronage of Presidents Julius Nyerere and Samora Machel had seen the takeover of both military and refugee camps in Tanzania and Mozambique by young left wing intellectuals. President Kaunda's decision to imprison the old leadership as well as more than 1,000 of the veteran freedom fighters left a vacuum in the leadership of the liberation movement that was soon filled by young men and women who had recently left the classrooms of high schools and universities. These were the Vashandi or Workers' Movement, led by Wilfred Mhanda and Sam Geza. Their heyday lasted only during the *détente* period of 1975 and 1976. By early 1976 they were in control of all the refugee and military camps in Mozambique.

As a better-educated group than the first guerrillas, they belonged to the two per cent of blacks who were allowed to enjoy secondary education by the colonial-settler regime. Most of the Vashandi were in their twenties. Some of them were teenagers who had just left school. Their education and their youth gave them a certain elitist arrogance that set them apart from the peasant majority. They were in strong contrast to the veterans, the freedom fighters who were mainly of peasant origin and who had formed the backbone of the liberation struggle in the 1960s and early 1970s. While the Vashandi assiduously studied the works of Marx, Lenin, and Mao Tse Tung, they had little time for the ideology of the peasants, which was dominated by ancestor worship and the power of the ancestral spirits, the *midzimu*, who controlled the day-to-day decision-making of the majority of the peasants and their veteran leaders. The Vashandi dismissed traditional religion as superstition, which had to be destroyed.

The Vashandi's disdain for traditional religion was one of their major weaknesses. It meant that they were unable to link up to the major ideology of the peasantry. Given the demographic reality of the liberation struggle, with the peasants constituting more than 70 per cent of the population, the armed struggle required the fullest cooperation of the peasantry if it was to be successful.

One of the effects of their antipathy towards traditional religion was that the peasants stood aside when the young Vashandi were ruthlessly captured by Tongogara's men. The tens of thousands of peasants who inhabited the refugee camps once dominated by the Vashandi watched in silence when the veterans stormed the camps and captured their former leaders. The takeover of one camp was described to me by a child witness in 1978:

> The veterans came in and captured the camp leaders. They tied them up and put them into sacks. I saw Comrade Wadzanayi trussed in a sack. She was one of the top commanders in our refugee camp. I thought she would be killed or was probably already dead. I was really surprised when I saw her returning to come and teach us.

Wadzanayi Mugadza survived the capture and subsequent yearlong imprisonment. She helped us to lecture in art and design in our teacher education programme, but died an early death on our return to Zimbabwe, her health probably compromised by the suffering she had undergone during the liberation struggle.

The release of Tongogara and the old military high command had brought the Vashandi's period of power to an abrupt and violent end. A seriously thoughtful and idealistic group, they believed that they should not use the weapons and tactics of war against their own organisation. Instead, they sought to dialogue with their leaders. They believed that Tongogara was capable of leading a socialist revolution, whereas very few of them believed that the old leadership, now led by Robert Mugabe, would be able to rise to the occasion. Having been trained by Tongogara, and having worked with him as their senior commander, these young freedom fighters had more faith in Tongogara than in Mugabe, but it was Tongogara who immobilised them in a ruthless military exercise.

After the abortive Geneva constitutional conference, the Vashandi group had agreed to have a meeting with Tongogara. When they arrived at the meeting spot in Beira, the place had already been surrounded by Tongogara's soldiers and the Vashandi were captured and imprisoned. Fortunately for them, Mugabe and Muzenda acted quickly to get the Mozambican authorities to take them over. They, thus, did not suffer the fate of the Nhari rebels. They spent the next four years in detention in Nampula. The Vashandi had misunderstood Tongogara's character as well as his ideological orientation. Because Tongogara was totally against racism and tribalism, he appeared to be highly progressive. However, while he had rejected the traditional forms of tribalism as evil, he had espoused the dominance of the military elite, with the veterans forming a new ruling class. The Vashandi had mistaken his traditional communalism for communism. This very basic error cost them the possibility of success. They had failed to foresee that Tongogara would use military tactics to capture them. The Vashandi also failed to ally with the older nationalist politicians now led by Robert Mugabe, whom they constantly criticised as "reactionaries".

The Vashandi themselves had done nothing to gain the support of the external political leadership, the *Dare*, which totally supported the military high command's decision to capture them by physical force. Moreover, they had also taken for granted their support from Presidents Samora Machel and Julius Nyerere, but ultimately those outside of the Zimbabwean liberation movement were not able to assist them. In other words, they lacked the basic political and diplomatic skills needed to survive as a political grouping. Idealism, dedication, and military skills turned out to be insufficient for political survival. Not surprisingly, when they were captured in Beira and subsequently held in every military and refugee camp, they found no voice raised in their support. Mugabe and Muzenda did not stop Tongogara from capturing them or censure him for doing so. The traditional religious leaders were also silent, seeing the conflict between the veterans and the Vashandi as of no concern to them. The Vashandi had condemned traditional religion as backward and based on superstition, and had made a point of condemning popular support for traditional religion. It was therefore not surprising that the traditional religious leaders were silent when the Vashandi were captured. The rank and file took no action either to defend or support the Vashandi. They remained passive bystanders when the Vashandi were destroyed, showing that the movement did not have deep roots among the common people.

The Vashandi leadership itself was divided, with the majority of young guerrillas under Wilfred Mhanda against any form of dialogue with Robert Mugabe. Mhanda, a formidable intellectual and brilliant speaker, was uncompromisingly against having anything to do with the old nationalists. He firmly believed that these old politicians would betray the socialist revolution, and was openly apprehensive about the new post-*détente* ZANU leadership. Mhanda's group was particularly opposed to Robert Mugabe, whom they had judged as an old-style nationalist who would create in Zimbabwe a neo-colonial regime. They did not accept Mugabe's socialist credentials and feared he would become a fascist dictator. There was already a deep suspicion of the old leaders within ZANU and ZANLA, going back to the overthrow of Joshua Nkomo in 1963 and of Ndabaningi Sithole in 1975. As noted earlier, Mhanda had originally refused to participate in the Geneva talks, but was forced to participate by President Samora Machel, who was determined not to accept the usual divisions within ZANU. If young leaders like Mhanda did not accept a peace agreement, then the war was bound to continue.

At the same time, a much smaller group, led by Sam Geza, and comprising only Felix Moyo and Augustine Mpofu, argued that it was essential to rejoin ZANU under Mugabe. The Mhanda group saw the smaller group as compromised, particularly so as their leader, Sam Geza, was then the brother-in-law of Mugabe. They were determined not to compromise themselves in any way. This adversarial approach meant that there was no meeting point for them. Geza's group, on the other hand, believed that Mugabe was a sound nationalist, and that at this stage of the nationalist struggle he should be supported. However, Mhanda's group was more dominant.

One of the weaknesses of the Vashandi movement was its glorification of the armed struggle, along the lines of Frantz Fanon, the powerful Algerian ideologue and psychologist who saw violence as a necessary cleansing of old decay.[1] Because of this idolising of armed struggle, Mhanda saw Tongogara, the perfect militarist, as the father of the revolution. He had himself trained and worked under Tongogara, and admired Tongogara's brilliant military skills, dedication, patriotism, and

---

1. Frantz Fanon, *The Wretched of the Earth*, Grove Press Evergreen Black Cat edition, New York, 1968.

personal discipline. He supported Josiah Tongogara, whom he saw as a new style and revolutionary leader. Tongogara had been his hero when he joined the liberation struggle as a young student, and he continued to idolise him. On the other hand, he despised the old politicians as corrupt and ideologically bankrupt. He was not prepared to compromise his principles by dialoguing with these old nationalists, but went out of his way to dialogue with Tongogara and his veterans.

In reality, Tongogara was very suspicious of the young radicals and had already branded them as "bandits". It was not difficult to predict that the young radicals would soon be crushed by the military might of the veterans led by Tongogara.

What would have been the outcome of the liberation struggle had the uncompromising, ascetic but highly popular Vashandi commanders retained their ascendance? Lacking experience in negotiations and bent on establishing a Marxist state in Zimbabwe, it is likely that they would have taken Zimbabwe in the same direction as Angola and Mozambique in the 1970s.

The rise of the right wing within the ZANU leadership as a result of the internal conflicts triggered by *détente* now led to some confusion. In order to retain the support of the communist bloc, the new right wing leaders purported to be more communist than those they had ousted. This was expressed through their propaganda. On the other hand, within ZANU itself there was an aggressive purge of the left wing. I soon found myself facing this challenge: I was seen as uncompromisingly left wing. Moreover, I was not black. Political orientation and race now joined together to my disadvantage. I was seen as too close to the arrested Vashandi. At the same time, I was naturally critical of how the leadership had unceremoniously dumped the young left wing group of university lecturers and students, who were now called "bandits" because of the uncompromising stand they had taken against *détente*.

The socialist rhetoric that ZANU espoused was born not out of conviction, but simply in order to gain support from important allies. Two of these were the Soviet Union and China, together with the communist blocs that they represented. In the period of the Cold War, socialism was a mantra that could bring support in terms of guns, military training, and food.

Various waves of ZANU leaders, who themselves had never read Marx or Lenin and had no interest in ever doing so, nevertheless realised that there was political gain in calling themselves Marxist-Leninists. By 1974, every ZANU leader claimed to be a socialist, and some even claimed to be Marxist-Leninists. These claims belied the fact that the formation of ZANU in 1963, a decade earlier, was based on anti-settler and anti-colonial sentiments, specifically focused on the two areas of contention: the land that had been taken away by the white settlers in the 1890s and the denial of education to the black majority. Anti-white racism was an integral though unspoken part of the movement. It had expressed itself upon the formation of ZANU in the opposition to the white advisors who surrounded the leader of ZAPU, Joshua Nkomo.

While the ordinary members of ZANU did not judge a person merely on the basis of race, for many leaders, race, like tribe, was a powerful tool to win support for themselves. This was a schizophrenia born of the racism of colonial Rhodesia, and ZANU was not able to overcome it. Not very surprisingly I was now attacked by the right wing on the grounds of race. Fortunately, I was supported by many of the rank and file throughout this difficult period.

My relationship with Rugare Gumbo, lasting from 1973 until 1977, ended before the birth of my daughter Chipo. Chipo was born in Dar es Salaam during a period when ZANU was fighting for its survival against external forces, and at the same time when internal rivalries had led ZANU to move from the left to the extreme right. It was a serious disadvantage for me to be both socialist and not black. I was not prepared to join the right wing. Nor could I change the colour of my skin to please them.

On the other hand, the fact that I was not black also provided me with protection. Both the Tanzanian and Mozambican authorities knew me, as did many of the support groups in the West who gave their unstinting support to the liberation of Zimbabwe. Being known was now a protection that I enjoyed, but which many of my black colleagues did not. I was also able to appeal to these supporters for help if I needed to.

With the rise of the right wing leadership, the racism that had characterised ZANU at its formation in 1963 re-surfaced, and people like myself now became easy targets and scapegoats. I was accused of "feeling superior" because I was not black. Accusations such as these were not based on anything I had actually said or done, but on a perceived "feeling". It was impossible to defend myself. Silence meant guilt, while self-defence meant insubordination. I was being condemned on the basis of race. I also personally felt that the right wing feared my close relations with the young freedom fighters, and would do anything to get rid of me.

The main reasons for conflict came from within ZANU itself. ZANU was formed in opposition to the Ian Smith regime. It united all forces that were against the Smith regime. One of the constant dangers it faced was that of fighting fire with fire, that is fighting racism with racism, fighting violence with violence. It constantly faced the danger of becoming a mirror image of the colonial racist regime. There was an underlying layer of counter-racism that expressed itself not only in pride in being black, but also in being against other races. The power struggle that followed the advent of *détente* in 1974 brought to the fore the underlying racism that had played a part in the formation of ZANU and of the liberation struggle for Zimbabwe. This counter-racism, which reflected a form of fascism, was directly in opposition to the socialism that was the official ideology of ZANU.

This was one of the most turbulent periods of the liberation struggle, when ZANU itself faced both external and internal conflict. I had developed a close relationship with Chipo's father, Rugare Gumbo, over the previous four years. Just at the time of Chipo's birth he was caught up in a ferocious leadership struggle within ZANU itself. This affected our relationship adversely. In a period of violent turmoil personal relations came under a great deal of stress, and my relationship with Rugare Gumbo was to founder.

It was in this situation that I realised that I was not going to receive any support from Rugare. Rugare has completed his master's degree at Toronto University, and chose to leave his academic career in order to join the liberation struggle. He rejoined ZANU as head of information in 1973. He was able to improve the information system quite markedly, stamping it with a left wing orientation. At that time, ZANU saw itself as a strongly socialist movement. He was also responsible for building up Ndabaningi Sithole as a gigantic figure, a leader surpassing all other leaders. This personality cult was to cause us a lot of problems, as Sithole failed to live up to his reputation.

By 1977, ZANU's ideology had swung to the right, and racism and tribalism had now become acceptable. Populism, always a very strong feature of ZANU politics, could as readily follow left wing socialist as right wing racist policies. Rugare had swung to the right with the flow of the tide in order to retain his position within the ZANU leadership. However, he was only to retain this position for a year. Despite his willingness to accommodate the new direction, he was to be imprisoned by ZANU. Fortunately, his life was saved by the intervention of Robert Mugabe and Simon Muzenda, who insisted that all ZANU prisoners should be handed over to the Mozambican government.

When I joined the University of Zambia branch of ZANU in 1973, my race was not seen as an issue by the student leaders. I was accepted as a Zimbabwean who could contribute to the liberation struggle, albeit through intellectual and academic work rather than through the barrel of a gun. However, by 1977, the time of Chipo's birth, the extreme right wing of ZANU had come to the fore.

Many thousands of children were born in the struggle. My daughter Chipo belonged to this group. She was born in Dar es Salaam in 1977. Through the help of Herbert Ushewokunze, the head of health in ZANU, it was arranged that I should remain in Dar es Salaam in order to have a caesarean operation. This was impossible in Maputo during this period. Herbert was correct: I received the best medical attention in Dar es Salaam. I was fortunate to be supported by my many comrades, colleagues, and friends there. The commanders in charge of the ZANLA forces in East Africa, Khumalo and later John Chimbande, did their best to help me. Chipo was born in August. I was delighted that she was a girl, as I thought it would be more difficult for me to bring up a boy on my own, something I realised I would have to do, like many other freedom fighters. We flew to Mozambique when she was five months old. Mozambique would bring me closer to the scene of the struggle. I believed I would be able to play a more active role in providing education for the tens of thousands of children who had fled from the war zones in Rhodesia. However, I also knew that there was a serious internal conflict within ZANU, and that I would be drawn into this conflict.

Despite my bitter experience of ZANU right wing racism, I remained very strongly committed to the liberation struggle. I believed it was essential to continue within ZANU, as leaving ZANU at that point would be equivalent to deserting the people, many of them young students like the Vashandi who were prepared to sacrifice their lives for the liberation of Zimbabwe. Many of them like Saul Sadza had already died in the struggle. It was important that we should not give up on their struggle and sacrifice.

After the despatch of the young Vashandi Marxists, the old conflict between Henry Hamadziripi and Robert Mugabe on the one hand and Henry Hamadziripi and Josiah Tongogara on the other came to a head. The antagonism between Mugabe and Hamadziripi probably dated from 1963, when ZANU was founded. In the elections for the leadership held in Gwelo (now Gweru), Hamadziripi is said to have engineered the victory of Ndabaningi Sithole in a set of political manoeuvres that left him many enemies. Ten years later, in the 1970s, Hamadziripi attempted to clip the wings of the emergent military leadership under Tongogara by trying to organise a more subservient military leadership, with Meyor Hurimbo as alternative leader. However, Hurimbo, who was well known for his absolute loyalty to his leaders, exposed the plan. Tongogara developed a profound dislike and distrust of Hamadziripi.

Hamadziripi had made a number of previous bids for leadership. He had challenged Chitepo continually during the latter's tenure in office. It was not surprising that Smith regime's propaganda portrayed this political challenge in a negative light, and implied that Hamadziripi was responsible for the assassination of Chitepo. Hamadziripi challenged both Mugabe and Tongogara. His group by this time included Joseph Taderera, as well as Mukudzei Mudzi, Rugare Gumbo, and Cletus Chigove. They claimed that Mugabe could not provide the Marxist leadership required for the success of the liberation struggle. Rather confusingly, the Hamadziripi group had openly supported the suppression of the Vashandi, the young Marxists. And, furthermore, Hamadziripi and many of his followers were also ardent supporters of Ndabaningi Sithole, who had over and over again stated his virulent opposition to any form of communism or of socialism.

The Hamadziripi group was particularly critical of Tongogara, whose killing of the Nhari group provided a portentous omen of what the future could be like under Tongogara. Mukudzei Mudzi, one of the most dedicated and morally upright of the external leadership, was determined to oppose Tongogara, even though he could see that such opposition would be disastrous for his own political career and could even lead to his elimination. His wife, Tracy, begged me to speak to him to stop his open opposition to Tongogara. She was afraid he would be killed like other Tongogara opponents. I was in Dar es Salaam at the time, and on one occasion when Mukudzei came there, I made a special effort to speak to him about his open opposition to Tongogara. I pointed out that Tongogara was a key player who would lead us to military victory. I also pointed out that he might be killed if he continued his open opposition. Despite what I said, Mukudzei was a man of principle and insisted on continuing to oppose Tongogara implacably. He saw leadership by Tongogara as potentially disastrous for Zimbabwe. Tongogara later arrested him, and immobilised him till after independence.

Probably the most problematic aspect of Hamadziripi's challenge was his strong reliance on his tribal base for support. People within ZANU were suspicious of calls to a return to the traditional leadership of the Karanga, who had dominated Zimbabwe in the 16th century. Although the Karanga are still a very powerful ethnic grouping within the country, ZANU politics was such that a national leader had to command the support of all ethnic groups.

Hamadziripi's bid for power was marked by very bad timing, that is, when he was bound to fail. This was mainly due to Tongogara's superb understanding of the advantage of timing in guerrilla warfare. Tongogara ensured that the battle between the two men, a political battle that would end in the political destruction of one or the other, took place at a time when he, as head of the ZANLA army, was bound to have the upper hand. This was the height of the military struggle, when the need for military victory superseded all else. Tongogara was able to get away with liberties that he would not have been able to in a different period.

Another of Tongogara's techniques was to surround the Hamadziripi group with his own hand-picked supporters, *agents provocateurs* who would claim to be supporters of Hamadziripi but whose real function was to gather or fabricate evidence against him in the now well-orchestrated show trials that Tongogara was so expert at organising. The Hamadziripi group was not well equipped to deal with an enemy of such political sophistication and ruthlessness. They tended to see the infiltrators and *agents provocateurs* as eager supporters, so filling their ranks with traitors. In early 1978, his group was captured by Tongogara, subjected to a humiliating imprisonment and a show trial. Fortunately for Hamadziripi's group, Mugabe and Muzenda quickly insisted on their being handed over to the Mozambican authorities, and they now joined the Vashandi group whom they had once opposed in detention in Nampula.

Many saw Mugabe falling into the category of upright and morally motivated leaders like Kenneth Kaunda and Julius Nyerere, as opposed to Sithole, who showed every sign of following in the footsteps of his mentor and supporter, Idi Amin. Idi Amin trained Sithole's military specialists. Zimbabwe would be very fortunate indeed to have a leader of the calibre of Kaunda and Nyerere, who had laid the foundation for a sound future for their countries, overcoming narrow ethnic loyalties to build up united and peaceful nations. Both of them had done a great deal to build up the human resources so essential for the future development of their countries. Although neither Zambia nor Tanzania had done well economically, they had done exceptionally well in nation building. Kaunda and Nyerere had devoted themselves to improving both the physical infrastructure and the weak political systems they had inherited after a century of colonialism. Mugabe already showed that he was much more likely to listen to the university than to the soothsayers, and it was natural that as university people we would regard him more favourably.

At the same time, Mugabe also had the good fortune not to have been involved in the internecine conflict of the early 1970s that had brought the political and military leadership of external ZANU into irreconcilable opposition with each other. Having just emerged from 11 years of imprisonment in Smith's jails, he could now serve as an objective arbitrator in that bitter dispute, a task in which he was ably assisted by his deputy, Simon Muzenda. His job was made even easier by the Vashandi's implacable opposition to his leadership as not Marxist enough and Hamadziripi's badly timed manoeuvres to oust him from the leadership of ZANU. He could thus safely exclude both the Vashandi and most of the external ZANU leadership, thereby cutting a very tricky Gordian knot. Of the old external ZANU leadership, only Kumbirai Kangai was to survive.

Mugabe was astute enough to see that military victory was paramount during that period, and that all efforts should be focused on gaining this aspect of the liberation struggle. Military victory depended on full support for the militarists under Josiah Tongogara, and Mugabe gave the commander his fullest support. By so doing, Robert Mugabe emerged victorious, with the military under Tongogara at his side, his old rival Ndabaningi Sithole politically irrelevant, and the Vashandi as well as the Hamadziripi group held in detention by the Mozambican government.

Mugabe's strength lay not only in the very favourable comparison with leaders from outside ZANU and with his predecessor within ZANU, Ndabaningi Sithole, but also from his character. Seen as honest and trustworthy by his political allies, the veterans, he was also known to have no control over the army, ZANLA. This made him heavily reliant on the veterans for any power he was to enjoy. The Vashandi's adamant and vociferous opposition to Mugabe, while weakening his position with the young left wingers within ZANU, strengthened his standing among the veterans. This meant that Mugabe would always be dependent on the military leaders for his power base. In the person of Mugabe, they found someone with a brilliant intellect, who could be a highly effective spokesman for the liberation movement, but who was inherently in a weak position. He could not use them as "cannon fodder" and "gun carriers" as former leaders had done. The military were suspicious of being utilised as instruments and weapons to achieve political goals, and then sacrificed and discarded once these political goals were achieved. This inherent suspicion made them a dangerous and powerful source of opposition to any political leadership which did not take their interests into consideration.

Mugabe's tendency to consult and to listen to his followers made him a highly democratic leader. His strength was that he would always listen to the interest groups who formed his political base, in this case the veterans. However, this ability to listen to his followers was both his strength and his weakness. Under the feudal traditional system, followers adopt the views of their leaders: Mugabe had only to drop a hint about his own opinions, and his followers would instantly adopt that point of view. At the same time, his own views were coloured by the views of those who had audience with him. Vociferous groups, for example, the veterans, would win more support than the Vashandi, who were his implacable critics. Thus, despite the fact that he saw himself as a Marxist socialist, putting him in the same political grouping as the Vashandi, in fact he was more likely to be influenced by the veterans who were virulently and implacably against Marxism-Leninism. Tongogara had warned that anyone claiming to be a Marxist-Leninist was a dissident and a bandit, and he kept to his word in ensuring that all the Marxist-Leninists were kept under lock and key. Thus, Mugabe's close alliance with Tongogara from 1976 until Tongogara's death in late 1979 meant that, in fact, he had to go against his initial Marxist Leninist principles.

It was during this period that Sally Mugabe, his wife, made an indelible mark on the revolution in support of her husband's claim to leadership. Sally Mugabe was a single-minded woman. She was characterised by her absolute dedication to the liberation of Zimbabwe. Born in Ghana, she had entered politics as a teenage activist at the time of Kwame Nkrumah. Nkrumah's vision of a free and united Africa became her vision of life. She retained this vision until the end.

She had a simple ambition: she wanted every woman in Zimbabwe to be educated and to have a job. She realised that economic independence was of critical importance to women. Without it, women could not be free. She spent a lot of time trying to strengthen the women's movement. In this area, she managed to win the unfailing support of poor women, particularly market women and peasant women. However, she was not able to win the support of many professional women. This fact rested to some extent on the nature of ZANU, with its very strong women's movement based on the needs of peasant and working class women. To some extent, it also reflected Sally's personality, that she was herself happier with grassroots women than with middle and upper class women. It also reflected the antipathy, even hostility, that many grassroots women feel against their more educated and better off counterparts.

A very practical person, Sally supported the liberation struggle in simple and practical ways. She collected cloth and sewing machines from donors. These were distributed to every refugee camp for Zimbabweans. She provided cloth to enable tailoring workshops to be established in every camp. She herself sewed shirts, skirts, and trousers, and distributed them in military and refugee camps. I myself received a skirt from her. These clothes were much appreciated in the camps. Young recruits in threadbare clothes, often exposing their backs and buttocks, appreciated the clothes she sent. At our school in Matenje we had a tailoring workshop equipped by Sally, and tailors worked everyday to provide basic clothing for teachers and pupils.

Sally understood the symbolism of politics. Although the sewing machines and cloth that she collected and distributed could never satisfy the needs of the hundreds of thousands of refugees and freedom fighters, her actions had important symbolic significance. She was seen as a caring and concerned person who was doing her best to alleviate the suffering of the freedom fighters and refugees. This was an important contribution to her husband's political popularity. Through her tireless work, she created the political image of a caring and dedicated leadership. This image followed her after independence, when she decided to devote herself to looking after lepers and prostitutes. Leprosy has been under control in Zimbabwe for several decades. Nevertheless, there were some hundreds of former lepers who lacked housing, clothes, and food. Sally decided that it was her duty to provide them with a house, blankets, clothes, and food. After her death, she gave her clothes to the lepers, and it is possible today to see an old leper woman wearing the expensive coat that Sally used to wear.

Her work with prostitutes in the Marondera area was also substantive. She provided funds to allow each former prostitute to build a house for herself. However, she was also very ruthless, cutting off further assistance to any woman who returned to her former trade. This was another aspect of her character, that she was also feared. Her intense personality, absolute honesty, and dedication made it difficult for anyone to relax in her presence. She was respected, feared, and loved, but she was not someone you could laugh and joke with.

After independence, she was seen as one of the few people in high positions who was not easily corrupted. This reputation was strengthened by her refusal to allow her Ghanaian relatives to utilise her position to enrich themselves in Zimbabwe. When government ministers and other high functionaries began to succumb to corruption, the poor always believed that she retained their interests at heart and would ensure they were cared for. This made her an important political asset to her husband.

Her help for the poor was very personal rather than systemic. An example of this was that she appealed personally to a white industrialist to employ handicapped workers at his Ruwa factory, and to gain her patronage dozens of handicapped workers were employed. Soon after

Post-Détente and the Defeat of the ZANU Left Wing

Sally Mugabe

her death, they were sacked. This revealed not only the cynicism of the white employer, but also the fact that she was not able to incorporate her work into a permanent and stable system.

Having entered politics as a teenager and having devoted her whole life to politics, Sally developed a high degree of political astuteness. She knew, almost instinctively, what would win political support. She was also a very astute and instinctive judge of character. Just before her death, when ZANU decided to move away from socialism, she appealed to me to make a statement at the central committee meeting to persuade members against this step, and to reject the new ideology of Structural Adjustment. I was reluctant to do this, as I knew that ZANU was an alliance of many groups and not strictly a socialist party. She was very disappointed with me as she was convinced that the abandonment of socialism as the party ideology would mean the death of the party.

Sally was never happier than when she was with young children. This reflected the years she had spent as a primary school teacher and teacher trainer. Tragically, her only son, Nhamo, died as a child. She was not able to have any more children, as by the time Mugabe was released from prison in 1974 she was already seriously ill with the high blood pressure that was to lead to kidney failure. For almost two decades of her life, she was on dialysis until her death at the age of 62 in 1992.

One of her main characteristics was loyalty. Those who worked for her earned not only her respect and loyalty, but she also helped them to build houses for themselves so that they could become economically independent. She was absolutely and always loyal to her husband, supporting him in every way she could.

One example of her loyalty to Mugabe was the way she protected him from real and sometimes what I saw as imaginary dangers. One day when we were together in Dar es Salaam, she recounted to me an incident when one of the top ZANU leaders who was later to oppose Mugabe openly, had come to give Mugabe a present of a tube of toothpaste. She said the bottom of the toothpaste tube had been opened, and a poison had been inserted into it so that when Mugabe used it to brush his teeth, he would also be poisoned. She was quite convinced about this. I tried my best to reassure her that it was quite impossible that a top ZANU leader would try to poison a close colleague. However, I was unable to persuade her. It was not long afterwards that the man she had suspected of being against her husband did indeed reveal his hostility towards Mugabe. She had instinctively sensed this.

She had to undergo dialysis twice a week. This was a heavy burden for her. Nevertheless, she continued her work in charge of the Child Survival Foundation, through which she gained support from the Asian business community and the white farming community within Zimbabwe to provide boreholes in remote rural areas, again a sign of her practical character. She had the ability to see beyond race and tribe to harness all resources towards her goals. In this she was helped by the fact that as a Ghanaian she did not have any ethnic or tribal links within Zimbabwe.

Yet it was this very ability to perceive and judge people's characters accurately beyond ethnic attributes that made her very unpopular with Mugabe's own ethnic group, the Zezuru. They felt that despite the fact that Mugabe the prime minister and later the executive president was Zezuru, they were not able to win dominance and privileges for their ethnic group. Sally was seen as a problematic obstruction to their tribal ambitions. Like all other tribal groups, powerful interest groups had formed, jockeying for power, positions, and additional funding for their own grouping. The Zezuru interest group was a particularly well-organised and aggressive one. The Zezuru group's steering committee, popularly known as the Group of 24, saw her as a particular problem, and they were determined that once she died, she would be replaced by a more pliable woman. Thus even before her death in 1992, moves were under way to find a suitable replacement.

Sally, a very sensitive and intelligent woman, was well aware of these machinations. She interpreted them as reflecting an inability of Zimbabweans to accept her wholeheartedly because she was a Ghanaian. In her last years, she was even contemplating returning to her home country. She remained only out of loyalty to her husband, despite the painful situation she found herself in of being replaced by a younger, more beautiful, and more fecund second wife who had already produced a child for Mugabe some years before Sally's death.

However, she was accused of sending a car from Zimbabwe to Ghana during the 1988 "Willowgate" car scandal, when a number of top politicians were accused of using their positions to obtain cars.[1] This was perhaps more a symptom of what had happened to her marriage by that time. Sally was terminally ill, and Mugabe had begun an affair with Grace Marufu, whom he was to marry in 1994, two years after Sally's death. Sally was considering moving back to Ghana.

She described to me once her first visit to Rhodesia as a very young woman to marry Robert Mugabe. The white magistrate who was responsible for registering the marriage took it upon himself to warn her that polygamy was one of the local customs, and that she should consider this before committing herself to marriage with a Rhodesian African. Sadly for her, this white magistrate's warning came back to haunt her in the last years of her life, when her husband decided to take a second wife.

Mugabe's bid for power was well supported by his deputy, Simon Muzenda. Because of his humble and unprepossessing manner, Muzenda was often able to diffuse highly explosive situations without appearing to have done anything. As one of the oldest politicians and a founder member of ZANU, he was able to win the confidence of the militarists under Tongogara as well as of the young leftists under Wilfred Mhanda and Sam Geza. The Vashandi group regarded and

---

1. See Chapter 18.

still remembers Muzenda as the person who saved their lives after they were arrested by Tongogara.

Just before independence, Muzenda was sent to negotiate with the two groups of ZANU prisoners held in Nampula. He asked them to rejoin ZANU so that they could return to Zimbabwe as a united party. Only three members of Vashandi group agreed to rejoin ZANU. They were Sam Geza, Augustine Mpofu, and the late Felix Moyo. All other members of the Vashandi group refused to rejoin, as did all of the Hamadziripi group.

With the demise of the young leftists and of the old external leadership, there was now need to build up a new leadership. Robert Mugabe embarked on this task with alacrity. He brought in a new group of university educated leaders such as Sydney Sekeremayi, a medical doctor educated in Sweden; Witness Mangwende, a student leader from Britain; Ibbo Mandaza, who had been lecturing at the University of Dar es Salaam; Ignatius Chigwendere, a trade unionist who had settled in Britain; Davison Mugabe, who had lectured in the United States for many years. In addition, many of the old ZANU leaders from the 1960s returned to the fold. Others who had integrated themselves into the ANC, such as Herbert Ushewokunze and Eddison Zvogbo, were also welcomed back into the fold as top leaders. Military leaders, including Josiah Tongogara, Robson Manyika, William Ndangana, Meyor Hurimbo, Solomon Mujuru, and Vitalis Zvinavashe, were integrated into the political leadership, while a new cadre of young military leaders who had not participated in the execution of the Nhari group or in the suppression of the Vashandi or the old external leadership, were ushered in. This enabled a new military leadership to emerge that had taken no part in the leadership conflicts of the past. These included Josiah Tungamirai and Perence Shiri, both of whom became consecutive heads of the air force after independence, and Dominic Chiwewe, later to become commander of the national army.

The ability of ZANU to renew itself despite seemingly irreconcilable internal conflicts was one of the most prominent characteristics of the liberation struggle. This was achieved each time through the entrance of a new and younger generation of leaders who rose above the conflicts of the past.

CHAPTER 12

I End Up in a Military Camp

It was thanks to one of the top right-wing leaders in the ZANU hierarchy, Edgar Tekere, that I had my first experience of life in a military camp, initially at Ossibissa, a military camp for women guerrillas, and then at Pungwe III, a very large military base, both in Mozambique.

I was teaching at Chindunduma School, the headquarters of the ZANU education department, then located at Gondola near Chimoio, in February 1978, when Edgar Tekere arrived at the school. He told me that he had decided I should leave the school immediately and accompany him to a military camp. I totally refused to obey, insisting that teachers had no business in military camps. I knew that in a situation of war, when thousands of my comrades had died, it would be all too easy to have an opponent killed "in crossfire", the usual terminology for unexplained deaths during that period. Although I had entered the struggle for the most altruistic of reasons, I soon found myself embroiled in the constant internecine conflicts within ZANU itself.

Herbert Ushewokunze, one of the few qualified doctors in ZANLA, was also at Gondola at that time. He advised me to obey my senior commander. I had known Herbert since my student days at university in Salisbury, when he was a student at Natal University. We now found ourselves as fellow freedom fighters, but apparently in opposing factions, as I was obviously considered a very dangerous person by the right wing of ZANU. I did not think it wise to follow his advice, as I felt I was fighting for my life and obedience would be suicidal. I therefore continued to defy the order. Instead, I informed both the Mozambican and Tanzanian authorities of my plight. Schools were guarded by Mozambican and Tanzanian soldiers at that time. The contest of wills continued for several days.

Many people were sent to persuade me to follow the orders to move to a military camp. The most pathetic of these was Edgar Moyo, the husband of Sheiba Tavarwisa, deputy secretary for education in ZANU. Moyo, a former ZIPRA guerrilla, was genuinely frightened by his experience within ZANLA. He told me I should obey or I would be killed. I told him it was more likely that I would be killed if I obeyed. Moyo was himself later killed "in crossfire".

Several days later, in the middle of the night, a group of men were sent to capture me and force me into a Land Cruiser. My training in drama came to my rescue, as I began to fight these men, at the same time shouting and screaming. As this was a school with more than 2,000 children, they soon streamed out of their mud and grass dormitories, and became witnesses to a fierce battle between their teacher and a group of men. The men were obviously very hesitant, and did not know how to handle the situation. Herbert was horrified by the spectacle as more and more children came out to spectate. He rushed forward to silence me by putting his hand across my mouth. This gave me a good opportunity to bite him. I knew that my safety would depend on having as many witnesses as possible, and I was fortunate enough to have 2,000 children present. I believe these children saved my life. Many years later the teachers and children from this school still recall this incident whenever they meet me. Today it is a joke, but at the time it was far from funny.

After a fierce and very noisy battle, I found myself bundled into the back of the Land Cruiser together with my daughter, Chipo, who was only about six months old. It was fortunate that because of the tendency of the Rhodesian forces to attack schools, we used to sleep fully clothed with our shoes on, so I was able to leave fully dressed at least. A year later, one of our headmasters, Jones Zvenyika, gave me a suitcase of my possessions that he had rescued for me. One of the most amazing things in the liberation struggle was the ability of the rank and file freedom fighters to keep a sense of balance as well as a sense of humour, despite the unbalanced leadership of which we were often victims.

This move against me was related to the internal conflict within ZANU. Despite the fact that I was not part of the Vashandi group, it was well known that I had close links to the group not only because of my own socialist political viewpoint, but also because of the work I did during the *détente* period when the Vashandi rose to power. I had worked closely with the Vashandi leaders, who provided brilliant leadership of the liberation struggle between 1975 and 1976, and through their clarity and dedication brought an end to *détente*. *Détente*, if it had succeeded, would have heralded a fatally weak and divided independ-

I End Up in a Military Camp

ent Zimbabwe, prone to warlord control and to continued exploitation and oppression. Instead, the Vashandi ensured that ZANLA emerged from *détente* as a united and coherent force, rather than as the divided fiefdoms of various warlords.

However, since the Vashandi consisted of young men and women in their late teens and early twenties, they exhibited very limited political understanding and skills, and were the victims of their own tremendous and early success. By the end of 1976 the main leaders, including Wilfred Mhanda and Sam Geza, had been arrested and were kept in custody by the Mozambican government until after independence. The Vashandi were at least still alive, having been protected by the Mozambican government, unlike their predecessors, the unfortunate Nhari group, killed in 1974.

In early 1978, a group of leaders comprising Henry Hamadziripi, Rugare Gumbo, Joseph Taderera, and Cletus Chigove were arrested by ZANLA itself and accused of attempting a coup. Their arrest had been preceded by an incident where Taderera and Chigove had managed to seize Edgar Tekere and Herbert Ushewokunze from the Chimoio ZANLA headquarters. On the night of the attack, I was asleep in the bedroom I shared with Oppah Machinguri[1], a young woman guerrilla in charge of the finances for ZANLA. I was awakened in the middle of the night and told to flee. Although I did not understand what was happening, I grabbed my daughter Chipo, and made for the surrounding bush.

I found myself hiding in the same area as Rekayi Tangwena, the famous traditional chief who had so courageously defied the Smith regime's various attempts to oust him from his ancestral lands. He had assisted Robert Mugabe and Edgar Tekere to flee across the mountains from Rhodesia to Mozambique. He then had joined the liberation struggle. Now we found ourselves hiding together in the Mozambican bush in the middle of the night, fleeing because of a machine gun attack by one ZANLA faction against another. This was too much for Chief Tangwena, who wept. He wept because he foresaw more bloodshed after independence. He told me of his fears: "What will happen

---

1. After independence, Oppah Machinguri Rushesha served as deputy minister and minister in a number of ministries in Zimbabwe and as provincial governor.

after independence if we are ready to kill each other now?" Some days later, Solomon Mujuru rescued Ushewokunze and Tekere, and in turn imprisoned Taderera and Chigove.

The Hamadziripi group was accused of organising to remove both Mugabe and Tongogara. We were now faced with choosing between Mugabe or Hamadziripi, this at a critical time in the liberation struggle when ZANU and ZANLA should have been totally united against the settler-colonial regime of Ian Smith. I had known Hamadziripi from the time I had joined ZANU in 1973, and was closely linked to Rugare Gumbo, who was the father of my daughter. Although in my view it was incorrect to begin these internecine conflicts when we had not yet won the war against the colonialists and settlers, my close relations with the Vashandi and with the Hamadziripi group were well known. My belief was that Tongogara was essential for the success of the military struggle. Obviously Mugabe had come to the same conclusion. It was in the context of the struggle within ZANU that the decision had been taken that I should leave the school for a military camp. Whatever the rationale for Tekere's decision, I was now to have my first experience of life in a military camp.

Ossibissa was a camp for women guerrillas. The young freedom fighters who had set up the camp had named it after a Ghanaian pop music group that was very popular during this period. As in all other military camps, rallies and military exercises were part of the daily routine. Some of the women had children. The women got up very early in the morning, and would bathe themselves and their children in icy cold water in the belief that this would strengthen them both physically and in terms of determination. Ossibissa was indeed the Zimbabwean equivalent of Sparta, characterised by arduous physical exercise and hardship. Women guerrillas came there to rest between assignments at the front.

The women conducted their own school in which they taught each other. Roughly half the women had some secondary education, whereas the other half had either never been to school or had had only a few years of primary education. As the skills required in the early stages of guerrilla warfare did not depend heavily on educational levels, some young peasant women had managed to gain leadership positions through their prowess in war. I remember one senior woman commander who was totally illiterate. She had to cope with the fact that she did not even know the days of the week, information she gained from me. The school thus played a critical role in enabling women guerrillas to share their knowledge, skills, and experiences through these classes.

One of the sad things I remember about Ossibissa was that each day a child died. This was due to the ignorance of these young mothers about nutrition and primary healthcare. Thus, while they immersed their young children in icy water every morning, they failed to give these children a balanced diet. These young children were fed a diet of tea, sugar, and biscuits. This was partly because of the shortage of milk. It was also partly because the women guerrillas, most of whom were from a peasant background, did not want to feed their children on the traditional diet for infants among the peasantry: maize meal porridge and peanut butter. The guerrillas felt that through their participation in the war they had risen above the peasantry, commonly called the "*povo*", and their new status as freedom fighters, now called "comrades", was reflected in what they fed their children. We began to include nutrition lessons in the school curriculum, and this did lead to a lowering of child mortality.

In addition to the ignorance of primary healthcare, it was also not possible to receive vaccination and other advantages of modern medicine. I was fortunate to have managed to get my daughter vaccinated against childhood diseases when I was still in Dar es Salaam, because such basic amenities were unavailable in the Mozambican camps. When I returned to Zimbabwe, I took Chipo to be vaccinated again against polio at the local clinic, which was run by a white nurse. The nurse nearly hit me as she thought I was irresponsible for not having had her vaccinated earlier. Chipo was two and a half years old at independence. I could not explain to her that this would have been impossible.

Medicines themselves were in serious short supply. Because of this, we began to utilise some of the natural medicines around us, including eucalyptus leaves boiled in water as cough mixture.

The sense of solidarity among the women at Ossibissa was extraordinary, with our minds focused on the rigours of warfare. It was there that I managed to understand in depth the dedication as well as the suffering of these women guerrillas.

I had not been long in Ossibissa when it was decided that I should go to Pungwe III, on the banks of the Pungwe River, one of the biggest rivers in Mozambique. Probably, this decision was made to ensure that I had absolutely no ability to contact the outside world, as this was still possible in Ossibissa. Pungwe III was one of the biggest military bases in Mozambique, housing several thousand guerrillas. It was located in a most isolated spot remote from any human dwelling. It was possible to walk for weeks without meeting anyone. I understand it was taken over a decade later by Renamo, the extreme right-wing guerrilla group fighting the Mozambican government.

One of my most vivid memories of Pungwe III was the severe shortage of food. Long lines of freedom fighters would queue up to receive a handful of *mangai*, dried grains of maize that had been boiled. In addition, each one received a bit of salt, literally in their hands, as there was a serious shortage of plates. This was the one meal of the day. I found the *mangai* quite inedible, as it would soon give me a severe stomachache. Sometimes, ground maize would be found for me so that I could eat *sadza* or maize porridge instead of *mangai*. This was a highly privileged diet. Oil and sugar were luxuries. I remember on one occasion the cook, a young woman guerrilla, decided to give me a special menu of spaghetti. Believing that I was too thin she added a cup of oil out of kindness. Unfortunately, this made the spaghetti totally inedible!

We managed to get some of the cooking oil from the cooks to use as skin cream, as this was the only oil available. It worked quite well.

At Pungwe III we also ran a school for those who wanted some education. In contrast to Ossibissa, our school was very small, as most of the camp dwellers were undergoing rigorous military training every day and had little time left for anything else. It was quite amazing to see the young recruits, fed on a handful of *mangai* with salt each day, following a physically strenuous training programme. Despite these harsh conditions, the morale was extremely high and you would hear voices raised in song every evening.

The sons and daughters from the richest families mingled and lived together with the sons and daughters of the poorest peasants. University graduates mingled with illiterate youths on an equal footing, all of them recruits in the liberation struggle. These graduates would have to take orders from officers much less educated than themselves, as some officers had had only a few years of primary education. Some were illiterate.

I End Up in a Military Camp

The young recruits were very poorly clad, often with much of their bodies visible through their threadbare clothes. The scarcity of clothes meant that the cloth and clothes sent by Sally Mugabe, often made by herself, were much appreciated.

There was also a serious shortage of blankets, with one blanket being shared by three or four guerrillas. The only way to keep warm in the cold winter nights was to sleep close to the fire. Shoes were also in very short supply. This became problematic and particularly difficult because of the prevalence of *matekenya*, or sand lice, which would burrow into the skin of your feet and under your toenails, causing excruciating pain. They could only be removed through an operation to prise them out using the only equipment available, needles and razor blades.

Many support groups in Europe, particularly Sweden, collected old clothes for us. The guerrillas were clothed in the cast-offs of Europe, collected from door to door by supporters composed sometimes of religious groups and at other times by young political idealists, who believed it their duty to assist us to overcome settler and colonial oppression. We would sometimes receive lorry loads of shoes from our supporters in Canada, organised by Brian Haddon and his friends. Haddon, a white Zimbabwean whose parents, Michael and Eileen, had fought a long struggle against the Smith regime, was one of thousands of supporters who provided the guerrillas with the basic necessities of life.

One of the major problems besides the lack of food and clothing was illness, in particular dysentery and malaria. These were both killer diseases that took as many lives as the enemy bullets. I was the victim of both, and valued the excellent work done by the medical officers. Although they had received only a few months of training, they literally saved lives every day. I was particularly lucky to have Tandayi, one of the nurses at Pungwe III, looking after me during a very serious attack of dysentery followed by a very bad bout of malaria. We were fortunate enough to have support groups in Europe providing us with essential drugs.

I had been in Pungwe III for about five months when Tongogara arrived one day and called me to speak to him in private. He made it clear that he would not allow me to continue my work in education if I did not support his leadership. I remained silent. Although I had never opposed Tongogara, I was critical of his execution of the Nhari group as well as his abuse of women.

It was Tongogara who made the decision that I should return to the school in June 1978. He had not been consulted about my violent transfer from the school to a military camp, and he was strongly opposed to it. Those months in Pungwe III were among the harshest of my years in the liberation struggle.

CHAPTER 13

Traditional Religion in the Liberation Struggle

One of the most striking characteristics of the Zimbabwean liberation struggle was the power of the traditional religious leaders, the *vana sekuru*. They held a special position in the psyche of the freedom fighters, particularly the peasant soldiers who constituted about half the freedom fighters. The other half consisted of high school students who had deserted their schools in their tens of thousands to join the struggle. Many of the peasants were poorly educated, having had little opportunity under the colonial regime to gain even primary education. However, they did have the traditional education offered through the religious teachings of the vana sekuru.

From the 1890s, when whites first entered the country, traditional religious leaders had opposed colonialism and were instrumental in organising opposition to it. One of the main leaders in the first *chimurenga* or just war against colonialism in the 1890s was Nehanda, a woman of outstanding religious and political leadership. When the military struggle began to escalate in 1972, one of the first acts of the ZANLA commanders was to persuade the traditional religious leaders to support their struggle. Some of these key religious leaders were persuaded to follow the guerrillas into Mozambique to provide spiritual and ideological leadership for the armed struggle. This was a decisive move in terms of gaining popular support, so strong was the influence of the spirit mediums over the popular psyche, in particular the peasant psyche. The peasantry constituted more than 70 per cent of the black population.

In every refugee and every military camp, the spirit mediums had their own separate encampment where they practised their religion. They dressed in traditional black togas, black being the colour of holiness. They were not allowed to wear trousers or shoes, these being seen as alien and colonial. The male spirit mediums sported long beards. There were an equal number of female spirit mediums, as the religion appeared to be an equal-opportunities area. Women spirit mediums could be more senior than male spirit mediums. Hierarchy depended on the authority of the spirit who commanded the medium, not on the political connections of the incumbent. Thus, one of the main characteristics of the spirit mediums was their absolute independence from the political leadership, and they were free to support or to criticise the political incumbents.

Despite their political independence, or perhaps because of it, the spirit mediums played a critically important role in persuading the peasantry to support a particular political group and a particular political direction. The Smith regime made a great effort to woo spirit mediums to support their rule, on one occasion even showering pamphlets purporting to come from the ancestors from aeroplanes. The liberation forces were equally assiduous in pursuing the support of these traditional leaders.

One of the key messages of the spirit mediums was that the ancestral spirits fully supported the struggle to regain the land. Freedom fighters firmly believed that they were protected by the ancestral spirits, because the ancestral spirits were committed to ensuring that the land be returned to its rightful owners.

Young children, particularly young girls, were given over by their parents to be brought up by the spirit mediums. This was a sign of the faith and trust placed by parents in their spiritual leaders.

The faithful believed that religious leaders were selected by the spirits, who would come and inhabit their bodies during spiritual trances. During these trances, it was believed that the spirits spoke directly to their children, the spirit medium being no more than a "pocket" or container for the spirit. Thus the person who provided the means for the ancestral spirit to speak could not be blamed for what he or she said during the trance.

Nightly spirit possessions by the ancestors, their arrival heralded by an eerie whooping sound, were a familiar feature of every camp in the liberation struggle, whether these were school camps, refugee camps, or military camps. One of the key tenets of traditional religion in Zimbabwe was the belief that the ancestral spirits protected their offspring and would guarantee their welfare, but only provided that the living kept to the rules of their ancestors. These rules were simple ethical rules, such as respect for life, sexual purity, and care of the environment. It was believed that those who transgressed these simple rules would be killed by the spirits.

Often, those possessed would ask to speak to particular people in the camp, and on several occasions I was awakened in the middle of the night and summoned to appear before a spirit medium. This was difficult for me, as I had developed very poor night sight as a result of the lack of Vitamin A in our diet. Moreover, I could not appear in slacks in front of a spirit medium. Consequently, I had to be led almost like a blind person through difficult forest paths to the hut where the possessed spirit medium was in a trance. I could not make out what was really happening during these meetings, except that I understood that the spirits were very friendly.

It appeared to me that spirit possession was a very entrenched cultural way for people to express whatever concerns and problems were on their minds. In such sessions, the "spirits" would speak freely, criticising anything that had displeased them during the day. Their displeasure could be against such matters as overwork or sexual abuse. The spirit mediums provided a very vocal and independent platform for expressing the people's views.

Spirit mediums saw themselves as protectors of the environment. They worked to ensure that their followers respected it: trees could not be cut down except for agriculture, firewood had to be collected from the fallen dead branches instead.

Such was the strength of the belief in the power of the spirits that the majority of ZANLA freedom fighters refused to kill anyone unless they were trying to save their own lives or the lives of their colleagues. This was one of the key characteristics of ZANLA fighters, distinguishing them from the Selous Scouts who posed as guerrillas and who tried to cause confusion by killing indiscriminately. Hundreds of prisoners of war, both white and black, were released rather than killed because of the strong influence of the traditional religious leaders. Respect for life applied to all forms of life. One example of this that I witnessed was the refusal of the freedom fighters to kill wild animals. The forests of Mozambique were full of snakes of all sorts. These were protected by the spirit mediums. Sometimes snakes would enter our thatched huts. The freedom fighters would chase the snakes away, but would never kill them. On one occasion, a huge snake entered my thatched house. I grabbed my daughter Chipo and my adopted son Arnold. Arnold, who was three years old, loved animals of all sorts, and he struggled against me, saying he wanted to play with the snake! Meanwhile the freedom fighters came and chased the snake back into the forest.

Killings of political opponents were resoundingly condemned by the traditional religious leaders, who constantly warned that people who indulged in such killings would be punished by the ancestral spirits. Such killings did take place, as evidenced by the execution of the Nhari group. Adherents of traditional religion believed that people who killed would never get into power, but would be punished by the ancestral spirits in due course.

Enemy soldiers were killed only if they resisted capture. A white agricultural extension worker, Nigel Hawkesworth, was held in captivity for many months, as were dozens of white and hundreds of black soldiers. When captured, they were treated humanely, and many of them eventually joined the liberation forces themselves. It was quite possible for an ex-enemy agent to become a top guerrilla commander. Many made this transition quite successfully.

I recall a visit to the ZANU storeroom in Dar es Salaam that held the clothes contributed by supporters from Scandinavia for freedom fighters. This was in 1977 at the height of the war. I met a number of black Rhodesian soldiers who had been placed in charge of the storeroom. I asked them why they did not escape, as they were living freely in a suburb of Dar es Salaam. They told me that they knew they would never be killed as long as they remained at their posts, but that if they tried to escape they would certainly be killed. This was a code of conduct based on the rules of the spirit mediums. These prisoners of war had been captured within Rhodesia itself and had been partly force-marched and partly transported to Tanzania, many thousands of kilometres away.

The sexual purity promoted by the spirit mediums meant that the freedom fighters were warned against any form of sex during war, whether sexual dalliance or rape. The mediums held that people who misbehaved sexually would be killed for their transgressions. These rules were generally adhered to by the rank and file, although they were generally disregarded by many top leaders. This was a point of constant conflict between the spirit mediums and specific leaders, who were condemned during their trances.

This spiritual rigour accounted for the fact that there were very few cases of rape during the prolonged guerrilla struggle from 1972 until 1980, a situation that made reconciliation between blacks and whites at the end of the war a relatively painless exercise.

The spirit mediums often gave warnings against imminent attacks the following day. On such days, the camp commanders would ensure that everyone left the camp at about 4 a.m. in the morning. Sometimes, these warnings turned out to be true, but on many occasions nothing untoward happened on the day. I was in Pungwe III military camp when we received report from the spirits of an imminent attack the next day. We set off at about 4 a.m. on a rainy day in March 1978, moving in single file into the dense forest that surrounded the camp. I had a cumbersome suitcase, which Jones Zvenyika had so kindly rescued for me from Maputo and delivered to Pungwe III. One of the soldiers gallantly offered to carry the suitcase for me on his shoulders. I felt guilty for imposing this burden on him, but it was quite impossible for me to carry the suitcase as well as my daughter strapped on my back. Everyone in the camp carried all his or her possessions, as what little they had would be destroyed by the bombs if left in the camp. Most of the recruits at Pungwe III possessed only the badly torn and worn out clothes on their backs. With a piece of plastic over our heads, we walked in driving rain for many hours until nightfall and remained in the forest the whole night, unable to sleep. We rested upright as the rain fell on us, with raindrops dripping from the ends of our noses. The ground was too wet for us to lie on. The next day we returned to camp. This time it had been a false alarm.

I had not been in Pungwe III for more than a few days when I received a message from the traditional religious leaders to visit them. Their camp was quite apart from the military camp. I was very hesitant about accepting this invitation, as I did not think I had much in common with the leaders of traditional religion. I did not know what I would say to them. Nevertheless, they sent messages to me again and again, and eventually I became too embarrassed to further refuse their invitations. I arrived at their camp, about an hour's walk away, and apologised for not coming earlier. My excuse was that I had failed to find a suitable interpreter. Although I have a reasonable grasp of Shona, it was not good enough for a conversation on complicated issues.

My discussion with the traditional religious leaders was very different from what I had expected. They wanted to know why the Soviet Union, the United States, and the Chinese were participating in our struggle for the liberation of Zimbabwe. We had a very profound discussion on the international implications of the Zimbabwean liberation struggle.

It was at Pungwe III that I first realised that there was serious antagonism between the veterans led by Tongogara and the traditional religious leaders. These leaders constantly condemned unnecessary killing as well as sexual promiscuity, and although as far as I knew they did not specify names, these frequent statements made in trances were fiercely resented by the veterans. Such was the antagonism that in a rally held in Pungwe III in 1978, Tongogara threatened the traditional religious leaders with imprisonment if they continued with their subversive allegations. He made the religious leaders stand up one by one in front of a crowd of thousands of people, and subjected them to a verbal tirade. These white bearded old men, dressed in their traditional black togas and without shoes, stood in silence. They did not deign to respond. Two years later, just a few months before independence, Tongogara died in a car accident. The adherents of traditional religion believed that this was the spirits' response.

CHAPTER 14

The Formation of the ZANU Department of Education

By 1975 tens of thousands of Zimbabwean refugees, including thousands of children, had fled from the war zones inside the country to refugee camps in Mozambique. The situation became desperate as more and more refugees fled Rhodesia. It was impossible for the newly independent Mozambique, itself under immense internal pressure, to provide adequately for these refugees. Many died from a combination of malnutrition and endemic diseases, such as malaria and dysentery. Death was a daily experience. It was essential to provide both medical and educational services for these refugees.

Schools started immediately with whatever materials were available. There were no textbooks, exercise books, or blackboards. Instead, the cardboard boxes that came from Norway through the World Food Programme, containing tinned tuna fish for the refugees, were the only available school materials. All the children knew there was a country called Norway that provided them with tuna fish! Charcoal and cardboard became the chalk and blackboards, the pencils, and exercise books for the eager teachers and children. Children usually wrote the words in the sand with their fingers.

Late in 1977, Dzingai Mutumbuka was appointed secretary for edu-cation. He was one of the first lecturers to leave his university post to join the struggle. I had known Dzingai from my student days at the University of Rhodesia and Nyasaland, through the Roman Catholic student network that linked students from all over the country. A brilliant thinker, Dzingai first became involved in politics while in Zambia. Many Zimbabwean lecturers at the University of Zambia were drawn into ZANU politics when the liberation war began to turn in favour of the freedom fighters at the end of 1972. Dzingai had just joined the school of natural science after leaving his post at the University of Dublin. At the University of Zambia, he became part of the group of

Zimbabwean university teachers and students who met each week to study aspects of the situation in Zimbabwe, looking at possible strategies for areas like agriculture, industry, and education.

UNICEF was the first organisation to assist with a grant of US$250,000 to buy books, pencils, and other school materials. I managed to purchase most of the equipment and books in Dar es Salaam, and these were sent to the schools that had been established in the camps in Mozambique. This was a great improvement on the makeshift teaching materials made of charcoal and cardboard. For the first time, children had paper, pencils, and ballpoints to write with. For the first time, they had textbooks. For the first time teachers, had blackboards and chalk.

The *détente* exercise had led to the arrest of the whole external leadership of ZANU. This leadership vacuum forced people like Dzingai and myself, who had devoted ourselves to our professional and academic careers, to take over the roles of political leadership, roles for which we were totally unprepared. From university lecturers, whose sole experience was teaching in the lecture room or performing experiments in the laboratory, we found ourselves making momentous decisions that would affect the future of our country.

Such were the dangers we faced in Zambia that we were forced to leave for fear of losing our lives. Dzingai had fled to London. I remember unpicking the lining of his jacket in order to insert some documents, and then sewing it up again. From 1975 to 1976, Dzingai worked tirelessly in Britain and Europe winning support for ZANU. He became one of the best-known proponents of the liberation struggle for Zimbabwe all over Europe. During a rally on behalf of Zimbabwe in Trafalgar Square in 1976, when tens of thousands of British people gathered to support us, Dzingai made his first political speech. Having played a critical role in salvaging ZANU and the liberation struggle during the *détente* period, we were again to work together in establishing an education system for the thousands of children who had been forced to flee from Rhodesia by the brutality of the Smith regime.

Dzingai decided to prepare a long-term education plan that would include not only the provision of primary and secondary education, but also research, curriculum development, teacher training, and administrative training. He also made plans for dozens of young people from the refugee camp schools in Mozambique to attend universities in friendly African countries, such as Sierra Leone, which then had one of the best university systems in Africa, as well as in Nigeria and Tanzania. The objective was to establish an education system in the Mozambican camps that would not only be educationally sound, but would also incorporate ZANU's political agenda of national unity and national consciousness, socialism, anti-imperialism, anti-colonialism, and anti-racism. He also went on an aggressive recruiting campaign in Africa and overseas to attract young Zimbabwean graduates to come and teach in our schools, and he succeeded in attracting quite a number.

Sheiba Tavarwisa, one of the first women to join the liberation struggle, was the deputy secretary for education. A strong leader, she had not only undergone military training, but had also been a pioneer in the early 1970s in transporting arms for ZANLA from Zambia to Mozambique, and then into Zimbabwe. Women such as Sheiba Tavarwisa spearheaded the struggle, making it possible for the men to follow after the ground was prepared. She was also one of the first trained teachers to join the liberation struggle. Her ability to organise thousands of teachers and children into orderly schools provided an excellent foundation for Mutumbuka's ambitious plans.

The first education department headquarters was established in Chimoio, but was destroyed by a combined air and ground force in November 1977.

The education department headquarters then moved to Gondola, where a former farm complex had been made available by the Mozambican government. The plan that had begun in Chimoio under Ephraim Chitofu and Peter Tsorai to develop a distance education course for teachers now continued under Chitofu and myself, as I had now moved from Dar es Salaam to Gondola. Ephraim Chitofu was an experienced primary school headmaster whose school had been closed down as the war began to affect large areas near the border with Mozambique. Like many others in the war zones, Chitofu had become a target of the Rhodesian forces, who accused him of sympathising with the guerrillas. People in positions of authority such as school heads were particularly singled out so that their torture, imprisonment, and often death would serve as a warning to the community. Chitofu had, therefore, fled to save his life.

In Mozambique, Chitofu became one of the major educational leaders, helping to establish a number of schools. His steady educational leadership and his dedication to the liberation struggle enabled him to thrive in this very difficult environment, and in the process to enable tens of thousands of children to obtain a sound education.

The headquarters of the ZANU education department was later moved to Pasi Chigare, near the Party farm. Pasi Chigare was a typical ZANU school, consisting of hundreds of large huts that served as dormitories for the children. A few smaller huts were inhabited by staff. The complex housed about 2,000 children. It was on a bright July morning in 1978 that our school was bombed. That morning, the young girls who lived with me and helped me had informed me that a lorry had arrived the night before containing shoes donated by our supporters overseas. These young teenagers did not have any shoes, despite the fact that the sand contained lice that burrowed into their feet and laid their eggs under the skin. Shoes provided protection. Knowing this, I decided to go to the storeroom to see if I could obtain some shoes for these girls. Usually, I would take a bath first thing in the morning before going to teach, but on that day I decided to take my daughter Chipo with me to the storeroom, which was situated on the outskirts of the camp. I arrived there at about 7 in the morning. The storekeeper decided to give me a cup of tea, a luxury in refugee camps where tealeaves and sugar were not easily obtained. I had not had time to take a sip when a schoolboy came running into the hut to warn us that planes were bombing the school. I grabbed Chipo and rushed out. Luckily, I had come with the *mbereko*, the traditional baby sling used for carrying infants on mothers' backs. I managed to tie Chipo on to my back and we all rushed out, in time to witness low-flying aeroplanes bombing the centre of the camp.

In order not to be seen from the swooping planes, we had to crawl on the ground until we reached the tall grass that surrounded the school. All around me I saw children running away from the planes, screaming and tearing off their clothes. Children believed that their clothes, particularly red clothes, could be seen from the planes and would lead to them being attacked. Red is the colour of danger in traditional culture. It was also believed that the pilots could easily spot people dressed in red as targets. Often the clothes donated from Scandinavian countries were very brightly coloured. I saw three year olds, five year olds running away from the planes. Some of the teachers were handicapped, and they too had to flee as best they could. One of the handicapped teachers at the school was Irene Ropa Mahamba. She had left university to become a teacher in the refugee schools in Mozambique. That day, she also had to flee into the bush as the planes bombed our school.

Once we reached the tall grass, which was over six feet high, we were able to get up and run. Running away from the scene of the bombing, I soon became separated from everyone else. I was alone with Chipo in the middle of a forest of tall savannah grass. Chipo, hardly a year old, knew that something serious was happening and throughout the hot day's walk she did not give any trouble. From time to time I would breastfeed her. I did not know where we were going other than away from the disaster area. I walked the whole day. On the journey I came across a huge red and orange snake on my path, but we just skirted warily around each other. I managed to find some large leaves to protect my head from the burning sun. Luckily, I had brought with me the "clip on" sunglasses that Sheiba Tavarwisa had given me. The clips had long disappeared, and I had to tie the dark glasses on with some string to my spectacles, but they worked very well. I think Sheiba had found them in the pocket of some donated clothes. In order to stave off thirst, I pulled up some grass stalks and chewed on them to get some moisture.

Dusk fell. I looked for some place where we could rest for the night and found an outcrop of granite rocks. I decided we could stay there for the night. The hot day had given way to a very cold night. July is the middle of the southern African winter. The only covering we had was the *mbereko* used for carrying Chipo on my back. I spent an uncomfortable night resting on the rocks and as soon as dawn broke, I climbed up to the highest rock and tried to see where I was. I saw some white buildings in the distance, and, thinking this was a nearby town, I made my way in that direction.

After about four hours of walking, I reached the buildings. It was not a town at all but a ZANLA military camp. As usual, while our school had been bombed, the military camp had been left untouched. The soldiers guarding the gates were surprised to see me and thought I was a Portuguese woman. However, I was soon warmly welcomed to a big breakfast of sweet tea and *fatkoeks* or doughnuts. This was very welcome after a day and night without food.

I discovered that our school had been destroyed. Two schoolgirls had been killed by fragments of granite which exploded when the area was bombed. Everyone else had escaped. Search parties had been sent out to find the children. Some of the school leaders had escaped to the nearby town, and had managed to get drunk. They were later arrested for neglecting their duties. Afterwards, they were imprisoned and demoted because they had failed to come back after the bombing to take responsibility for the search for the 2,000 missing children. During the liberation struggle the military wing of ZANU had the final say. When they arrived at the school after the bombing and failed to find the person in charge, they took drastic action. This was an example of military discipline, which was always severe. However, other teachers had assumed this responsibility and soon everyone was accounted for. The exercise of finding 2,000 lost children who could die of thirst, hunger, and exposure had been trying, but was eventually completed.

All our belongings had been destroyed, but I soon found a new wardrobe, as the women guerrillas came and gave me a piece of clothing each. Although most of these clothes were too large, I was soon able to adapt them to my size. As we did not have such luxuries as cotton to sew with, it was necessary to pull some threads from the cloth to use as cotton. Needles were important tools that we guarded jealously. Chipo had to give up her milk bottles immediately and be fed directly from a cup, as spoons were in short supply. She adapted straight away and gave no trouble at all. The bomb attack also spelt the end of napkins for Chipo, as all the napkins were lost: however, she adapted to this very easily as well. I probably missed them more than Chipo did. I had failed to find babies' napkins in Dar es Salaam where she was born, but Beatrice Ng'onomo, a good friend of mine, had managed to send some from Lusaka through the good offices of Tommy Sithole, a Zimbabwean journalist working in the *Daily News* of Tanzania. Tommy had been on a business trip from Dar es Salaam to Lusaka and had kindly brought back the napkins. Now they were lost forever as a result of the bombing of our school.

Numerous other refugee camps and schools were bombed that day in July 1978, making it impossible to continue with educational work in Chimoio. By this time many school children had experienced as many as six bomb attacks, and were beginning to suffer from psychological traumas of various types. Symptoms included incurable hiccups and a strange disjointed and jerky walk. Malnutrition may also have added to the psychological strain. Soon after the July 1978 bombings, hundreds of school children began to fall into nightly trances during which they were possessed by spirits. The familiar barking sound that preceded these encounters would resound eerily through the night, heralding another spirit possession in a dormitory. Spirit possession was as much an expression of hysteria as a form of protest against oppression and suffering. This phenomenon only ended when the children were transported to Tete province, then considered beyond the range of the Rhodesian planes.

One of the reasons schools were bombed so often may have been the infiltration of refugee camps, particularly schools, by Rhodesian agents. They were sent in their hundreds to infiltrate the camps and found it easy to infiltrate refugee camps, but apparently more difficult to infiltrate military camps.

It was only a few months later that a Rhodesian agent was discovered among our students at Mabvhudzi School in Tete. He had entered the school as a student. We did not suspect anything, but one day he was arrested by the Mozambican peasants in whose midst we lived. They reported that he behaved strangely, and was always wandering among them instead of attending classes. He also had a taste for luxury, in this case meat, and was always trying to barter clothes for meat. He was searched, and in the heel of his shoe a radio transmitter was found. This must have been one of the ways in which the Rhodesian military were able to spot the schools and refugee camps. He was handed over by the school authorities to the ZANLA military who visited our school about once a month. I believe he was executed by the military.

The Mozambican authorities decided to transport all refugees away from areas bordering on Rhodesia, leaving only guerrillas there. ZANLA had developed a system of underground bunkers that were apparently not identifiable by the Rhodesian reconnaissance planes that circled the camps every night. Throughout the war, the Rhodesians were either unable or unwilling to attack military camps, but consistently bombed schools and refugee camps. The Rhodesians refused to distinguish between schools, refugee camps, and military camps, regarding all of them as equally legitimate targets.

Large trucks arrived to transport thousands of children and their teachers on the more than 1,000 kilometre journey from the Chimoio area to Tete. I had not experienced sitting in the back of a crowded lorry before, but I was only too happy to leave the insecurity of Chimoio for the relative security of Tete and did not mind the lack of comfort. A site had been selected near the Matenje River, which proved an essential source of water for the thousands of refugees. Unlike the military camps, which were located very far away from the local population, Matenje camp was placed very close to the local inhabitants.

Matenje was to be the new headquarters of the education department. As soon as we arrived, we made some rough shelters to protect us from the wind and the cold. Luckily, it was not the rainy season: it was August 1978. We celebrated our arrival and Chipo's birthday with a sumptuous dinner of chicken, which we had managed to buy through *chirenje*[1], a system of barter by which freedom fighters exchanged some of the clothes they received from Scandinavian donors with the local peasants for food.

Within a few weeks, a large camp of grass-thatched pole and mud houses ("*posto*s") and dormitories was built by the teachers and the 2,000 children. The main building materials were bamboo and grass, which were plentiful in the area. Beds, tables, and benches were also made of bamboo. The camp commander, Chiridza, who was in charge of construction, displayed an extraordinary organisational ability. Although he had only enjoyed primary education, he gained his very impressive administrative skills in ZANLA, with which he had served as a military commander at the front. By 1974, he had retired from ZANLA and had joined the education department. He was able to engender both hard work and aesthetic appreciation as various building teams competed to see which houses and dormitories were the best. The sanitation system, which had been chaotic at first, now became well organised with the construction of pit latrines. The achievement of building their own school and dormitories and the establishment of the daily routine of school brought about an extraordinary spirit of pride and unity in both teachers and students.

---

1. *Chirenje* comes from the name of a Lusaka suburb, Chilenje, where presumably the system of barter was common.

The Formation of the ZANU Department of Education

The staff of the department of education included former school heads such as Ephraim Chitofu, John Machokoto, and Tovadini Mwenje. As experienced primary school heads, they provided invaluable experience. Chitofu and I worked in the teacher education and research department. One of the other school leaders who had been in charge of Pasi Chigare School, John Machokoto, was in charge of the schools, and remained in charge until we all returned to Zimbabwe. He became the head of Chindunduma Primary School after independence.

There were a number of teachers who had gained their experience in the struggle, such as Hoyini Bhila, Jones Zvenyika, Gertrude Vimbisai Nyakupinda, and James Mushamba. These young teachers were able to take on the onerous responsibility of running schools with remarkable success. It was truly amazing to see these young people in their early twenties run schools with thousands of young children. Jones Zvenyika, for example, was the headmaster in charge of over 2,000 pupils. Only a few years earlier, he had been a young student. Despite his youth, he turned out to be both a superb teacher and a brilliant organiser. Much of his success depended on his human relations and leadership skills. Sadly, his wife Prudence was killed by the Smith forces. She was in one of the first groups to return to Rhodesia after the Lancaster House talks. Although the freedom fighters had been told that they were now free to return home, the Rhodesians nevertheless felt that they were a legitimate target. Jones himself died of a heart attack after independence.

Hoyini Bhila, Gertrude Vimbisai Nyakupinda, and James Mushamba were involved in teacher training with me. They too had been young students when they joined the liberation struggle, but they were now able to shoulder the responsibility of educating thousands of children.

Our team also included graduates like myself, Darlington Chitsenga, who had a masters' degree in mathematics from Columbia University, Josephat Nhundu and Stephen Nyengera, who had left the University of Sierra Leone on completion of their studies to join the struggle, and Farai Karonga, who had just completed an honours degree at a British university. Chitsenga was a brilliant mathematician, but unfortunately the suffering he had endured as part of the liberation struggle, particularly the humiliating treatment of graduates by some of the war veterans, had taken its toll, and he was gradually giving way to alcoholism. Josephat Nhundu, Stephen Nyengera, and Farai Karonga were typical of the enthusiastic and idealistic young graduates who were willing to leave their universities to come and help in the liberation struggle. They were involved in teacher training and curriculum development.

There was also a team of graduate and undergraduate students from the University of Rhodesia, including Morgan Borerwa, who had a degree in accountancy, and Simon Matsvai, Khulukane Ndebele, Martin Makomva, and Kenneth Munyarabvi, who had been undergraduates. Others had come from universities in neighbouring countries, like Mike Munyati and Irene Ropa Mahamba from the University of Botswana. These young graduates and undergraduates in their early twenties were able to contribute to the educational programmes as teachers, teacher trainers, and curriculum developers. For example, Simon Matsvai, who had completed second year economics, managed to write a basic textbook on economics in Shona: this remains one of the few serious textbooks for adults available in the Shona language and is still the only economics book in that language. He later obtained a degree in economics with distinction after independence, and also succeeded in doing well in his MBA. He served as one of the best directors of the Zimbabwe Foundation for Education with Production (ZIMFEP), a non-governmental organisation formed by Dzingai Mutumbuka and myself to provide education, training, and job opportunities for ex-combatants and ex-refugees. Morgan Borerwa was able to run valuable courses on accountancy and to write an accountancy textbook. Irene Mahamba contributed valuable inputs into the teacher-training programme before she left for Maputo to be Simon Muzenda's administrative assistant.

Their dedication to the liberation struggle was to be tested not only by the physical hardships, but also by the problems of setting up a whole system of education without the necessary infrastructure, the trained and experienced personnel, and the educational materials. We had to build the system literally from nothing. Particular physical hardships included the chronic shortage of food; the physical labour of constructing houses and school shelters; the endemic diseases which plagued us such as dysentery, malaria, and the parasitic disease known as *matekenya*; but most of all the constant vigilance against bombing attacks. Food shortages and unbalanced diets led to night blindness, a problem that could become chronic. Constant attacks of malaria led to many people involved in the struggle developing diabetes, apparently a side effect either of malaria or of the chloroquine that was used to cure it.

A problem more difficult to solve was that of the tensions between the university group and the less educated leadership, some of whom had left the military to join the education department. The history of ZANU and ZANLA had been marked by such tensions, with the less educated harbouring serious suspicions about the educated, whom they saw as elitist and prone to opportunism. On the other hand, the educated often suffered from an unwarranted arrogance and superiority complex. These tensions were perhaps inevitable when only two per cent of the population in colonial Rhodesia was allowed access to secondary education and less than one per cent access to any form of tertiary education. The Nhari and Vashandi conflicts in 1974 and 1976 had exacerbated the tensions between the educated and the veterans. Both rebel groups had consisted of the young intelligentsia and had expressed opposition to the old leadership either of the nationalists, who were the founders of ZANU, or of the veterans, who were the original, mainly peasant guerrillas who had spearheaded the liberation struggle.

Some of the leaders at the school had chosen to leave the military to join the education department. This may have been because of their war injuries or because they genuinely did not want to participate further in the military struggle. These ex-military officers played an important role in organising and defending the schools, particularly because of the Rhodesian forces' tendency to bomb schools. In addition to class work, it was necessary to construct shelters, build up water and sanitation systems, establish agricultural programmes in order to provide fresh food to supplement the rice and tinned fish provided by the World Food Programme, and also to cook meals for thousands of children.

The daunting task of ensuring that these children we were responsible for received a good education minimised these inherent tensions. The training courses that allowed the less educated to improve their academic and professional qualifications also played a critical role in knitting together these two disparate groups into a united team.

Tensions often grew when a less educated person was placed in charge of a programme. For example, the early childhood programme was under the control of one of the women military commanders. Her grasp of English was poor, and she had to rely on her secretary to write letters and reports on her behalf. During the liberation struggle, military seniority was more important than academic achievement. However, many of the university graduates were able to handle this situation very pragmatically and wisely, and to accept the authority of the military specialists.

On one occasion, the military leadership decided to bring some 300 severely injured guerrillas to the school to allow them to recuperate. Schools were relatively well catered for, as the World Food Programme provided food for the refugee children. In the military camps, food was in serious short supply. Moreover, the injured were a serious liability in a situation of war. Military camps could be attacked, and it was difficult if not impossible for the severely injured and handicapped to escape to safety during a bombing raid. Speed was of the essence in escaping from a bomb attack, as the aeroplanes would drop the first bombs, swoop up into the air, circle, and return to drop further bombs. Those who survived were those able to flee from the target area as quickly as possible.

The children saw the injured guerrillas as heroes of the revolution. Naturally, they idolised the freedom fighters. However, we teachers were thoroughly taken aback when the war veterans quickly brought all school activities to a halt. They reorganised the school, removing the children from the dormitories, and instead housed them in their own *posto*. They told the children that they need no longer go to school or do any of the normal work that the children were responsible for. School and work were oppression, according to the war veterans. They encouraged the children to boycott both classes and work. Instead, the children's new duties entailed going to fetch beer for the war veterans from the local population.

After only three weeks, we who made up the school authority had to request the removal of the injured war veterans. They had managed to stop all school activities. These injured war veterans were full of bitterness. They had lost limbs that could never be replaced, they had received bullet wounds, and some had lost their sight. They had seen their roles as being that of military heroes, freeing the country from the colonial oppressors. Now their injuries embittered them. They had no respect for education. I remember seeing some of them tearing up the pages of a precious textbook in order to roll a cigarette. I watched in silence. I had personally purchased some of these textbooks in Dar es Salaam, and we had carefully transported them to our schools in Mozambique. Fortunately, the military authorities under Tongogara accepted our pleas and the war veterans were removed from the school. Only then were we able to resume our educational activities.

It was decided to bring teachers from the other schools at Doeroi, Chibavava, Mabvudzi, Nampula, Xai Xai, and Chindunduma itself to do teacher training and school administration courses at Matenje. These activities, together with curriculum development and research, could now take place in a more stable and peaceful atmosphere away from the war front.

A number of training courses soon started. A 20-week intensive teacher-training course began, using a combination of face-to-face teaching, distance education materials, microteaching, a case study, and four weeks of supervised teaching practice. Four such courses were held before the end of the war. The course, known as Teacher Education Part One (TEI), was a basic teacher-training course for primary school teachers. It consisted of in-depth study of the primary school curriculum, combined with study of the philosophical underpinnings of education, as well as child psychology and educational methodology. This was later to become the model for the Zimbabwe Integrated Teacher Education Course (ZINTEC) that was developed after independence to train 9,000 primary teachers to cope with the vast expansion of the primary education system. Zimbabwe's primary enrolment was to rise from 0.8 million children to over 2 million within two years, and it was necessary to provide the children with education while simultaneously allowing their teachers to receive professional training. The TEI model developed under war conditions was ideal for this purpose, allowing the teachers to be trained while at the same time providing education to the children.

One of the more hilarious incidents was a scientific experiment set up by Darlington Chitsenga. Utilising bits of pipe and rubber, he managed to construct a sophisticated distillation set-up during the course. We later found out that this was to be the prototype for the distillation of alcohol by the local people, a successful example of the transfer of technology! Alcohol was in serious short supply, and it appeared that our science lessons contributed towards developing a solution. Sadly, this may have been the beginning of the chronic alcoholism of a few of our colleagues who had been traumatised by their war experiences. They found solace in the alcohol they had learnt to brew for themselves.

Science and mathematics were very popular subjects, with the teacher trainees showing a great deal of creativity in developing suitable experiments for the children. I remember an excellent lesson on soil erosion that consisted of pouring water on a bare patch of soil and comparing this to pouring water on a well-grassed patch. This gave a graphic idea of soil erosion. Another trainee invented a way of teaching graphs by getting groups of children to measure their heights on the ever-available bamboo sticks. The different heights were then put together to form a graph.

One of the most useful sections of the TE1course was a two-day course on how to run a library. A very practical course, it turned out to be essential training for every teacher.

Another section dealt with primary healthcare, including immunisation. Rather tragically, one of our trainees was dying of tuberculosis. He had been a student at the United Teacher Training College in Bulawayo before joining the struggle, and during 13 years of formal education he had never been taught the value of immunisation. I remember his question in class: "Do you mean to say that if I had been vaccinated I would not have caught tuberculosis?" He subsequently died.

Students had to choose one technical subject on which they spent three hours a week. The choice was limited because of the shortage of staff and of equipment and materials. The subjects offered included agriculture, building, art, and tailoring. The most popular course was definitely tailoring. During the course the students made a shirt and a pair of trousers for themselves. As there was an endemic shortage of clothes, practical necessity accounted for the popularity of the tailoring course. Sally Mugabe had obtained some rolls of material and four sewing machines for us. We found it possible for as many as 70 students to use four sewing machines through a system of group work. Each group would concentrate on a different activity each week, with one group enjoying the use of the machines. This proved to be a very effective course.

The teacher trainees were required to attend classes from 7 a.m. to 4 p.m., with a short break for lunch. Such was the enthusiasm of these trainees that nearly all of them spent long hours studying and doing homework in the evenings, using little home-made diesel lamps for light. Matenje was fortunate in having an up-to-date library of over 3,000 teacher education books contributed by a donor and purchased in Britain. The library, run by sixth form students, was invaluable to the trainees.

A smaller group was selected to do Teacher Education Part Two (TEII). This was a 12-month course, with subject specialisation. Because of the war conditions, the only subjects offered at this level, which was equivalent to first year university level, were mathematics, English, geography, and biology. In addition, the teacher trainees studied educational philosophy, psychology, and methodology in greater depth. These teachers were being prepared to teach at secondary level. During their training, they also worked as tutors for the TEI course, enabling us to do group work with five to eight students in a group. This was aimed at redressing a problem that arose from the first TEI course, which consisted of 50 teacher trainees. Because of the shortage of lecturers, we always divided the students into four groups for group work. The result of this became very evident: this class always did group work, and always broke the classes into four groups, irrespective of the size of the class! The lessons they learnt from practice were much better learnt than those they had studied theoretically about group dynamics. We had to introduce more flexible group work in our teacher training.

A ten-week course on school administration was established for those in administrative positions who had completed TEI. The course combined theory and practice. Each student had to choose a practical programme through which to practise his or her theoretical premises. Many of the projects related to health and sanitation, and these were areas where a high standard of administration was obviously necessary. We were thus able to train a cadre of school administrators who could cover a variety of aspects of school life, including both the academic and the practicalities of life.

Although I had begun the teacher training programmes, I was fortunate to be able to hand over responsibility to some of my younger colleagues. Josephat Nhundu, who had joined the struggle after completing his master's degree in education at the University of Sierra Leone, soon took over this programme. This was an exacting as well as exciting experience for him, and enabled him to gain invaluable experience. After independence, he was able to utilise this experience in his various posts, including as a secondary school head and as a lecturer in charge of the distance education degree course at the University of Zimbabwe. He later became head of the distance education department at the University of Botswana.

The secretarial course was a three-month course in which secretarial skills such as note taking, accountancy, typing, and business practice were taught. A very high level of skills developed such that we were able to produce our own textbooks using manual typewriters and manual cyclostyling machines.

A separate school of administration was set up in Maputo under the then secretary general of ZANU, Edgar Tekere, and Robson Manyika, who was in charge of manpower development. Sister Janice McLaughlin, a Maryknoll sister, played a key role in establishing this important school. The intention was to train a strong cadre of administrators in preparation for independence. A small core of administrators was trained, but plans to transfer the school to Zimbabwe after independence failed. However, the schools that had been under the ZANU education department were transferred to Zimbabwe.

Sister McLaughlin had been imprisoned by the Smith regime for her work in the Roman Catholic Commission for Justice and Peace. She became one of the most ardent supporters of the liberation struggle and joined us in the education department of ZANU PF. She was a popular figure in the schools. Her journalistic training and skills contributed to our training programmes. For example, she started a newspaper at Matenje. She also managed to gain overseas support for the education department. We were fighting a psychological battle as well as a battle for survival. The former entailed winning support for ZANU worldwide, and as an American volunteer she was able to play an important role in this. The battle for survival meant we needed antibiotics and books, and she also managed to secure this type of support.

Another teacher training programme took place in Denmark under the auspices of the Development Aid from People to People (DAPP). Students were sent to Denmark to a DAPP college for one year. The programme proved to be expensive and its results were rather disappointing. Students spent a year doing many different things, with little specialisation – an expression of DAPP's philosophy of learning from life rather than from academic instruction.

At the same time, large numbers of students were sent to universities in Africa, in the West, and in the Eastern bloc under various scholarship programmes organised by ZANU. There were several hundred Zimbabweans at the University of Zambia as a result of President Kaunda's determination that Zimbabwe would have more graduates at independence than Zambia had had. Universities in Nigeria and Sierra Leone also took many Zimbabwean students. Others went to universities in the surrounding countries, including Botswana, Lesotho, Kenya, and Tanzania. Britain and the United States had several thousand Zimbabwean students. It was estimated in 1979 that there were over 4,000 Zimbabwean students in universities outside Rhodesia, leading to a situation where more Zimbabweans graduated outside the country than from the University of Rhodesia.

On one occasion, the Algerian government offered our school a scholarship for a telecommunications trainee. I selected a young man from our sixth form class on the basis of his excellent performance in mathematics. On the day he was to depart from the school, I went to say goodbye. He was to travel to Maputo in the back of the huge Scania lorries that brought supplies to the camps from Maputo. He was dressed in khaki shirt and trousers. I asked him where his clothes were, as he had no luggage at all. He replied, "I've got them on." Many years later, after independence, a young engineer showed up at my office. It was my young student with only one set of clothes. He had successfully completed his degree in telecommunications in Algeria.

Research was essential in a situation where there were many unknowns. It was mainly concentrated on an analysis of what was actually taking place in the schools and camps, such as the language used in different age groups, actual practice in the preschool, the educational levels of the people in the different camps, and so on. Military camp residents seemed to be divided equally between those who had never been to school and those who had. Most of those who had been to school had managed to complete their primary education, but only a minority had attained secondary education. We found out that some of our Grade 2 pupils already knew 400 words of English, although they could not speak English fluently. Nor could they read English. English had penetrated the culture so thoroughly that, for instance, all colours were in English. New concepts had entered African languages in an English form, as little work had been done to find equivalents in the African languages. An example of a word that every Grade 2 student knew in English was "camouflage", a concept that I remember my Form 4s once had problems with. Every child in the war had to know this word, as they were faced with the problem of their schools being bombed so often.

Curriculum development was part of the responsibility of the research department. It was essential to develop our own materials for languages, history, and other social sciences, as the existing materials were sometimes openly racist and misleading. For example, the white colonialists were always depicted as the bringers of civilisation to benighted blacks, whose sole pre-colonial occupation was to slaughter each other in tribal warfare. This was, of course, a serious distortion of the truth, but served to justify colonial rule. It was also important to provide the children with a vision of their future and the roles they would play in an independent Zimbabwe. Part of this vision was the elimination of the very tribal prejudices that had been enhanced by the colonialists as part of the tactic of divide and rule. Nine textbooks were developed during this period.

A number of English books were developed, mainly by James Mushamba. They dealt with the concepts that were an important part of the liberation struggle. Vimbisai Gertrude Nyakupinda developed a popular series of Shona primers, and Wadzanayi Betty Magadza developed an excellent set of teaching materials for primary art. Basic Ndebele was developed by Stotombi.

The history of one of our teacher trainers, Wadzanayi Betty Magadza, was typical of many of the former Vashandi leaders. Having trained as a primary school teacher in Waddilove mission, she joined the struggle out of youthful nationalism and enthusiasm. During the imprisonment of the majority of ZANU leaders during the *détente* period of 1975-76, people like Wadzanayi rose to leadership positions in the refugee camps under the umbrella of the Vashandi group. However, as noted earlier, Vashandi ascendancy lasted less than two years. When the main Vashandi leaders were, first, imprisoned by Tongogara's high command and, later, handed over to the Mozambican government, by whom they were held in Nampula, Wadzanayi remained a prisoner of ZANU for almost two years. One of the children in the school, a boy of 11 called Gift, described how she was captured. He told me that she had been forcibly captured at a refugee camp where she had been a leader and a teacher. She had been thrust into a sack and tied up. "I thought she was dead", he told me. Two years later, she was freed and returned to the school as a teacher, and later became a teacher trainer and curriculum developer.

By the time she joined the education department as a teacher, Wadzanayi had a small baby boy, Stephen. She had borne this child when she was in semi-incarceration. She hoped and believed that she would be able to marry Stephen's father after the war had ended, but this was not to be. After independence, she found, like many other women guerrillas, that she had been deserted by her former lover. As a single parent she sought respectability by marrying one of her other guerrilla admirers, but this marriage ended badly when she gave birth to an albino child. Traditionally, the woman is blamed for the birth of an albino, although it is a well-known scientific fact that albinism is caused when both parents have a recessive gene for albinism. This union ended in a divorce. Wadzanayi died prematurely after independence, as did her son Stephen. The war had blighted her life, as it has blighted the lives of many of its participants.

Many of the other teachers did not suffer such tragedies. The ZANU education system allowed them to be trained as teachers. After independence large numbers of both teachers and students went on to teachers' college and to university. Many became university teachers and school heads, as well as serving as primary and secondary school teachers. The education programme enabled some 300 teachers to be trained as well as several thousand children to receive a good education. The ZANU education programme proved an exhilarating experience as well as a peaceful haven for many guerrillas and refugees during the difficult war years. Much of this was due to the thirst for education found in almost every Zimbabwean.

Jeans Cassiah Rayo was an example of one of the young secondary school students who was able to build on her education through the education department. After independence she was able to continue her education at a teachers' college and at the University of Zimbabwe. Today she is the headmistress of one of the largest girls' schools in Harare,

Queen Elizabeth High School. She is typical of many young people who gained their initial teacher training in the refugee schools for Zimbabwean children in Mozambique.

Many of the thousands of children who attended our schools also benefited from having the opportunity of a sound education. Thus, our work meant that the war years were not lost years, but years of opportunity for these young children. Many of them have managed to go on to university.

There was also planning for education in semi-liberated zones where the Rhodesian authorities had closed down schools. By mid-1979, ZANU believed that it was appropriate to reopen schools under its own jurisdiction in areas that were seldom entered by Rhodesian forces. A number of educational personnel, including Bassie Bangidza and Emias Munemo, were sent to the war front to prepare for the reopening of schools. The plan was never effected, however, as the war came to a sudden end towards the end of 1979 as a result of the Lancaster House negotiations.

Plans were also made for the takeover of the country's education system after independence. Primary education was to be provided for all and secondary education was to be expanded by about 20 per cent per annum. After independence, primary education for all became a reality, utilising the model we had developed in Mozambique where we knew that education consisted of the knowledge and skills learnt by the pupils rather than of the buildings. In Mozambique, we did not have any permanent shelters as classrooms. The plan to expand secondary education by 20 per cent per year was quickly abandoned after independence, when government decided to expand secondary education more quickly because of popular demand. However, the secondary education model was also one we had tried out in Mozambique, where every child who passed the primary school leaving examination automatically entered secondary school.

Examinations for all levels from Grade 1 to Form VI were developed at Matenje by the research and curriculum development department under Chitofu and myself, and were taken in all the schools run by ZANU. Entry into secondary education was by examination, but both Grades 6s and 7s were allowed to sit for the end-of-primary examinations. 75 per cent of Grade 7s and 50 per cent of Grade 6s qualified to enter Form I. Education from preschool to Form IV was provided at all the schools set up by the ZANU education department. However, Form V and tertiary education was only available at Matenje. In addition, classes were organised at all refugee and military camps where those who were not directly undergoing arduous military training were able to attend some ordinary classes. Military camps that offered educational programmes included Ossibissa, Tembue, and Pungwe III. Even so, education was only a peripheral activity at military camps.

Matenje housed a large *crèche* or early childhood education centre, with over 200 preschool age children. The war situation meant that fathers and mothers were often freedom fighters whose duties might take them away from their families, in which case the children were left in the care of the *crèche*. There were also a number of war orphans who were looked after in the *crèche*. Children were divided into groups of six, each group under a caregiver who had received training in childcare.

The need for training of the preschool staff was important. While the young women who looked after the young children were caring and well intentioned, sometimes traditional beliefs about children would be so strong that they would interfere with the well being of the children. One strong belief was witchcraft, which is believed to be hereditary. One of the children was obviously suffering from some form of mental and emotional disability. This little girl of one or two years of age could not react with her surroundings. She did not cry, even when the adults pinched or punched her. The workers became quite convinced that the child was a witch. While they treated her with care in order not to provoke the witch in her, they also isolated her. One night, one of the dormitories in the *crèche* caught fire. The grass-walled and grass-thatched dwellings easily caught fire. The teachers rushed in to save the children, but this poor child decided to hide under a bed and was burnt to death.

Another serious problem was the staff's failure to understand nutrition and its links to emotional welfare. Some of the children refused to eat, for example. Suddenly separated from their mothers, surrounded by crowds of children all demanding attention from the strangers who looked after them, and subjected to bombings, many of these children were traumatised. One striking example led me to adopt one of the children, a small boy named Arnold. I used to take my daughter Chipo to the *crèche* every morning. Being very sociable, she loved going there to play with so many other children. One day I noticed a little boy of about two years of age. He was suffering from extreme malnutrition. Although there was a chronic shortage of food, the *crèche* was always favoured and had enough food for the children. The *crèche* teachers told me that the boy refused to eat, and that nothing they did could persuade him to take food. After some days of watching his self-imposed fast, I decided to take Arnold home with me. He at first refused to eat, but after I resorted to force-feeding for some days, he began to eat and behave normally. His mother had been sent on a military training mission in North Africa and, as was the custom, he had been left in the care of the *crèche*. So traumatic was the experience of separation from his mother that he lost the ability to speak and began to refuse to eat. After independence, I was able to find his mother and to effect a reunion.

Later, we managed to create a system by which small preschool children could be placed individually with teachers, rather than living in the large impersonal dormitories. They spent the day at the *crèche* and came home to live with the teachers who had taken responsibility for them as individuals. This new system worked well.

In our schools, classes were small, often with two teachers in charge, because we had a large number of teachers in training. Team teaching was the norm. The constant threat of bombing led to the practice by which all teachers left the camp at dawn with their classes and returned at sunset. The "classrooms" were literally grass shelters under trees. All classes had desks and benches made of bamboo, which was in plentiful supply in the area. They were situated around the periphery of the camp, one to two kilometres apart from each other. Supervisors had to walk about half an hour to the next class. The idea behind this wide scattering of classes was to avoid a direct hit by bombs on a considerable number of students at any one time.

Most of the time Matenje housed 2,000 to 3,000 students, split up into over 80 classes, although for a short period the number rose to over 9,000 students. The strategy of scattering the classes worked very effectively: the Rhodesian reconnaissance system easily identified the camp itself, but as there were very few people in the camp during the day, the frequent bomb attacks led to few casualties. Sometimes the camps were left with only about 20 cooks preparing the food for the day. The school cook, John Mapepa, preferred to work with a small team.

Pupils were required to attend five hours of lessons every day as well as to do manual work such as house-building, furniture making, gardening, and cooking for a further four hours a day. Some children went to classes in the morning and to their workstations in the afternoon; others worked every morning and went to classes in the afternoon. Right through the day you would find children singing while they were working. They felt empowered when they were able to build their own houses and make their own furniture, skills that were to stand them in good stead after independence. Many years after independence, I was to visit the beautiful house built by one of our former pupils for himself. Unfortunately, this was at his funeral. The young man never fully recovered from the half-dozen bombing raids he had endured during the liberation struggle, and had committed suicide.

Our schools provided the opportunity for many peasant children to receive education for the first time. As the colonial regime had accepted responsibility for school provision for blacks only in urban areas, and from 1968 had also banned Christian missionaries (the traditional providers of education to blacks) from opening any more schools in the country, many children were unable to obtain any form of schooling. Furthermore, the war situation had disrupted schooling, forcing schools in war zones to close down. The traditional thirst for education asserted itself even in the midst of war and the people welcomed the establishment of schools enthusiastically. This was one activity for which there was unanimous support.

The language policy we followed was to allow all children to learn the two main African languages of Shona and Ndebele, as well as English. As most of the children were Shona speaking, they learnt Shona and English as soon as they began Grade 1. At Grade 4 level they were introduced to Ndebele. The children had no difficulty coping with the three languages. It was wonderful to find children becoming literate in their mother tongue within a few weeks of entering school. Ndebele was also particularly popular. Probably the common Bantu roots of the two languages facilitated learning. Unfortunately, this policy could not be adopted after independence because of the cost factor.

We followed the traditional mathematics curriculum. However, in primary school science we concentrated on primary healthcare, emphasizing hygiene, balanced nutrition, and immunisation.

Gardening was an important as well as essential part of school activity, as the only fresh vegetables we had were grown at the school. The school was fortunate to have the services of a senior foreman from a commercial farm, who brought a high level of expertise to the task. Gardening was compulsory for every class. After independence, gardening continued to play an important part in the school system under the ministry of education's Education with Production policy.

One of the results of colonialism, combined with the effects of the war, was the large number of teenagers who had never been to school before. It was inappropriate to place them in the same classes as the young children or to make them follow the same curriculum as six year olds. It was also inappropriate to make them undergo the usual six to seven years of primary education. Instead, we developed a three-year primary education course for teenagers.

Large numbers of teenagers, some of whom had been child soldiers, were able to complete their primary education within three years and to go forward to secondary education. Most of these teenagers were boys, but the ferocity of the war was also beginning to force large numbers of young peasant girls to flee to Mozambique. These girls were able to go to school for the first time.

As education was free and compulsory, we soon developed a large secondary school section, from Form 1 to Form 6. All those who passed the primary school leaving examinations were allowed to enter secondary school. This was a far cry from the small percentage allowed to enter secondary schools in Rhodesia, and was an important model for what was to happen after independence.

The challenge before us was how to provide a good quality secondary education without the normal facilities of science laboratories, workshops, buildings, electricity, etc. We were fortunate in having a large number of teachers and teacher trainees, some of whom had done O levels (Grade 11). We also had a handful that had done A levels (Grade 13) as well as about a dozen who had done some years of college or university. These were trained under the secondary teacher-training course known as Teacher Education Part II (TEII).

Working in the less than ideal conditions of a refugee camp we were able to establish a high quality secondary section at a number of schools, although the A levels course was only offered at Matenje. We offered core subjects such as English, mathematics, general science, based on the Scottish science syllabus, history, and geography. Incidentally, the Scottish science syllabus was to become the foundation for the secondary science course after independence. For A levels we were limited to the subjects where we had graduate teachers, so the only subjects on offer were English literature, which I taught, mathematics and physics taught by Farai Karonga, geography taught by "Zizi" Mukanduri, and biology taught by Stephen Nyengera.

We were able to definitively break away from the colonial heritage of providing secondary education to only a minute percentage of the age group. The quality of secondary education even in the difficult conditions of refugee camps was high. Particularly impressive were the young students who entered the Sixth Form. Sixth Form education was open to all students who passed the equivalent of O level examinations. Many of our students were able to do well at university after independence. We also found that many banks were keen to employ our sixth formers after independence.

Adult education classes, mainly literacy classes, were held for refugees. Matenje school was situated a few kilometres from a refugee camp, and our teachers would go from the school to the refugee camp to run classes. The Paulo Freire method was used. This began with discussion of people's concerns. From this discussion a few key words would be chosen. For example, the word chibage, Shona for the staple diet of maize, would lead to the formation of words beginning with chi-. The Bantu languages' classificatory system, in which classes of concepts begin with a specific phoneme, was well suited to the Freire method. This method also fitted well into the ZANU political mobilisation system, which required the people to voice their grievances and to find solutions for them. Contrary to our experience after independence, when it was mostly women who came to literacy classes, in Mozambique our classes mainly attracted men.

The provision of education for children and for adults, and the professional training for teachers and administrators proved to be one of the most important achievements of the liberation struggle, transforming the sacrifices and suffering undergone by both pupils and teachers into achievements. Many thousands of children and adults received their education under these difficult conditions. These programmes provided an invaluable testing ground for policies that were to be pursued after independence, such as the six to seven years of primary education for all; the three year primary education programme for teenagers; combining education with production; secondary education for all; the combination of distance education, in-service, and full-time teacher training that was to become ZINTEC; adult literacy classes for those who demanded it; and preschool education for all, as well as upgrading courses for administrators and support staff. The liberation struggle was the birthplace of the ambitious education programme that followed Zimbabwe's independence.

CHAPTER 15

The Internal Settlement and Intensified Armed Struggle

The failure of the Geneva conference to come to an agreement on an interim government was followed by Ian Smith's attempt to install a black government of his own choice in power. Immediately after Geneva, he took the monumental step of changing the land laws that had prevented black people from owning land in so-called "white" areas. Now they would be able to buy and own agricultural, commercial, and industrial land, although it would still be impossible for them to own residential land in white areas. Although this change would affect only the wealthiest of blacks, it was, nevertheless, a step that could have far-reaching consequences in terms of dismantling the century old apartheid set-up of Rhodesia. Allowing wealthy blacks to buy land formerly reserved for whites could only win middle-class blacks to his side. If he himself could provide what the better off and better-educated nationalists were fighting for, he could divide the richer nationalists from their poorer counterparts and seriously undermine black unity within the country. Smith proceeded to follow a dual strategy, one of internal negotiations with the more pliable black leaders, such as Bishop Abel Muzorewa and the Reverend Ndabaningi Sithole, while at the same time making indiscriminate and frequent attacks into the neighbouring countries of Mozambique, Zambia, and Botswana. Refugee camps were routinely attacked.

Abel Muzorewa, who had won a great deal of popular support during the 1971 British-backed testing of black opinion within Rhodesia, became the closest of Smith's allies. Such was Muzorewa's popularity, that he was able to draw crowds of between 50,000 to 100,000 to his rallies during 1976. With this support, Muzorewa was certainly a credible leader. Meanwhile, Chief Jeremiah Chirau, a Smith supporter, agreed to form his own political party, the Zimbabwe United People's Organisation (ZUPO). This would give the impression that Smith's internal settlement was supported by the traditional leaders within the country, a major victory in a country where more than three-quarters of the people remained tied to peasant agriculture and to traditional mores. A third plausible leader was Ndabaningi Sithole, until recently the much lionised leader of ZANU and ZANLA, and still claiming to stand at the helm of the liberation movement, and more aptly of the liberation army. If these three leaders were to come to an internal agreement with Smith that brought about some credible form of "majority rule", Smith would have made his opponents in the Patriotic Front less relevant. The question was how credible could Smith be. Already his choice of partners revealed his real intentions.

Muzorewa was a peace-loving and obedient cleric who had little political experience and constantly revealed negotiating weaknesses and inexperience. His willingness to obey the Smith regime's authority unquestioningly was to cause his undoing. Moreover, he had been unable to gain any support from within the liberation armies. He was eventually to agree to the formation of a coalition government with Smith's Rhodesian Front, in which Smith was to retain the reins of power. Smith, in the final analysis, was willing to transfer only the cosmetic aspects of power to Muzorewa. Meanwhile, the critical areas of the army and the police remained in Smith's hands, resulting in a period of the most intense bloodshed both inside Rhodesia and in neighbouring countries. Consequently, Muzorewa's regime came to be identified with a devastating period of bloodshed combined with the rhetoric of liberation.

Chief Jeremiah Chirau fell into the mainstream of traditional chiefs. The colonial regime's utilisation of chiefs in their system of indirect rule had weakened the chiefs' traditional powers. Chiefs had become part of the Rhodesian civil service, paid a handsome salary by consecutive settler-colonial regimes. Those who questioned settler-colonial excesses, such as Chief Mangwende, were unceremoniously removed. The impotence of chiefs had been amply demonstrated, to the chagrin of their followers. Moreover, the counterbalancing power of traditional religious leaders made it possible to question the chief's exercise of power if it was felt to be against the people. This was constantly being done, with chiefs' powers being regularly put under scrutiny by traditional religious leaders. Thus, chiefs, particularly among the majority Shona people, had to constantly prove that they were the voice of the people rather than the voice of the colonial government. In such a situation, it was unlikely that people would follow their chiefs blindly.

An internal settlement to establish an interim government was signed on 3 March 1978 between Smith, Muzorewa, Sithole, and Chirau. Broadly based on the original Kissinger proposals made before the Geneva conference, Smith agreed to an executive council of four, with himself as the only white, the other three members being Muzorewa, Sithole, and Chirau. Blacks had half the seats in the executive council. However, knowing the weak position of the three black signatories, whose power derived from Smith himself, it was clear that Smith knew that he would always have the upper hand.

The ministerial council would consist of an equal number of blacks and whites, the blacks nominated by the three black leaders and the whites by Smith. Each ministry would have two ministers, one black and one white.

Parliament was to consist of 72 seats elected through universal suffrage, and a further 56 selected in three different ways, but representing whites. A constitutional amendment would require only 51 votes, but a change of the Internal Settlement Agreement would require 78 votes. White concerns were well articulated in the Agreement, and included:

– Property rights would be sacred. This would ensure the entrenchment of the land ownership system that allowed 3 per cent of the population, the whites, to control the best agricultural land as well as commercial, industrial, and residential property in the cities.

– The Rhodesian judiciary and public service would be retained intact.

– The police, army, and prisons would remain "efficient" and "free from political interference", vague expressions that were interpreted to mean retention of the colonial security services.

– The new government would bring about a ceasefire, reconsider the composition of the armed forces, look into the rehabilitation of war victims, deal with the release of political prisoners, remove racial discrimination, draft a new constitution, and register voters.

– Other areas of concern to whites, such as the retention of dual citizenship and pensions, were guaranteed.

It was clear that the negotiations had made no significant gains for blacks, who constituted more than 97 per cent of the population. Nevertheless, there was now a new "interim" government, half of whose members were blacks. The new government's racial composition could be deceptive. The later constitution agreed upon by the interim government and placed before whites only in a referendum lowered the number of seats for whites to 28, but retained control of the civil service, army, and judiciary in the hands of the whites.

Immediately after signing the Internal Settlement Agreement, both Muzorewa and Sithole flew to Britain to try to persuade the British government to accept the internal settlement. If the British government, which was still the legal constitutional authority in Rhodesia, could be so persuaded, the new government would have the recognition it sought. Despite concerted efforts to persuade the international community to accept the internal settlement, they were to fail.

As soon as he was appointed prime minister, Muzorewa again went to the United States at the invitation of Senator Jesse Helms, a Republican known for his extreme conservative views. Once again, Muzorewa's ignorance and insensitivity to the American political scene was evident, as he was apparently indifferent to the fact that President Jimmy Carter, a Democrat, would not necessarily view an alliance with Helms as the best recommendation. Nevertheless, Carter received Muzorewa for half an hour, listened to him, but promised nothing.

The interim government had only been in office for two weeks when it faced its first crisis: the new co-minister of justice, Byron Hove, had criticised the use of force by the Rhodesian police against black civilians. He suggested the restructuring of the police force to include some blacks in positions of authority. For this radical statement, he was instantly sacked. Muzorewa was unable to stop the expulsion. His decision to remain in a government in which he was so patently powerless now demonstrated beyond doubt his role as a puppet of Ian Smith.

As part of the agreement, the Smith-controlled forces began a programme of releasing political prisoners. Several thousand political prisoners were being held. It was decided to release over 700, but at the same time the trials and executions of freedom fighters continued. Apparently only the supporters of Muzorewa and Sithole were being released. Those who supported the Patriotic Front of ZANU and ZAPU remained in prison, as did members of the People's Movement, an internal movement set up by ZANU and ZAPU, and led by Canaan Banana.

A year later, in January 1979, the so-called interim government organised the referendum for whites only. Out of just over 67,000 white voters, 84.4 per cent supported the new constitution that guaranteed them a further period of white rule. It was noteworthy that black opinion was not tested.

Following the referendum, elections were held in April 1979, with universal suffrage for the 72 black seats. The main contenders were Muzorewa's ANC, Sithole's faction of ZANU, and Chief Chirau's ZUPO. Despite instructions to the people from both ZANU and ZAPU to boycott the elections, 1.8 million people, roughly half the electorate, voted. Some signs of dissent were evident, with teachers in Shabani being arrested and imprisoned for refusing to act as election officials. Despite such protests, the large voter turn out indicated that the people were eager for an end to the war and for an opportunity to return to normal life. More than 64 per cent voted for Muzorewa's ANC. Sithole's group managed to obtain 14 per cent of the votes, whereas Chirau's ZUPO obtained only 6 per cent. The new parliament was to be dominated by the ANC, which had won 51 seats. With Smith's Rhodesian Front holding 28 seats, the new government was to be a coalition of the ANC and the Rhodesian Front. However, the constitution guaranteed white control of the civil service, judiciary, army, and police, and it was Muzorewa's willingness to relinquish these critical areas to Smith's control that was to bring about his downfall.

Soon after Muzorewa's accession to power, splits began to appear in his party, the ANC that had been hastily formed during *détente* to include as many well-known nationalists as possible. James Chikerema left to form his own political party, the Zimbabwe Democratic Party.

The alliance with Ndabaningi Sithole also came under serious strain, with Sithole accusing the Smith regime of having cheated to bring Muzorewa to power. Despite evidence of white employers ferrying their black workers to the polling booths, it was clear that a substantial section of the black electorate was prepared to give Muzorewa a chance to demonstrate whether his government would be able to improve the lot of Africans in the country. This realism typifies much of Zimbabwean politics, with voters willing to choose the best option from a limited number of choices. In this case, among Muzorewa, Sithole, and Chirau, they clearly saw Muzorewa as their best choice.

Now that Muzorewa had the opportunity to prove his mettle, he revealed his Achilles heel: his willingness to see Ian Smith and his Rhodesian Front party as his backers and to regard the outside world, in particular the Frontline states, the Organisation of African Union (OAU), Britain, and the United States as his enemies. He publicly spoke of the sanctions still supported by both Britain and the United States as examples of "insanity". He particularly saw the Patriotic Front alliance of ZANU and ZAPU as his enemies, calling the freedom fighter "terrorists". The continued air raids into neighbouring countries, as well as in the contested and liberated zones within the country, did not win him support at a time when almost every black family now had a son or daughter in the liberation struggle, working either as chimbwidos or mujibhas, the young girls and boys who helped guerrillas within the country, or as freedom fighters themselves. Many more had enrolled in schools in Mozambique and Zambia, and the bombardment of these schools was to cause much concern to their parents. Muzorewa proudly proclaimed that he, as minister of defence, had ordered the bombing of "terrorist bases" outside the country, particularly in Zambia, as he appeared to have an obsessive preoccupation with the position of Joshua Nkomo. Nkomo had been an earlier rival in the bid for an internal settlement.

An incident that was to highlight Muzorewa's complicity in the killings was the massacre of 183 auxiliaries belonging to his rival, Ndabaningi Sithole. At a stage when each black political party had established its own army, both Muzorewa and Sithole had received recognition and assistance from the Smith regime in setting up their own armies, known as auxiliary forces. These auxiliaries numbered about 11,000 and were generally under the control of the Rhodesian army and police. They were being used to control the local population. In July 1979, 183 auxiliaries belonging to ZANU (Sithole) were massacred. The Rhodesian army communiqué announced that they had been killed in "crossfire", then a popular expression for unexplained killings. Muzorewa made a statement blaming the auxiliaries themselves. He described the incident as a "regrettable affair", but said the "mutinous behaviour" of the militiamen left the regular government forces with no other option. Officials belonging to ZANU (Sithole) present during one of the two massacres, gave a different account. *The Guardian* newspaper of London, published reports by Timothy Mapuranga and Dipuka Nyaka, two auxiliaries who survived the massacres:

> ... auxiliaries were gathered in four groups by the white military instructors on the morning of July 20, close to the village of Gokwe in western Rhodesia. The groups were allegedly told that they would be taught how to communicate with an aircraft and how to use the new NATO gun.
>
> When an aircraft appeared over the seated auxiliaries, however, it allegedly opened fire and troops placed around the camp did likewise. Mr. Mapuranga said: "There was a lot of dust and smoke. Helicopters were hovering over our heads to stop us from leaving the place where we were being shot in cold blood. I ran away from the scene. The soldiers saw me and began to aim at me. Bullets tore my clothes."
>
> Other survivors also claimed that they were fired on by aircraft as well as ground troops after being assembled by the instructors... "We were told to put our weapons down as the aircraft approached, so as not to make the pilots nervous", said one survivor, Dipuka Nyaka. "As the plane was passing, machine gun fire was coming from it. We just scattered, stepping over the bodies of our comrades." Another survivor said helicopters then pursued the auxiliaries fleeing into the bush.[1]

Sithole's auxiliaries had been trained in Uganda by Idi Amin, and were described by the Rhodesian forces as "mafia-type gangs" guilty of intimidating the "tribes people". They were accused of murder and rape.[2] The Rhodesians were prepared both to ally with as well as to kill Sithole's forces when it suited them. Sithole remained within the new government, although he made some feeble protests. His inability to

---

1. "Muzorewa Describes Auxiliary Massacre as 'Regrettable'", *The Guardian*, London, 18 August 1979. Published in Goswin Baumhögger, *The Struggle for Independence*, Vol. V, Institute of African Studies, Africa Documentation Centre, Hamburg 1984, p. 993.
2. Radio Salisbury broadcast of 20 July 1979. Published in Goswin Baumhögger, *The Struggle for Independence*, Vol. V, Institute of African Studies, Africa Documentation Centre, Hamburg 1984, p. 993.

protect his followers was exactly what had led ZANLA forces to reject him earlier in 1976. History was repeating itself.

Another example of this was an accusation by Muzorewa in June 1976 that Sithole had organised a squad to assassinate him. This was the same accusation that had been made by Ian Smith in the trial of Sithole, where the infamous "Mrs. X", an emissary of Sithole, gave evidence against him. Ironically, the very same accusation was to be made twenty years later in 1995, when Sithole was once again accused of sending assassins, this time to kill Robert Mugabe. None of these attempted assassinations ever succeeded.

The credibility of Muzorewa, Sithole, and Chirau suffered mainly because of the continued slaughter of civilians by the interim government's security forces. Controlled entirely by the Rhodesian Front, their aim was to wipe out any sign of support for the freedom fighters. If guerrillas were sighted in a village, the Rhodesian forces were prepared to wipe out the whole village. And this was indeed what they did, killing women and children in the process. Numerous massacres of villagers followed. Muzorewa himself protested against the killing of 105 "tribesmen", apparently oblivious of the fact that this was committed in the name of his government. Unable to engage the guerrillas, the Rhodesian forces struck the people among whom the guerrillas lived.

This was also a period when a number of missionaries were killed, most notably at Elim mission in Eastern Rhodesia and at Makumbe Roman Catholic mission. The Smith regime placed the blame on the liberation movements, whereas the liberation movements blamed Smith's Selous Scouts, Smith's own guerrilla group formed to fight the guerrillas at their own game. To date, it has not been possible to state definitively which side was responsible the massacres of missionaries, although there is circumstantial evidence that the Smith regime's failure to investigate the Makumbe mission massacres indicated that they might have been complicit. The Smith regime's tendency to look upon missionaries as accomplices of the guerrillas may have led its forces to make these attacks. Moreover, the use of the Selous Scouts and of mercenaries brought out the more criminal characteristics of war.

Because they were unable to win the war within the country, the Smith regime adopted the strategy of attacking the neighbouring countries of Mozambique, Botswana, and Zambia. Flaunting their aerial superiority, they even attacked ZIPRA guerrillas within the capital city of

Lusaka on several occasions in 1978 and 1979, seriously humiliating President Kenneth Kaunda and his government. Smith was prepared to undermine Kaunda's government, even though Kaunda had done so much to destroy communism, the same policy that the Smith government claimed motivated their war. The late Ariston Chambati, a prominent member of ZAPU and later to be minister of finance in Zimbabwe, was caught up in an attack on the centre of Lusaka during this period. Zambian railway lines and wagons were attacked, for example at Magoye in October 1978.

Mozambique alone suffered more than 120 attacks, with over 1,000 Mozambican civilians killed. In particular, the Smith regime attacked economic and infrastructure targets in Mozambique, such as railway lines. An agricultural research station in Mozambique was also attacked in an attempt to disrupt agricultural activity. There was no attempt to hide their intentions. By December 1978, Mozambique was being attacked on virtually a daily basis, and this was to continue until the successful completion of the Lancaster House constitutional conference.

Botswana was also mercilessly attacked because it allowed Zimbabwean refugees to remain in the country. The objective was clear: to intimidate the Frontline states into ceasing all support for nationalists and their guerrilla armies.

Refugee camps, particularly schools, were easy targets, and these were attacked again and again.

Although ZANU itself was banned within Rhodesia, it had formed an internal party known as the People's Movement led by the Reverend Canaan Banana, and including in its midst a large number of well-known leaders such as James Bassoppo Moyo, a well respected social worker. The main task of the People's Movement was to ensure that the country remained united behind ZANU while at the same time mounting a campaign to recruit freedom fighters and to win support for them. So effective was the People's Movement, that the majority of them were imprisoned during the period of the internal settlement. As a result, Canaan Banana was arrested and was to spend the next few years in prison.

Meanwhile, the war was intensifying within the country. Attempts to crush guerrilla support by vicious attacks on civilians resulted instead in increased support for the guerrillas. The Rhodesian forces, told to hit as hard as possible, and bolstered by white mercenaries with a thirst for blood, were now seen more and more as enemies of the people. In the first nine months of 1978 alone the regime claimed to have killed more than 3,300 people. The tally over the previous few years was said to be over 10,000 within Rhodesia, with a further 1,600 in neighbouring countries.[1]

The intensification of the war meant that guerrillas were no longer fighting as isolated groups, but were now able to adopt the tactics of conventional warfare. The blowing up of railway lines, fuel depots, air force and army bases, meant that Smith was in effect losing the war. The rail link between Bulawayo and Wankie was blown up in July 1978, and the main rail link between Salisbury and Bulawayo was blown up in September 1978, causing a disruption of the flow of goods to and from South Africa, the only neighbouring country that had not applied sanctions to Rhodesia. These attacks were part of a coherent programme to disrupt trade links.

It was during this period that the guerrillas began to enter the capital city, then known as Salisbury, and to attack targets within the outskirts. The bombing of Woolworths, a shop in the centre of the city, in August 1977 brought the reality of the war to the heart of white settlement. The daring attack on a fuel storage depot in Salisbury in December 1978 hit the Rhodesian regime very hard, as the fuel shortage was already very severe. The subsequent fire that lit up the whole city to a radius of 25 miles made it difficult to continue the myth that the Rhodesians were winning the war. Fuel depots were to be blown up elsewhere in Rhodesia, including Fort Victoria.

By now, more than 70 per cent of the country was under martial law, with the population driven into the unpopular "protected villages", and constant battles taking place between the Rhodesian forces and ZANLA and ZIPRA forces, who continued to operate separately. Guerrilla incidents were now taking place on a daily basis, with the Rhodesians unable to control the situation. The only action they could take

---

1. Figures given by the Rhodesian regime and reported in the *Daily News*, Dar es Salaam, 11 September 1978. Published in Goswin Baumhögger, *The Struggle for Independence*, Vol. IV, Institute of African Studies, Africa Documentation Centre, Hamburg 1984, p. 662.

was to attack targets in neighbouring countries, and this they did mercilessly.

The downing of a commercial aircraft by ZIPRA, using Soviet SAM 7 anti-aircraft missiles, in September 1978, left a traumatic mark on the Rhodesian psyche. The killing of white civilians had so far been very limited, as ZANLA guerrillas had been instructed to strike at military personnel only. Now the use of anti-aircraft missiles as well as the slaughter of civilians would bring the war to a different stage, with a potential for civilian targets being more common. A second attack on a commercial aircraft in February 1979, once again by ZIPRA, added to the consternation. The only area where the Rhodesian forces had maintained their superiority was in the air. They had carried out many aerial attacks, both within the country and in neighbouring states. The entrance of ZIPRA into the war in 1978, with their highly trained as well as better equipped forces, could spell a drastic change in the fortunes of the Rhodesian forces. They were now likely to lose their one and only advantage. With ZANLA controlling the situation on the ground, and the possibility of ZIPRA destroying Rhodesian superiority in the air, the Rhodesians had no possibility of military victory. The Rhodesian army leaders could clearly see this: a political solution was the only way out.

The severe shortage of manpower within the Rhodesian army was also being felt, despite the forced conscription of all able-bodied white men. Young white men were leaving the country to avoid conscription. My brother Allan was one of those who had left the country rather than serve in the Rhodesian army. Such was the desperation that by October 1978, the regime had decided to conscript blacks, targeting African males between the ages of 18 and 35 who had had three years of secondary education. University students were to be one of the main targeted groups, leading to protests by black students. The forced conscription of young black men was to have the opposite effect, causing many young undergraduates and graduates to flee the country, some of them entering Mozambique to join ZANLA, in preference to fighting for the Smith regime.

During this period ZANLA forces were able to capture many enemy forces. Four white prisoners were released in early February 1979. One of them, a seasoned British army major, said: "I was impressed with the guerrilla efficiency in the field, their discipline and particularly their high morale."[1]

While the Rhodesian forces continued to bomb neighbouring countries now almost on a daily basis, they were rapidly losing control within the country itself. The ZANLA guerrillas were now fighting in three-quarters of the country, and were making more frequent attacks on the capital city. There was every likelihood that Rhodesian air superiority would soon be decimated by ZIPRA, and the visit of Soviet leader Podgorny to Angola and Zambia could herald the entrance of more sophisticated Soviet armaments into the war to support ZIPRA. This could end any possibility of a Rhodesian victory. Many areas of the country could now only be reached by the Rhodesian forces by air and helicopter, with freedom fighters taking over administrative control. In 1979, the ZANU education department, of which I was a member, was making plans to set up schools in liberated and semi-liberated zones, for example. At the same time, the economy had been totally disrupted by the war, with all able-bodied white men having to serve in the army. Sanctions were definitely biting.

It was in such a situation that only the most unrealistic of Rhodesians could go on believing that they could win. The majority saw the need either to flee or to have a political solution. Tens of thousands of Rhodesians had now left the country. Reality could not be avoided. Signs that the end was near came when even members of Smith's government began to resign. The resignation of Rollo Hayman, co-minister of internal affairs, in early 1979 and of General Hickman in March 1979 were ominous signs that the regime's end was near.

The British elections at the end of April 1979 brought Margaret Thatcher to power. For more than a decade and a half, the British government had washed its hands of the Rhodesian problem, leaving Ian Smith to do as he wished. Economic sanctions had been applied, sometimes half-heartedly, but by 1979 their effects were being felt. Now the change from a Labour government to a Conservative government was to see a rapid movement to re-establish British responsibility for

---

1. Article by Anthony Lewis entitled, "Talking with Mr. Mugabe", *New York Times*, 8 February 1979. Published in Goswin Baumhögger, *The Struggle for Independence*, Vol. V, Institute of African Studies, Africa Documentation Centre, Hamburg 1984, p. 805.

Rhodesia and to bring about a conclusion to the political impasse and to the escalating war.

The British foreign secretary, Lord Carrington, believed that the election of the Muzorewa government through universal suffrage had brought about a significant change in the situation. Both he and his prime minister, Margaret Thatcher, met with Bishop Muzorewa, and gave every indication of being willing to accept the Muzorewa regime as legitimate. There was now the possibility of an end to economic sanctions, allowing the regime to re-establish its economic lifeline with the outside world.

However, Thatcher, a shrewd politician, was eager to win the support of the Commonwealth, which met in Lusaka in August 1979. The Commonwealth secretary general, Shridath Sunny Ramphal, played a key role, as did President Julius Nyerere, in persuading the British government to accept whichever government the majority of Zimbabweans elected. In Lusaka, a deal was hammered out that would enable Zimbabwe to be born through a constitutional conference that would remove the impediments that still remained under the Muzorewa-led government, namely white minority control of the civil service, judiciary, army, and police. In other words, Zimbabwe would have a constitution similar to those that other former British colonies had received at independence.

CHAPTER 16

The Lancaster House Agreement

Lord Carrington, the British foreign secretary and chairman of the Lancaster House constitutional conference, made it clear that the British had decided to grant independence to Rhodesia under the same conditions that it had done other African countries. This would entail "that the principle of majority rule must be maintained and guaranteed; that there must be guarantees against retrogressive amendments to the constitution; that there should be immediate improvement in the political status of the African population; that racial discrimination is unacceptable; that we must ensure that, regardless of race, there is no oppression of the majority by the minority or of the minority by majority; and that what is agreed must be shown to be acceptable to the people of Rhodesia".[1]

The Patriotic Front alliance of ZANU and ZAPU were intent on ensuring that the post-independence government actually controlled the army, police, judiciary, and civil service, unlike the situation under the Muzorewa regime. They therefore posed a number of questions:

1. Will the people of Zimbabwe be really sovereign and be able to exercise their sovereign authority?

2. Whose army shall defend Zimbabwe and its people? It must be noted here that 60 per cent of the present white army are mercenaries.

3. Whose police force shall protect the people of Zimbabwe?

4. What type of administration and judiciary shall serve the people of our country, Zimbabwe?

5. Will any ethnic, religious, tribal or other group be able to hold the rest of the people of Zimbabwe hostage?

---

1. Opening speech by Lord Carrington, 10 September 1979. Published in Goswin Baumhögger, *The Struggle for Independence*, Vol. VI, Institute of African Studies, Africa Documentation Centre, Hamburg, 1984, p. 1049.

6. How do we create the situation for the holding of free and fair elections?
7. Whose laws will govern such elections?
8. In particular, apart from the British supervisors and the Commonwealth observers, who will administer the elections and ensure the safety of the voters and candidates?
9. What will be the future of the people's land?[1]

There was clearly some nervousness that the elections would be rigged to favour Muzorewa if they were administered and supervised by the settler-colonial regime.

Muzorewa, on the other hand, saw the Lancaster House conference as a way of legitimising his government, which he believed had been democratically elected. His main aim was to convince the British and the world to lift sanctions. While he expressed gratitude to the British government, he once again attacked the Frontline states, particularly their chairman, President Nyerere of Tanzania, for trying to be "kingmakers" by supporting the Patriotic Front alliance of ZANU and ZAPU against the will of the Zimbabwean people. He claimed to be for "unity", while denouncing the Patriotic Front as representing "disunity".[2] This was at a stage when national unity was so critical that every political party and every politician claimed to be supporting it.

Ian Smith hoped to use the conference to steer world opinion towards accepting the solution he had engineered of establishing a majority of black parliamentarians, with an equal number of black and white cabinet ministers, while real power was maintained by the whites. In particular, he sought to retain veto power by the white minority as a safeguard. In other words, the small group of whites in parliament could negate any decisions made by the rest of parliament.

---

1. Opening speech by J. Nkomo on behalf of the Patriotic Front, 11 September 1979. Published in Goswin Baumhögger, *The Struggle for Independence*, Vol. VI, Institute of African Studies, Africa Documentation Centre, Hamburg 1984, pp. 1050–51.
2. A. Muzorewa's message for the People of Zimbabwe Rhodesia, 15 September 1979. Published in Goswin Baumhögger, *The Struggle for Independence*, Vol. VI, Institute of African Studies, Africa Documentation Centre, Hamburg 1984, pp. 1057.

One of the first requirements was for Ian Smith to drop his insistence on the white minority's veto power in parliament over any changes to the constitution. Smith stubbornly refused to back down, even going to the extent of leaving the conference to return home. He finally capitulated when his own delegation, now led by Muzorewa, voted against his stand. That meant that even his closest supporters, Chris Anderson and David Smith, who had loyally served him as ministers, had decided to go against him. The final straw was reported to be a sharp message from the head of the Rhodesian army, Lt. General Peter Walls, which stated that the Rhodesian conflict could not be ended by military means and required a political settlement. Smith's capitulation was the first victory leading to a negotiated settlement at the Lancaster House conference. An agreement would require equally serious compromises by the other negotiators.

Next it was necessary to persuade Muzorewa to accept new elections, a step he was loathe to take as he insisted that he had been elected democratically and that those election results had to be respected. In the spirit of generosity, Muzorewa conceded on 5 October 1979, after almost a month of negotiations, that he would accept a new round of elections. He said: "Although we feel that another election is unnecessary and unfair to our electorate in Zimbabwe Rhodesia, we are, however, confident that our people will reaffirm their desire for and commitment to genuine democracy through the new election, in the same manner as they did during that which took place as recently as April."[1] This confidence in the loyalty of the electorate was to prove mistaken.

Finally, there was the problem of how far the Patriotic Front of ZANU and ZAPU would accept constitutional provisions that were not wholly to their liking. A number of issues related to race, such as the reservation of seats for the minority white population, the granting of citizenship and passports to settlers who had entered the country after 1965, the year of the illegal Unilateral Declaration of Independence by the Smith regime, and the holding of dual citizenship by settlers. The Patriotic Front eventually agreed that 20 per cent of the seats would be

---

1. Statement by A. Muzorewa on accepting the British proposal, 5 October 1996. Published in Goswin Baumhögger, *The Struggle for Independence*, Vol. VI, Institute of African Studies, Africa Documentation Centre, Hamburg 1984, pp. 1097.

reserved for whites for at least seven years, and this provision lasted until 1987. While citizenship was granted to all those who had lived in the country for more than five years, dual citizenship was not accepted.

A more serious disagreement occurred over the Bill of Rights, which would ensure that ownership of land remained in white hands after independence. Land could not be confiscated from whites, but would have to be bought on a "willing seller, willing buyer" basis. The British government made vague promises to provide some money for the purchase of farms, and argued that the United States and other countries could provide more money for this purpose. It was strange that a highly developed and wealthy country such as Britain felt it could not afford to pay for the compensation of white farmers, but, nevertheless, expected a black government of a much poorer developing country to do so. However, despite their virulent objections, the Patriotic Front was forced to accept this part of the independence agreement.

The Bill of Rights gave anyone the right to open a school. This caused a furore, as the Patriotic Front interpreted the clause as tantamount to allowing whites to open racially segregated schools. It remained part of the Bill of Rights, but turned out to be much less problematic than expected, as government had both financial and regulatory powers to control the opening of schools.

The stipulation that the public service commission include at least two former civil servants, which, of course, meant they would be white, was accepted. However, it was agreed that the army, police, and judiciary would be appointed by the president on the advice of the prime minister. The Patriotic Front's contention that an executive presidency would be preferable to a constitutional presidency was rejected.

The Patriotic Front's major victories at the constitutional conference table included the right of the post-independence government to control the police, army, and judiciary. The post-independence government would have the right to appoint the members of the public service commission. However, the commission was to have virtual autonomy in the designation and promotion of civil servants, once it was appointed. This was to provide some protection for the civil service against political interference in the carrying out of its duties.

In the end, all parties made some concessions. The Patriotic Front, whose military victories had made the political settlement urgent and inevitable, were forced to make major and quick concessions by their backers, namely Presidents Samora Machel and Julius Nyerere. President Machel in particular made it clear that he would not allow ZANU, one of the main partners in the Patriotic Front, to continue its military offensives from Mozambican territory. This momentous decision was probably due to a combination of war weariness and the conviction that the settler-colonial regime had already made very major concessions. Machel's close rapport with British Prime Minister Thatcher contributed to Mozambique's determination to stop further military support for the Zimbabwean guerrillas.

On the other hand, ZANLA leaders such as Josiah Tongogara, who had led the main military offensive against the settler-colonial regime now led by a coalition of Abel Muzorewa and Ian Smith, were well aware of the growing criticism of their leadership within ZANLA. The Nhari and Vashandi rebels were precursors of future opposition movements from within, and the challengers were likely to be younger, better educated, with access to higher technology, and probably more left wing. The settler-colonial regime's last stronghold, its control over technology and air power, would need to be broken. There was a possibility that this could be achieved by the rival liberation army ZIPRA, under ZAPU. If ZANLA itself were to fill this gap, it would need access to higher technologies controlled by more highly educated military personnel. This was clearly a dangerous trend for a military leadership whose personnel mainly had only primary education or, at best, a few years of secondary education. Thus, there was pressure from within ZANLA itself to accept a compromise.

At the political level, it was clear that those leaders who took over an independent Zimbabwe would remain in place for the next few decades. The Lancaster House negotiations offered the incumbents this golden opportunity. If they did not grasp this chance, the next opportunity would come to a new set of leaders.

The Muzorewa-Smith regime was also anxious to conclude the war before the economy completely collapsed. White Rhodesians were fighting for the economic advantages that the continuation of the war was rapidly destroying. The Rhodesian regime knew it was totally unable to win the war by military means. Continuation of the war would only lead to certain defeat. It would also lead to greater bloodshed and further destruction of the infrastructure. Most feared of all was the clear radicalisation of the black population. It was better to capitulate before all was lost. Their control of the air still enabled them to bomb both Zambia and Mozambique in a show of strength and as a form of coercion during the Lancaster House conference. A bridge on the Tazara railway line linking Zambia to Tanzania was bombed. A British schoolboy and some British lorry drivers who happened to be near the bridge were even captured by the Rhodesians. A ZANLA military camp was attacked, but the Rhodesian casualties were so high that press reports had to be heavily censored. Both the capture of the British civilians and the high Rhodesian casualties proved an embarrassment to the regime.

Thus, all sides were ready for a compromise and a compromise was reached.

CHAPTER 17

Prelude to Independence

Having agreed to the main features of a post-independence Zimbabwe, the challenge was to steer the country towards independence as quickly and as peacefully as possible. Britain, which had shrugged off responsibility for the situation in Rhodesia for so long, now agreed to reassert its authority through the appointment of a governor, Lord Soames, to take over until the elections. Soames's task was to ensure a ceasefire and a peaceful changeover of government.

The Lancaster House agreement demanded that the Rhodesian army remain in barracks and that the liberation movements place all their soldiers in camps guarded by British policemen and Commonwealth soldiers under British command. This involved an enormous act of trust on the part of the liberation movements, as it was possible that once the guerrillas were confined to assembly points, they could be attacked and killed. The fear that the Rhodesians would bomb the disarmed guerrillas assembled in enclosed spaces where casualties would be high was real. The Rhodesians had indeed done just that to Sithole's Ugandan trained guerrillas less than six months before.

Tongogara once again showed his superior grasp of both political and military strategy. While officially accepting the Lancaster House agreement for all freedom fighters to surrender themselves to the British forces at these holding camps, ZANU and ZANLA secretly decided that only a section of their forces should surrender. Some 20,000 guerrillas were to enter these camps. Another group, consisting of several thousand experienced political commissars, were deployed in every village, ostensibly to protect the people from attacks from enemy forces, but in addition to this role, to attempt to influence the outcome of the elections. The third group remained poised outside the borders, ready to enter the country if any unexpected catastrophe took place, such as the killing of their comrades in the holding camps. ZANU and ZANLA were prepared for every eventuality. This clever strategy was to lead to serious disagreement with ZANU's Patriotic Front partner, ZAPU, which was to dispute the results of elections in which a large proportion of the ZANLA guerrillas had remained in every village.

This strategy was transparent to all, but it was not possible for the British, the Rhodesians, or for the ZAPU partners in the Patriotic Front to change the situation. ZANU asserted that all its guerrillas had entered the assembly points, and it was quite impossible to check the veracity of their claims.

Meanwhile, a serious debate began within the Patriotic Front alliance on whether they should fight the elections together, or whether they should fight it as separate political parties. ZAPU believed it would be more advantageous for the two parties to remain united throughout the election. This view was shared by all the Frontline countries, and President Samora Machel was its most eloquent proponent, using Tongogara's funeral to underline this point with heartfelt words. Unmindful of such sentiments, many in ZANU, led by Eddison Zvogbo, believed that ZANU would be able to win virtually all the seats in the areas dominated by the Shona ethnic group, which comprised 80 per cent of the population. This victory was assured by the fact that ZANLA now controlled most of the rural areas, and its political commissars remained at their stations throughout the election period.

Tongogara, who was fiercely opposed to ethnic analysis and ethnic loyalty and, therefore, to Zvogbo's views, believed that it would be more advantageous for the two parties to remain together throughout the election period. This was not because he had any personal loyalty to the ZAPU leader, Joshua Nkomo, whom in reality he regarded with some suspicion, but because he saw the potential increase in his own power through the unification of ZANLA and ZIPRA under his leadership. Tongogara regarded all politicians with scepticism, and certainly Mugabe was not exempt from this suspicion. A united ZANLA and ZIPRA would wield immense power after independence, and would place politicians from both ZANU and ZAPU at the mercy of a powerful, united, and victorious army. Tongogara enjoyed the confidence and support of both armies and had succeeded in eliminating his opponents politically, if not physically. He was now poised for greater challenges and victories. Josiah Tongogara was a serious challenger for the leadership of ZANU.

His unexpected death on Boxing Day 1979, just at the advent of independence, brought an end to the dominance of the military led by

Tongogara's veterans. They had won the war, but now that the war was over, they were soon to lose their political dominance after the loss of their brilliant, charismatic, and ruthless leader. Tongogara died in a bizarre accident. Given the potentially powerful role he would have played in an independent Zimbabwe, there were natural suspicions that he had been killed by rivals within ZANU, but there was no evidence to support these suggestions. Within ZANU, those who trusted fervently in the intervention of the ancestral spirits in the affairs of their offspring believed that the ancestral spirits had ensured that Zimbabwe was saved from the rule of Tongogara, as had been foretold by the spirit mediums. His death brought deep sorrow to his supporters and admirers, and rejoicing among his opponents.

Another problem had to be solved during this transitional period: the opponents of Mugabe and Tongogara, some 70 of whom were still detained in Mozambique, had to be dealt with. These opponents were the Vashandi and the Hamadziripi groups. Simon Muzenda was sent to offer reconciliation so that ZANU would return to an independent Zimbabwe as a united group, but only a handful of the Vashandi returned to the ZANU fold under Mugabe's leadership.

The Hamadziripi group subsequently joined Ndabaningi Sithole's ZANU Mwenje to fight the 1980 elections, and were to face a resounding defeat. Many of them were resolutely opposed to Mugabe as a person and had remained loyal to Sithole. Sithole was fortunate to have attracted a large amount of money for his election campaign, which at least enabled his top lieutenants to secure property for themselves as compensation for their long years in the struggle. Most of them were able to buy either a house or a farm during this period when property prices were at an all-time low. It was enlightening to see the ZANU Patriotic Front leaders concentrating on winning the elections and the ZANU Mwenje leaders concentrating on the acquisition of personal property at that crucial stage.

Danger also lurked from the Rhodesian side. Its army as well as its undisciplined auxiliary forces continued to behave as they had before. The question was whether the British governor, Lord Soames, would be able to control them, or whether he would become their victim. The first sign of danger was Soames's decision to use the Rhodesian army to assist in keeping law and order, despite the fact that the Lancaster House agreement had stipulated that all armies would be kept within barracks. Soames had to stop their attacks on guerrillas. Two attempts were made to kill Mugabe. In the first attempt, his house was attacked with grenades. He was uninjured. A later attempt came in the guise of a landmine placed on the route that his car would follow on the election trail. By sheer luck, the landmine detonated between cars in the cavalcade, and Mugabe escaped unscathed once more. The bomb left a huge cavity in the road, but injuries were minimal. Both these attacks were later traced back to the Rhodesian security forces. A third incident concerned a bomb being carried in a car by two Rhodesian security officers. The bomb detonated near the Anglican cathedral in Harare and both officers were killed. Questions were naturally raised regarding their possible intentions. Other members of the guerrilla armies were not so fortunate. A substantial number were killed during this period by the Rhodesian forces. These fatalities heightened tensions based on the conviction that Soames would use his power to support the Muzorewa group during the elections. Such suspicions were heightened by Soames's decision to disallow Enos Nkala, a well-known ZANU hothead, from taking further part in the political campaigning.

An equally dangerous situation arose over Soames's decision to allow South African troops to remain in Rhodesia, despite the decision at Lancaster House that all foreign troops should leave. His excuse was that the South Africans were only there to protect the railway route to South Africa, an unconvincing argument as the railway route was more essential for Rhodesia than it was for South Africa.

Elections were held at the end of February 1980, with more than 2.6 million voters taking part in that historic event. There was estimated to be an over 90 per cent turnout. ZANU won the majority of seats, 57 of the 80 common roll seats, gaining 71 per cent of the votes. ZAPU won 20 seats and 25 per cent of the votes, mainly in the Ndebele ethnic strongholds of Matebeleland and Midlands. Muzorewa's ANC, which had less than a year before won overwhelmingly, now suffered defeat, winning only 3 seats and less than 4 per cent of the total votes. As Zvogbo had predicted, the electorate had voted ethnically. The majority Shona, who comprise some 80 per cent of the population, voted overwhelmingly for ZANU, with defections going to ANC rather than to ZAPU. The minority Ndebele voted overwhelmingly for ZAPU, with only Bulawayo in the Ndebele heartland wavering, and this only because some cities in Matabeleland actually had a predominantly Shona population.

More than 200 foreign observers came to check on the validity of the elections, the largest contingent being from the Commonwealth. The British government had appointed an election commissioner as well as parliamentary observers from both the Conservative and Labour parties. The United Nations sent a small delegation, which incidentally included the future Secretary General, Peres de Cuellar. The United States sent its own observers. Other independent groups were also represented, notably a group of independent observers from Canada and the USA. The official British election commissioner, Sir John Boynton, was thought to favour the Muzorewa group, whereas other groups of observers favoured the liberation forces. The consensus was that there was a certain degree of intimidation from both ZANU PF and from the Muzorewa auxiliaries, but that the conduct of the elections was sufficiently free and fair as to ensure that the results generally reflected the wish of the electorate.

The large turnout for the election reflected the wish of the people for peace after many years of conflict. Peaceful elections had replaced military conflict as a way of resolving differences. This was a monumental breakthrough for Zimbabwe. For the majority of people, this was their first experience of elections, and they appreciated the opportunity to express their wishes.

ZANU's strategy of only one-third of ZANLA forces entering the holding camps became a sore point with ZAPU after the elections. ZAPU believed that ZANU would not have had such an overwhelming electoral victory if it had not deployed its most experienced political commissars in the field, whereas ZAPU, which had a smaller guerrilla force, had apparently obediently ordered all its troops into these camps. ZAPU's conviction that it had been cheated of electoral victory by this strategy was to be a major factor in its taking up of arms against the ZANU dominated government from 1982 to 1987. ZAPU's conviction that it would have fared better in the 1980 elections is, of course, a matter for conjecture. However, by 1980, there were a number of factors that supported ZANU victory. One was ZANLA's control of a sizeable part of the country, particularly of the rural areas, where they had won the battle for minds and hearts as well as military control. Areas controlled by ZANLA were likely to vote for ZANU. A second factor was the drift of the two major liberation movements towards ethnic identification: despite efforts by ZANU to convince everyone that it represented the Ndebele as well as the Shona, and by ZAPU that it represented the Shona as well as the Ndebele, in fact the population was poised to vote ethnically.

The wish of many Rhodesians to nullify the elections was counterbalanced by the decision made by the British and the South Africans not to support further violence from the Rhodesian regime. The Rhodesians knew that on their own they could not win a military victory, and Britain was anxious not to allow Rhodesia to become the British Vietnam. The South Africans, despite the presence of their troops in Rhodesia, had decided that an election victory not wholly to their liking was better than the continuation of the un-winnable guerrilla war. Muzorewa protested that the elections had not been free and fair, but he decided to accept its outcome. Zimbabwe was now born. The first post-independence government was a coalition of the Patriotic Front partners of ZANU and ZAPU, under the leadership of Robert Mugabe.

CHAPTER 18

The Fruits of Independence

The announcement of the Lancaster House agreement to give Zimbabwe independence was greeted with joy at Matenje School. The teachers and pupils danced and sang the whole night long. I felt both joy and apprehension. The liberation that we had fought and suffered for was now at hand. We would need to make the best of the opportunities that would be offered to us. Independence meant the beginning of another liberation struggle, possibly even more difficult than what we had just gone through. Our struggle had so far been primarily a military one. We were about to enter a period when we would be the government of the country.

I was given the privilege of flying back to Harare in May 1980 in a special plane that carried a few dozen of the elite. I travelled with my daughter Chipo, then aged two and a half, and Pedzisai, the teenager who had been living with me and helping me with Chipo. Mrs. Angeline Tongogara was on the plane. She was newly widowed, and had just given birth to a baby girl.

We were met at the airport by Solomon Mujuru, now the head of ZANLA and soon to be head of the Zimbabwe army. We entered the country without passports and were taken to houses that ZANU PF had bought with the contributions it had received for accepting independence along the lines advanced by the Western allies. Our house was for the education department, and was located in the upscale suburb of Chisipite.

My family was delighted to see me, as they thought I had been either imprisoned or had died. The enemies of ZANU PF had spread stories about conditions in the rear camps, some of them based on guesswork rather than reality. In particular, the Hamadziripi group, to which Rugare Gumbo belonged, had now joined Sithole's ZANU Mwenje, and they had been determined to destroy the chances of Robert Mugabe getting into power. To this end, they had spread all sorts of stories, tinted with their political bitterness.

The majority of the Vashandi group had refused to return to ZANU PF, as they believed that it had betrayed the socialist revolution. However, they also refused to join Sithole's party because, in their view, that group had rejected the liberation struggle during the *détente* period. They wanted to join ZAPU as the only other liberation movement that had the support of the masses of Zimbabwe, but their attempts to do so failed.

I managed to find my adopted son Arnold Marira, and went out to look for his mother, Gloria Mvududu. She had been placed in a hall in Mbare township with many other war veterans and refugees. The dilapidated hall was crowded, with each family enjoying just a couple of square metres of space on the dusty cement floor. I managed to reunite mother and son.

Gloria had joined the liberation struggle as a high school student. She had given birth to Arnold during the war, but Arnold's father died in battle soon afterwards. 1976 was a period of intense fighting, as the war resumed after the hiatus of *détente*, and thousands of young freedom fighters died. She lived in Ossibissa camp with me in 1978, when Arnold was only a year and a half old. Not long afterwards, ZANLA was offered a medical training programme in Libya for women and Gloria was selected to participate. The practice then was for children of women called to work at the front or to go overseas to be kept by ZANU PF at one of our schools, and that is how Arnold came to Matenje School at the age of two. I adopted him when I found that he was on a hunger strike at the *crèche* where he was kept with 300 other children. It seemed that he had lost the will to live after the disappearance of his mother.

Not long after our return home, Gloria was employed as an officer in the CIO, which was trying to fill its ranks with freedom fighters. She was able to study for her degree at the University of Zimbabwe, since there was a well-organised programme to enable former freedom fighters to obtain university education. The army, the CIO, the ministry of health, and the ministry of education were foremost in providing training for former guerrillas, who were given leave to complete their studies.

She married a few years later. Her husband, a brilliant and dedicated freedom fighter who had been part of the Vashandi group, died a decade later of HIV-AIDS, the scourge that was wiping out so many of the best people in Zimbabwe, and Gloria was widowed for a second time. She finally left the CIO in the 1990s to become an independent entrepreneur as well as computer teacher. She eventually joined the diaspora of Zimbabweans who left the country in the economic crisis of the late 1990s.

It was during the first week we were in Salisbury that Pedzisai and I went into town. We passed Second Street and saw a white policeman, a *mujoni*, on duty. Pedzisai began to cry, as the white policeman was a symbol of the torture that she had suffered at the hands of the Rhodesian security forces. It was an inauspicious beginning. White policemen dressed in exactly those uniforms had perpetrated horrendous torture on young girls like Pedzisai, trying to extract information from them regarding guerrilla movements in the countryside.

Soon after that, Ruth First, a prominent South African freedom fighter working at the Eduardo Mondlane University in Maputo, came to visit. I took her around Salisbury. She was very upset to see that the Rhodesians were still in charge of everything. This was not her vision of independence after a fierce war of liberation during which over 10,000 freedom fighters had died. She began to cry. Ruth was murdered a few years later by a parcel bomb sent by the South African apartheid regime.

Having lived for more than nine years in Mozambique, Tanzania, and Zambia, I knew that the first decade of independence would be critical and that it would provide the opportunity to make some definite advances. It would provide us with the opportunity to address the two major aims of the liberation struggle, the redistribution of land held by white commercial farmers and the democratisation of educational opportunity. Attaining these two goals in the first decade of independence would be an enormous achievement. In addition, we had to ensure that the war veterans, who had played such an important role in the liberation of Zimbabwe, should be suitably catered for.

An immediate problem was that the Lancaster House agreement was based on the preservation of all the settler-colonial institutions and systems. This would make it difficult, if not impossible to attain some of the most dearly held goals. For example, it had been agreed that the land resettlement programme would be based on the "willing seller-willing buyer" system, which meant that perhaps not enough land would be made available to the land hungry peasants. Moreover, land resettlement might prove impossibly expensive, although both the British and the American governments had made vague promises to fund the purchase of white-owned farmland. Retaining the settler-colonial education system might also be a problem, as this could make it impossible to provide education for all.

POLITICAL CHANGES WITHIN ZANU PF

Zimbabwe's independence presented a mass of contradictions. While the new government headed by Robert Mugabe as prime minister and Canaan Banana as the constitutional president largely represented the liberation movements, the civil service remained wholly controlled by the white civil servants who had worked under the Smith regime, and who remained loyal to their old masters. The institutions and systems built up over more than a century of settler-colonialism remained intact, and it was our challenge to work within these institutions and systems. For example, Dzingai Mutumbuka, head of the ZANU PF education department, had been appointed minister of education, with Victoria Chitepo, an educationist, veteran political activist, and wife of the late ZANU leader, Herbert Chitepo, as his deputy. They were totally isolated among the old bureaucrats. The top echelons were all white, although a couple of blacks had been appointed a year or two earlier at the middle levels. These blacks were generally hostile to those of us who had been in the liberation struggle. In fact, when the election results were announced, officers and secretaries in the ministry of education were so upset that many of them wept.

The political compromise had been strongly supported by both Presidents Julius Nyerere and Samora Machel. Mozambique and Angola had been destroyed by the departing colonialists and settlers under a scorched earth policy. The two presidents feared that the same thing would happen to Zimbabwe. They put heavy pressure on Mugabe and on ZANU PF to adopt a policy of reconciliation rather than revenge. In fact, they wanted Mugabe to include Ian Smith in the new cabinet, but this Mugabe refused to do.

One of the first signs of compromise was in the cabinet, which included some prominent members of the Rhodesian Front government. One of the cabinet members was Chris Anderson, who had been minister of law and order under Ian Smith. It was through his ministry that hundreds of guerrillas had been sentenced to death as "terrorists" before independence. ZANU and ZANLA had assiduously avoided fighting against or killing civilians, as they regarded themselves as freedom fighters who were fighting against the settler-colonial regime's soldiers. However, the Smith regime termed all its opponents terrorists, "*mangandanga*", a word for "legendary monsters" in Shona.

John Conradie was so disturbed by the incorporation of the Rhodesian Front into the independence cabinet that he decided to leave the country. I tried to persuade him that it was essential to bring in the old Rhodesian Fronters, in particular people like Chris Anderson who had been earmarked as Smith's successor, in order to have a peaceful handover of power to the liberation movements. I told him that white Rhodesians would follow leaders like Chris Anderson, whereas they regarded whites like John Conradie, who had joined the liberation struggle, with intense suspicion and hatred. Conradie found this logic very difficult to accept. He was unconvinced that such a compromise was needed or would work. It was ironic that Conradie, a gentle person who could not kill an ant, had been found guilty by the Rhodesian regime of helping ZAPU to bring arms into the country. Upset by the compromises, he left for self-imposed exile in Botswana. He was to return only many years later. He died prematurely in the 1990s, his health permanently compromised by his years in prison, where he had contracted tuberculosis. Like other political prisoners, he had been kept together with criminals. His long years of imprisonment meant that he now knew every thief in town. They usually greeted him as a long lost friend!

Another example of compromise was the attempts by white farmers and businessmen to incorporate the new leaders into their power and property-owning structures. The new leaders were soon able to obtain personal properties, not only because these were now cheap with the outflow of tens of thousands of panicky whites from the country, but also because they were offered many properties at bargain prices by whites who had decided to stay. Many Rhodesians realised that it was essential to form alliances across racial lines with the new leaders, and they were not slow to do this. Beautiful houses and farms were changing hands. For those in power, there was a special price, often a fifth of the market price. This was not considered as corruption, but as a bargain. For example, many successful white farmers owned five or six farms, and one use for surplus farms was their sale at bargain prices to the new ruling elite. The new leaders were also offered directorships in old established companies. ZANU PF itself was offered a number of such free shares in companies that sought government patronage. Patronage had long been a feature of colonial politics. Big and moneyed business was able to extend its influence after independence too. The millions of dollars of demobilisation money, while providing a cushion for the tens of thousands of newly demobilised peasants, also enriched some of the military leaders.

One of the changes taking place in ZANU PF was that it was rapidly transforming itself from a liberation movement into a business conglomerate. Initially, this was part of a plan to ensure the financial survival of the movement. It began to acquire businesses in a number of economic sectors, mainly the commercial rather than the industrial sector. These businesses were under the control of Emmerson Mnangagwa and a family of Indian businessmen who had worked with ZANU PF in Mozambique, the Joshis. Over the next two decades, ZANU PF began to grow into a formidable economic player. Rumours of corrupt deals and practices could not be verified, given the veil of secrecy that surrounded these businesses. ZANU PF's stable of companies was said to number over 100. In 2004, Mugabe initiated a clean-up in the country, after corruption had reached such proportions that it was threatening to destroy the whole economy. This included an internal investigation of the corruption within ZANU PF companies. To date, no evidence has been made public.

While ZANU PF members during the 1970s consisted of a small group of dedicated intellectuals, business owners, and peasants, dominated by the military elite of ZANLA, independence brought into its fold hundreds of thousands, soon millions, of new members, eager to play a part in the new form of governance. Among these newcomers were white farmers eager to ensure prolongation of their land tenure, black workers who now enjoyed the protection of the government, the unemployed who hoped that their future prospects would improve with the new black government, rich businessmen of all races – indeed anyone who had any hope of anything for the future joined up. As a nationalist movement, ZANU PF had always been open to all comers, and now the doors were wide open. New cells, branches, and districts of ZANU PF were being formed at a brisk pace. These bodies had the right to elect their representatives at the provincial level, and those representatives became members of the central committee. This committee voted for national leaders at the annual party congress. The central committee, which had consisted of a few dozen members, now began to swell to several hundreds of members.

The political education programme dominated by socialism and the identification of the people's grievances during the liberation struggle came to a halt. Instead, ZANU PF became captive to its electorate's wishes. In the 1980s, black workers and peasants believed that the governing party represented their interests and they were enthusiastic supporters. This support was only lost in the 1990s, when workers felt abandoned by the new philosophy of Structural Adjustment. Enthusiastic white farmers soon integrated themselves into the party at all levels. In subsequent elections held in 1985, 1990, and 1995, black peasants were quite capable of eagerly electing members of parliament who were white farmers or Indian businessmen. In fact, it was often easier for whites and Indians to be elected by peasants than it was for their own traditional leaders, as peasants believed that such members of parliament were more likely to represent their interests than traditional leaders, who took their support for granted. As a result, those whites and Indians who participated in ZANU PF politics could win parliamentary elections with huge majorities, whereas black members of parliament were scraping by with majorities of only a few hundred votes. Quite often, a black candidate would win by about 300 votes, garnered at the last moment by appealing to the local army barracks to come out and vote. These narrow victories by many black candidates showed that their constituencies were not satisfied with their performance, but, on the other hand, voters were also not satisfied enough with rival political parties to make a decisive break with ZANU PF.

Elections were seen as opportunities to change personnel rather than to change policies. Policies, especially national policies, were taken for granted. Politics was about satisfying local practical needs. Local needs included boreholes, better medical facilities, improvement and upgrading of the many schools that had been established, the establishment of libraries, better roads, grinding mills, etc. Candidates who could provide these needs were supported. Those who failed were voted out at each election. Richer, better-educated, and harder working candidates were better able to provide than poorer, less-endowed candidates. For example, a member of parliament who could access the government's large water development programme could ensure that boreholes were drilled in his or her constituency. Such a candidate would receive more votes than a candidate who failed to produce anything substantial.

On my return from Mozambique, I stayed for a few months in the ZANU PF house in Chisipite, but then managed to buy a house in Avondale by borrowing money from my uncle. There were many houses for sale in 1980, as a lot of whites were leaving. Although prices were very low, few blacks could afford to buy. I began to participate in the local ZANU PF branch and was popularly elected to become a member of the district leadership of the Women's League. Most of the other women leaders were street vendors or housemaids, although a few of the educated elite were also voted in. Most of the members were blacks, but there were a few of us of different races. In the Avondale Women's League, the leadership included Doris Hollander, a white psychiatrist who was head of the psychiatric unit of the ministry of health, and Lydia Chikwavaire, a prominent women's movement leader whose husband was then mayor of Harare.

Nine out of ten members of the women in our district were illiterate, the tenth usually having only a few years of primary education. This was an inherited situation, since girls were less likely than boys to have gone to school. I tried, unsuccessfully, to help the street vendors to improve their planning and budgeting.

It was at election time that our members became active. This was also the time when the important leaders would come to the local level to win support. The parliamentary candidate for our area was Bernard Chidzero, senior minister of finance and economic planning for over a decade. He would come and meet with the district leaders in the months preceding the elections. The district party machinery was crucial for victory. ZANU PF provided the platform for the workers and the unemployed to meet with the political elite. In return, the political elite was expected to provide practical rewards for this support, which could be in the form of summer jobs, such as grass cutting, or housing. Blacks were now allowed to own housing in cities, something forbidden under colonialism, but there was inadequate availability of low-cost houses and plots. Membership of ZANU PF could and did lead to a housing application going on to the priority list, if the applicant's member of parliament was prepared to vouch for him or her. In other words, party members could jump the queue. This system of patronage established itself from the very beginning, but came to play a more and more powerful role as the leadership became more firmly established.

Almost everyone believed that a one-party state was the right solution, as such a state would guarantee national unity. This conviction was very strongly reinforced during the civil war that ensued between 1983 and 1987, when ZAPU dissidents were on the rampage in Matabeleland and Midlands, and the government responded with harsh and ruthless suppression of the rebellion.[1] The unification of ZANU PF and ZAPU in 1987 was hailed by almost everyone as a monumental achievement in nation building by strengthening the one-party state.

With the ending of socialist political education, and its replacement by a more traditional form of patronage politics, the way was open for ZANU PF policies to become more populist than socialist. One example of the popular understanding of patronage and its relationship to legal ownership soon came to my attention. One of our strong but very modestly educated women leaders, Angeline Chikaka, had noticed a derelict house with a very large garden in the Avondale area. Avondale included many flats and houses built initially for the white middle class. Doris Hollander helped her to go to the municipal offices and find out who was the registered owner. This turned out to be a retired Englishman who had long since returned to England and had probably forgotten that he owned a house in a leafy suburb of Harare. When Angeline Chikaka wrote to him, he replied that he was prepared to sell the house for Z$11,000, by then about US$3,500, a bargain by any standard. However, as a self-employed street vendor, Mrs. Chikaka did not have access to such funds. Through her enormous energy and effort, she managed to obtain funding from a well-known indigenous women's NGO, and the transfer was made to the NGO. She was allowed to live there, where she ran a modest and run-down pre-school for the children of the poor in that area. Many years later, the NGO leader, who had been away overseas for some years, returned and claimed the property. Mrs. Chikaka believed that she was the owner, as she had paid for the mortgage and rates for more than five years. She did not understand that the legal transfer had been to the NGO and not to herself. She believed that since she was a prominent party leader she would

---

1. See "Post-Independence Wars" below.

win the land dispute between herself and the NGO. She appealed to all the top party leaders, whom she knew through the ZANU PF hierarchy. However, the property was taken by the NGO, and sold for a huge profit to a private apartment developer. I tried to assist by negotiating for the NGO to pay her the money she had expended over the years on the mortgage and rates. This amounted to about Z$3,500, then enough to buy a township house, but Mrs. Chikaka refused to accept this compensation, saying she insisted on having the property in Avondale. She lost everything.

The traditional concept of ownership was that the chief, as a custodian of the interests of his followers, would allocate land to all in need. In the modern context, the government was now the chief. Mrs. Chikaka believed that the government would support her legal ownership of the house because she was a faithful party member. This principle that ownership would go to faithful party supporters remained very strong, and came into play when white farmlands were confiscated in 2000 and distributed to party supporters, irrespective of their agricultural skills.

Another example of traditional concepts came into play after the 1985 elections. We held our weekly meeting after ZANU PF had won the elections. The leadership of our Women's League, dominated by street vendors and house workers, suggested that as a victory celebration they would go and beat up members of the minority ZAPU party. I objected, saying this was not part of our party programme. Doris Hollander, who did not speak Shona, did not understand what our colleagues were threatening to do. I asked them how they would identify the ZAPU members, and they told me contemptuously that this was obvious, as the ZAPU members owned televisions and wardrobes. These women who did not own such luxuries were preparing for battle with the more privileged middle class who owned such items. I suggested that they were not allowed to beat up anyone without the permission of the district chairman, a businessman. Their sense of hierarchy and of male superiority led them to request permission for the beatings. The chairman unilaterally decided to forbid such actions, so there were no beatings in our district. However, in other areas all over the country alleged ZAPU members were beaten up. One of the freedom fighters who had been with us in Mozambique and who had chosen to live in a township house rather than in a former white suburb for ideological and not economic reasons was almost beaten up: unfortunately he owned a television and a wardrobe in his modest township house.

The use of violence as a political tool was well entrenched, especially among the poor, for whom violence against the rich was a way of expressing their frustrations. Violence had been used during the war when "sell-outs" who supported the settler-colonial regime suffered beatings, or were even executed by freedom fighters. In the politics of the 1960s, when I had begun my career as a schoolteacher in the townships, violence was also endemic, with ZANU and ZAPU youths meting out violent punishment on their rivals. This violence escalated during the farm takeovers in 2000.

During the liberation struggle, negative power was strongly balanced by positive power, as the freedom fighters enjoyed immense prestige and support from the peasantry and the youth. Popular meetings, known as "*pungwes*", a term taken from the Pungwe River in Mozambique, were held to persuade people to support the liberation struggle. Popular music strengthened this sense of solidarity against the colonial oppressor. By 2000, the state media were trying to revive nationalist fervour by linking the land takeovers to a key objective of the liberation struggle: the return of the land from the settler colonialists to the indigenous people. The fact that more than 100,000 peasants received land won ZANU PF renewed popularity.

Growing Political Power of the Black Middle Class and the Change in ZANU PF's Political Ideology

Independence led to the strengthening of the black middle class, which had been suppressed under the settler-colonial system when it was subordinated to the interests of the white minority. Because the Smith regime tried to crush this class, most of its members were fervent supporters of the liberation struggle. However, the middle class did not necessarily see its interests as coinciding with those of the peasants or workers, and this became more and more apparent after independence. The unity of all blacks against the settler-colonial regime was beginning to break down, the first sign of this being the dissident problem. Another sign was the open opposition of many of the ruling class, whether politicians or bureaucrats, to the free distribution of land to landless peasants and to the democratisation of educational opportunities for the children of workers and peasants. Thus, the post-independence period could be defined as a change in the class dominance in the ruling party, from a peasant-dominated movement governed by the values of traditional religion, to a black middle class political party geared to promoting the interests of that class.

Many peasant values, such as traditional religion, were not understood or respected by the more sophisticated and educated urban dwellers, who despised and rejected such "superstitions". On the other hand, some residual traces of traditional religion remained in the habit of many of the ruling class to consult seers and spirit mediums to predict the future leadership of the country, and, in particular, to obtain spells and charms to protect themselves from harm or to enhance their chances of re-election. The belief that the traditional spirits are powerful players on the political scene remained strong among some powerful politicians. Even those who did not really believe in the powers of the traditional spirits nevertheless knew that such beliefs still influenced the electorate, and that it was therefore pragmatic to win the support of their terrestrial representatives.

The situation was exacerbated by the change in ZANU PF's ideology from nominal socialism in 1992 to Structural Adjustment's version of liberal capitalism. While Marxism-Leninism had already been abandoned by 1976, long before independence, nevertheless its rhetoric still lingered for a decade after independence. It also served an important function as a benchmark for measuring what was being done by government. The poor regarded socialism, however ill defined, as representing their interests. This rhetoric expressed itself in concern for the welfare of the poor, often symbolised by the first lady, Sally Mugabe. This care for the poor was expressed through the distribution of food and clothes to the destitute. Although this was charity rather than system change, it had a powerful symbolic significance. In the eyes of the poor, they had a representative within State House who would ensure that their interests were not forgotten. With her death in 1992, this symbolism also died. The poor felt themselves totally discarded. Hundreds of thousands of Zimbabweans filed past her coffin at State House. Her traditional wake offered the opportunity for everyone to enter State House, whether they were political opponents like Ndabaningi Sithole or James Chikerema, or the destitute from the streets. The funeral was an expression of deep sorrow by the poor that they were no longer represented in State House.

The decision to espouse Structural Adjustment in 1992 was interpreted as an open door for the entry of neo-liberal capitalism. As the newly liberated black middle class consisted of traders and professionals, rather than of industrialists, Structural Adjustment did not give a boost to new industrialisation. Instead, it led to very rapid de-industrialisation, as locally manufactured products were replaced by cheaper imports from East Asia. New black-owned import companies and retail stores sprang up at the same time as the white-owned industries folded. Higher levels of consumerism than ever before were achieved by the small black elite, while tens of thousands of black workers lost their jobs in the old industries. At the same time, fees were introduced for hospital and clinic services: as a result the poorer half of the population could no longer enjoy even the most rudimentary of medical services. In the education sector, I managed as minister to stop the introduction of primary school fees in rural areas where 70 per cent of the population lived, but they were introduced in the urban areas.[1] This eventually led to the problem of "street kids" without schooling, a problem that had existed in colonial days but had disappeared during the first decade of independence.

Structural Adjustment was interpreted by the ruling political class as licence to enrich itself. The first decade of independence had seen a small number of blacks becoming rich through property ownership rather than through industrialisation. A small number had managed to link up with large multinational companies, which still continued to lever enormous political power. Structural Adjustment ushered in a period of increased corruption by the political class, which saw the opportunity to secure a larger share of the economy through the political support they were able to give to private sector ventures from outside. An outstanding example of this was the construction of the airport, which was given to a foreign company that had managed to ally with Leo Mugabe, the nephew of Robert Mugabe. Thus, the regulation agreed by cabinet that only Zimbabwean companies should be allowed to compete was breached in spirit, though not in the letter of the law. Cabinet itself sanctioned this tender. Leo Mugabe's company was not an architectural or engineering company, but merely a front for a foreign company. Later, allegations were made by the foreign company

---

1. Note that fees were charged for secondary education from the beginning.

itself that it had provided bribes to leading politicians, in effect becoming a channel for state funds to corrupt politicians.

It was in 1988 that the "Willowgate" scandal broke. This was linked to the purchase and resale of cars. The combination of control of the economy by an economically powerful white elite and the control of political power by a nominally Marxist-Leninist socialist party brought immense challenges. One of these was the tendency of the moneyed class, then mainly white, to expatriate their funds, causing a dearth of foreign exchange. As a result, there were shortages of imported products, such as motorcars. These were relatively cheap and affordable because of price control, but they were unavailable. Ordinary people now began to obtain cars through their political contacts. One of the most popular ministers at the time was Maurice Nyagumbo. A veteran nationalist with communist leanings, Nyagumbo was soon a source of cars: a letter recommending sale of a car to a member of his constituency would result in the company selling a much coveted car to that individual. Nyagumbo apparently wrote over 30 such letters. He himself did not possess a car.

Despite government price-control regulations, many of these cars were resold at market prices rather than at the controlled price. The market price was in fact twice the controlled price. One of the ministers caught up in this scandal was Dzingai Mutumbuka, our very high level, dedicated, and hard-working minister of education. His wife had bought and resold one of these coveted cars at a profit, and had then bought another one. He was removed from government for this transgression.

One of the showpieces of the Willowgate scandal was the open court "trials" presided over by a senior judge, Justice Wilson Sandura. Ministers such as Nyagumbo and Mutumbuka were brought before a jeering public of unemployed spectators and street people, rather like the trials during the French Revolution depicted by Charles Dickens. These politically powerful people had not broken a law, but had transgressed against a price-control regulation. They were not allowed lawyers, but had to defend themselves before the jeering crowds. After his public appearance, Nyagumbo committed suicide.

After his death, the "trials" ceased, and dozens of other "accused" got off scot-free. A few ministers lost their posts. There was a consensus that the Willowgate trials had been used to remove political rivals. Two precedents had been set: one was that by sacrificing a few high level people, public anger could be assuaged; and the second was that any corruption scandal could be used to remove political and ethnic rivals.

Another example of a breach of the spirit of the law was the sacking of 10,000 lower level civil servants, mainly cleaners and cooks, in the mid-1990s, in response to the demand made by the International Monetary Fund and the World Bank that the civil service should be cut by this number. These cleaners and cooks, nominally civil servants, were paid the minimum wage, at the time the equivalent of about US$30 a month. At the same time, the bureaucracy was not made more efficient by their dismissal. Tasks such as cleaning and cooking were outsourced to private companies owned by the ruling class, and they charged a great deal for their services. This was obviously an unsuitable model, as these services became much more expensive and deteriorated in quality. As a result of these changes, many university and college students could no longer afford to eat at student canteens and began to cook on paraffin stoves in their parquet-floored rooms. The damage caused to the fine middle class accommodation was serious. Students also had to provide their own sheets and blankets. The end result was that many poor students pulled down the curtains for this purpose.

Even more damaging to the civil service was the option given to civil servants to receive a very tempting "golden handshake" to persuade them to leave government employment. Large numbers of experienced civil servants decided to take this large cash incentive, seriously weakening the service.

Structural Adjustment saw the entry of new leaders into ZANU PF. These leaders had not taken part in the difficult pre-independence liberation struggle of the 1960s and 1970s, but had joined the ruling party after it got into power in order to promote their business prospects, which remained closely linked to political patronage. Economic opportunities were available to those who identified with the ruling party and denied to those who opposed the ruling party. Using their newly acquired wealth, they soon came to hold key positions in the ruling party, displacing the militarist peasant-dominated veterans and the socialist Vashandi, dominated by high school and university students, who had vied for leadership during the liberation struggle. Known as the Mafikizolo, or newly arrived, they integrated themselves into the party leadership. They gained support from some of the top ZANU PF leaders who now saw the ability to "buy" power as critical to political success. Whereas during the liberation struggle, support for ZANU and ZANLA would mean deprivation and even death at the hands of the forces of the settler-colonial regime, now many ZANU leaders and supporters saw financial gain and opportunities to make more money as the main reason for supporting politics. Patronage from the political elite was now the key to success.

One phenomenon of patronage politics was that the masses could vote for the best patron who would provide the most for the community, irrespective of ideology or race. Some of the Mafikizolo had even supported the settler-colonial regime before independence. Neither they nor their supporters saw their new positions as top leaders of ZANU PF as contradictory: their consistency lay in that they always supported those in power. Thus by the 1990s, the new leadership within ZANU PF began to outnumber those who had been in the liberation struggle. These new leaders had become millionaires and billionaires through their political connections. They, like the wealthy whites before them, tended to expatriate their wealth, rather than investing it inside the country.

An example of the Mafikizolo's business acumen is that they soon began to buy up essential products, for example fertiliser. They would then have monopoly control over the product, despite the fact that they had not participated in producing it. Through this monopoly, they increased the price to unaffordable levels, such that most farmers were no longer able to afford fertiliser. They were able to export most of it at a handsome profit. Thus, whereas previously fertiliser was available to all farmers, it now became a luxury commodity. The artificial shortage and the high price affected the productivity of farmers, particularly of peasant farmers who traditionally produced most of the food for Zimbabwe. This was exacerbated by the fact that white commercial farmers had long cut down on and even stopped producing staple foods, having begun to concentrate on cash crops such as tobacco and horticulture. The food shortages that have characterised recent years were caused in part by severe drought, but Zimbabwe has a history of severe droughts and had always managed to feed its people in the past. The role of the Mafikizolo in undermining national food security was critical.

Another reason for the food shortage was the sale of Zimbabwe's strategic food reserve for profit. Structural Adjustment economists believed that the storage of food was too expensive, and that in times of need food could be purchased from overseas at a cheaper rate than locally produced food could be stored.[1] This strategy led to disaster, as the drastic devaluation of the Zimbabwe dollar in the late 1990s made the importation of food virtually impossible.

Mafikizolo symbols now filled the capital city, Harare. They drove around in luxury cars, dressed in the latest foreign fashions, built luxury houses. Harare had never before seen such splendour. It was rumoured that one of the main Mafikizolo had a computer-controlled wardrobe, which allowed him to select his daily garb through high tech.

The Mafikizolo bought factories not to increase production, but to strip them of the assets for a profit. Their main power concentration was in the new indigenous banks, which soon began to compete with each other in fabricating pyramid-type investment schemes. The madness of these schemes was such that it was claimed to be possible to increase one's investment by 1,000 per cent in a year. Tens of thousands of the middle class invested in such schemes, many of them to lose their life savings.

The Inherited Bureaucratic System: "We are as good as Ian Smith"
Zimbabwe's independence meant that some of the programmes that had begun during the liberation struggle could continue, such as the expansion of education to cover the majority of children. However, the fact that the Rhodesian system, in terms of the army, the police, the bureaucracy, and the economy was intact, meant that compromises had to be made on a daily basis. In some cases it was possible to work within the inherited system. In other cases it was possible to change the inherited system. However, on many occasions the inherited system was impervious to change. Many of the new bureaucrats had also come in with their own agendas, which could be very different from the agendas developed during the liberation struggle. For example, some of the new bureaucrats had tribal agendas. Others were bent on utilising their new-found powers for corrupt purposes, leading to distortions of government programmes.

---

1. The huge subsidies for agriculture given by the European Union and by the United States government to their farmers mean that their food is generally much cheaper than locally produced food.

Examples of these diverse objectives soon came to the surface. One example affected me personally very soon after independence. As a head of a department in the ministry of education, I was very politely requested by my superior officer to promote a young teacher to become an officer in my department. I interviewed the young lady and found her to be quite reasonable, but without the requisite experience, so I did not promote her. I was surprised to find that this led to a huge conflict, during which I was accused of not "following directives". It turned out that the young lady was the girlfriend of my superior officer. This became a fierce battle, as soon afterwards a promotion post became vacant, for which I believed I was the most qualified and experienced officer, but I was turned down, in my opinion because I had not cooperated in promoting the girlfriend. I should mention that one of my more accommodating colleagues did promote her. Having spent more than five years in the liberation struggle, I would not accept people's relatives and girlfriends being promoted even when they were not suitable for such posts. I held the opinion that this was not what we had fought and died for, and we should not allow it. The ensuing and very public conflict brought me into greater prominence, and one of the results was that I was appointed minister of education and culture in 1988.

I did manage during my period in office to ensure that promotions in the ministry of education at least were as professionally based as possible. Tragically, however, the promotion of friends and relatives, particularly of the larger family of ZANU PF supporters, came to play a larger and larger role as the party became more deep-rooted. The Ian Smith government had passed legislation to ensure the survival of their bureaucracy. The effects of this legislation were mixed, with the public service commissioners ensuring that promotions were confined to those who were politically acceptable.

One major achievement during my term as minister of education and culture was that we were able to improve the promotion process to enable more women to be promoted. In the first decade after independence, only about four per cent of leadership positions such as school principals and education officers were held by women, and even this minority tended to be non-black women, like myself. We were able to identify the barriers to the promotion of women in the civil service, in particular in the ministry of education, where more than a third of teachers were women. One barrier was the colonial-era rule that women who were pregnant were dismissed, and upon return to teaching would be considered as new entrants. A man who entered the service in the same year as a woman could be considered ten or fifteen years senior to the woman if the woman had left to give birth to a child. We were able to change this iniquitous regulation. The other barrier was that before the 1970s very few women were able to go to university, so that when age was taken into consideration, the top positions would have to go to older men. We managed to change this by placing men and women on separate lists, and comparing men to men and women to women. The top two candidates from each list were then compared to each other. If they were considered equal then the new regulation stated that the woman had to be selected.

The most serious problem was the strong pull of the whole bureaucracy, whether it consisted of whites or of blacks, to repeat the colonial system. Their model of excellence was the Rhodesia model, and they sought to imitate and replicate it. Many of the new bureaucrats measured their success in terms of how well they could imitate their white predecessors. This they succeeded in doing. While those of us who had been in the liberation struggle were critical of the inherited system, this was not the case for the majority of newcomers. Most blacks saw independence as their opportunity to enjoy what the whites had previously enjoyed. The Rhodesian system of values, with its emphasis on ethnic loyalty, remained strong.

Another early problem was that the new politicians wanted to exercise their power over all decisions, destroying our efforts to plan effectively. They strongly believed that the benefits of development should go only to their political supporters. If the politicians were given full power to control school expansion, for example, there would be lots of schools in areas controlled by powerful politicians and no schools in areas where there were none.

Powerful ZANU PF politicians now placed pressure on us to stop providing educational facilities in areas that had not voted for ZANU PF. As head of educational planning (1980-82), I had to take a strong stand against members of parliament and government ministers politicising the school location and planning processes. It was fortunate that I had been in the liberation struggle, and succeeded in ensuring that school provision would be based on the number of children in the community and not on the political affiliations of their parents. This stand was supported by both Dzingai Mutumbuka, the first minister of education after independence, and Robert Mugabe, the first prime minister.

The new black bureaucrats who had not participated in the liberation struggle were dependent on the new political leadership for their positions and for their promotion prospects. They saw their professional survival as governed by the whims of the new political forces. Despite the powerful institution of the public service commission in support of civil servants, many of them were nevertheless afraid of the power of politicians. They were eager to please individual politicians, although they were often instinctively and ideologically against some of the new policies. They saw clearly that the new policies would bring about major changes in the social hierarchy. For example, the policy of primary and secondary education for all, while wildly popular with the peasants and workers, was opposed by most of the new black bureaucracy, who could see that education of the masses would endanger their privileged positions as a tiny elite who had had the opportunity to gain access to education. Education, information, knowledge, and skills had been jealously guarded and made inaccessible to the poor. Thus the tenets of the liberation struggle were assiduously opposed, utilising bureaucratic regulations to stop the establishment or improvement of schools for the poor.

Bureaucratic opposition to the government's land resettlement policy was also quite violent. White bureaucrats saw the resettlement programme as an opportunity for white farmers whose land was adjacent to the communal areas to exchange their farms for better farms closer to other white-owned farms. Many of the new black bureaucrats saw the redistribution of white farms to the black middle class as a sensible policy. However, the redistribution of good farmland to poor and landless peasants was fiercely opposed. It was argued that giving land to such people would transform the rich commercial farming areas into degraded communal areas. While there was some truth in this assertion, it was also true that many of the middle class who now wanted to own farms were not themselves farmers by profession. There was a serious danger that they would become exploitative landlords rather than productive farmers. The age of the "telephone" farmer had begun. Telephone farmers were those rich politicians and bureaucrats who remained in Harare to promote their careers and interests, but who now owned farms controlled and operated by telephone.

One of the most fearful institutions inherited after independence was the Central Intelligence Organisation (CIO), the colonial secret service that had been responsible for not only trailing us during the long years of the liberation struggle, but that had also placed its *agents provocateurs* so successfully within the heart of ZANU PF. These agents had succeeded in causing havoc in our midst as well as in killing many of our colleagues. They acted under the belief that they had the right to kill those who opposed the colonial government. Many of us had suffered attempts on our lives. Now the newly independent government had inherited the CIO intact. It was still headed by its old director, Ken Flower, after independence. The majority of officers who had so faithfully served the colonial regime decided to remain at their posts, with their skills in infiltration and killing opponents of the government accepted as part of the new order. They were reinforced by former freedom fighters, mostly from ZANLA. Their terms of reference and their procedures were to remain almost the same as they had been before independence. They infiltrated all opposition parties as they had done before independence, often acting as *agents provocateurs*. One of their most famous acts was the infiltration of the Movement for Democratic Change (MDC) and involving their leader, Morgan Tsvangirai, in a televised plot to overthrow the government in 2000 through a Canadian Israeli named Ari Ben Menashe.

Another example of the survival of colonial officers involved Lionel Dyke, one of the most notorious Rhodesian military officers, who had virulently opposed the liberation struggle. He became one of the military leaders in charge of suppressing the dissidents in Matabeleland in the early 1980s. He was later responsible for training the 6th Brigade. In 2002, he allegedly claimed that he was sent by very high level ZANU PF leaders to negotiate a transitional government with Tsvangirai, but after being trapped in the Ben Menashe plot, Tsvangirai was so suspicious of this gesture that he decided to publicise it.

EDUCATION

One of the first examples of opposition to the new government in 1980 was what happened to the tens of thousands of children who had been in schools in Mozambique and Zambia. They were hastily placed on government and mission-owned farms, together with their teachers. However, the Rhodesian authorities were still in power, and their first manoeuvre was to try and starve out the children. I went to the social services department to see if they could provide food for the children. I was told by a white official that since these children were "communists", they should not be allowed to remain together, and that the best strategy was to force them to disperse by not providing them with food. This strategy was now in force. These children had been relatively well fed by the United Nations High Commission for Refugees (UNHCR) and the World Food Programme (WFP) while we were in Mozambique and in Zambia. Now they were at the mercy of white officials, who totally refused to provide them with food. The strategy to starve them into dispersal partly worked: those students who could find any relatives left the temporary camps. However, there were many thousands who were orphaned or had lost contact with their families. They were now starving.

In order to cope with the challenge of providing food and schooling for these children within Zimbabwe, Dzingai Mutumbuka, the first minister of education after independence, decided to form a non-governmental organisation to be known as the Zimbabwe Foundation for Education with Production (ZIMFEP). This was a good strategy in view of the fact that we could not get any money or support from the organs of government. Although ZANU PF was now the official "government" of Zimbabwe, it did not have the power to provide basic food and facilities for the children it had cared for so well in the refugee camps in neighbouring countries. We now had tens of thousands of starving children being looked after by unpaid and equally starving teachers.

I was the first chairperson of ZIMFEP, and we were responsible for the children from our schools in Mozambique as well as the ZAPU schools in Zambia. The ZIMFEP board consisted of war veterans who had supported the education programme in the struggle. Its first staff consisted entirely of war veterans. Our self-chosen responsibilities included providing war veterans and ex-refugees with a good education, with job training, with job placement, and, where necessary, creating employment opportunities for them. We also took upon ourselves the task of providing education and training for war veterans who wanted to have educational and training opportunities. The war veterans we catered for had not been able to receive primary and certainly not secondary education because of the settler-colonial education policies.

ZIMFEP began as a partnership with Patrick van Rensburg's Foundation for Education with Production (FEP), an organisation that had been operational for over a decade in providing education combined with work in Botswana. We were able to benefit from van Rensburg and FEP's considerable experience. However, we soon parted ways because of FEP's need to establish a resoundingly successful pilot programme in order to secure its future donor funding. This meant bringing in highly skilled and experienced management from overseas. On the other hand, my experience in Zambia had taught me that highly successful programmes managed by foreigners would have only a short lifespan: they would be brilliantly successful for about five years and then would die a natural death when the foreigners left the country. It was essential for us to ensure that the ZIMFEP schools continued as a permanent feature of the education system, incorporating the precepts as well as the programmes that had been developed in the refugee schools during the liberation struggle. Our task was not to have an instant and brilliant success, but to integrate our values, achievements, and systems into the settler-colonial education system we had inherited. I knew from my experience in Zambia that success would be difficult, and that once we were successful, we would face even stiffer opposition, this time not from the white Rhodesians but from within ZANU PF itself. Any development that was vaguely left wing, such as providing education for all and strengthening peasant and worker education, was likely to meet with stiff opposition from both the traditionalists and from the middle class. Both of these groups benefited from having a largely illiterate majority who would be dependent on them for everything. Van Rensburg's idea of having brilliantly run schools with foreign managers was, in my view, a recipe for future failure, as the schools would no doubt be attacked as foreign influenced and foreign controlled. It was essential for us to have successful models that were as home grown as possible.

However, the inherited Rhodesian bureaucracy was determined to stop any attempt to re-establish schools that had operated outside the Rhodesian system. These schools did not conform to the Rhodesian idea of a school, whether this was a school for whites or a school for blacks. The bureaucrats were uniformly against the idea of education

The Fruits of Independence

ZIMFEP school, 1980

with production. White bureaucrats saw this as undermining the white-controlled industrial sectors. "If the children are taught to make their own furniture, this will destroy the furniture industry," one white official solemnly told me. It was part of settler-colonial government policy to support the white-owned furniture industry through purchases for the schools. Many furniture factories depended largely on government purchases for their survival. For the black educators, education with production was demeaning: they saw education as a preparation for someone to become part of the ruling elite and they had little time or patience for the concept of educating peasants or industrial workers. We therefore faced active hostility and practical barriers from within the ministry of education as well as from other ministries. We had to fight for money to feed the children. We had to fight for the positions and pay of our teachers. The bureaucracy had a good excuse that no provision had been made in the state budget for food, teachers' pay, school materials, etc., for these children. The teachers and other staff who selflessly remained with the children did so without pay. I was fortunate enough to obtain some funds from donors to pay these teachers once. They received only Z$300 each for several months of work.

I took a high official from the Swedish International Development Agency (SIDA), Birgitta Berggren, to visit some of these locations. We visited Loreto mission near Gwelo, one of the places where teachers and children had been located. The Roman Catholics had kindly allowed us to use their property. We saw the dire conditions under which the teachers and pupils were living. Unfortunately, when we ended the visit we found that one of the refugee children had stolen the rear view mirror from the Swedish embassy car. Despite this embarrassing incident, SIDA decided to provide generously for these children through ZIMFEP.

We were able to obtain some urgent funding to buy basic foods for the children. Generous donors included SIDA, the Danish World University Service, HIVOS, Bread for the World, the Swiss Christian Aid, Save the Children UK and USA, and UNICEF. The first months of independence were fully occupied with trying to feed the tens of thousands of children from the refugee schools. A lot of my time was spent raising funds and purchasing food. SIDA provided generous funding to allow us to establish schools for the refugee children who had been in Mozambique and Zambia. These supporters who had helped us through the long years of the liberation struggle continued to support us after independence. Without these faithful supporters of the liberation struggle we would have found it much more difficult to establish education for all on a firm basis in the first decade of independence. With their help, ZIMFEP was able to purchase a number of farms where schools could be built. SIDA also assisted us to establish the War Veterans and Refugee Scholarship Fund, which was to allow tens of thousands of war veterans and refugees to obtain primary and secondary education and job training. SIDA insisted on establishing this scholarship on a dollar for dollar basis, with government paying for half and SIDA for the other half. This condition helped to integrate the scholarship fund into the government's financial system, and the fund was able to survive for about fifteen years after independence. It was destroyed in the mid-1990s when bureaucrats in the ministries of education and finance concluded that war veterans no longer needed an educational input. Many of them felt that much too much had already been done for war veterans.

The ZIPRA freedom fighters, with their well-integrated and organised network, benefited immensely from this fund. I remember on one occasion when we handed over the list of more than 3,000 awards a year to SIDA, they questioned the number of "Dubes" being awarded scholarships, as they suspected some form of corruption. "Dube" is a

The Fruits of Independence

ZIMFEP school, 1980

very common Ndebele name. At a time when ex-ZANLA forces were being integrated into the army and police, the ex-ZIPRA forces were unemployed and had to devote their time to study. We were giving large numbers of scholarships to ZIPRA at a time when their leadership had withdrawn from government.

In 1980, ZIMFEP managed to buy several farms. Taka Mudariki, the director of ZIMFEP, and I personally visited over 200 farms before we selected nine on which we were to build agriculture-oriented schools for the refugee children who had returned from Mozambique and Zambia. At the time there were many former white farms for sale at a very low cost. Only two of these farms were registered in the name of ZIMFEP, and this was at the insistence of the donors. I personally registered the rest under government ownership. I did not realise then that this would cause ZIMFEP immense problems in the future, as local politicians manipulated government ownership of the farms to take away the farms from the schools. These farms were the best that we could find. We were fortunate enough to be able to retain some parts of these farms through the five-year leases we were given in the 1990s.

My fear that ZIMFEP would be attacked for being too successful materialised in 1990, at the height of its success. ZIMFEP suffered a fierce attack based on tribalism. We were accused of being too "Manyika". The Manyika are an ethnic group located near the border with Mozambique, and many freedom fighters hailed from this group. It was also the ethnic group of ZUM opposition leader, Edgar Tekere. This accusation led to the loss of key staff who had worked for ZIMFEP for a pittance in order to support the education of ex-refugees and war veterans. In the words of a departing staff member, "I've done my best, but now I am being accused to belonging to a certain tribe by one of the highest ranking leaders in ZANU PF. I don't have to continue – I can get three times more in salary by working for private enterprise."

This was to be one of several attempts to take over ZIMFEP by ethnically based political groups who were jealous of ZIMFEP's success in providing educational and job opportunities to veterans and former refugees. These takeover attempts have continued up till today. Opponents use the ruling party's hostility to NGOs to undermine ZIMFEP's work. Some of them saw ZIMFEP as a milk cow that could provide funds and jobs for their tribe. Others saw ZIMFEP's work with war veterans as a suitable platform to launch their political ambitions. Politicians who had never done anything for war veterans or ever helped ZIMFEP in any way, suddenly began to claim to be its founders, and attempted to take it over.

In the ministry of education, the only two multinational publishing companies in the country in 1980 were vying with each other to be "nationalised", as most of the neighbouring countries had "nationalised" one publishing house and then banished all the rest. I did not see the need to nationalise either of them, as it would be better to have the advantages of both in competition with the other. Instead, we followed a policy of encouraging local publishing companies to provide all the school textbooks. As a result, over 40 publishing companies began to flourish. State investment in education included generous fixed subsidies for educational materials such as textbooks, and this gave a big boost to the local publishing industry.

One of the examples of confusion was the arrival of a large contingent of Ghanaians soon after independence. Some of them claimed to be relatives of Zimbabwe's first lady, Sally Mugabe. They made a beeline for the ministry of education, which had been given the lion's share of the state budget, including some Z$85 million for the construction of schools. This was then equivalent to about US$85 million. This

Ghanaian group had arrived with a couple of engineers and offered to build all our schools. In 1981 we were planning to build about 400 new secondary schools. Their rationale was that the settler-colonial system would not allow us to build so many new schools, whereas they were willing and able to do so. Their fee was to be US$4 million to be paid overseas. As the first head of educational planning after independence, it was my responsibility, together with the deputy secretary in charge of finance, Hugh Vickerstaff, to deal with this contingent. Meanwhile, Mutumbuka, as minister, was being threatened with dismissal by the Ghanaians who claimed to be close relatives of the first lady. He reacted by wining and dining them endlessly, while claiming that decision-making over building contracts was vested in the bureaucracy, i.e., with me and Vickerstaff. My instinctive reaction was that we could not give a contract to a company whose work we could not inspect. Moreover, if we were building 400 schools it would be more sensible to have 400 contractors rather than only one. I therefore asked the Ghanaians to allow two technical specialists from the ministry of education to visit Ghana to inspect the schools they had previously built. This they would not agree to. We were not able to overcome this impasse. It was a credit to the first lady that despite appeals from the Ghanaians for her to intervene on their behalf to "discipline" us into giving them this monopolistic contract, she refused to do so. After two years of attempting to force the ministry of education to give them the monopoly, they left Zimbabwe empty handed. Instead, we managed to give the contracts to 400 local companies, many of them small contractors who were to enjoy their first government contracts. The use of these indigenous contractors lasted for more than a decade, when they were replaced by more expensive large companies. The bureaucrats in charge of giving contracts did not want to handle hundreds of little companies owned by contractors who only had primary education, and instead favoured large companies owned by university-trained graduates. One of the results of the use of urban-based large companies to construct schools in remote rural areas was a serious escalation in building costs.

Meanwhile, Mutumbuka was struggling to see if he could incorporate some of the staff who had been running the schools in Mozambique into the ministry of education system. Those of us who had degrees and diplomas fared much better than those whom we had trained ourselves. Only a few of us, Stephen Nyengera, Tovadini

Mwenje, Ephraim Chitofu, and I, were able to work at the ministry headquarters and regional offices. A larger contingent was able to have their positions in our schools confirmed as school heads and as teachers. Many of our teachers from Mozambique and Zambia had already left, a large group having been trained as magistrates by Prof. Bob Seidman of Boston University. Our teachers were among the best educated of the freedom fighters, many of them having been high school students before joining the liberation struggle. They had received some years of further education in Mozambique and elsewhere, and they were now to fill key posts in other government ministries. I managed to get the two training programmes that we had conducted, as well as the training programme that had been conducted in Denmark by the Development Aid from People to People (DAPP) recognised by the ministry of education as suitable qualifications for appointment and pay purposes. We also managed to have the schools registered and funded by the ministry of education, no mean feat given the fierce opposition at the time.

Mutumbuka had a good grasp of political possibilities, and he now had the responsibility of transforming the colonial bureaucracy, which was so hostile to anything new and particularly to any change in the established system, into a bureaucracy that would be responsive to the educational needs of the black majority. He had to transform a pure white bureaucracy into one that integrated black professionals. This he did by forming an alliance among black professionals who then held relatively junior positions in the education system, black professionals who had been outside the country, and those of us who had been in the liberation struggle. Mutumbuka was not afraid to make decisive changes in the system. The experience of running schools in refugee camps had enabled him to see that schooling had to do with intellectual and affective development, and not just with buildings. Thus, many of the first schools started literally under trees, but through a system of careful planning and phased implementation, these schools were able to graduate into good buildings within the first few years of independence.

Two of the major successes of the first year of independence were that we managed to incorporate our policy of primary education for all and secondary education for the majority and to establish an innovative teacher education course known as the Zimbabwe Integrated National Teacher Education Course (ZINTEC). I was the first acting head of

ZINTEC, through which we managed to spearhead an expansion of the primary education system from an enrolment rate of 35 per cent of the age group to over 100 per cent within a short period. The entrenched bureaucracy fiercely opposed our attempt to start. We were unable to obtain offices within the ministry. Nor could we employ anyone to do secretarial work. Fortunately, the UNICEF office, headed by a Tanzanian, Mr. Shomari, provided us both with offices and with funds to employ temporary secretaries until the programme could be officially established within the ministry of education.

Another problem was the refusal of the ministry to order the furniture and other materials required to start the programme. Assisted by a UNESCO consultant, Jinapala Alles, who had been director general of education in Sri Lanka, I was able to check what was happening at every stage of the bureaucratic chain. I discovered that middle level officials were not allowed to order the needed furniture by a senior official. Despite discovering where the blockages were, we were, nevertheless, unable to take control of the logistics. As a result, when ZINTEC started, the students had only one chair each, so that they had to carry their chairs from the dormitory, to the dining room, to the lecture room! However, despite these minor hiccups, ZINTEC managed to succeed.

I became the first head of educational planning in the ministry of education after independence, in September 1980. I was able to ensure that the educational plans were done in such a way that primary and secondary education would expand, while at the same time ensuring that the quality of education was improved. While education for whites, Coloureds, and Asians had been of high quality before independence, African education had been of very varied and in many cases dubious quality. Primary education in particular had been of very low quality in most schools for blacks, and it was a major challenge to ensure that these primary schools improved substantially, while keeping costs to reasonable levels. Primary schools increased from about 1,800 to over 4,500 schools, and secondary schools from less than 200 to over 1,500.

Secondary education for blacks had been of high quality during the colonial period through the system of severely restricting opportunity for blacks to obtain secondary education to two per cent of the age group. There were very few secondary schools for blacks. The challenge was to open up opportunities without lowering quality. We managed

ZIMFEP, Girls learning tie and dye

to provide good quality secondary education to more than half the age group. We also managed to increase tertiary education substantially. Whereas only about 300 black students were enrolled a year at university level before independence, we were able to increase this to more than 10,000 within a few years.

The thirst for education was enormous, and we were able to tap into the resources of the community to build up the education system so that every child would be able to gain a primary education. By establishing a system of partnerships between state and community, we were able to share responsibilities. The state provided technical assistance in terms of building regulations, standards, and plans, with building officers assisting the communities, while the communities, mainly the parents, built the schools. They were able to obtain grants from the ministry of education that partly covered the cost of the buildings. The ministry of education paid the teachers' salaries and the cost of teaching and learning materials through a per capita grant to the school authorities. This community-based school system meant that the government school system was not expanded, except for a few model schools that we built in rural areas where government schools had never existed before. The majority of schools were community based and community

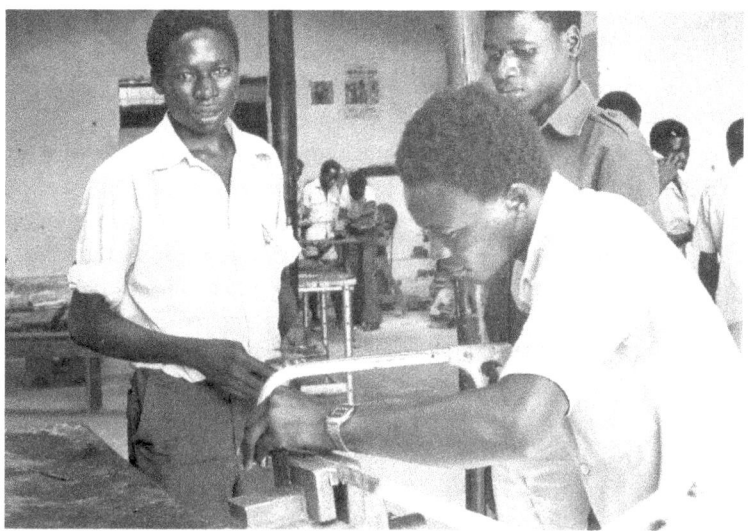

ZIMFEP, Boys woodwork

owned. As a result, even today only 11–12 per cent of schools are government owned, but all schools receive government support in terms of teachers' pay and grants for the purchase of school materials.

Despite the opposition of many bureaucrats, we managed to organise upgrading programmes in teachers' colleges and universities for the teachers who had taught in the liberation struggle. Most of these teachers did very well. Professor Walter Kamba, then vice chancellor of the University of Zimbabwe and a leading legal specialist for the Zimbabwean liberation movements, established a special programme for qualified war veterans to enter the university. The freedom fighters were required to have the same entry qualifications as other candidates, but because of the fierce competition for university places, 24 places were specially earmarked for them each year. Sadly, this programme was discontinued in the 1990s after Kamba had retired and Mutumbuka and I had left our posts in government. The black middle class exhibited its traditional hostility towards war veterans by closing down even these humble opportunities for self-improvement.

The University of Zimbabwe established a special programme on military strategy for army personnel. The main lecturer was a former member of the Rhodesian army. The Zimbabwean army employed him as a major, and seconded him to the university to enable it to begin this special programme to upgrade army officers.

One important compromise that mainly affected the privileged white community and the better-off black middle class was the government's decision to allow new private high fee schools to be established. I was initially very much against this move, but Robert Mugabe, as prime minister, insisted that we should allow them to be established, as this was a guaranteed right under the constitution. Soon there were over 40 such privileged schools, in comparison to about a dozen before independence. We were, however, able to impose regulations on these schools, such as insisting on them having a certain percentage of scholarships.[1] All schools in Zimbabwe were to follow the same core curriculum, although a large degree of freedom was given regarding additional options. Some of the most privileged Roman Catholic schools began to provide scholarships for the best pupils from their poorer mission schools, thus enabling them to have the most brilliant children from all over the country in their top schools. This infusion of new talent strengthened their education system considerably.

We also managed to construct and establish schools for the refugees and war veterans in nine ZIMFEP schools. Job training and job placement programmes for war veterans were established outside the government structure through non-governmental organisations, such as the Zimbabwe Project and ZIMFEP. After this training, we organised cooperatives for our graduates. Many of them were resettled on farms that government leased out to them. Others formed furniture and textile companies. ZIMFEP continued to provide technical and managerial support for two years after their graduation. Some 24 such cooperatives were formed.

The democratisation of educational opportunities was achieved within the first decade of independence and remains one of the most important achievements of the liberation struggle. I knew that once the majority of the population was educated, this achievement could not be totally reversed. By embarking on these changes, we had irrevocably changed the human resource map that we had inherited. With a highly

---

1. However, scholarships for the brilliant poor were not a satisfactory solution for the black middle class, who wanted privileged entry for their children at fees they could afford. In 2004, this led to a conflict between these schools and the ministry of education.

educated population, Zimbabwe could be transformed both politically and economically. The poverty that made bread a luxury to be enjoyed only at Christmas could become a thing of the past.

However, the democratisation of education also led to growing criticism of the government, as education enabled the newly educated young to voice their opinions eloquently and openly. The two frustrations facing the young were the lack of employment opportunities after the first decade of independence, and what they saw as the growing corruption within the ZANU PF government. Corruption and lack of employment opportunities were closely related, as they reflected on the ZANU PF policy of redistributing existing wealth, but without due emphasis on increasing wealth to cover the whole population. Thus, although education had been democratised, the economy had not.

Tensions and Conflict between the University and Government

One of the priorities of the ZANU PF government after independence was the expansion and improvement of university education. At independence, there was only one university, the University of Zimbabwe. The University had played a key role in the liberation struggle, providing intellectual leadership against the settler-colonial regime in the 1960s and 1970s. In the 1970s, large numbers of students left their lecture halls to join the liberation struggle. Many of them refused to serve as soldiers under the Smith regime, when, towards the end of the war the shortage of white conscripts and mercenaries led the government to make the decision to recruit university students. These young intellectuals played an important role in providing education to the largely peasant refugees in Mozambique during the liberation struggle.

ZANU had been characterised as a party of the black intelligentsia when it broke away from ZAPU in 1963, and it retained this reputation after independence, when many of the cabinet were recruited from the intellectuals who had joined the liberation struggle.

The post-independence expansion of the University of Zimbabwe from a few hundred black students to over 10,000 had a number of effects. One was that, whereas there had once been a severe shortage of graduates in the country, with only about 4,000 graduates at independence, there was soon to be a glut. The surplus increased in the 1990s when a number of new state and private universities were established. But the number of jobs within government for graduates was not growing, except for teachers, where the demand remained high. One result of this was that graduates with law or engineering degrees were soon being forced to become secondary school teachers, and the ministry of education had to make special regulations and adjust their pay scales to accommodate them. The labour market could not absorb the great increase in graduates.

Another problem was that university courses trained graduates to work for government or to seek jobs in established companies. Graduates were unlikely and, indeed, unable to start their own private companies. There was no programme to assist new graduates to establish themselves in new areas. For example, the majority of engineering graduates, some of the most brilliant students in the country, could not find jobs as engineers. Yet if government had had a vision of supporting the expansion of engineering industries after their graduation, either by building more much-needed village dams or by expanding the narrow base of engineering companies dominated by white engineers in the private sector, it would not have been difficult to absorb about 50 graduates a year.

The expansion of university enrolment also meant that the student population now included larger numbers of students drawn from the peasant and worker population. Before independence, the settler-colonial governments had ensured that not only was university education restricted to a few hundred blacks a year, but these few hundred were more likely to be representative of the richer peasantry who owned land in the African Purchase Areas, traditional chiefs, or the professional middle class. This was because of the fee structure, which would automatically exclude poorer peasants and workers from secondary education. After independence, although fees continued to be paid for secondary education, the establishment of more than 1,500 new secondary day schools and of more than 100 high schools that provided advanced or A level education, opened up university entrance to students who would not have been able to go to university before independence. Entry into secondary school increased from just over 12,000 a year before independence to more than 250,000 a year by the mid-1980s.

The expansion of the University of Zimbabwe also meant that it was necessary to recruit many young and brilliant lecturers who were not much older than the students themselves. They were closer in age and interests to the students than to the generation that was now in power. Their lack of maturity and experience meant that they were a more volatile group. With the history of political commitment of the university, and with the natural tendency of young people to criticise the older generation, the university soon became a hotbed of opposition to the ZANU PF government. This was apparent during the suppression of the dissidents in the 1980s, when an ethnic divide emerged at the university, with Ndebele students virulently critical of the government's fierce and violent handling of the situation.

One of the most prominent intellectual leaders at the university was Jonathan Moyo, who spent two decades attacking the ZANU PF government, in particular its top leader, Robert Mugabe. However, by 2000 Moyo had decided to join ZANU PF, and re-emerged as the minister of information under Mugabe after the 2000 elections. This about-face surprised Moyo's former supporters.

The honeymoon between the government and university lasted through the 1980s. By the end of the 1980s, it was clear that government was moving away from its original vision of empowerment of peasants and workers, and had become more committed to empowerment of the black middle class. Corruption was becoming endemic. The Willowgate scandal showed that the political elite had used their political power to break their own regulations. The way Willowgate was handled added fire to the growing criticism, for although a handful of ministers were removed, a few hundred of the political elite were seen to have escaped any form of censure. None of them was imprisoned. The Willowgate "trial" showed that it was possible to humiliate members of the ruling elite in front of large crowds, a satisfying display. The combination of corruption and the showy but inconclusive trials led to greater disrespect for the governing class.

The acceptance of Structural Adjustment in the 1990s as a panacea for Zimbabwe's economic ills led to a drastic shrinkage of the economy and a concomitant increase in corruption. Student unrest culminated not only in anti-government demonstrations, but also in their support for the newly formed opposition party, the Zimbabwe Unity Movement (ZUM) established by veteran politician, Edgar Tekere, to fight the 1990 elections. Within a few months of its establishment, ZUM was able to gain a quarter of the votes in the 1990 elections, its support coming mainly from the youths in urban areas, including enthusiastic support from the students. The formation of the MDC a decade later again found the students as enthusiastic supporters.

The conflict between university and government is in line with the traditional role of the university as the conscience of the nation. It is also in line with the long conflict that had dogged ZANU and ZANLA throughout the formative years of the liberation struggle of the 1970s between the privileged and educated university elite and the less educated freedom fighters, who had been recruited from the neglected peasantry. The peasant freedom fighters had seen the educated elite as a highly privileged and unreliable partner, likely to betray the struggle at any moment to serve its own interests. The conflict between intelligentsia and the less educated poor has remained one of the most critical political dividing lines up till today.

THE POSITION OF WOMEN AFTER INDEPENDENCE

Women played a critical part in the liberation struggle before independence, since they were able to move into areas controlled by the settler-colonial regime without arousing suspicion. Thus, much of the ground-breaking work in liberated areas during the war had to be done by women. As a result, a sizeable number of them became military commanders, responsible for commanding men as well as women.

At independence, this translated into having a number of prominent women freedom fighters included in the new political leadership as parliamentarians and as cabinet ministers. This was possible because in the 1980 elections political parties were able to nominate their candidates independently. However, within the first decade of independence it was decided that there should be primary elections in which parliamentary candidates would be elected by people at the grassroots. The introduction of primary elections saw an immediate drop in the number of women candidates, as both peasants and workers selected mainly male candidates. There was no sensitisation campaign to support the need for the election of more women. In the absence of a framework that would ensure that women had equal representation at parliamentary level, ZANU PF members returned to a more traditional trend of voting for men. This included large numbers of women members voting for men in preference to women candidates. The number of elected women parliamentarians has continued to be meagre. Today, women constitute 15 per cent of parliamentarians.

As a result of the loss of women political leaders in parliament, it became necessary for President Mugabe to include a large number of women parliamentarians for the 20 nominated seats. These nominated seats are a leftover from the Lancaster House agreement, which had reserved 20 seats for whites only. When these racially reserved seats were eliminated in 1987, it was understood that they would be reserved for under-represented groups, and women were now the most under-represented group. Had Mugabe not used his prerogative to nominate a number of women to parliament, there would have been even fewer women in parliament.

The first decade of independence saw many changes in the law intended to benefit women. At the time, the minister of women's affairs was a young freedom fighter, Joyce Mujuru[1], and she was able to use her powerful position to inaugurate a number of new laws. She was supported by the then minister of justice, the late Eddison Zvobgo, and by a powerful group of women lawyers, including Elizabeth Gwaunza, now a Supreme Court judge. One of the laws that produced a fundamental change in the status of women was the *Legal Age of Majority* (1982). This law enabled women to enjoy equal rights in the eyes of the law. Previous to this, indigenous women were treated as minors who had to be legally assisted by male relatives or husbands. They were not even allowed to open their own bank accounts. The new law made every Zimbabwean, whether man or woman, equal in the eyes of the law at the age of 18. Daughters could now inherit property and women could qualify as guardians of their own children and administer deceased estates. Property ownership by women was of critical importance to the independence and freedom of women. The 1991 *Deeds Registry Amendment Act* went further to clarify that women could register immovable property with title deeds in their own names. However, over the past 20 years traditional forces have continued to oppose this law, and have tried to have it rescinded.

Traditional inheritance laws meant that women generally could not inherit property. However, the colonial Roman Dutch law allowed non-indigenous women to inherit property. There were thus two contradictory laws in place at independence. Ownership of immovable property in cities and in former white-held farmlands was governed by

---

1. Joyce Mujuru is the Vice President in Zimbabwe since January 2005.

Roman Dutch law. Before independence, black people were not allowed to own such property, but were allowed to own land in the African Purchase Areas. The Purchase Areas represented only a minute proportion of the country's land: the majority of black people lived in the communal areas, which were governed by African traditional law. After independence, when black people were allowed to buy property in cities, Roman Dutch law could now apply to middle class women, although in the communal areas, where land ownership was not based on title deeds, women still could not own or inherit land. In the 1990s, government sought to correct this contradiction by reverting to traditional law for all indigenous women, so preventing them from inheriting even property that had formerly been governed by Roman Dutch law. However, by the 1990s women lawyers comprised one of the best organised groups in the country, and they were able to spearhead opposition to this return to feudal property rights. The proposed legal change was thus blocked by the activism of women lawyers, supported by middle class professional women. However, in practice traditional laws remained powerful, as shown in the Magaya case in 1999.

This case concerns inheritance of a house in a city area. On the death of the father, the eldest child, Venia Magaya, believed she was the rightful inheritor. This was contested by her stepbrother, who was much younger than herself. The Supreme Court of Zimbabwe decided that even though this was an urban property that was not governed by traditional law, Venia Magaya, as a woman, had no right to inherit, and the property should go to her brother. Thus the Supreme Court upheld the view that indigenous women could not inherit property. According to their ruling, a woman belonged to the family of her husband, and therefore could not inherit property within her natal family.

The adherence to traditional property ownership law, which disinherits women, reflects the strength of feudal power within modern Zimbabwe. Moreover, it is not clear whether the issue of women's rights resonates for the majority of women, who are peasants. It is quite possible that many women will still vote for a parliamentary or presidential candidate known for his opposition to women's rights.

Other laws were passed that strengthened the position of professional and urban women. Before independence, professional as well as working class women were paid less than their male counterparts. The Equal Pay Regulations (1980) provided for equal pay for equal work, and also allowed breastfeeding time for women who had recently given birth. The *Labour Relations Act* of 1984 allowed for three months of maternity leave and outlawed any form of discrimination. However, an adverse aspect was that many employers stopped employing women, as they were unwilling to pay for maternity leave.

The *Matrimonial Causes Act* of 1985 enabled women to seek the equitable distribution of matrimonial assets upon divorce. Despite the generous provisions of this act, in fact most women do not feel they can use it for their benefit. One reason is that a woman who is divorcing for whatever reason may not want to alienate her husband's relatives within a strongly patrilineal system, as this may be harmful to her children. I know of a case of a young educated woman involved in a divorce case. She lost the house and furniture as well as custody of her four-year-old son, even though she had partially paid for the house and furniture. This was because she believed it was essential to maintain amicable relations with her former husband and his family. Another case involved a traditional woman whose husband had taken several more wives. She was not happy that her marriage had now become a polygamous one, but she felt unable to accept divorce even though the law now allowed her to claim half the property, as her traditional belief was that a woman who "betrayed" her husband would go insane. Divorce was interpreted as disloyalty and betrayal.

In the same year, 1985, women were allowed to contribute to public service pensions and medical schemes in their own right: before independence women depended on their husbands' pension and medical aid schemes, creating a crisis for women who were divorced. Such women could find themselves totally destitute in their old age. This applied to both black and white women civil servants. Many white divorced women found themselves destitute both before and after independence because of these iniquitous laws.

The *Deceased Person's Family Maintenance (Amendment) Act* of 1987 allowed the surviving spouse and children the right to continue occupying the matrimonial house; to use the household goods and effects they were using before the deceased's death; and to use and enjoy the crops and animals. This act made property-grabbing by the men's relatives illegal. One of the problems with traditional inheritance laws was that the wife had few or no property rights: at the death of her husband, his relatives, sometimes very remote relatives, could come and claim the property of the deceased, often leaving the wife and children destitute. Some interpretations of traditional inheritance laws had maintained that the wife could only claim her clothes, pots, and pans. She also lost custody of her children, as in a patrilineal society children belong to the father's family. She could only retain some property rights if she agreed to be inherited by a male relative of her husband. This was particularly the case if there was no son over the age of 18.

The constitution of Zimbabwe outlaws gender as a basis for discrimination. However, in practice, foreign-born wives had the right of residence, whereas foreign-born husbands did not. The *Constitutional Amendment Act* of 1996 put male and female spouses of Zimbabwean citizens on a similar basis in terms of right of entry into Zimbabwe based on the marital relationship.

Despite the changes in the legal system, the majority of women lacked both knowledge and sufficient money to make use of the new laws. A concerted effort was made by the ministry of women's affairs to obtain donor funding to support its education programme on women's rights, and it was able to obtain generous funding for this purpose from Nordic countries and Britain. These new laws were translated into local languages, and many courses were held to enable some women to learn about how to exercise their rights. However, the end of donor support for such progressive educational programmes in the late 1990s meant that most women were unable to access their basic human rights.

The heavy dependence of the women's rights programme on donor funding reflected on the failure of government structures after independence to support women's rights in terms of financial investment. Instead, much depended on the strength of individual women leaders. The women's rights movement has visibly weakened. Despite the incorporation of women's rights into the statutes, it is still possible for magistrates and judges to make judgements in contravention of the laws.

Nevertheless, there were some gains made on behalf of women. It was possible to include many more women in promotion posts in the civil service by changing the inherited regulations. Changes also took place in police stations, where a special officer, usually a woman, was in charge of dealing with cases of sexual violence and rape. Courses were held to ensure police officers could handle issues related to sexual violence without causing the victims of such violence further problems.

Over the years, the position and prestige of the war veterans also began to deteriorate, and war veterans, particularly women war veterans, began to hide the fact that they had participated in the war. The post-independence mores did not value women who had held positions of authority during the war, or who asserted their independence. At the same time, traditional feudal values reasserted themselves: under feudalism, a woman's position in society generally depended either on her father's status or on that of her husband. Some women now tried to ensure that they held respectable positions in society by linking themselves to men in high positions, rather than by trying to prove their independent worth.

Polygamy, and its more modern mutation of having a number of mistresses, grew among the rich and powerful, with many prominent leaders distinguishing themselves by the number of wives and girlfriends that they were able to attract. Financial affluence made the practice of polygamy more feasible, and it is still considered a social distinction by some to be able to have many wives. The more affluent were able to establish these additional wives in what are termed "small houses", but for the less affluent, casual liaisons became more common.

From the mid-1980s, the scourge of HIV-AIDS began to decimate the population, striking down the affluent as well as the poor. Wives were particularly vulnerable, as under customary law wives could not refuse unprotected sex, even when they knew that their husbands indulged in promiscuity and there was a strong possibility of their being infected with HIV-AIDS.

LAND RESETTLEMENT

The key area of land resettlement received immediate attention after independence. Sam Geza, a university lecturer in the economics department at the University of Zambia and a leader of the left-wing Vashandi movement of freedom fighters in ZANLA, was appointed the director of land resettlement. This was an important post in terms of attaining the most critical aim of the liberation struggle. Geza had spent more than four years in forced exile in Nampula, Mozambique, because of his left-wing political views. He was one of only three of these exiles who had agreed to rejoin ZANU PF. Now he was to play a definitive role in achieving an historical land resettlement programme.

He immediately embarked on an ambitious programme for landless peasants, settling over 62,000 families between 1981 and 1987 on 2 million hectares of land that had been purchased by the government under the "willing seller-willing buyer" system, and partially funded by the British government under Margaret Thatcher, who had been as good as her word.

However, it was not long before Geza faced enormous opposition, when his superiors tried to remove him from his post. In order to retain his position he had to use the regulations instituted by the Smith regime: these regulations made it virtually impossible to dismiss a civil servant unless he or she had been found guilty of a crime in a court of law. He retained his post, despite all these machinations. However, the battle and Geza's victory were at a severe personal cost. He was identified as a civil servant who did not unquestioningly obey his political masters. This was totally against traditional procedures, where obedience to authority was the only acceptable form of behaviour. In the words of one minister, "Who is this man who has failed to recognise the ruling family of Zimbabwe?" Traditionalists considered the ruling family to be above the law.

The basic cause of this conflict was the issue of who would get the land. Already the middle class was appalled at the idea of so much good land going to the peasantry. Government was apportioning land free of charge to landless peasants when the up and coming middle class were expected to purchase land at market prices. Many of the middle class openly opposed the policy of giving land to the peasantry, and by 1984 they had become powerful enough to stop this type of land resettlement. The argument was that the peasantry could not use this land optimally.

There were other reasons for halting land resettlement. Feudal chiefs, especially those in Matabeleland, opposed providing land to peasants. Under the Matabele feudal system, chiefs owned hundreds and even thousands of cattle, and they would distribute these to be looked after by their retainers. The retainers were allowed to keep the milk, but would return the cattle and any offspring to their benefactor in due course. The benefactor might choose to give the retainer a cow after many years of faithful retainership. This whole comfortable social order was seriously upset by the government's land resettlement programme. Peasants with their own land were no longer prepared to be retainers. The right form of land resettlement for the feudal lords was the extension of the communal areas that they controlled, and after the unity agreement between ZANU PF and ZAPU in 1987, Vice President Joshua Nkomo insisted that an additional form of land resettlement be introduced through which communal areas could be extended. One of the reasons for the traditional chiefs' support of the dissidents in the 1980s was this very opposition to giving poor peasants independent land holdings. However, this traditional form of land resettlement was very much opposed by the bureaucratic and technical specialists, and although the new form of resettlement was officially on the books after the 1987 unity agreement, it was never implemented.

One of the things I observed was the increase in the practice of polygamy as a result of the resettlement programme. It also resulted in higher birth rates. When I was minister of education, I visited a former commercial farm that had been bought by three brothers. They managed the farm successfully with their bevy of over 20 wives. They also managed to produce over 200 children, and government had established a primary school where their children could obtain free education. As these formerly landless peasants and new farm owners could not afford to employ workers, they instead married and gave birth to their labour force. Providing land to the poor had some unforeseen social consequences, and feudal marriage systems that reinforced the weak position of women remained very powerful social institutions.

The changes of government in the United Kingdom provided another excuse for halting land resettlement. While Margaret Thatcher had faithfully kept to her promise to fund the purchase of white-owned farmlands, her successors did not feel any such responsibility. She provided a total of 44 million pounds for the resettlement projects.[1] This was sufficient for purchasing the initial 3 million hectares of land in the early 1980s. Her fall from power in 1990 was a serious blow to land resettlement in Zimbabwe. Her successors within her party and from the Labour Party easily found one excuse or another to stop funding land resettlement. One excuse was that there was some corruption and

---

1. BBC News Online: the Zimbabwe Crises, the Battle for Land, http://bbc.co.uk/hi/English/static/in_depth/Africa/2000/zimbabwe_crisis/slideshow.

patronage in the land resettlement processes. In fact, if they had been sincere, their participation would have helped to lessen and control such corruption. Another was that the Labour government had no responsibility for problems created more than a century before by successive colonial governments. In a letter to the Zimbabwean government, British Labour minister Clare Short, who was responsible for foreign aid, clearly stated that the British government had no responsibility whatever for funding land resettlement in Zimbabwe. This letter directly triggered unilateral action by the Zimbabwe government to confiscate land without compensation. Both the British government and the Zimbabwe government adopted intransigent positions on this issue, culminating in a violent land seizure in 2000.

Meanwhile, the Zimbabwe government had taken the stand that they would not use government funds to purchase white-owned farms, as they considered this to be the responsibility of the British government as agreed at Lancaster House in 1979. As a result, few farms were purchased after 1983, despite the regulation that farms could only be bought after the state had been given the right of first refusal.

Probably the main reason for the British refusal to fund further land purchases was that the status quo appeared to be stable, with white commercial farmers and British companies continuing to own some 12 million hectares of land. Many of these white farmers had joined the ruling party, and were on extremely cosy terms with both the peasantry and the ruling elite. There appeared to be no reason to disturb a status quo in which millions of hectares were owned by British-based multinationals. This comfort zone was destroyed by the 2000 elections. For over a decade the British government had refused to provide funds to buy out white farmers. In 2000, when white-owned farms were confiscated by the Zimbabwe government, the British government decided to provide political and financial support to the newly formed opposition party, the MDC. They obviously believed that the MDC would restore the farms to their white owners.

I asked Geza early in the 1980s why he was carrying out the resettlement programme at such speed, when in fact it might be better to slow down. He replied that the resettlement programme would soon be stopped, and he was determined to take it as far as possible while he had the power to do so. Unfortunately, his prediction came true. Geza was soon promoted upwards to the position of permanent secretary for the ministry of commerce and industry, and with his removal the resettlement programme for the peasantry came to an abrupt halt. It was only to recommence in 2000, after a hiatus of thirteen years. Later, Geza left government after they attempted to "promote" him out of his position: he strongly supported a Zimbabwean form of Structural Adjustment, whereas government believed it was much more appropriate to faithfully follow the IMF/World Bank recommendations. There was an almost naive belief in government that obedience to IMF/World Bank principles would lead to automatic economic growth. For almost a decade, the Zimbabwean government proved to be the perfect student, faithfully following the recommended Structural Adjustment strategies.

In the 2000 parliamentary elections, land again became the key issue, and it was because of ZANU PF's land redistribution policy that it was able to win this election. Land proved to be the trump card. Knowing that land was such an emotive as well as economically critical issue, Mugabe and ZANU PF chose to make it the main theme of their 2000 and 2002 election bids. For the landless and for the peasantry, the revival of the liberation struggle gave them hope that they would receive land to mitigate their increasing poverty. Many of those who had participated in the liberation struggle of the 1970s felt that their revolution had been betrayed, and this was an opportunity for them to regain some of the lost ground.

One of the tactics of the ruling party and government was to utilise the war veterans as a tool to intimidate white farmers to abandon their farms. War veterans who had been neglected for almost a decade and a half suddenly found themselves recalled to duty. This was under the then minister of home affairs, Dumiso Dabengwa, once head of the ZIPRA armed forces. The ZIPRA former dissidents, united with unemployed ZANLA war veterans, now came to the fore. Their recall to duty was revivifying, and enabled them to rejuvenate their membership through the new recruitment of unemployed youths from the townships. The post-independence population explosion without a commensurate increase in the economy and number of jobs now meant that millions of young people were on the loose, with no prospects of employment. They were hastily trained through short political orientation courses, armed, and let loose on the commercial farms. Soon they were also to be used in the townships, where large numbers of disaffected urban workers, whose earnings had been seriously affected by inflation, were ready to vote for the opposition MDC.

A few white farmers were able to buy off land takeovers through various manoeuvres, such as persuading the new would-be settlers to allow them to continue farming through cash payments or by employing prominent war veterans as highly paid security guards. This additional rent increased the price of produce for the ordinary consumer. The hurriedly organised land resettlement programme differed from the orderly land resettlement of the 1980s, with many disputes arising from the different claimants for land, such as the white farmers themselves, the political elite, the war veterans, and the peasants. Severe technical problems also arose, such as the shortage of funds for investing in the newly acquired farms, the shortage of fertiliser and draught power, and also the shortage of expertise and experience.

The new land resettlement coincided with a severe shortage of fertiliser.[1] The well-established commercial banks, most of them branches of international banks, had never specialised in supporting agricultural production by the peasantry. It was also a period when a number of new indigenously owned banks were being established, but their core business was foreign currency speculation. All banks were nervous about lending money to the newly resettled farmers, who did not have title deeds to their newly acquired properties to offer in return for mortgages. In other words, the banking sector as a whole failed to support agricultural expansion.

THE CHANGING ROLE OF WAR VETERANS AFTER INDEPENDENCE

The return of a triumphant liberation force to a country that had agreed to retain all the settler-colonial institutions intact was bound to be problematic. Moreover, the ZANU PF political elite headed by Robert Mugabe had never been in complete control of the guerrillas, as the late militarist leader, Josiah Tongogara, had assiduously ensured that the military would remain largely outside the control of the traditional politicians. This meant that ZANLA, a highly politicised army, was

---

1. The shortage was caused by the Mafikizolo, who increased the price to unaffordable levels and exported most of the fertiliser at a huge profit.

nevertheless not under the political control of the leaders who took power after independence.

On the other hand, the army was a powerful force that could make or unmake any political leader in Zimbabwe. Anyone who wanted to take power in Zimbabwe would need to win the backing of the freedom fighter-dominated army.

Immediately after independence, the guerrillas from ZANLA and ZIPRA were integrated into the national army, with training and retraining under officers from the former colonial power, Britain. The liberation movement officers were now trained at Sandhurst. This was brilliant political symbolism, aimed at placating the West, which had been so apprehensive of a "communist" government taking power. Mugabe was well able to understand the need for such a placatory symbol at that stage of the liberation struggle, and this brilliant political stratagem worked.

A large demobilisation exercise began almost immediately in 1980. Half the guerrillas had been recruited from high schools, whereas the other half had come from the largely unschooled peasant population. While the demobilisation exercise was voluntary, most of the illiterate and semi-literate guerrillas decided to leave, having been given the princely sum of Z$3,500 (then about US$3,500) as a demobilisation grant. They did not see themselves as professional soldiers and were eager to return to civilian life. At the time, the demobilisation grant was sufficient to purchase a township house. While during the settler-colonial regime blacks were not allowed to purchase or own any property within a city, this had now changed, and the more far-sighted used their demobilisation grants wisely. Some war veterans pooled their money and purchased commercial farms – farms at that time were going for about Z$20,000–50,000. This form of cooperation was particularly common among former ZIPRA guerrillas. Some of these farms were later confiscated by government during the dissident period of the mid-1980s. There was an old colonial regulation that the property of those who opposed the government could be confiscated, and it was still in force after independence. The confiscated farms were never returned to the former ZIPRA war veterans.

After a few years, the demobilisation money was dissipated, and many war veterans found themselves stranded without education, without jobs, and without land. The ministry of education provided scholarships for war veterans for the first 15 years of independence, and this gave educational and job training opportunities to about 10,000 war veterans and ex-refugees, mainly in the ZIMFEP schools.[1] However, there was a core of war veterans who did not believe in the need for education, and they were now suffering the degradation of pauperisation. This was a far cry from their status as war heroes in the early years of independence.

John Conradie, together with many of us in ZIMFEP and the Zimbabwe Project, struggled to convince government that the freedom fighters should not be bought off with individual grants. Rather, training and job creation programmes should be created to cater for the demobilised. The tens of millions of dollars being handed out to war veterans should instead be utilised for the purchase of farms on which they could be settled. However, these pleas fell on deaf ears. We believed this was because many in government feared the power of war veterans if they remained as a united and organised group. It was better, it seemed, to disperse the former guerrillas, and if a generous grant could do this, they were prepared to pay it.

Year after year we tried to persuade government to devote about Z$40 million for employment creation programmes for war veterans, but we failed, as the bureaucrats, now entirely black, rejected the idea of spending more money on them. Ministers too were happy to let sleeping dogs lie. The War Veterans Association did not take a confrontational stand on behalf of the war veterans until 1997.

Only a few years after independence, Zimbabwe was plunged into a civil war between the two former liberation movements, ZANU PF and ZAPU. Their partnership had lasted for over six years from 1976 until 1982. It fractured after a violent confrontation between groups of guerrillas just outside Harare. This was based on the suspicion on the part of ZANU PF that ZAPU intended to stage a military coup, after arms originating from ZAPU were discovered and ZANU PF concluded they would be used to overthrow the ZANU PF-dominated government. These arms were discovered on ZAPU-owned farms near Harare airport, seen as a strategic military location. In fact, both liberation movements had retained a great part of their weaponry after independence.

---

1. See "Education Section" above.

There were other reasons for the civil war. One was the dispute that arose between ZANU PF and ZAPU, the two partners in the Patriotic Front, over ZANU PF's election victory in 1980. As noted earlier, ZAPU believed that the ZANU PF strategy of retaining its guerrillas in every village had led to an unfair electoral advantage over ZAPU, most of whose guerrillas had been in holding camps, as agreed at Lancaster House. The decision of the two liberation movements to contest the 1980 elections separately meant that the political unity needed to build a united army from the two separate liberation armies did not exist.

Some of the former ZIPRA guerrillas, now known as "dissidents", made it their duty to destroy all government structures, including wells and schools, in Matabeleland and Midlands, provinces where they had a lot of ethnic support. Teachers were intimidated, mutilated, and killed if they insisted on continuing with their duties in rebel-held areas. As a result, these areas began to lag in educational development.

The dissidents killed anyone who did not follow their orders. Our security guard at J.Z. Moyo School, which ZIMFEP was in the middle of building for war veterans and ex-refugees from ZAPU, was killed for not allowing the dissidents to remove all the building materials that we had purchased for the construction of the school. Two ZIMFEP teachers disappeared from George Silundika School: it is presumed that they were killed either by the dissidents or by the security forces. The headmaster of George Silundika, Mutobi, was arrested, and was only released after intervention by ZIMFEP.

I visited a very successful cooperative farm that was being run by ex-ZIPRA freedom fighters in Filabusi in Matabeleland. This cooperative had been formed with technical and financial assistance from ZIMFEP. I was surprised when they asked to have a police station established on their farm. When I asked them why, they responded it was because they wanted to prove they were not dissidents. One of the pressing problems they faced was that, because they now had a very successfully run farm on state land, they were afraid local government officials would confiscate it on the pretext that they were dissidents.

The government reacted violently to the dissident violence. Unfortunately, this suppression included violence against and killings of civilians who supported the dissidents. Government troops, mostly from the majority Shona ethnic group, ruthlessly put down the dissidents, who belonged to the Ndebele ethnic group, killing any men whom they suspected of being dissidents. This conflict continued for about five years, and only ended with the unity agreement signed in 1987 between ZANU PF and ZAPU. President Canaan Banana played a leading role in bringing the two parties together.

Many of these very same ZIPRA dissidents of the 1980s became the leaders of the joint ZANLA and ZIPRA War Veterans Association in the late 1990s and early 2000s, forcing the Mugabe government to embark on a large-scale land redistribution programme, so resuming the land resettlement programme that had been halted in 1987. Former ZANLA freedom fighters voted in ZIPRA freedom fighters as their leaders, because they believed their own ZANLA members were too subservient to the ZANU PF political leadership. ZIPRA freedom fighters had no loyalty to Mugabe and his government, and did not mind fighting ferociously, even destructively, against the government for their rights. The war veterans forced government to provide them with compensation and pensions. It was the revolt of the war veterans in 1997 that first shook the government out of its complacency. However, it would be incorrect and misleading to blame the fall of the economy on the war veterans' revolt. The symptoms of economic malaise had been there since the early 1990s. Senior minister of finance, Bernard Chidzero, fell ill in 1992 during the critical period immediately after the espousal of Structural Adjustment. His replacement, Ariston Chambati, died shortly after his appointment. A series of acting ministers filled the gap between 1992 and 1997, a period of intense financial turbulence globally. Thus, the economic downturn was exacerbated by a coincidence of internal and external crises.

The willingness of ZANLA veterans to support ZIPRA veterans as their representatives reflected on their shared experience of being neglected after independence. Only by threatening government were they able to assert their rights. They took a lesson from the trade unions, which had also begun to wield their power through threats. Under the leadership of Hunzvi, the war veterans were able to force government to disburse billions of Zimbabwe dollars in compensation in 1997. President Mugabe, faced with the war veterans' revolt and the resulting political instability both in Zimbabwe and in the region, gave in to their demands. In 1996, the ministry of labour, which was in charge of the war veterans compensation fund, decided to disburse about Z$1 billion in compensation, ranging from about Z$100,000 to

Z$850,000 each to a few hundred members of the ruling elite. The then minister of labour, Nathan Shamuyarira, presided over this distribution, with most of the medical accreditation being done by Hunsvi, who had trained as a medical doctor in Poland during the war years. Hunzvi was a key figure both in organising the scam and in pressuring the government to extend the handouts to larger numbers of war veterans. This proved to be the straw that finally broke the economy's back, by ushering in a sudden and unprecedented level of inflation.

By 2000, popular support for ZANU PF had waned as a result of rising unemployment and corruption. The ruling party had weakened considerably: its political education programme had fallen into disuse. Hunzvi led a burst of intense violence against any political opponents of the government. He led war veterans from ZIPRA and ZANLA, reinforced by unemployed township youths, to beat up or kill anyone resisting the farm takeovers. This negative power of violence received sanction from the ruling party and government as a political tool.

While most educated former ZANLA guerrillas were able to gain high positions in the security forces, the diplomatic service, and the civil service after independence, the same was not true for most of the former ZIPRA guerrillas. In particular, the ZIPRA guerrillas who had taken up arms against the government in the 1980s had been left with little or nothing. Their fate was in the hands of an NGO, the Zimbabwe Project, run by Paul Nyathi and Judith Todd.[1] The Zimbabwe Project, funded by donors, took over responsibility for the former dissidents.

It is a commentary on the political understanding of the MDC that it never tried to win over the war veterans to its side, given the immense discontent of unemployed war veterans.

One result of the resuscitation of the war veterans and the arming of the youths was that these paramilitary forces soon acquired a life of their own, with the government and party losing control over them. This loss of control was evident when war veteran leaders challenged their political leaders, at times physically attacking the families and representatives of the political elite. Rivalry over possession of specific farms occurred, with politicians, war veterans, and local peasants

---

1. Nyathi became a leader of the MDC at its formation in 2000. Judith Todd is also a supporter of the MDC. Nyathi and Todd were well-known long-time members of ZAPU.

claiming the same farms. It was also evident in some gratuitous violence, which saw physical attacks on and killings of some white farmers and MDC officeholders and supporters.

ZANU PF AND PEASANT SUPPORT

The liberation war had begun to succeed in 1972 only after ZANU PF and ZANLA had managed to gain the support of the peasantry, in particular through the traditional religious leaders, the spirit mediums who spoke on behalf of the ancestral spirits. The ancestral spirits urged their offspring to wage a war of liberation for their land. Right up until independence the peasants played a critically important role in liberating the country. The peasantry continued to play an important role after independence, particularly at election time, when their votes counted.

The loyalty of the peasantry to ZANU PF after independence was based on the fact that the government had immediately delivered on their promises of land resettlement, improved and expanded education and health services, a clean water supply, and food provision during drought periods. However, while the peasantry's short-term needs were well catered for, their long-term needs were not. The peasant population continued to increase, as Zimbabwe managed to double its population over 20 years. As a result, the communal area resources were becoming more and more overstretched. The halting of the resettlement programme in 1987, while acceptable for a short period, was becoming a serious problem, with peasants beginning to take the law into their own hands by squatting on commercial farmland owned by whites. Moreover, the failure of the government to address the issue of economic expansion through both agricultural and industrialisation programmes, meant that youths from peasant families found it difficult to get work. While youth unemployment had been a problem for many decades before independence, the youth now were better educated and more vocally critical than their predecessors. Education thus led to a greater propensity to criticise the government.

The peasantry were more likely to concentrate on personality than on policies. They expressed their dissatisfaction with their members of parliament by throwing them out at every election if the incumbents did not respond to their expressed needs, but the changing of the

The Fruits of Independence

guards at every election did not change the fact that ZANU PF had not yet been able to provide long-term solutions.

One of the interesting aspects of peasant politics was the tendency to ignore racial lines. This a-racial perspective showed quite a high degree of sophistication. I believe this was due to the peasants' experience in the war of liberation, where leaders had to be judged independently of their regional origins. This is in contrast to the political elite's perception of the peasantry as tribal-bound. The political elite has been quick to try to use tribal and racial differences to foment division and to win support, and no doubt there are some groups within peasant society who might respond to such divisions, but the experience of the first decades of independence shows the peasantry to be above such simplistic prejudices. I have personally found that peasants who had been involved in the liberation struggle were well able to judge issues outside the narrow tribal context.

An example of the elite's failure to understand the peasantry was apparent when Morgan Tsvangirai, leader of the then highly popular opposition MDC, decided to stand in his home area of Buhera, a district that had borne the brunt of the liberation struggle. Contrary to MDC expectations, the peasantry did not vote for their "home boy". Tsvangirai had not been able to provide the development over several years that peasants expect from their political aspirants. MDC attributed their losses to intimidation by ZANU PF supporters. However, MDC managed to win almost 50 per cent of the seats in the 2000 elections despite these threats.

After independence, government tried to play down the role of traditional religious leaders, who had been so powerful during the war years. Instead, it actively cultivated the support of more established religious leaders, in particular the Roman Catholics. Roman Catholic Archbishop Patrick Chakaipa presided over the second marriage of President Robert Mugabe to Grace Marufu in 1994 in a splendid ceremony intended to demonstrate divine support for Zimbabwe's rulers.[1]

---

1. The Catholic church has been very openly critical of the violence used in the 2000 and 2002 elections, much to the chagrin of ZANU PF, which well understands the electorate's belief in the need for moral probity in government. Most traditionalists believe that the ancestral spirits will destroy a leader who opposes their moral rules.

However, the lack of prominence given to traditional religious leaders did not mean that they disappeared. They remained and remain powerful opinion-makers. Traditionally, they were supposed to voice the people's needs and to criticise secular leaders who transgressed ancestral rules of morality and good governance. A number of prominent ZANU PF leaders continue to consult with these spiritual leaders. Their support will remain critical in influencing the predominantly peasant vote.

THE WORKING CLASS AND THE LABOUR MOVEMENT AFTER INDEPENDENCE

The black working class and the labour movement had been fiercely suppressed during the colonial period. One of the first acts of the newly independent government was to try to unite the weak trade unions into a strong union under the aegis of the ruling party. They succeeded in this, forming the Zimbabwe Congress of Trade Unions (ZCTU). The liberation movements had fought for the rights of black workers, and it was a natural step to establish a representative body to be the voice of workers in their negotiations with the white-owned companies.

Workers were also delighted when the minimum wage was established at Z$30 (then about US$30) a month in the early 1980s, a trebling of the wages that most workers had earned before.

However, the honeymoon between government and trade unions lasted only for the first decade of independence. Workers soon faced the problem of unemployment for their well-educated children. Whereas before independence, the two per cent of blacks who gained a secondary education were more or less guaranteed a job in the modern economic sector, albeit probably as messenger or "tea boy", now the over 50 per cent who obtained a secondary education found themselves unemployed, as the economy was growing slowly compared to the galloping population growth. While both parents and youngsters were prepared to wait patiently, using the opportunity to improve their academic qualifications, joblessness was a cancer that would soon destroy the friendly relationship between government and workers.

The regulations introduced to protect workers became a double-edged sword, as employers took care not to expand their workforce. Neither government nor private company owners accepted the responsibility of expanding the economy or of expanding employment, and the result was that workers found themselves with more and more dependents. Workers themselves paid little attention to enlarging the economy and the number of employed, instead concentrating on higher wages for themselves.

The situation took a definite turn for the worse with the introduction of Structural Adjustment in the early 1990s. This was intended to boost the private sector, while diminishing the government's role in the economy. The theory was that by freeing the private sector from bureaucratic control, it would prove its mettle through competition with outside industries to create a stronger economy. Ten years of Structural Adjustment led to the destruction of hundreds of factories, with the resultant loss of employment for tens of thousands of workers. The economy was shrinking instead of expanding. In a situation of declining employment and growing inflation, workers began to revolt, led by the ZCTU with a narrow strategy of organising strikes for higher wages. Other areas of worker power and organisation, such as worker technical education and training and worker ownership of the means of production, did not receive much attention from the trade union leadership.

Labour unrest at a time when government was weakening and the economy shrinking led government to depend more and more on deficit budgeting to satisfy the demands for higher salaries, but deficit budgeting increased the government's debt burden, such that soon more than 30 per cent of the budget was being used to pay for the exorbitant interest charged for these loans. At the same time, government's propensity to allow the money supply to increase to pay for the budget deficit meant that banks were now the only profitable enterprises. Other industries were starved of investments.

A confrontational rather than problem-solving approach developed over the years between labour and government, with trade unions resorting to strike action whenever they had grievances. Government, on the other hand, used strong-arm tactics to break up strikes. The political polarisation was very harmful to national interests. The discourse between government and trade unions concentrated on the narrow area of salaries and benefits. There has been little discourse on the broader areas of development. Some elements within ZCTU did see a need for the trade unions to broaden their field of discourse, and in the process they devised an excellent economic development framework, probably the best development plan that has come out of Zimbabwe so far.[1] This farsighted plan was not adopted by government or by the MDC, and faced the prospect of being a mere academic exercise. The plan could still be a foundation for closer collaboration between government and trade unions so that they can work jointly to solve national problems. Instead, each has sought to destroy the other. The growing polarisation between the government, which was increasingly representative of the new and growing black middle class, and the workers' movement led finally to a divorce between ZANU PF and its progeny, ZCTU. Leaders of ZCTU, such as Morgan Tsvangirai and Gibson Sibanda, decided to form their own political party, the Movement for Democratic Change or MDC.

THE FORMATION OF OPPOSITION PARTIES

The Zimbabwe Unity Movement (ZUM) and the Movement for Democratic Change (MDC)

Not long after independence we heard of an incident during which a senior government minister, Edgar Tekere, the third in the ZANU PF party and government hierarchy, had attacked a white farmer in a military style operation and killed him. Tekere was put on trial and defended by a famous South African lawyer. Using one of the laws enacted by the Ian Smith regime, which excused crimes committed in a state of war, Tekere was acquitted. However, Mugabe decided to dismiss Tekere from his post as a cabinet minister. Tekere's killing of the white farmer was a harbinger of what was to happen 20 years later, when some white farmers and opposition supporters were killed as part of the land seizures by war veterans and peasants.

After being excluded from power, Tekere decided to form his own party, the Zimbabwe Unity Movement (ZUM). In the 1990 elections, youth disenchantment with the ZANU PF government, particularly with the lack of employment opportunities, enabled ZUM to gain 20 per cent of the vote after only a few months of existence. Tekere's politics and policies found popular support particularly among young university students. The University of Zimbabwe, which had been the centre of opposition to the Smith government, now became a centre of opposition to the ZANU PF government. A key criticism by the youth

---

1. Zimbabwe Congress of Trade Unions, *Beyond ESAP*, Harare, 1996.

was government corruption. Fighting corruption was ZUM's main policy. Other than that, ZUM's policies seemed very similar to those of ZANU PF. Some confusion ensued when Tekere decided to form an alliance with Ian Smith. This was in some ways a surprising alliance, as at one time it appeared that they represented opposite political poles. Tekere's youthful university supporters were taken aback by the alliance. However, ZUM's ability to galvanise such substantial support within a short period indicated that it was quite possible to challenge ZANU PF seriously, and ZANU PF recognised this. Tekere's party managed to win several seats in parliament. Those who voted for ZUM did not care that he had allied with Ian Smith.

By the early 1990s, Ian Smith enjoyed a revival of support from some of the urban blacks who believed that they had been better off under him than under the ZANU PF government. Smith had carried out a policy of strong industrialisation as well as house building in urban areas, and these two programmes had benefited the urban working class. A couple of UNESCO education experts who had come to provide specialist training in Zimbabwe in 1992 were astounded when they saw Ian Smith walking on his own in First Street in Harare, the main shopping street in the city centre. Black passers-by stopped to clap for him. They asked me about the significance of what they had seen. Ian Smith had remained a political force after independence. In the initial years of independence, he used to meet regularly with Mugabe, but these meetings ended when Smith boasted that he was able to give instructions to his successor. Nevertheless, he continued to play an active political role, with his right-hand man, Peter van der Byl, even claiming to be more socialist than anyone else in parliament. He based his claim on the fact that the Ian Smith government had done more than any other government to establish new state-owned and state-supported industries. Smith continued to farm in Shurugwi, while maintaining a city house in Avondale, Harare. I would sometimes find him in the same queue at the bank.

The phenomenon of overnight and fervent support for the opposition again occurred a decade later in 2000 when the MDC was formed. Without time or opportunity to lobby for support, it nevertheless managed to gain 50 per cent of the votes. For both ZUM and MDC, this could be interpreted as protest votes rather than real support for the new opposition leaders and their newly formed parties.

MDC was composed of everybody who was against Mugabe and ZANU PF. It instantly became a powerful, well financed, but seemingly directionless opposition, with its various components having different goals and strategies. Built on the foundation of the labour movement, unemployed youths, and the black intelligentsia, MDC soon also attracted the support of the white farmers whose farms were being invaded by peasants led by war veterans. Foreign support, particularly from the former colonial power Britain, which still had major economic holdings in farming and mining in Zimbabwe, was soon to follow. The very dispersed nature of MDC's support led inevitably to its inability to pull together a credible political and economic strategy. In particular, it failed to win the support of the peasant majority. As the peasantry still constituted 70 per cent of the population, an electoral victory by MDC would be difficult if not impossible. Its strong identification with white farmers soon made it appear to represent white land interests.

Despite the fact that MDC did not enjoy the support of the rural majority, ZANU PF and government launched a fierce and violent attack against it. The MDC decided to "fight fire with fire", i.e., to retaliate by using violence against violence. The common people were the victims of both sides. Old rivalries and old scores could also be settled under a period of *laissez faire* violence. Such transitional political periods had characterised Shona history in the Middle Ages, and had been experienced in the rivalry between ZANU PF and ZAPU both in the 1960s and 1980s.[1] Both ZANU PF and the MDC consider the use of violence to be an important factor in influencing voters, although this consensus reflects more on the two parties' failure to understand and respect the electorate's wisdom and judgment. Violence had been a feature of traditional political systems as well as of settler-colonial regimes, and remained a feature of the post-independence political scene.

---

1. See Stanislas Mudenge, *Political History of Munhumatapa 1400-1902*, Zimbabwe Publishing House, Harare, 1988. His study shows that lawlessness and violence characterised the interregnum in the Middle Ages, according to Portuguese observers. Once the new ruler came into power, he was able to re-establish law and order.

The MDC was able to overwhelmingly defeat the government's proposed new constitution in the 2000 referendum, and to win half votes in the parliamentary elections later that year. The rejection of the new constitution actually had the adverse effect of prolonging the term of office of Robert Mugabe, who had been prepared to bow out gracefully by taking on a less powerful role as a constitutional president. The sudden support for the MDC from white farmers and from the British government also had an adverse effect, namely the sudden and badly planned takeover of thousands of white-owned farms. The reaction of ZANU PF was to return to the rhetoric of the liberation struggle, with the MDC seen as a surrogate for the settler-colonial government.

The MDC was born out of opposition to the proposed new constitution. In 2000, government had appointed a 400-strong constitutional commission to canvass opinion, and had then drawn up a new 100-page constitution, copied largely from the recently developed South African constitution. Such was the confidence of the ZANU PF government in the content and processes followed that they believed they would win an overwhelming vote of confidence through a referendum. However, MDC lobbied for support on the grounds that the new constitution could allow the 76-year-old president to enjoy a further two terms in office, since it did not clearly state that two terms of office included office held before 2000. Mugabe had already enjoyed two terms before that date. Such was the unpopularity of Mugabe in 2000, as a result of urban joblessness, that this single issue led to a large majority voting against the constitution. Despite the high literacy rate in Zimbabwe, most people voted against the constitution without having had the opportunity to read it.

The polarisation of the political platforms between ZANU PF and MDC reflected the historic polarisation between the liberation movement and the settler-colonial regime. Some of the white farmers who had been staunch supporters of ZANU PF were the first to support the new opposition party. The ruling party believed that land and property belonging to opposition members, whether white or black, should be confiscated, and the 1960s legislation was still in place to enable them to do so. This legislation had been further elaborated and applied to both white farmers and to MDC supporters. An interesting example of this political polarisation concerned the white farmer Roy Bennett[1], formerly a staunch ZANU PF member of parliament who decided to stand as an MDC candidate in his constituency. The largely peasant population in his area, Chipinge, continued to support him, making him one of the few MDC members of parliament to come in on the peasant vote. Despite his huge success as a commercial farmer, his farm was confiscated. Had he remained on the ZANU PF platform he could have retained his farm.

POST-INDEPENDENCE WARS

Zimbabwe went through three wars after independence in 1980. The first was the internal conflict between ZANU and ZAPU that lasted from 1982 to 1987 and ended with the unity accord between the two former liberation movements. The second was the participation of the Zimbabwean army in the Mozambique war, on the side of the FRELIMO government against the Renamo rebel movement. This took place between 1980 until 1994, when a political accord was signed between FRELIMO and Renamo. The third war was the incursion into the Democratic Republic of the Congo (DRC) from 1998 until 2003, in support firstly of the government of Laurent Kabila, and later of Joseph Kabila.

The participation of Zimbabwe in three wars over two decades requires serious analysis. While the first internal conflict between ZANU and ZAPU had its roots in centuries-old conflict between the Shona and Ndebele ethnic groups, it also had its genesis in more recent Zimbabwean politics. When ZANU split off from ZAPU in 1963, the reaction of the ZAPU leadership was to squelch the upstarts violently, to fight back fiercely. The subsequent conflict gave Ian Smith the pretext to ban both parties and to imprison their leaders for the next decade.

---

1. Roy Bennett was imprisoned by the Zimbabwe government in late 2004 up until the middle of 2005 after a parliamentary committee found his guilty of disrespect for parliamentary procedures. This was in after an altercation between the minister of Justice, Patrick Chinamasa, and Bennett: Bennett had accused the minister of illegally taking more than one farm under the land resettlement programme, whilst the minister accused Bennett's ancestors of being "thieves". Bennett reacted by jumping up and pushing Chinamasa down to the floor. The incident was televised. This incident made it impossible for Bennett to campaign for a parliamentary seat in the March 2005 elections.

To recapitulate, outside Rhodesia, the two liberation movements continued as separate rival entities, although there were many exchanges between them. The biggest exchange took place in the late 1960s when the bulk of the ZAPU army, ZIPRA, joined ZANU's army, ZANLA. This amalgamation was very successful, and contributed immensely to ZANLA's military success a few years later. Another attempt at amalgamation took place in 1975-76, when the Zimbabwe People's Army, ZIPA, was formed under the auspices of Presidents Nyerere and Machel. This unity ended tragically when many ZAPU guerrillas were killed by ZANU guerrillas at Mgagao and Morogoro military camps in Tanzania. The differences were overcome again later in 1976 when ZANU and ZAPU joined together to form the Patriotic Front. It was at this stage that ZANU became ZANU Patriotic Front or ZANU PF. The Patriotic Front was united against the British at Lancaster House. However, ZANU decided to fight the 1980 elections separately from ZAPU, a decision intended to weaken the military might of Josiah Tongogara, who could have successfully joined the two liberation armies into an indomitable force that would threaten the power of the traditional politicians. Politicians valued a strong army, but wanted it to be a tool of political power rather than an independent force. The election strategy was master minded by Eddison Zvobgo and led by Robert Mugabe: the two liberation movements fought the elections separately, along ethnically divided lines. Thus, the birth of Zimbabwe began with a division between the two liberation movements and the two major ethnic groups.

The civil war ended in a truce brokered by President Canaan Banana, who persuaded both sides to lay down their arms for the sake of Zimbabwe. However, the six-year war aroused intense bitterness in Matabeleland against the government of ZANU PF, and this surfaced again in the 2000 and 2002 elections, when Matabeleland voted decisively against ZANU PF. The government forces had committed many atrocities in Matabeleland. This was itself a reaction to the atrocities committed by dissidents against government officials.

The Mozambique war was well supported by the populace, who understood it as a continuation of the liberation struggle. Zimbabwe could not be free unless its neighbours, Mozambique, Namibia, and South Africa were also free. The apartheid regime of South Africa had taken over support for Renamo from the Rhodesians. Renamo, formed out of the Shona ethnic group in Mozambique, the same ethnic group as the majority Shona in Rhodesia, was opposed to the FRELIMO liberation movement because of its socialist policies and the ethnic dominance of southerners. Renamo was not only supported by the Rhodesians and the apartheid South African regime, but also by traditional Shona religious leaders in Mozambique and by fundamentalist Christian sects from the United States. The termination of the war came about when the government of Joachim Chissano decided to make an historic political compromise with Renamo, and Renamo became the official opposition party in Mozambique in 1994.

The participation of Zimbabwe in the DRC war is more clouded, and did not enjoy popular understanding or support within the country. It began in 1997, coinciding with the revolt of the war veterans against Mugabe and his government. The war did not threaten Zimbabwe's independence and sovereignty in the same way that the dissident and the Mozambique wars had done. Zimbabwe at the time enjoyed the chairmanship of the defence committee of the Southern African Development Community (SADC). The government of Laurent Kabila was being threatened on the one hand by rebels, and on the other hand by Western mining interests, as Kabila had ended ownership of the DRC's rich mining concerns by the French and Belgians, given them temporarily to American and Canadian companies, and then reneged on the deals with the Americans and Canadians. Laurent Kabila faced serious opposition, with the possibility of the rebels enjoying enormous financial support from his Western opponents. He now offered some of these mines to Zimbabwe, with a number of mines going to individual Zimbabwean generals and others to official Zimbabwean government-supported companies. Zimbabwe had and has one of the best military forces on the continent, and Kabila needed a strong army to defend his regime. He could no longer trust the Rwandans and Ugandans who had supported his takeover of the government from Mobuto Sese Seko a year earlier, in 1996-97.

One of the controversial powers enjoyed by the president in Zimbabwe is the power to declare war without consultation with cabinet or parliament. This law was passed in 1987, and I made my maiden speech against this specific clause. However, I was totally unable to win support and the law was passed. Nearly all parliamentarians believed that their responsibility was to vote loyally for anything presented by the government. Very often they had not even read the details of the bills they were passing. Loyalty was the most important quality. Criticism would be interpreted as disloyalty. Mugabe's decision to enter the DRC war was thus within his powers as executive president.

While it is true that both SADC and the Organisation of African Unity (OAU) had passed resolutions not to accept any governments brought in by military coup, it is also true that there was no unanimous decision by SADC to wage a war in support of Kabila's government against the insurgents. The DRC had become the latest member of SADC when Kabila overthrew the Mobuto regime. His government was perilously weak, and the wealth of the DRC, in particular its diamond wealth, attracted predators both from among its neighbours and from overseas. The Zimbabwean army thus became the army defending the Kabila government. It succeeded in maintaining the Kabilas in power, and many Zimbabweans made personal fortunes in the DRC.

However, as had happened in Mozambique, Zimbabwe did not benefit from the postwar recovery period in the DRC. Instead, in both cases, South African industrialists and engineers began operations once peace had been restored. This is a matter of some resentment within Zimbabwe itself. The situation testifies to the superiority of the Zimbabwean armed forces, and the weakness of the Zimbabwean industrial and commercial sectors, which were unable to make use of the strong position of Zimbabwe in these two countries. We won the wars, but lost the commercial and industrial contracts. South African enterprises marched in after peace was won, and began large-scale industrial and commercial enterprises in both countries.

LACK OF ECONOMIC GROWTH

One continuing reality two decades after independence was that the economy remained almost wholly in the hands of the white minority. By 2000, some 12 million hectares of commercial farmland were still in the hands of white farmers and of multinational companies. The retention of commercial agriculture in white hands was predictably a time bomb waiting to explode. To some extent, this was redressed by the 2000 land resettlement, but not only was valuable time lost, with a hiatus of 13 years, but the 2000 programme was executed in technically unsound ways. As a result, some of the land that was taken could not be farmed at all, due both to bureaucratic delays and to the shortage of fertiliser. Devising a technically, legally, and politically sound land resettlement programme is of crucial importance to Zimbabwe's future economic growth.

One triumph of the early days of independence in the 1980s was the salvaging of the industrial system. Industries were white owned, and many of these owners had decided to shut down their factories and leave under a destroy-and-leave strategy. Government decided to take proactive steps to purchase these factories through the Industrial Development Corporation (IDC) so as to prevent de-industrialisation. In this it was highly successful. The IDC had been set up by the settler-colonial government to establish new industries. Once these industries were well established, they were sold to the private sector to run, usually to political supporters of the Rhodesian Front. Thus, the first decade after independence did not bring about a high degree of de-industrialisation, as had happened in Mozambique and Angola.

However, the ZANU PF government did not share the Smith regime's vision of industrialisation spearheaded by government initiative and investment. Instead, it took the white-owned industries as a static resource, which should be maintained if possible. In this it was supported by many white industrialists who continued to enjoy the position of being in monopoly control over the economy, and saw it in their interests to destroy their new struggling black competitors. White industrialists often used the government to destroy challenges from newcomers, especially black newcomers who had no connections with the ruling party.

An obvious failure was that the positive growth of the 1980s, albeit modest, was replaced by the shrinking of the economy in the 1990s. The white-owned industries established before independence, particularly the manufacturing industries, did not expand. White industrialists were not confident about the government's policies and preferred to invest their money either in high interest bank accounts or overseas, rather than in the difficult task of expanding their factories. Moreover, most whites between the ages of 20 and 60 had already left the country at independence, leaving mainly those who were too old to want to settle elsewhere. These old industrialists were unlikely to start new enterprises, although many of them bravely continued to work well into their 70s and 80s. Courageous veterans of the Second World War, they did their best to maintain the industrial infrastructure intact, but could not start new industries or adopt new technologies. Both the management and technology of these factories were not as good as those of their East Asian rivals. Government did little or nothing to protect these industries, partly because they were seen as white owned, whereas their domestic competitors, the import companies, were black owned. Meanwhile, coincidentally, mineral prices dipped, and oil prices trebled. All these economic ills were blamed on the ZANU PF government.

There was no government policy to nurture black industrialists. This would have been premature in the 1980s, as the settler-colonial regime had deliberately stopped blacks from gaining industrial skills or starting industrial enterprises. Blacks who had such skills were educated and trained after independence. However, by the 1990s, the time was ripe for such an initiative. Instead, Zimbabwe decided to embark on Structural Adjustment, or non-interference by government in any economic area.

Another reason for the shrinkage of the economy was the government's indigenisation programme, which did not bring about an increase in productivity. Indigenisation, as practised, decreased productivity, while at the same time creating a class of super-rich blacks.

The collapse of the Zimbabwean currency as a result of printing billions of dollars to satisfy restive workers and the angry and implacable war veterans created immediate currency instability in Zimbabwe. The government had been indulging in increasing the money supply unwisely since the early 1990s in order to buy peace with its labour movement, and it decided to use the same strategy to please the war veterans. The instability of the currency, for example moving from US$1:Z$1 in 1980 to US$1:Z$27,000 in 2005, was a symptom of the total loss of control over the economy. The situation was exploited by the new indigenous businessmen and bankers. The coincidence of crises brought Zimbabwe to the verge of economic collapse. The middle class that had benefited from independence found itself pauperised, the young found themselves jobless.

Government had never seen its role as employment creation, and this reluctance increased after the advent of Structural Adjustment. According to the tenets of liberal economics, government's role should be limited to infrastructure and services, such as roads, education, and health. The economy should be left to private enterprise. Ideology triumphed over practical realism, as 100 years of colonialism and settlerism had left a lopsided private sector dominated by white industrialists and white commercial farmers. Black entrepreneurs had been confined to petty commerce and the bus services from urban to rural areas, as the colonial system had divided the black family, allowing only male workers to live in cities, while wives and families had to remain in the rural areas. After independence, black traders were rewarded with import licences through which they could import goods for sale. Some of the new entrepreneurs sold these import licences to their white colleagues at a premium, so immediately doubling the cost of goods on the market.

The fact that the population has doubled since independence, whereas the number of jobs has actually shrunk during the same period, constituted a major challenge.

ECONOMIC DOWNTURN LEADS TO LOSS OF NATIONAL UNITY

The post-independence achievements, substantial though they were in the fields of infrastructure building, education, and other social services, were marred by the failure of the economy to grow during the Structural Adjustment period. The drastic shrinkage of the economy, coinciding with spiralling international petrol prices, the war veterans' revolt, the disastrous devaluation of the Zimbabwe dollar, the ostentatious and openly vaunted corruption of the ruling class, the DRC war, and the often violent take over of white-owned commercial farmlands, led to growing disaffection of the population, in particular the urban population, which suffered the most from Structural Adjustment.

The economic breakdown led to a destruction of the national unity that had defined the country in the 1980s, when Zimbabwe was seen as a model of good development in Africa by both its own citizens and the international community. Whereas the 1980s had been a period of racial harmony between blacks and whites, despite the Shona/Ndebele ethnic conflict, the 1990s saw a gradual descent from harmony to continuing conflict and polarisation. The social "glue" that had united all Zimbabweans was destroyed. The traditional honesty and helpfulness of the Zimbabwean was replaced by a rapacious and often criminal pursuit of money, and in this pursuit anything was allowed. Crime levels rose, whether this was petty crime or large-scale sophisticated crime by the political and economic elite. In particular, crime became the order of the day in the area of foreign exchange.

The replacement of socialism by Structural Adjustment as the national ideology, with the replacement of the freedom fighter by the Mafikizolo as the symbols of the ZANU PF government, led gradually to the disaffection of the general population. President Mugabe's two wives served as the symbols of the change, with Sally Mugabe identified by her work with lepers, prostitutes, the poor, the ill, and in rural water development, and Grace Mugabe identified as the fashion leader of the up and coming young, beautiful, fashionable, and wealthy. Sally was loved by the poor but hated by the powerful; Grace is the darling of the fashionable but hated by the poor, who somehow blame her for their poverty. Actually, she is not to blame for their poverty or for what has gone wrong in Zimbabwe, just as Sally's alleviation of the suffering of a few was not enough to change the system that traps the majority of people in poverty.

There was an exodus of an estimated 3.4 million young people. The majority of them went to South Africa, where the post-apartheid economic boom meant that there was a serious shortage of educated, qualified, and experienced personnel. A substantial number went to the former colonial power, Britain, where a shortage of professional personnel, particularly of nurses, doctors, and teachers, meant that they could be utilised as a cheaper labour force.

ZANU PF's return to its roots in terms of turning to the war veterans for support during its time of crisis, and its return to the discourse of the war period of the 1960s and 1970s when ZANU was fighting against settlerism and colonialism, managed to win it some respite, particularly when the new opposition party failed to win the support of the war veterans or of the peasantry, instead depending on the support of the urban workers and white farmers. Unfortunately, the MDC leadership was unwise enough to make disparaging remarks about war veterans and peasants, oblivious to the fact that the peasantry comprise 70 per cent of the electorate. Disenchanted as the peasantry was with the hiatus in the land resettlement programme between 1987 and 2000, they were nevertheless not prepared to vote for an opposition party that was initially against land resettlement.[1] ZANU PF was able to reassume

---

1. The MDC has since changed its stance on this issue.

its role as a liberation movement fighting for land for the peasant masses.

Zimbabwe's downturn in the second decade of independence must be analysed within the post-independence history of sub-Saharan Africa as a whole, rather than by looking at Zimbabwe as an isolated and peculiar case. It should also be analysed within the historical developments that took place in the 1990s, including the fall of the Soviet Union and of communism as a credible ideology. The freeing of Nelson Mandela in 1992, followed shortly afterwards by the granting of majority rule in South Africa in 1994, was another historical landmark that affected Zimbabwe's development substantially.

Like Zimbabwe, many African countries were initially very successful at the very same things that Zimbabwe was successful in, namely, educational provision, improvement of the social services in general, and infrastructure building. Nearly all were relative failures in the areas of economic expansion, particularly in the areas of industrialisation and industrial expansion. While the ideology of African countries varied, from socialism in Tanzania, to humanism in Zambia, to capitalism in Kenya, most countries have not yet made the transition from being the primary product economies inherited at independence, with the majority of the population dependent on traditional farming, to more multifaceted industrialised economies. Nearly all these countries were ruled during the first two decades of independence by the parties that had led the people through a liberation struggle. These liberation parties established one-party states as a way of uniting all ethnic groups into one nation. In the absence of industrialisation and its concomitant class distinctions, political parties tended to form around tribal groups. Moreover, the colonial policy to limit education, particularly secondary, technical, vocational, and university education for blacks meant that professionalisation was also severely limited.

One-party states were replaced either by breakaway groups from within the liberation movement, as happened in Kenya, or by parties supported by the former colonial power, as happened in Ghana when Nkrumah was overthrown by a military coup. In the case of Zimbabwe, the popular MDC was very quickly commandeered by forces that had fought against the liberation struggle.

The collapse of the Soviet Union in the early 1990s, and the gradual shift of China from a centrally planned economy to a market-based economy, meant that the communist form of socialism that had so inspired some of the freedom fighters in the 1970s was now seriously discredited. In Zimbabwe it meant the death of ideology, and, as in the early years of the Soviet collapse, it led to an increase in criminality and gangsterism. The death of ideology meant a fatal weakening of the state in Zimbabwe.

In the first decade of independence, Zimbabwe had been well favoured by donors. Indeed, it was the darling of the donors, who were prepared to pour in about 300,000,000 U.S. dollars into the country each year. With the fall of the Soviet Union, this largesse towards Africa in general ceased. Africa had been seen as a contested area between the West and the communists. Now that the Soviet Union had imploded, most Western countries, in particular the United States and the United Kingdom, no longer saw any advantage in providing aid, however meagre, to Africa. With the removal of Thatcher as Prime Minister in 1990, Zimbabwe was to receive no more of the promised aid to buy out white farmers. Whatever monies Western powers had reserved as "aid" now went largely to Eastern Europe, which was in need of large development funds for its recovery from communism.

One effect of the loss of donor funding in Zimbabwe was the weakening of the non-governmental (NGO) sector, which had enjoyed generous donor funding. This sector had been largely dependent on outside funding, and was not able to adjust speedily to depending on local funding, in particular because it was providing services to the poorest sectors of society. At the same time, Structural Adjustment had weakened government's control in general, the clearest indication of this being the weakening of the police force, which no longer had funds to enable it to investigate crime or to chase criminals. The relatively poorly paid police were now more likely to want petty bribes than to pursue criminals. The police became part of the problem. Thus, both state and non-governmental organisations were seriously weakened in the 1990s.

The liberation of South Africa, coinciding as it did with the espousal of Structural Adjustment in Zimbabwe, the fall of the Soviet Union, and the end of generous donor funding, meant that Zimbabwe's role as the frontline against apartheid had ended. Its weakened economy, already only about two per cent the size of the South African economy, was taking a serious battering with the closure of hundreds of factories.

Zimbabwe's role as a political and economic leader in the region was very much overshadowed by the emergence of the South African political and economic giant. The new South Africa, comprising a partnership between Afrikaner nationalists and African National Congress (ANC) nationalists, was not prepared to countenance any form of Structural Adjustment imposed from outside. It perceived Structural Adjustment as against the nationalist interests, and refused to accept loans from the World Bank and IMF, because of the attached conditions.

Zimbabwe was not able to re-establish its previous dominant leadership in the region except through military adventurism. Utilising its position as chair of the SADC security committee, Zimbabwe entered into a period of military adventurism in 1997, ostensibly to protect the sovereignty of the Kabila government against rebel insurgents. Of course, Kabila had himself been a rebel insurgent only a few months earlier.

In the same year, the government faced the war veterans' revolt. President Mugabe decided to placate war veterans by issuing billions of Zimbabwe dollars of compensation on 13-14 November 1997.

Several years of drought, usually interpreted by the highly religious Zimbabwean population as punishment by the ancestral spirits for the misdemeanours of their rulers, led to further disaffection.

By the end of 2003, Zimbabwe faced possible economic collapse, in particular because of the almost hysterical expatriation of foreign currency by all and sundry, but particularly by the political elite, which now controlled the indigenous banks. The wealthy were in the process of feathering their own nests, not in Zimbabwe, but in overseas bank accounts. They recognised they were at the end of an era and wanted to have enough insurance against the future. They did not care that by robbing Zimbabwe of what little foreign currency it had earned they were destroying the economy even further. The black market owned by big business and well connected political leaders now became the official banking system in the country, and even government departments and parastatals had to rush to the black market, known euphemistically and good naturedly as the "World Bank", if they wanted any foreign currency. Much-needed petrol was reportedly being purchased with foreign currency obtained from the black market.

The resignation of the reserve bank governor, Leonard Tsumba, towards the end of that year enabled President Mugabe to appoint Gideon Gono as the new governor. Gono immediately embarked on a rectification programme aimed at halting the dishonest exploitation of their clients by marauding banks. It is not clear whether Gono will be able to sustain such a massive clean up, given that so many members of the political elite are heavily embroiled in the corruption. This led to the flight overseas of a number of bank owners and managers, as well as of top ranking businessmen. A number of indigenous banks were shut down, and others brought under reserve bank curatorship.

Not surprisingly, the Mafikizolo attacked Gono's measures as a way of weakening "indigenisation", the populist word for the enrichment of a small number of the ruling elite. They also alleged that Gono himself had been corrupt, using as proof the fact that the bank he had headed had utilised the black market to obtain foreign currency. In fact, in 2003, almost the only source of foreign exchange was the black market.

It was also alleged that the corruption clean up was a way of weakening the political power of the Mafikizolo. The latter were in a life-and-death power struggle for control of ZANU PF. They were opposed by the old-style politicians of the 1960s, who were supported by those who had taken part in the liberation struggle.

President Mugabe sought to curb corruption by arresting a few of its most notorious perpetrators. A new presidential directive allowed imprisonment without trial for more than 20 days. Previously, anyone arrested had to appear before a magistrate within 24 hours. This new draconian measure was aimed at enabling the police to carry out their investigations unhindered. The fear that police investigations would be compromised by bribes is based on experience: evidence collected by the police is known to "disappear" on payment of large sums of money, and this still constitutes a perennial problem. ZANU PF companies were also to be investigated for corruption by an internal ZANU PF committee.

The cancerous spread of corruption among the ruling elite can be blamed not only on their personal lack of integrity, but also on the weak institutional systems whose processes were shrouded in secrecy. This secrecy was born out of a combination of Ian Smith's sanctions-breaking economy and ZANU PF's struggle as a liberation movement against enemy infiltration and attack. For example, for more than 20 years there was no public audit of ZANU PF businesses, contrary to the normal practice of annual audits. Combined with the new bureaucracy's use of secrecy to dominate and control a hapless, passive, and supplicant population, secrecy was one of the commonest features of the post-independence government. In this culture of secrecy, the public was unaware of how decisions were made, and even of what decisions had been made. For example, the processes regarding the redistribution of land after 2000, despite the formation of several committees, was not in the public arena, thus allowing corruption to flourish.

The weakening of the state led to the collapse of development and of law and order. Other manifestations of the weakened state included the emergence of regional lords who could challenge the government. ZANU PF politics now were more and more controlled by ethnic considerations, with regional lords within the ruling party threatening to remove their support if they were not given posts and privileges. Many of those holding political power openly used their positions to gain wealth.

CHAPTER 19

A Vision of Zimbabwe Tomorrow

Zimbabwe is at a crossroads: Zimbabweans are ready for transformation. They have shown their criticism of the ruling party through the 2000 referendum on the constitution and the 2000 and 2002 elections. They have also shown their scepticism of the MDC by the fact that the MDC was unable to win an outright majority both in the 2000 elections and in the presidential elections in 2002. By making land the only issue in both elections, Robert Mugabe showed his well-known political astuteness. The majority of the people in Zimbabwe want land, and they voted for land. Land was the trump card. The MDC was not able to trump this trump card because of its close alliance with white farmers, resulting in its mixed and confused messages on the land issue.

THE SURVIVAL OF FEUDAL AND SETTLER–COLONIAL INSTITUTIONS AFTER INDEPENDENCE

In looking at the development of Zimbabwe in the future, it is necessary to examine very critically the political, social, cultural, and economic institutions within the country. The combination of colonial and feudal institutions under the mantle of nationalism has produced some of the contradictions that we are experiencing today. These feudal-colonial institutions affect both the ruling party and the various opposition parties that have developed since independence. They have all worked within a system that inevitably reproduces some of the social effects that we now experience.

One of these is the high tolerance of corruption, as long as it is being perpetrated by someone who is politically loyal to your side. However, when corruption is exhibited by a political opponent or a potential political rival, it is necessary to clamp down on it as viciously as possible. Under Ian Smith and previous settler-colonial regimes, political supporters were richly rewarded with ownership of farms and industrial companies that were initially developed with state funds.

Opponents had their property summarily confiscated.[1] These powers of government have survived independence, and they have been used against white farmers and members of the opposition MDC. Most people who witnessed the confiscation of the property of peasants and of black businessmen who supported the liberation movements in the 1960s and 1970s do not see anything wrong with the confiscation of white-owned property.

The political polarity that leads to the killing of opposition party members has its roots in the colonial-settler heritage. Under Ian Smith, the CIO was licensed to kill anyone in the liberation movements, and this they did ruthlessly. Unfortunately, they have continued to perform these duties after independence, acting as an extra-judicial assassination squad.

POLITICAL TRANSFORMATION

It is clear that political transformation is needed in Zimbabwe. The inherited political system is one of polarisation between the government under ZANU PF and the various opposition parties and groups that have existed since independence, such as ZAPU, ZUM, MDC, the trade unions, the churches, and the NGOs. This is very much a repetition of the settler-colonial past, when the Ian Smith regime brutally suppressed the liberation movements.

Democracy was born at independence in Zimbabwe in 1980. However, democracy is still very fragile. This was very much in evidence when Chenjerai Hitler Hunzvi gained ascendance in 1996 until his death a few years later. Although he was not a member of the cabinet, he was nevertheless powerful enough to make decisions that cabinet ministers could not make. He forced government to make huge disbursements, firstly to an elite group of a few hundred, and then to some

---

1. Thousands of black people were affected by these laws. Members of nationalist parties were taken away from their homes and their property confiscated. Some of them were kept in exile in the Rhodesian equivalent of Siberia, the Gokwe region, which was infested with malaria. Others were detained in game parks, such as Gonakudzingwa, or imprisoned with common criminals. The late vice president of Zimbabwe, Joshua Nkomo, spent a decade in Gonakudzingwa, whereas President Robert Mugabe spent a similar period imprisoned with criminals. Hundreds of thousands of peasants in war-torn regions of Rhodesia in the 1970s had their cattle confiscated.

50,000 of the rank and file of former guerrillas. In both disbursements, he himself was involved in criminal fraud, but he was not convicted, an example of the weakening of the justice system for reasons of political expediency. Instead, he was buried in Heroes Acre, generally reserved for the politically powerful and for those who had fought for the liberation of Zimbabwe. He forced on to the country a huge devaluation of its currency, a power generally reserved for the minister of finance and the governor of the reserve bank. These were examples of political power being exercised outside the formally elected decision-making systems.

One of the reasons that Hunzvi was able to take over the powers of government was that government itself had weakened considerably in the 1990s. Partly, this was due to Structural Adjustment, which aimed at lessening state power and strengthening private enterprise. However, the nature of private enterprise in Zimbabwe, with its aging white industrialists and its non-productive patronage-dependent Mafikizolo, was that industrial productivity became much lower than before. Moreover, the strength of the Commercial Farmers Union (CFU), which represented mainly white commercial farmers, was such that it was able to prevent wholesale land resettlement. Government supporters saw the taking of white farmlands as an expression of the democratisation of property ownership: land re-distribution strengthened support for government among those in the middle class and peasantry who were able to obtain farms. Those who opposed the land confiscation, particularly the white farmers, saw the process as a denial of the democratic right to property ownership protected under the constitution.

During the liberation struggle, a number of forms of democracy were practised, but after independence these were largely displaced by the more dominant settler-colonial practices, as well as by the strongly held feudal mores. One of the liberation struggle's practices was that of self-criticism and group criticism. This has completely disappeared. I recall meetings where someone as powerful as Tongogara was criticised for his exploitation of women freedom fighters, for example. Tongogara was also criticised by the spirit mediums, the *vanasekuru*, for his execution of those he saw as enemies of the revolution, sometimes his personal rivals. These forms of criticism were seen as ways of strengthening the liberation struggle.

The respect for all forms of life and the need for sexual discipline promoted by the *vanasekuru* have largely been forsaken. The dependence on violence as the main if not the only way of resolving conflicts is in stark contrast to the tenets of traditional religion.

More recently, new forms of criticism have arisen through the opposition press and through NGOs funded by outside donors. Many "democratic" NGOs have been established to support the land rights of white farmers and British companies, but they have paid little attention to the very poor land rights of peasants, including those who have been resettled. The political discourse needs to be broadened beyond the property rights of the formerly economically mighty to also encompass the property rights of the formerly dispossessed.

In examining the conflict between government and the opposition press, in particular the *Daily News*, the mouthpiece of the MDC,[1] what is notable is the personalised nature of the attacks on government. The opposition press and the government press extol their own side, with each exposing corruption among their opponents but covering it up when it is from their own side.

Less powerful politicians are not able to suppress criticism, while more powerful and equally corrupt figures may not be criticised at all. This is in line with the practice of removing the less powerful but allowing the more powerful to remain, even though both may be equally guilty of corruption and even of criminal activities. The showy removal of a few corrupt figures wins public support for the more powerful politicians, but may in fact cover up larger scale corruption. It is essential to ensure that criminal activities and corruption are not protected by political considerations.

Generally, there is inadequate criticism of policies and strategies, other than the land seizure policy. The opposition press has been generously funded by big business and foreign interests, which have been desperate for a change in government in order to reverse the land takeovers. President Mugabe has staked his reputation on the land resettlement programme, and his removal has been seen as critical to a change of the land policy. The opposition press in general is still highly supportive of Structural Adjustment and blames Zimbabwe's woes on the

---

1. The *Daily News* is presently banned, but the case is still going through court challenges.

government's failure to obey the strictures of Structural Adjustment closely enough. I tend to see the opposite: that the government has been too obedient to a failed theory, without sufficient attention to the details as they apply to the real situation.

One of the problems over the last decade is the internal instability caused by the ad hoc manner in which policies and strategies have evolved. In a situation where government has lost control over some of the regional politicians, very local decisions are being made, often in contradiction of enunciated national policies. An example of this has been the land resettlement programme, which has witnessed very different implementation strategies from province to province: in some provinces local politicians have even been able to utilise the scheme to give themselves and their relatives ownership of a large number of farms, in contravention of the established regulations. Sometimes an individual politician has been able to utilise the volatile situation to get rid of his political and economic rivals and to obtain their property. This could be at the expense of destroying a productive enterprise. There is a need to establish a more stable and predictable economic environment. This will entail establishing a new political climate that will allow both criticism and political diversity without resort to violence. Zimbabwe has yet to build a strongly democratic and tolerant society.

Corruption has played a major role in weakening the ZANU PF government. A renewal of political legitimacy will need to see very firm control over corruption, in particular strengthening institutions to make corruption more difficult.

Democracy requires the protection of a strong government. Since the weakening of state power in the 1990s, democracy has also weakened considerably. Threatening government has become a very common political ploy, utilised by trade unions, by war veterans, and by regional "chefs".[1] Some of the regional chefs have threatened to withdraw their support or to split the ruling party, ZANU PF. Strong government that protects and supports the human rights of all its citizens, while nurturing economic freedom and a greater democratisation of property ownership rather than through command economics, is

---

1. "Chef" is from the Portuguese, and is the term of honour used for the new rulers belonging to ZANU PF. It is similar to the English word "chief". It developed during the liberation struggle, when Portuguese-speaking Mozambique was the home of most freedom fighters.

essential for democracy. Only a strong government can bring about a peaceful and stable government in Zimbabwe.

SOCIAL AND CULTURAL TRANSFORMATION

For the poor and deprived, the new governing elite has come to resemble the settler regime. Leaders have access to power and property. Leaders are known as "chefs", and they are the suppliers of positions and goods to their followers. The peasants and workers remain as supplicants, while the leaders are chiefs who are able to favour their supporters.

In an underdeveloped economy such as in Zimbabwe, ethnic and regional differences have a larger political role than in industrialised economies, where ethnic and regional loyalties may constitute only one of many other institutions and interests. However, there are already many other institutions in Zimbabwe, such as professional and trade organisations, educational and research institutions, religious institutions, women's groups, industrial institutions and companies, etc. Presently the democratic discourse is confined almost entirely to political parties and to NGOs, and is distorted by blind partisanship. Expanding the discourse to cover these other groupings can provide a more robust foundation for the development of democracy within the society.

Culture defines the aspirations and values of a people. Zimbabwe has many novelists, poets, and musicians who are interpreting the Zimbabwean psyche and forming the future values of the people. Zimbabwean aspirations and values derive from ancient tradition and history; the feudal past; the still dominant settler-colonial heritage; the religious experiences of the people; the liberation struggle; the post-independence experience; and the country's exposure to the world. The strongest strand today appears to be the settler-colonial experiences and values, with the ruling elite seeking to take over the symbols of the former colonial rulers, such as their housing, their farms, their cars, their holidays, their education system, their violent repression of opposition, etc. The boast "we are as good as Smith" is unfortunately true. But do we really want to be as good as Smith? This is an important question that Zimbabweans need to address today. I think we need to revive some of the principles and values of the liberation struggle, which included looking at the lives and needs of the underprivileged.

These have been lost since the 1990s, when the liberation struggle was reversed. For Zimbabwe to renew itself, it needs to re-examine its heritage from the past and to create a new culture and values for the future.

ECONOMIC TRANSFORMATION

Without economic expansion and improvement, the social gains of the early days of independence cannot be maintained. One of the biggest challenges for Zimbabwe is to move from a primary production economy to a more balanced production base, which will include greater self-sufficiency in industrial consumer products. This was a process that the Ian Smith government had already begun in terms of import substitution of major consumer products. However, these industries used low and medium level technologies, and were not able to modernise after independence. Now that these industries have been destroyed, the challenge will be to replace them with industries with higher-level technology and management systems. This will entail government support for re-industrialisation that will be totally different from the asset stripping that has characterised the last decade.

One of Zimbabwe's chief challenges is the expansion of the economy in order to cater for the whole population. This problem was there before independence, when the settler-colonial regime had developed a sound but small economy: it was only large enough to cater well for a minority of the population, the whites, who were at most four per cent of the whole. The post-independence government enjoyed the benefits of this economy, and did manage to expand it in the first decade after independence, after which it began to shrink. At the same time, the population has doubled in the 25 years since independence. A serious contradiction has arisen through the democratisation of education: the children of peasants and workers have been able to obtain a very high level of education, but property and economic rights have remained in the hands of a tiny minority.

A number of economic plans have been published over the last few years, several by government, one by the ZCTU, and one by the MDC. None of them is operational. Probably the only operational plan has been that made by the new reserve bank governor, Gideon Gono, as a way of stabilising the currency. This is not a full economic plan, but can be used as a foundation for building a more consensual and more detailed economic development plan for the country. A blueprint is very much needed, instead of the present crisis-ridden and crisis management approach.

Such a blueprint will need to look at each economic sector in detail, such as the textile sector, the engineering sector, the electronics sector, etc. Present economic plans are very broad and lack details. They appear to be attempts to appease outside opinion, being very faithful to the tenets of Structural Adjustment. Moreover, those who are supposed to implement the programme such as the industrialists have not been consulted about the plans, a fatal flaw.

Land remains and will always remain one of the key natural resources of Zimbabwe. The division of land between commercial farmlands and peasant farmlands that was institutionalised by the successive settler-colonial regimes has been retained in the 2000 land resettlement programme as the A1 and A2 farmlands. There is a need to unify and modernise the land ownership system.

While it is too early to judge the strengths and weaknesses of the resettlement process, it is probable that between a third and half of the resettled farmers will be able to make a success of their enterprises. By adopting transparent technical criteria for the removal of land from unsuitable farmers, and utilising the support of outside agencies such as the United Nations Food and Agricultural Organisation (FAO), which is the specialist United Nations agency in charge of agriculture, to increase transparency, it will be possible for the Zimbabwean government to reorganise the resettlement programme in such a way as to ensure that the land is held by practising, competent, and experienced farmers. The United Nations Development Programme (UNDP) has already initiated a programme to assist in the resettlement process, and this can form the basis for support for resettlement.

My vision for the former commercial farmlands is that they will be divided into farms of different sizes, according to technical, geographic, and individual needs. The housing area for workers will be turned into villages, where owners will have freehold tenure. There is no reason why housing land should not be based on freehold tenure, but farmland in the wrong hands can bring starvation to the country. Farmland will be sold on leasehold for 99 years, but only to serious farmers who have either done a course in agriculture or who have shown their skill through a record of success as a farmer. The price of the leaseholds should not be purely subject to market forces, because this will lead to land hoarding and land speculation. The rich will begin buying up all the farms. However, land should be sold rather than given away free of charge. The price of land should be controlled in such a way that it is affordable to the ordinary peasant farmer. At independence, white farmers were being paid Z$200 (then about US$200) per hectare. Similar price guidelines can be developed that will suit the real farmer. There is an urgent need to establish a landownership system that would provide security of tenure to good farmers, while enabling the state to protect agricultural land as a fundamental and key national resource. The present system by which land is given to those who are politically powerful mixes-up the criteria: the politically adept are not necessarily the best farmers.

Communal farmlands should follow a similar land ownership pattern, with freehold for housing areas and 99-year leaseholds for farmland. Unifying the system so that all land ownership follows clear and transparent rules that are not subject to patronage or political manipulation is of critical importance for stabilising the key industry in Zimbabwe, agriculture.

Loans should be made available to enable serious farmers to purchase the leasehold farms.

Inheritance of farmland should be studied and new rules established. Presently, two laws exist for inheritance of land, with former white lands being inheritable by the wife, and communal lands being inherited only by male heirs. In neither case is there a rule regarding the technical competence of the heir. A simple rule would be that the farm should be inherited by someone who has done a farming course or who has devoted his or her life to farming. Inheritance of farmland by non-farmers should not be allowed: instead the state should compensate such heirs, and the farmland should return to state ownership. A lesson should be learnt from the African Purchase Farms, which were initially very well farmed by dedicated farmers, who educated their children: but very few of these children returned to farm. Some of these farms are now derelict, or are used mainly as housing areas or retirement homes.

Present land resettlement programmes do not take into consideration the fact that over 70 per cent of farmers are women. The continuation of land ownership patterns through which women have no control over the fruits of their labour is a recipe for low productivity.

Women, as the main workers in the communal and resettlement areas, presently have to hand over income earned to their husbands. The likelihood is that the husband may use any savings to marry another wife. Most first wives do not welcome the idea of having younger and better educated second or third wives joining the household to usurp their positions. The wiser first wives therefore ensure that there are no savings.

The issue of the expropriated white farmers needs to be addressed very seriously. The land ownership problem in Zimbabwe is shared by other Southern African countries, for example South Africa and Namibia. It is also problematic in countries as far afield as Kenya, Rwanda, and the Sudan, where land hunger has been a pretext for violence and, in the case of Rwanda, genocide. The international community has a role to play in the farm resettlement programme in Zimbabwe. In my view, dedicated white Zimbabwean farmers should be allowed to return to their profession of farming. However, the farm sizes of about 2,000 hectares per commercial farm obviously cannot be continued. These farms have already been broken up to a maximum size of just over 200 hectares each in prime areas, and white farmers should also be able to access such land. The issue of compensation to these farmers needs to be addressed in a fair way. The British and US governments' promise of funding for land resettlement at Lancaster House has not been adhered to: it needs to be revived, reviewed, and supported by other donors.

Zimbabwe did not undertake sufficient water development to overcome its regular and perennial droughts. Government has made a tremendous effort to provide clean borehole water to all communities, thereby eliminating the need to walk many kilometres every day to fetch water, an onerous and time-consuming task that every woman and girl in rural Africa knows so well. For irrigation purposes there was a tendency to build large prestigious dams, which mainly benefited white commercial farmers, rather than smaller village dams that could have benefited communal and resettlement farmers. And even where dams were built for small-scale farmers, issues such as responsibility for upkeep and rights to water were not clear. Courses on the optimal usage of dam water were not in place, whereas little dams could do much to address the nutritional needs of the peasants through fish farming, and through irrigation during the droughts that plague Zimbabwe.

These dams need to be linked to greater productivity, e.g., including training and/or marketing for fish farming, horticulture, food processing, dam maintenance, etc. Ten thousand dams could transform the economy in the same way that the 6,000 schools built since independence have transformed the education scene. These dams could be built by the government through the ministry of water development, through the District Development Fund (DDF), and with the private sector. Close cooperation of all engineers is essential for such a massive programme.

Engineering is one of the strengths of Zimbabwe. It should be further strengthened and utilised for the development not only of infrastructure such as dams, roads, and bridges in Zimbabwe but also throughout Africa. Engineering necessarily plays a particularly important part in the early days of development. Zimbabwe should see its role as an important builder for the whole region. This will require close collaboration between government and the engineering private sector.

Engineering can be linked to employment creation within the country. The very high unemployment rate in Zimbabwe can be addressed by increasing the public works programme to absorb a larger number of the unemployed. If something like 30–35 per cent of the government budget were spent on public works,[1] this would boost demand for consumer products while increasing the supply of infrastructure. This would be a virtuous circle. A very ambitious public works programme over the next two decades can provide the cushioning for the re-industrialisation of the economy.

One of the focuses for public works could be housing construction in urban areas. There is an enormous shortage of urban housing. After independence, government stopped building housing for rental purposes, assuming that all urban houses would be owner-built and owner-inhabited. Private enterprise would take the place of government in housing construction. The result of this policy has become evident over the past ten years: the private sector has provided quite well for the middle class but not for the poor. The demand for housing increased, but the supply did not. There is a large demand for housing for low-

---

1. This is approximately the amount being spent on interest payments for government debt.

income workers. Even teachers find it difficult to find housing in urban areas. Rental housing built by municipalities and funded by government grants can also be sold to tenants. Housing could be utilised as one of the engines of growth. A return to building about 20,000 houses a year for the poor might do a great deal to overcome the present housing crisis. In particular, there is now a need to move to build more flats.

One symptom of the economic malaise in the country is the exodus of several million young Zimbabweans. It is only recently that this diaspora has been recognised as a rich resource for the country. To date, the diaspora has been seen only as a source of foreign exchange. However, it is possible to see this dispersion of the population as a great advantage to the country, providing a network of Zimbabweans all over the world. The diaspora could contribute to growth and development through the formation of companies and networks that could enable Zimbabweans to tap external opportunities and markets, particularly through Internet and email-created jobs. Investment by the diaspora in housing, agriculture, and industrial development is also possible. The skills and experience of the diaspora can be utilised. Special programmes should be developed to cater for the special needs as well as the special skills of the diaspora.

On the service side, Zimbabwe has the potential for providing first class medical and educational services to the whole of Africa. These are areas of growth that could benefit users inside Zimbabwe as well as being extended to people overseas.

The reserve bank governor has initiated a cleaning up and strengthening of the banking institutions. What has been done in the last few months is only a beginning, and requires concerted and sustained effort if the banking sector is to be strong enough to cater for real development. To date, banking services have not been extended to small-scale farmers and entrepreneurs.

BUILDING ON THE HERITAGE OF ZIMBABWE

Zimbabwe has a rich heritage. By the 11th century it was already sufficiently organised to be able to begin the construction of the first Zimbabwe.[1] A system of imperial government was balanced by the

---

1. "Zimbabwe" means houses of stones, and refers to the beautiful stone city built in southwestern Zimbabwe in the Middle Ages.

powerful spirit mediums, who represented the interests not only of their ancestors, but also of the common people. Leaders had to ensure that they promoted the interests of the people as a whole, and not only of themselves. The country has had a long history of struggle for democracy throughout the colonial period, and ending in independence. The people of Zimbabwe fought valiantly against political and economic oppression for 100 years. In the more recent liberation struggle of the 1970s, tens of thousands of freedom fighters died in order that Zimbabwe should be born. The newly revitalised Zimbabwe needs to return to the democratic and ethical values for which those freedom fighters died.

Underprivileged groups, including the peasants, workers, and women in general, have fought valiantly to gain equal and democratic rights. This struggle continues, and although some gains are apparent, the battle has not yet been won.

Zimbabwe also has a long history of industrial development, spearheaded in part by the Jewish refugees who were fleeing the Nazi holocaust. They brought with them their industrial skills as well as their respect for democracy. Its engineering industries were founded by Scottish engineers. White farmers developed commercial agriculture, based largely on tobacco, horticulture, and wheat, while peasant farmers have traditionally fed the nation. These economic players provide a strong foundation for the future. Today, Zimbabwe needs to recreate itself on the basis of its heritage, selecting the best features from all its history.

APPENDIX 1

The Mgagao Declaration by Zimbabwe Freedom Fighters (October, 1975)

We hereby express out deepest gratitude and appreciation for the efforts made by the OAU Liberation Committee in the struggle to liberate Zimbabwe from the clutches of imperialism, colonialism, and fascism. Without the support of the OAU Liberation Committee, the Tanzanian government, and Frelimo, the struggle to liberate Zimbabwe would not have developed to its present state. We sincerely hope and are fully determined to reward these noble efforts by securing the liberation of Zimbabwe people so as to make our contribution to the African revolution and the world revolution. In line with our sworn pledge to liberate Zimbabwe we hereby submit the following points for your consideration. After a careful, deep, and analytical study of the current situation in the Zimbabwean Liberation Movement in particular and the Zimbabwe revolution in general, we, as the people who have vowed to sacrifice our very lives for the liberation of our fatherland, wish to make our feelings and standpoint unequivocally clear to you in the interest of the liberation of Zimbabwe.

1.
We hereby state our unswerving and unequivocal commitment to the liberation of Zimbabwe through an arduous Armed Struggle. Events and facts have clearly shown that any other course of action would be tantamount to an open betrayal of the Zimbabwe people. We therefore strongly, unreservedly, categorically, and totally condemn any moves to continue talks with the Smith regime in whatever form. We, the freedom fighters, will do the fighting and nobody under heaven has the power to deny us the right to die for our country. We vowed to fight

for our fatherland and the bloodshed in the struggle to liberate our fatherland is ours and strongly not anybody else's.

2.
We hereby reaffirm our support for the Unity Accord signed on 7-12-74 by which the four organizations, ZANU, ZAPU, old ANC and FROLIZI were merged under the ANC. We strongly register our support for national unity, but to us unity is not an end in itself but a means to an end. Unity is not a magic formula to liberation but is one of the weapons in the struggle for liberation. For Unity to be meaningful in the Zimbabwe revolution, it should be based on an arduous and relentless armed struggle because any other course of action would make this same unity inimical to the Liberation of Zimbabwe. We know of three forms of unity:

    (a) Revolutionary Unity
    (b) Counter-Revolutionary Unity
    (c) Reactionary Unity.

Revolutionary Unity is for the purpose of promoting and accelerating the revolution. In this unity lies the strength of revolutionaries and we, as revolutionaries, stand for such unity.

Counter-Revolutionary Unity is for the purpose of arresting and setting brakes to the revolution. It is a weapon in the service of reactionaries int heir struggle to sabotage the revolutionary struggle and is aimed at stamping our the flames of the people's struggle. This is the sort of Unity advocated by Smith, Vorster, and their allies. We strongly condemn and will wage a relentless struggle against such a form of unity. Such a counter-revolutionary unity can be brought about by puppets and stooges of the reactionaries as a means of containing the revolution.

Reactionary Unity is unity of the reactionaries themselves in the struggle for the perpetuation of their existence, their evil rule and the suppression of the broad masses of the people. We are totally opposed to it because it is a sworn enemy of the people. In your efforts to strengthen the unity of the people of Zimbabwe, we strongly hope that you will take the three forms of unity into consideration and direct your efforts accordingly.

3.

We strongly condemn and completely disassociate ourselves from the Nkomo faction of the ANC. The move taken by Nkomo in holding his congress in Salisbury is clearly reactionary and divisive in the eyes of all revolutionaries and progressives of the world. It is a manifestation of various schemes worked out in the political laboratories of Salisbury and Pretoria aimed at depriving the Zimbabwe people of their right to independence based on majority rule, one man, one vote.

4.

We wish to register our strong criticism over the way the ANC leadership has been exercising leadership over the revolution. These are namely:
  (a) Bishop Abel Muzorewa
  (b) Reverend Ndabaningi Sithole
  (c) James Chikerema.

These three have proved to be completely hopeless and ineffective as leaders of the Zimbabwe revolution. Ever since the Unity Accord was signed on 7-12-74 these men have done nothing to promote the struggle for the liberation of Zimbabwe, but on the other hand, they have done everything to hamper the struggle through their power struggle. They have no interest of the revolution or the people at heart, but only their personal interests. They cherish an insatiable lust for power.

(a) They have failed to produce a most general line which can form a basis for all theoretical and practical activities of the party.
(b) They have failed to produce machinery capable of prosecuting and effecting the Armed Struggle.
(c) They have failed to make the necessary arrangements for our trained freedom fighters to go and reinforce our fellow freedom fighters at the front during this painful period, so as to lighten their burden.
(d) They have failed to make arrangements for the thousands of recruits in Mozambique to undergo military training.
(e) They have failed to take any practical steps to meet the problems of our comrades in Zambia and Mozambique.
(f) They have jumped from capital to capital raising funds which have never been put to the service of the revolution.

(g) They are fond of shouting slogans about Armed Struggle as a means of gaining popularity and raising funds for their own use, but make no effort whatsoever to take practical steps to prosecute the Armed Struggle. They are good only at fighting through the press and on paper.

(h) The relationship between them is characterized by mutual mistrust and intrigues which divorce them from the realities of the struggle. In our opinion the three leaders are incapable of leading the ANC. An Executive Member who has been outstanding is Robert Mugabe. He has demonstrated this by defying the rigors of guerrilla life in the jungles of Mozambique. Since we respect him most, in all our dealings with the ANC leadership, he is the only person who can act as a middle man. We will not accept any direction discussions with any of he three leading members of the ANC we have described above. We can only talk through Robert Mugabe to them.

5.
We lastly wish to register our strong disapproval of and condemnation of the set-up of the Zimbabwe Liberation Council as it is, for the following reasons:

(a) The Chairman of the ZLC, Reverend Ndabaningi Sithole, appointed people who were deeply involved in the internal strife within ZANU before the Commission of Enquiry had complete its task and cleared them. To the best of our knowledge, these people are namely:

(a) Noel Mukono
(b) Simpson Mutambanengwe
(c) Felix Santana
(d) Kenneth Gwindingwi

who occupy high posts with the ZLC were responsible for the death of many people in former ZANU. Another striking feature is that they are all from the home district of Reverend Sithole. This is no time for village politics. All four men have a sectarian record of corruption and subversion in former ZANU and this we can testify. Why Sithole appointed them in spite of their notorious record of which he is fully aware we just do not know. This is no time for surrounding oneself with tribal puppets. We will therefore not be part and parcel of whatsoever is done by the ZLC as currently constituted. We strongly disapprove of whatsoever actions and appointments that may be made by the present ZLC. We do, however, accept the ZLC in principle, provided the necessary rectifications and restructuring are made.

(b) We also level deep criticism against the Chairman of the ZLC, Reverend Ndabaningi Sithole for the following reasons:
  (a) In practical terms he has done nothing to promote the Armed Struggle.
  (b) He has associated himself with people who caused great loss of lives in ZANU before the Commission of Enquiry probing into the matter has cleared them.
  (c) He has referred to the former ZANU leaders now in Zambian prisons as murderers before they have been convicted before a court of law. Is he the judge responsible for trying their case?
  (d) He was given funds from America and Britain for the maintenance of the families of ZANU leaders now in Zambian prisons, but not a penny of them has been used for this purpose. He remarked that he w would never feed the families of murderers. He was also given funds for the defence of the ZANU leaders but not a penny of them has been used for the purpose.
  (e) He failed to challenge the interpretation of the shooting incident at Mboroma in spite of the fact that he had the full knowledge of what happened. Instead of going to see the victims of the shooting incident in the Zambian hospitals, he decided to fly to America to one of his slightly indisposed daughters because he considered her life to be more valuable than those of the freedom fighters shot at Mboroma.
  (f) He told our representatives in Zambia that Chairman Chitepo was murdered by ZANU leaders in prison. We wonder where he got this information? Is he also a Commission of Enquiry member looking into the murder of Chairman Chitepo? If so, why did he unofficially and prematurely disclose his findings to us?

6.

We strongly condemn the cold-blooded murder of our fellow freedom fighters at Mboroma and subsequent mendacious interpretation of the cause of the massacre given by the Zambian Government. The explanation given by the Zambian Government is a complete distortion of what actually transpired. There was no justification whatsoever for the cold- blooded massacre of our comrades. The blood of freedom fighters is sacred and precious and is never intended to water the soil of African States, but that of our beloved fatherland in the Zambian Government clamour for a peaceful settlement of the Zimbabwean problem affecting 6 (six) million people when it fails to solve peacefully the problem at Mboroma which concerned only a handful of people. How does the Zambian Government reconcile the two situations? When Smith shot 13 (thirteen) of our Zimbabwe patriots the Zambian Government condemned the massacre, so, naturally, we expected the Zambian Government to condemn its own actions. Since they agreed that Smith could have found another way of resolving the problem peacefully, they, too, could have found a way of resolving the Mboroma problem peacefully. After all, all the Zimbabwe Freedom Fighters at Mboroma were disarmed by the Zambian Government itself. In our opinion the shootings of our comrades at Mboroma was a carefully calculated move aimed at eliminating the militants within the ANC army. Clearly and beyond any doubt the Zambian action has generated hostilities between itself and the Zimbabwe Freedom Fighters. It is for his reason that we seek for cooperation of the OAU Liberation Committee, the Tanzanian Government, and the Mozambican Government in ensuring the evacuation of our Comrades in Zambia into a safer territory. After having shot the leading cadres, including girl cadres of our fellow freedom fighters at Mboroma, it will be ridiculous and stupid of anyone to expect cooperation between our fighters and the Zambian Government. The earlier they get out of Zambia the better, it is therefore for this reason that, on humanitarian grounds we sincerely and earnestly implore both the Tanzanian and Mozambique governments to allow entry of our fighters into their territories. If this fails, we shall appeal to the International Red Cross to investigate the conditions of our fighters in Mboroma since they are virtually prisoners of the Zambian Government. In our opinion Freedom Fighters cannot become the private property of an African State. We are not Zambia's property. We sincerely hope that the OAU Liberation Committee, the Tanzanian Government, and the Mozambique Government will give urgent and serious consideration to the evacuation of our fellow freedom fighters from Zambia.

7.

In view of the great problems affecting the Zimbabwe revolution, we strongly appeal to the OAU Liberation Committee, to the Tanzania Government and the Mozambique Government to make the necessary arrangement for the persecution and intensification of the armed struggle inside Zimbabwe. This can be done by giving passage to our trained fighters to go back home and fight, and giving us our consignment of arms and ammunition that came from China. Another of our present problems is the training of our thousands of recruits currently in Mozambique. We shall be mos grateful if your make the necessary arrangements for the training of our fighters. We have at present sixty military instructors without any work at all because of the current situation. You can either allow our fighters to undergo military training in Mozambique or hee in Tanzania so long as hey are out of Zambia or not in Zambia.

If the OAU, the Tanzania and Mozambique Governments cannot do anything to support the Armed Struggle in Zimbabwe, we shall kindly request to be deported back to Zimbabwe where we shall start from throwing stones. The fighting skill is already here, the weapons we shall get from the enemy, and food we shall get from or masses of the people who always have supported our Armed Struggle. We just cannot afford to stand and stare at the Smith regime and allied forces of reaction whittle away every ounce of the rights of the people of Zimbabwe. If we cannot live as free men, we rather choose to die as FREE MEN.

Signed by ZANLA Officers at Mgagao. (Doc.31)

APPENDIX 1

Curriculum Vitae
FAY CHUNG

Fay Chung is a Zimbabwean. She was educated at the university in Harare, now known as the University of Zimbabwe, where she received her first degree (1962), her postgraduate Certificate in Education (1965) and her Doctorate (1999). She also studied at Leeds University, where she obtained her M. Phil. in English Literature (1971) and has undertaken research at St Antony's College, Oxford (1995). Latterly, she has diversified into economics and completed a distance-education degree at the School of Oriental and African Studies, London in this area (2002). Following her recent retirement, she decided to enrol in an honours degree programme in economics at the University of Zimbabwe.

Her career has been almost exclusively in education. She began by becoming involved in the university night school as an undergraduate, organising university students to teach house servants and workers in the vicinity of the campus. One of the main tasks was the eradication of illiteracy. From 1963 to 1968 she taught at high school level at Ascot and Harare High Schools, Rhodesia. While studying for her M. Phil. at Leeds University, she taught as a part-time lecturer at Leeds Polytechnic and at the Kitson College of Engineering from October 1968 to June 1970. She was a lecturer in the School of Education, University of Zambia, from 1971 to 1975. From 1975 to 1980 she worked full-time for the Zimbabwe African National Union (ZANU), then one of the major liberation movements, mainly in Mozambique and Tanzania. She was in charge of teacher education and curriculum development for Zimbabwean refugee schools in Mozambique.

After Zimbabwe's independence in 1980, she worked in various capacities in the ministry of education, including as the first acting director of the ZINTEC (Zimbabwe Integrated National Teacher Education Course) programme, which was initiated at independence with the aim of training 9,000 primary teachers through a combination of face-to-face teaching and distance education; as head of educational planning in the ministry, with responsibility for planning the expansion of the primary, secondary and teacher training programmes; as head of the curriculum development unit, tasked with transforming the curricula for primary and secondary schools; as deputy secretary in charge of school administration; and finally as minister of education and culture. She spent a total of 14 years in the government of Zimbabwe.

Fay has been involved in a number of non-governmental organisations. She took part in the formation of the Zimbabwe Foundation for Education with Production (ZIMFEP), set up to provide education for war veterans and returning refugee children from Mozambique and Zambia. School leavers were assisted through placement in further training and in jobs, or through the establishment of cooperatives. She has been a board member of the Zimbabwe Institute of Development Studies, ZIDS. She is a founder member of the Forum for African Women Educationalists (FAWE), a network of education ministers, women university vice-chancellors and other women educational leaders in Africa, focused on strengthening the education of girls and women in Africa. In addition, she is a founder member of the Association for Strengthening Higher Education for Women in Africa (ASHEWA) and has helped to establish the Women's University in Africa (WUA), located in Marondera, Zimbabwe.

Her work has also had an international dimension. She was a member of the Delors Commission on Education and worked as the chief of the education cluster at UNICEF, New York (1993-98), and then as the first director of the UNESCO International Institute for Capacity Building in Africa (IICBA) in Addis Ababa (1998-2003). Between 1998 and 2003, she served as an honorary special advisor to the Organisation of African Union (OAU) and later to the African Union (AU).

Her publications include:

Socialism, Education and Development, Zimbabwe Publishing House, Harare, 1985, co-authored with Prof. E. Ngara.

"Education for a Changing Zimbabwe," in *Education in Zimbabwe, Past, Present and Future,* ZIMFEP, Harare, 1986.

Basic Principles of Administration, College Press, Harare, 1988.

"Government and Community Participation in the Financing of Education in Zimbabwe," Address to the 1989 conference of the *International Journal of Education Development,* Oxford.

"Educational Expansion, Cost Considerations, and Curriculum Development in Zimbabwe," in Jill Ker Conway and Susan C. Bourque, eds., *The Politics of Women's Education – Perspectives from Asia, Africa and Latin America,* University of Michigan Press, Ann Arbor, 1993.

"Community Participation in School Development with Special Reference to Zimbabwe," Paper presented to South African Seminar on Community Participation, Johannesburg, May 1995.

"Education and Training in Dynamic Economies, Creative Approaches to Public/Private Partnerships," Paper presented to World Bank Seminar, Washington DC, October 1995.

"Education for All: the Zimbabwean Experience," in J.Balch et al., *Transcending the Legacy: Children in the New Southern Africa,* AEI, SARDC, and UNICEF, Nairobi, 1995.

"Education and the Liberation Struggle," in N. Bhebe and T. Ranger, *Society in Zimbabwe's Liberation War,* Vol. 2, University of Zimbabwe, Harare, 1995.

Making Development Work Without Forgetting the Poor: Re-thinking Our Common Future, paper presented at the Michigan Law and Development Symposium, Michigan University, 1996.

Challenges for Women in Developing Countries: Technology, Democracy and Institutions, UNESCO Futures Studies, 2003.

Acronyms

ANC	The African National Council
CFU	Commercial Farmers Union
CIA	Central Intelligence Agency
CIO	Central Intelligence Organisation
CONEX	Conservation and Extension
DAPP	Development Aid from People to People
DDF	District Development Fund
DRC	Democratic Republic of the Congo
FAO	United Nations Food and Agricultural Organisation
FEP	Foundation for Education with Production
FRELIMO	Frente para o Liberação do Mocambique
FROLIZI	Front for the Liberation of Zimbabwe
HIVOS	Humanistisch Institut voor Ontwikkelingsamenwerking
IDC	Industrial Development Corporation
IMF	International Monetary Fund
LONRHO	Name of company originally owned by Tiny Rowland
MDC	Movement for Democratic Change
MPLA	Movemento Popular par o Liberacao do Angola
OAU	Organisation of African Unity
RENAMO	Mozambique National Resistance/ Resistência Nacional Moçambicana
SADC	Southern African Development Community
SIDA	Swedish International Development Agency
TE1	Teacher Education Part One
TEII	Teacher Education Part Two 215
UCRN	University College of Rhodesia and Nyasaland
UDI	Unilateral Declaration of Independence
UNDP	United Nations Development Programme
UNHCR	United Nations High Commission for Refugees
UNICEF	United Nations Children's Fund
WFP	World Food Programme
ZANLA	The Zimbabwe African National Liberation Army
ZANU	Zimbabwe African National Union

ZANU/PF	Zimbabwe African National Union/Patriotic Front
ZAPU	Zimbabwe African People's Union
ZCTU	Zimbabwe Congress of Trade Unions
ZIMFEP	Zimbabwe Foundation for Education with Production
ZINTEC	Zimbabwe Integrated Teacher Education Course
ZIPA	Zimbabwe People's Army
ZIPRA	Zimbabwe People's Revolutionary Army
ZLC	Zimbabwe Liberation Council
ZUM	Zimbabwe Unity Movement
ZUPO	Zimbabwe United People's Organisation

www.ingramcontent.com/pod-product-compliance
Lightning Source LLC
Chambersburg PA
CBHW070807300426
44111CB00014B/2447